Garden Gate

The YEAR IN GARDENING

— VOLUME 15 —

SPECIAL PUBLICATIONS

"No matter how long the winter, spring is sure to follow."
—Proverb from Guinea

Please contact us to find out about other *Garden Gate* products and services:

By Phone: 1-800-341-4769
By Mail: 2200 Grand Avenue, Des Moines, IA 50312
By E-mail: GardenGate@GardenGateMagazine.com

OR VISIT OUR
Web Sites: www.GardenGateMagazine.com
or www.GardenGateStore.com
or www.GardenGateSpecials.com

Copyright 2009 August Home Publishing Co.

Welcome

You hold in your hands a wealth of information from the pages of *Garden Gate* magazine 2009. Each year the editors bring you great stories about the plants you love, design ideas for your garden and basic how-to information from our test garden, along with tips and questions from our readers, before and after gardens and plans straight from our drawing board. We're here to help you create a beautiful place of your own!

In this new book, not only are all of the year's stories at your fingertips, but we've organized them in an easy-to-access format. Whether you're looking for inspiration from gardens we've photographed or how to plant and care for daylilies, you'll be able to find the information quickly and easily. It's like having the editors of *Garden Gate* in your own back yard.

Each section has its own contents and in the back of the book you'll find an index for the entire book along with zone maps.

So sit back and enjoy a full year of gardening!

The Illustrated Guide to Home Gardening and Design®

PUBLISHER **Donald B. Peschke**

EDITOR **Steven M. Nordmeyer**

MANAGING EDITOR **Kristin Beane Sullivan**

ART DIRECTOR **Eric Flynn**

ASSOCIATE ART DIRECTOR **Carrie Topp**

SENIOR EDITOR **Stephanie Polsley Bruner**

ASSOCIATE EDITORS
Jim Childs, Deborah Gruca, Sherri Ribbey, Amanda Wurzinger

SENIOR GRAPHIC DESIGNER
Kate Corman
Kevin Venhaus

ILLUSTRATOR **Carlie Hamilton**

SENIOR PHOTOGRAPHER **David C. McClure**

CORPORATE GARDENER **Marcia Leeper**

VIDEOGRAPHERS **Mark A. Hayes, Jr.**

Garden Gate® (ISBN 978-09801046-8-4) *Garden Gate*® is a registered trademark of August Home Publishing Co., 2200 Grand Avenue, Des Moines, IA 50312. © Copyright 2009, August Home Publishing Company. All rights reserved.
PRINTED IN CHINA.

TO ORDER ADDITIONAL COPIES
OF THIS BOOK
VISIT, WRITE OR CALL

www.GardenGateStore.com

Customer Service
P.O. Box 842, Des Moines, IA
50304-9961

800-341-4769
(Weekdays 8 a.m. to 5 p.m. CT)

To learn more about
Garden Gate magazine visit

www.GardenGateMagazine.com

Garden Gate contents

The YEAR IN GARDENING VOLUME 15

great plants — p. 8

- 'Red at Night' Bearded Iris — 10
- Catmint — 12
- Chrysanthemums — 14
- Climbing Roses — 18
- Corydalis — 24
- Daylily — 26
- Frosty Kiss Mix Gazania — 28
- Japanese Painted Fern — 30
- 'Elizabeth' Magnolia — 32
- Moss Phlox — 34
- Naked Ladies — 36
- Red Barrenwort — 38
- Shasta Daisy — 40
- Soapwort — 44
- Zinnias — 46
- Did You Know — 50

top picks — p. 58

- New Plants for 2009 — 60
- Spring-Blooming Flowers — 68
- Flowers That Plant Themselves — 74
- Readers' Favorite Shade Flowers — 80
- Bulbs for Three Seasons of Color — 88
- Easiest Clematis Ever — 96

before and after — p. 104

- How to Work Less! — 106
- Three-Season Color — 110
- Season-Long Color — 112
- Water-Wise Beauty — 116
- A Whole New Level to Your Garden — 120
- Quick and Easy Update — 124

garden design — p. 128

- Start from Scratch — 130
- Set the Style — 134
- Welcome Change — 138
- Think Outside the Trellis — 142
- Triangles Make a Point — 144
- Rain Gardens — 148
- The Big Picture — 152
- Time to Relax — 158
- Nature's Masterpiece — 160
- Color — 164
- 4 Fabulous Fall Combos — 168
- Warm, Winged Welcome — 172
- Butterflies Welcome — 174
- Bird Friendly Garden — 178
- Did You Know — 182

design challenge drawing board — p. 186

- Enter Here — 188
- An Entry Garden for Everyone — 190
- Make the Uglies Disappear — 192
- Hide an Eyesore — 194
- Fill in a Big Berm — 196
- Easy Tips to Fill a Big Garden — 198
- Too Much Going On! — 200
- Keep it Simple! — 202
- Tame a Steep Slope — 204
- Beauty on Many Levels — 206
- From Simple to Simply Stunning — 208
- Plant a Little Peace and Quiet — 210

COVER CREDITS:
Daylily border, Design: Rita Ward

all about containers p. 212

Containers 1-2-3 .... **214**
Instant Spring! **218**
Basket of Flowers **220**
Sunny Sizzler **221**
Getting the Hang of it **222**
Grasses = Great Containers **228**
Readers' Best Containers **230**
Create a Super Bowl **234**
Warm Sunshine **235**
Cool Idea **236**
3 Ways to Shape Up
 a Container **238**
Container Cleanup **240**
Overwintering Plants **241**
Did You Know **244**

gardening basics p. 248

Off to a Great Start **250**
Fertilizer: Get the Facts **254**
Feed Your Plants
 What They Love! **256**
No Pests, No Chemicals **258**
The Secrets to Dividing
 in Summer **260**
Lots of Lovely Lilies **262**
Garden Smarter:
 7 Easy-Does-It Tips **264**
Point, Click, Plant! **266**
Get Your Garden
 in Shape Now! **268**
15 Years of Readers'
 Best Tips **270**
Deer Diary **274**
Attack of the Invasives **276**

Garden Coverups **280**
No-Mow Slope **282**
Sharpen Your Edges **284**
Digging Tools That Work **286**
Bulb Tools That Really Work ... **288**
Think Small, Save Time! **290**
Did You Know **292**
Beneficials
 You Should Know **304**
Pests to Watch **305**
6 Weeds to Know **306**
Know Your Zones **308**

index p. 310

Throughout the book, you'll find this icon indicating additional tips, videos and information on our Web site. Visit www.GardenGateMagazine.com, click the Web extras button and look for this information in issues 85-90 of *Garden Gate* magazine. And while you're there, be sure to browse the rest of our helpful online content!

Meet 'Elizabeth', a beautiful yellow-flowered magnolia on page 32.

great plants *for* your garden

GROW BETTER PLANTS We can help. Whether you're looking for how to get your daisies to bloom longer, how to prune your climbing roses or even just need to know the best plant for a tough spot in your yard, we have it. Planting, feeding, watering, pruning tips, even variety recommendations. Find them all here.

'Red at Night' Bearded Iris **10**	'Elizabeth' Magnolia **32**
Catmint **12**	Moss Phlox **34**
Chrysanthemums **14**	Naked Ladies **36**
Climbing Roses **18**	Red Barrenwort **38**
Corydalis **24**	Shasta Daisies **40**
Long-Blooming Daylilies **26**	Soapwort **44**
Frosty Kiss Mix Gazania **28**	Zinnias **46**
Japanese Painted Fern **30**	Did You Know **50**

PLANTS | EDITOR'S CHOICE

'Red at Night' Bearded Iris

Iris 'Red at Night'

Size	2 to 3 ft. tall, 1 to 2 ft. wide
Bloom	Dark-red flowers with orange beards in early to midspring
Soil	Well-drained
Light	Full sun
Pests	Iris borers can be a problem
Hardiness	Cold: USDA zones 3 to 10 Heat: AHS zones 10 to 1

You've heard the rhyme: "Red sky at night, sailor's delight…" Well, 'Red at Night' iris would delight any *gardener*, with those velvety dark-red flowers. And there are plenty of them: In catalog-speak, this iris is "well-branched," meaning it produces lots of flowers.

So how do you work those big flowers into a garden? Below, in "Hot spot, cool garden," irises are the star of the show, with the other plants creating a backdrop. Tucking irises near shrubs, a fence or a wall gives them shelter from wind. A many-flowered cultivar like 'Red at Night' can be top-heavy, so you may need to stake the flower stalks in a windy garden.

CARE AND CULTURE

A spot in full sun with well-drained soil is perfect for irises. Most irises will flower with only five or six hours of sun, but the stems will be floppy.

Irises spread quickly, so you'll need to divide them in three or four years. It's time to divide when there's a dead space in the center of the plant. Split irises in late summer when they're semi-dormant — they'll have plenty of time to develop new roots before winter.

Dig up the clump and cut or break off divisions, each with a section of rhizome and a fan of leaves. Make a shallow hole, and mound soil into a ridge in the bottom. Set the rhizome on the ridge, then fill in soil around it, so it's just covered.

Water your irises in well, but don't use bark mulch; it'll hold moisture around the rhizomes and they may rot. You can scatter all-purpose granular fertilizer around in the spring, but irises don't need much feeding.

Rake up iris leaves in the fall. They can harbor iris borer larvae, the only serious iris pest. In spring, larvae burrow into rhizomes, causing them to rot. Often, the first sign of damage is brown streaks on the leaves. If you find rotted rhizomes when you split your iris, discard the rotten areas and let the rhizomes dry a couple of days in the shade before replanting.

'Red at Night', like any iris, will steal the show in any garden. It's one hot plant! □

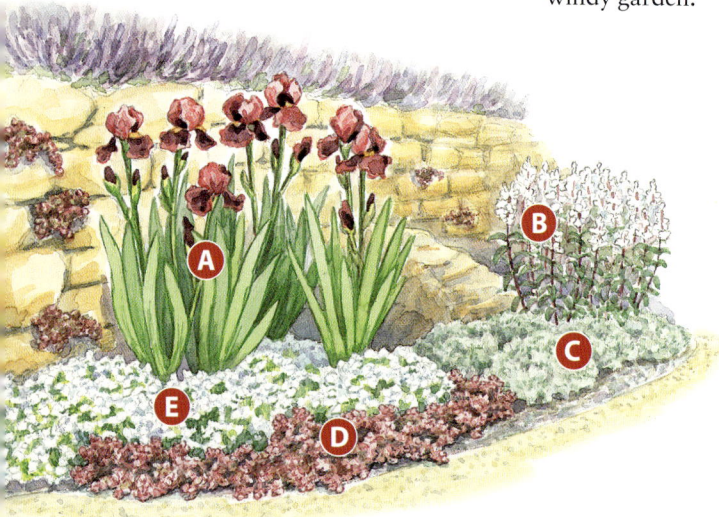

Hot spot, cool garden
Is this one hot look? Or is it a cool design? You decide! White-flowered dianthus, white penstemon blooms and silver artemisia foliage cool things down. But big, bold iris flowers, and burgundy creeping sedum and penstemon foliage keep this sunny corner looking hot.

A **Iris** *Iris* 'Red at Night' 2 to 3 ft. tall, 1 to 2 ft. wide; cold-hardy in USDA zones 3 to 10; heat-tolerant in AHS zones 10 to 1

B **Penstemon** *Penstemon digitalis* 'Husker Red' 2 to 3 ft. tall, 1 to 2 ft. wide; cold-hardy in USDA zones 3 to 8; heat-tolerant in AHS zones 8 to 1

C **Artemisia** *Artemisia schmidtiana* 'Silver Mound' 8 to 10 in. tall, 10 to 15 in. wide; cold-hardy in USDA zones 3 to 7; heat-tolerant in AHS zones 7 to 1

D **Sedum** *Sedum spurium* 'Red Carpet' 4 in. tall, 12 in. wide; cold-hardy in USDA zones 3 to 9; heat-tolerant in AHS zones 9 to 1

E **Dianthus** *Dianthus plumarius* 'Itsaul White' 6 to 9 in. tall, 12 to 18 in. wide; cold-hardy in USDA zones 3 to 9; heat-tolerant in AHS zones 9 to 1

Mail-order sources

Cooley's Gardens
www.cooleysgardens.com
503-873-5463. Catalog $3

High Country Gardens
www.highcountrygardens.com
800-925-9387. Catalog free

PLANTS | LONG-BLOOMING PERENNIAL

'Six Hills Giant'

CATMINT
Nepeta spp.

6 to 48 in. tall, 18 to 48 in. wide

Flowers in shades of purple, blue, pink or white in summer

Full sun

Well-drained, slightly alkaline soil

No serious pests

Cold-hardy in USDA zones 3 to 9

Heat-tolerant AHS zones 9 to 1

PHOTO: Courtesy of Proven Winners ('Blue Ice')

Botanical Names

Foxglove
  Digitalis purpurea
Lamb's ear
  Stachys byzantina
Snow-in-summer
  Cerastium tomentosum

Easy-care, fragrant and a butterfly magnet
Catmint Has It All!

Lots of perennials bloom in mid-May, but come August, not many of those same plants are still blooming. Catmint is one of those rare summer-long-blooming perennials. But its benefits don't stop with just its longevity.

All catmints are heat- and drought-tolerant. They're also extremely pest-resistant as well as very hardy. On top of that, they're fragrant, too. Brush the foliage and you'll get a pleasant herbal scent. And did you know that catmint flowers are popular with butterflies and hummingbirds, too? Well, it's all true!

CHOOSE A GOOD CATMINT The two most popular cultivars you'll find are probably 'Six Hills Giant', in photo 1, and 'Walker's Low', below left. They're also among the longest-blooming members of this family. Leave some room for these large perennials — they grow nearly 3 feet tall and up to 4 feet wide.

But not all catmints are this big. Others are better as ground covers. 'Blue Wonder', white 'Snowflake' and the new variety 'Blue Ice', below center, grow as 10- to 14-inch mounds. The blue-tinted flowers on 'Blue Ice' begin in early May and fade to white as they age. You'll have a constant supply of flowers on the plant until at least September.

And although most catmints are purple, blue or white, there are a few pink varieties. 'Sweet Dreams', below right, and 'Dawn to Dusk' both have pink blooms and more upright habits than some of their blue or white cousins.

ADD THEM TO YOUR GARDEN In photo 1, you can see how beautiful a scattering of catmints can be when planted in several places through a perennial border. Their rich flower colors and gray-green foliage make them amenable neighbors for almost any perennial.

Tall catmints, like 'Six Hills Giant', often have a spiky form. In a perennial design it's always a good idea to mix shapes. Pair it with a mounding plant, such as the snow-in-summer or lamb's ear you see here.

'Walker's Low'

'Blue Ice'

'Sweet Dreams'

'Six Hills Giant'

(1) Long-blooming 'Six Hills Giant' catmint will add color to this garden long after the spikes of the pink and white foxglove and drifts of white snow-in-summer have finished blooming.

One traditional use for catmints, especially the low-growing cultivars, is as a ground cover in a rose garden. The catmints do a good job of covering up old roses' bare knees. And some folks think that catmint helps repel rose pests, although there's no scientific evidence to back this up.

Catmints are tough — any of them will be terrific along your hot concrete sidewalk or driveway. However, because it is very popular with bees, it may not be a good choice near your mailbox.

Try a catmint in a container "recipe" that needs full sun and well-drained soil. In fall, go ahead and move the catmint into your perennial border and you'll get to enjoy it again next year.

KEEP THEM TIDY AND TRIM Catmints are long bloomers, but many tend to "relax" after their biggest flush of flowers. The stems splay out from the crown and the center opens up. They'll keep right on blooming and new growth will often fill in the center on its own. Or you can be ruthless, cutting the entire plant to within just a couple inches of the ground. It'll recover quickly, usually starting to bloom again in about four or five weeks. And while you're cutting, be sure to enjoy the fragrant foliage. There is an exception to the lax stems — 'Sweet Dreams.' In most spots it stays standing. I still like to just deadhead its spent flowers. That encourages the side branches to grow out and bloom.

There's another reason you may want to remove spent flowers — catmint can reseed. The resulting seedlings will look similar to the parent. But if you don't want or need them, they're easy to pull or hoe out.

You can usually find several catmint cultivars at most local garden centers. Not there? Check out one of the mail-order sources listed at right so you can discover why this is a must-have perennial. □

— *Jim Childs*

Mail-order sources

Bluestone Perennials
www.bluestoneperennials.com
800-852-5243. *Catalog free*

Busse Gardens
www.bussegardens.com
800-544-3192. *Catalog $3*

PLANTS | FALL PERENNIAL

You don't *have* to replant mums every year!

Sure-Fire Color

CHRYSANTHEMUMS
Chrysanthemum spp. and hybrids

1 to 3 ft. tall,
  1 to 2 ft. wide
Flowers in
  most colors
  except blue
Full sun
Moist, well-
  drained soil
Cold-hardy in
  USDA zones 4 to 9
Heat-tolerant in
  AHS zones 12 to 1

'Grape Glow'

Chrysanthemums are the quintessential autumn flowers. There's something about the way the autumn light shines on the colors that gives them a warm glow you don't find in many other flowers. Even the spicy, pungent scent is intoxicating in the cool fall air. And there are so many ways to enjoy mums.

INSTANT COLOR Potted mums in full autumn flower are immediate garden gratification. All the work of pinching and feeding has been done for you to make them dense, compact and colorful. As you see in the photos below, you can pop them into a garden at a moment's notice or in a spur-of-the-moment seasonal container. Once the buds begin to show color, you can set budded mums even into shaded areas and they still bloom just fine. I'll give you tips about how to buy and plant them in "Potted pointers" below. If you live where the ground freezes solid, potted mums are best treated as seasonal annuals: Enjoy them while they're in front of you and remember them fondly when they're gone.

GROW FOR THE LONG HAUL There are ways to avoid replacing your mums every year. To start, look for plants in the perennial section at the garden center in spring — this way they'll have time to get established before fall. And some cultivars are hardier than others. In "Eight indestructible mums" at right, I'll tell you about a few of my favorites, including 'Samba', which is cold-hardy in USDA zone 5. Several on the list are hardy even into zone 4. And if you toss winter mulch over them, they'll survive a zone colder yet. Some of the cultivars, such as 'Sheffield', have been around for a long time. However, 'Maroon Pride' and 'Centerpiece' were bred in recent years specifically for cold climates. They stay more compact than many of the older cultivars, even without much pinching.

Like most perennials, hardy mums have a few unique growing quirks. If you've had problems getting them to survive, don't give up! On the next pages I'll show you what you can do to help them come back every year. And I have design tips with plant combinations that will keep your garden colorful all season long. Let's take a look. ☐

— *Jim Childs*

Potted pointers To get the most bloom time, choose potted mums that are just starting to show color. And if you're moving them into containers, don't worry about using a high-quality potting mix or even fertilizing — they're ready to go. Actually, no matter how you're going to enjoy them, you can simply slip the mum, pot and all, into place and you're set for the season.

14   *the* YEAR IN GARDENING   www.GardenGateMagazine.com

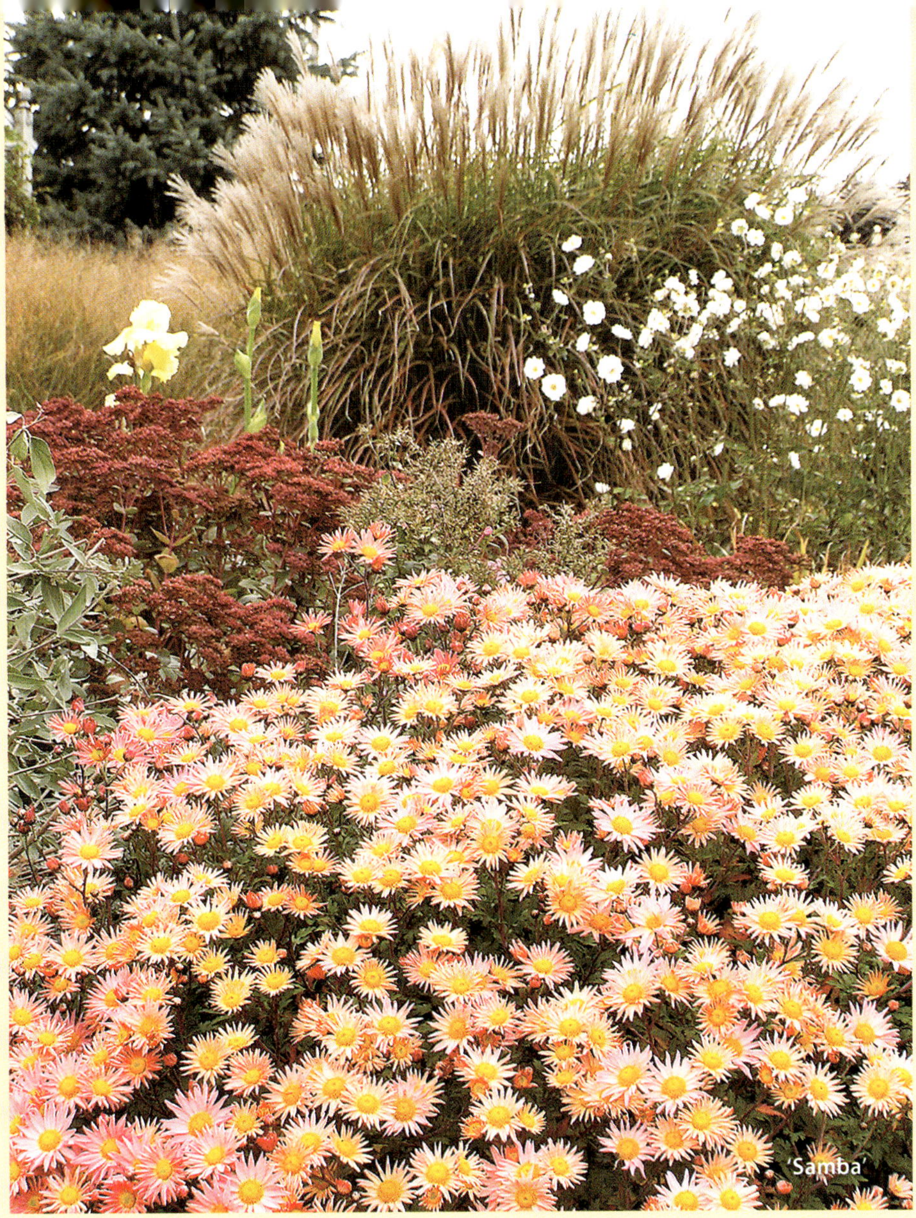

'Samba'

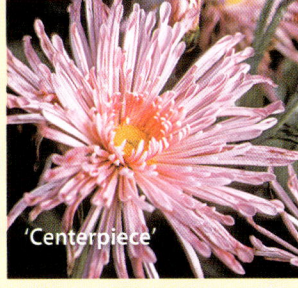

'Centerpiece'

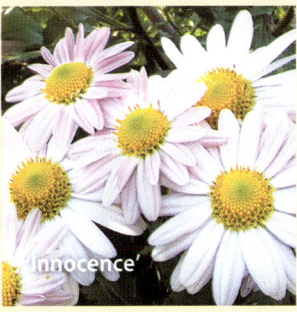

'Innocence'

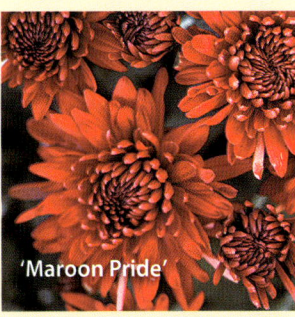

'Maroon Pride'

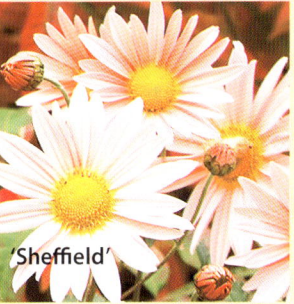

'Sheffield'

PHOTOS: Courtesy of Walters Gardens ('Samba'); Courtesy of University of Minnesota ('Centerpiece' and 'Maroon Pride'); Courtesy of Avant Gardens ('Innocence')

eight indestructible mums

While all mums are colorful, some are hardier than others. Cultivars that have stood the test of time are a good bet, as is buying from mail-order sources in cold locations, like those below right.

'Centerpiece' (in photo) Up to 2 ft. tall and wide; 4-in.-wide rose-lavender flowers bloom in early autumn; cold-hardy in USDA zones 4 to 9; heat-tolerant in AHS zones 9 to 1

'Grape Glow' 15 to 18 in. tall, 24 in. wide; 3½-in.-diameter, double rose-purple flowers bloom in late summer; cold-hardy in USDA zones 4 to 9; heat-tolerant in AHS zones 9 to 1

'Innocence' (in photo) Up to 3 ft. tall, 2 ft. wide; 2-in. single white daisies blushed with pale pink open in midfall; cold-hardy in USDA zones 5 to 9; heat-tolerant in AHS zones 9 to 1

'J.C. Weigelan' 2 to 3 ft. tall, 2 ft. wide; single wine-red daisies bloom in early autumn; very frost tolerant; cold-hardy in USDA zones 5 to 9; heat-tolerant in AHS zones 9 to 1

'Maroon Pride' (in photo) 18 in. tall, 24 in. wide; 3½-in.-diameter, double dark red flowers open in midfall; cold-hardy in USDA zones 4 to 9; heat-tolerant in AHS zones 9 to 1

'Samba' (in photo) 18 to 20 in. tall and wide; 2-in. single rosy peach to pink daisies with gold centers open in late summer; one of the Autumn Crescendo™ series; cold-hardy in USDA zones 5 to 9; heat-tolerant in AHS zones 9 to 1

'Sheffield' (in photo) Up to 36 in. tall, 15 to 18 in. wide; soft apricot bloom in midfall; also listed as Hillside Pink Sheffield; cold-hardy in USDA zones 4 to 9; heat-tolerant in AHS zones 9 to 1

'Will's Wonderful' 2 to 3 ft. tall, 2 ft. wide; red buds open to creamy yellow and strawberry pink flowers in late October; cold-hardy in USDA zones 5 to 9; heat-tolerant in AHS zones 9 to 1

Mail-order sources

Avant Gardens

www.avantgardensne.com
508-998-8819. *Online catalog only* (Mums listed as *Dendranthema*)

Busse Gardens

www.bussegardens.com
800-544-3192. *Catalog $3*

White Flower Farm

www.whiteflowerfarm.com
800-503-9624. *Online catalog only*

YOUR GUIDE TO **PERFECT MUMS**

Start with a good design
One of the biggest concerns with hardy mums in the perennial border is how to disguise them until they flower. After all, for much of the growing season they're only mounds of green leaves. I've put together this small vignette and shown it to you in two seasons to illustrate a technique that helps disguise the mums early but lets them shine in autumn.

THE SPRING SHOW Look closely at this late-spring garden and you can see some of the mums peeking out behind the bergenia. There are more mums woven into the spaces between the white Shasta daisies and blue peachleaf bellflowers. And just like mums, late-season grasses can be difficult to work into a border, too. In this colorful spring view you just see a few of their tips beginning to poke through.

AUTUMN APPLAUSE It's prime season for mums. The bergenia foliage in front is beginning to take on rosy tints in the cold fall weather. Autumn grasses are at their zenith. The Shasta daisies and bellflower are finished blooming so they've been cut back — it's their turn to hide while their foliage continues to feed the plant for the show next year. And while you could stake the mums to stand straight, I like the casual way they billow up and over the perennials that were cut back. To see exactly how this garden fits together, check out our plan below.

SPRING

Spring bloomers fill in for the mums while they're still growing early in the season.

Mums are visible, but not the focus of the garden.

AUTUMN

Let the mums grow tall so they cover the spring bloomers.

Cut back early season perennials when they finish blooming.

Like the garden above?
Follow this easy plan to create it in your own yard. Want it bigger? Where there's just one plant, adjust the spacing so there's room for two or three. Or for a long border simply repeat the entire plan.

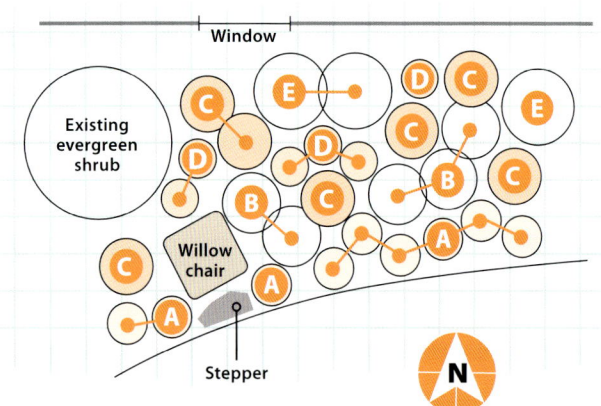

Scale: 1 square = 1 square ft.

A **Bergenia** *Bergenia* 'Bressingham Ruby' **(9)** 12 to 16 in. tall, 12 to 18 in. wide; large evergreen foliage with rosy red tints in fall and winter; cold-hardy in USDA zones 3 to 10; heat-tolerant in AHS zones 10 to 1

B **Shasta daisy** *Leucanthemum* ×*superbum* 'Esther Read' **(5)** 18 to 24 in. tall, 16 to 24 in. wide; fluffy, double white flowers; cold-hardy in USDA zones 5 to 9; heat-tolerant in AHS zones 9 to 1

C **Chrysanthemum** *Chrysanthemum* 'Sheffield' **(7)** 36 in. tall, 15 to 18 in. wide; for this look, pinch once then let the stems sprawl over the daisy foliage; cold-hardy in USDA zones 4 to 9; heat-tolerant in AHS zones 9 to 1

D **Peachleaf bellflower** *Campanula persicifolia* 'Telham Beauty' **(6)** 24 to 36 in. tall, 12 to 15 in. wide; spikes of porcelain-blue flowers in early summer; cold-hardy in USDA zones 3 to 7; heat-tolerant in AHS zones 7 to 1

E **Korean feather reed grass** *Calamagrostis brachytricha* **(3)** 3 to 4 ft. tall, 2 ft. wide; late-season grass with airy seedheads; cold-hardy in USDA zones 4 to 9; heat-tolerant in AHS zones 9 to 1

survival tactics

While hardy perennial mums are usually quite durable, you'll reap huge rewards with a bit of extra care. Here are tips to reduce the risk that you'll have to plant new mums every year. And there are pinching tips below to show you how to get the plant habit that will look best in your perennial border.

☐ **Start early** Spring is the time to get mums in the ground. That gives them lots of time to send out a strong root system that will keep them from being heaved out of the soil over the winter. Buy young starts in early spring. If they have flowers, snip them off so the mum puts its energy into growing more roots and branches.

☐ **Rejuvenate frequently** For the most flowers, divide mums every spring. Toss out the weak and woody centers and reset only healthy young sprouts from the edge of the clump.

☐ **Choose the best spot** Always plant hardy mums in full sun and well-drained soil. Avoid locations that stay wet, or where water collects, especially in winter. With too much moisture, the crown rots and the plant will die.

☐ **Feed regularly** Mums are heavy feeders. Start with a granulated 10-10-10 fertilizer as soon as you see new growth. Give them another dose in early August, or when you spot the buds forming. Or apply a slow-release fertilizer in spring. But if you irrigate or it's been a rainy season, give your mums a little extra 10-10-10 as the buds form. Never feed after mid-August or the plant will try to keep growing rather than wind down to get ready for winter.

☐ **Best survival tip** Mums left standing will survive cold winters better than ones cut to the ground. And it's a good idea to spread 2 to 4 in. of straw or other loose mulch to keep the roots evenly cold and protected.

☐ **Be patient** Wait to uncover the crown and cut the old stems down until spring, about the time the forsythia blooms. Late cold snaps can kill tender new growth.

Reset mum divisions with the largest leaves and biggest pieces of root.

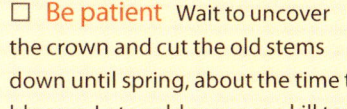
The first stems poking through the mulch may look spindly. Uncover them and prune old stems to perk them up.

Tall and casual Pinching is the way to get the most flowers, but if you want a taller, more natural-looking mum, do it just once. When the plant is 4 to 6 in. tall, pinch or snip out the tip. You'll get four or more side shoots that will each produce a cluster of flowers.

When the mum is 4 to 6 in. tall, pinch off the top inch or two of the stem.

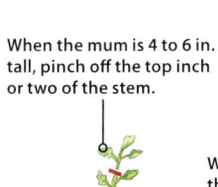

With just one pinch, the end result will be tall stems with clusters of flowers at the top.

Mounds of color Looking for shorter plants with more flowering branches? You'll want to start pinching in spring and repeat the process every time new growth stretches to 4 to 6 in. long. Stop pinching in mid-July so your mum will have time to set flower buds.

Pinch each time the new side shoots grow to be about 4 to 6 in. long.

By fall you'll have a compact plant covered with lots of colorful flowers.

PLANTS | SHRUB

'John Cabot'

CLIMBING ROSE
Rosa spp.

6 to 20 ft. tall
Flowers in white, yellow, pink, orange or red
Full sun
Moist, well-drained soil
Blackspot, Japanese beetles, powdery mildew, rust, aphids
Cold-hardy in USDA zones 3 to 11
Heat-tolerant in AHS zones 9 to 1

Botanical Names

Barberry *Berberis* spp.
Catmint *Nepeta* spp.
Shrub rose *Rosa* spp.
Weigela *Weigela florida*
Yellow wax bells *Kirengeshoma palmata*

Mail-order sources

Antique Rose Emporium
www.antiqueroseemporium.com
800-441-0002. *Catalog free*

High Country Roses
www.highcountryroses.com
800-552-2082. *Catalog free*

Northland Rosarium
www.northlandrosarium.com
509-448-4968. *Online catalog only*

Orion Farm
www.orionfarm.com
800-558-4180. *Online catalog only*

Witherspoon Rose Culture
www.witherspoonrose.com
800-643-0315. *Catalog free*

Our regional guide makes them easier than you think!

Gorgeous Climbing Roses

I used to think climbing roses were too hard to grow — that these finicky shrubs needed too much extra pruning, protection and fussing. But then I found the secret to growing beautiful climbers: Get one that's right for my region. For instance, 'Lillian Gibson', at right, is cold-hardy to USDA zone 4 without a lot of protection, so it does great in this Midwestern garden. Since it's fragrant and nearly thornless, it's perfect near a path like this one to the back yard.

FAMILY MATTERS The term "climbing rose" is a catch-all for any type of rose with extra long canes. Since they're not really vines, climbing roses don't have any tendrils to help them hold on to structures. In nature, these roses just "scramble" over whatever happens to be nearby. If you want them to go somewhere specific, like onto an arbor, you have to attach them with twine or other soft material.

Technically, there are two types of climbing rose: climbers and ramblers.

Climbers have stiff, fairly vertical canes. They're easy to train onto any upright structure, such as a wall, arbor or pillar. They typically have large flowers and bloom from spring until frost.

Ramblers have a more relaxed, draping habit that's perfect along a fence. They bloom only once, usually in late spring, but the show is well worth the wait.

SHOWING OFF Because of their height and beauty, climbing roses are magnets for attention, so you want a planting that really sets them off. Notice how the bright pink shrub rose in an equally vibrant container at right balances out the mass of pale pink above? Large roses like this one often have woody "legs." Cover them with taller perennials or shrubs, such as catmint, yellow wax bells, barberry or weigela.

Care for a climber is the same as for any other rose. Give these shrubs at least six hours of sun, well-drained soil, regular water, and an application of an all-purpose rose fertilizer in spring for happy, healthy plants.

The structure that holds your rose up is just as important as the rose you grow. Make sure to get something that will fit its mature size. For example, a trellis or obelisk will support a 6- to 7-foot rose easily. But a huge rambler that's 15 feet or more needs a sturdy pergola or arbor to keep it up. Practical matters aside, a big structure is more in proportion to a big rose, helping to balance it out visually.

Whether summer's humidity or winter's plunging temperatures make it hard for you to grow climbers, you'll find tips to help on the following pages. Then I'll introduce you to five of the best varieties for your region. You'll find lots of heights and flower colors there. Most of these roses are climbers; I'll let you know if one's a rambler. If you can't find one of these beauties at a local garden center, check out the mail-order sources at left. They all have a great selection.

Now let's start our tour of the best roses around North America.

'Lillian Gibson'

THE RIGHT ROSES FOR YOU!

If you've been frustrated by climbing roses in the past, you may not have the right rose for where you live. The rose lists you find here will help remedy that. Where winters get well below freezing, be sure to ask your nursery if the rose is own root or grafted. Own-root roses tend to be hardier. Grafted roses are less hardy varieties grown on a hardy root stock. You can still grow them in cold-winter areas, but they need some help. The graft is a knot where the top of the rose meets the roots. Plant it 2 to 4 inches below the soil's surface. This isn't a big deal in the South, where winter die-back isn't such a problem.

To help you find the right rose, I've divided the United States and Canada into five regions: Midwest/Northeast, Mountain West, Northwest, Southwest and Southeast. The Midwest and Northeast are combined because they have a lot in common when it comes to growing roses. Now let's look at some roses that *thrive* instead of just survive in your region. □

— *Sherri Ribbey*

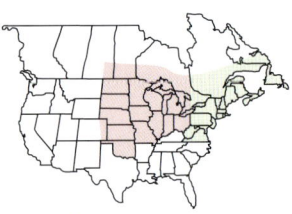

Midwest/Northeast

The biggest challenge to growing beautiful climbing roses in both the Midwest and Northeast (including parts of Canada) is winter cold. Frigid temperatures kill the canes back to the ground so even if the plants survive winter, they don't bloom much the next summer. Plus, shrubs that would, in milder climates, grow 10 to 15 ft. tall, reach only 4 or 5 ft. Snow cover helps a lot because it acts as a layer of insulation. But not everyone can rely on it every year.

Though all of these roses are hardy, they'll do better with some extra protection if they're in an exposed area or windy corner. After the last hard frost, take the canes off the structure and lay them on the ground. Then add an insulating layer of straw or pine boughs. If the rose is too big to lay down, wrap burlap around the canes as far up as you can reach to protect them from drying winter winds. The less winter dieback there is, the bigger your rose will be the following year.

FIVE GREAT ROSES

'Autumn Sunset' 8 to 12 ft.; double apricot-gold; fragrant; cold-hardy in USDA zones 5 to 8; heat-tolerant in AHS zones 8 to 1

'Dortmund' 8 to 10 ft.; single red flowers with a white center and yellow stamens; fragrant; cold-hardy in USDA zones 5 to 9; heat-tolerant in AHS zones 9 to 1

'New Dawn' 12 to 18 ft.; double blush-pink; cold-hardy in USDA zones 5 to 9; heat-tolerant in AHS zones 9 to 1

Ramblin Red® ('RADramblin') 6 to 10 ft.; semi-double red; cold-hardy in USDA zones 3 to 7; heat-tolerant in AHS zones 9 to 1

PHOTO 'William Baffin' 10 ft.; semidouble pink; Canadian Explorer series; cold-hardy in USDA zones 4 to 9; heat-tolerant in AHS zones 9 to 1

LOCATION: The Ewing and Muriel Kauffman Garden of Kansas City

'William Baffin'

Fourth of July

Mountain West
Gardening in the Mountain West is always an adventure. From freezing temperatures to torrential rains alternating with drought, weather can be wild here. In addition, the sun is more intense at higher altitudes, and soils drain quickly and aren't very fertile. There's not much you can do about weather, but you can nourish the soil with compost to help the roses on the list at right beat the heat, survive the cold and look good, at the same time.

FIVE GREAT ROSES
Awakening ('Probuzeni') 16 ft.; double pale pink; fragrant; cold-hardy in USDA zones 5 to 9; heat-tolerant in AHS zones 9 to 1

'Félicité Perpétue' rambler; 15 ft.; double pink to white; fragrant; cold-hardy in USDA zones 5 to 9; heat-tolerant in AHS zones 9 to 1

PHOTO **Fourth of July™ ('WEKroalt')** 9 to 10 ft.; semidouble red and white; fragrant; cold-hardy in USDA zones 5 to 9; heat-tolerant in AHS zones 9 to 1

'Henry Kelsey' 6 to 7 ft.; semidouble red; fragrant; Canadian Explorer series; cold-hardy in USDA zones 3 to 7; heat-tolerant in AHS zones 9 to 1

Seven Sisters* (*Rosa multiflora* **'Grevillei'**) rambler; 10 ft.; deep pink to white; cold-hardy in USDA zones 4 to 7; heat-tolerant in AHS zones 9 to 1

Northwest
Mild temperatures and plenty of rainfall make gardening in the Northwest a real pleasure. On the other hand, all that moisture is a haven for fungal diseases, such as blackspot. No rose is immune to blackspot, but the ones you'll find here are disease-resistant so they won't lose all their leaves if this fungus does flare up. To treat blackspot, get a fungicide with neem oil. This organic vegetable oil is made from the pressed seeds of neem (*Azadirachta indica*), an evergreen tree from Asia. It's also effective against insects.

FIVE GREAT ROSES
Altissimo ('Delmur') 9 to 10 ft.; single red; cold-hardy in USDA zones 5 to 9; heat-tolerant in AHS zones 9 to 1

Dublin Bay ('MACdub') 10 ft.; double red; fragrant; cold-hardy in USDA zones 5 to 9; heat-tolerant in AHS zones 9 to 1

PHOTO **Graham Thomas ('Ausmas')** 6 to 10 ft.; double yellow; fragrant; gets taller in warmer climates; cold-hardy in USDA zones 5 to 9; heat-tolerant in AHS zones 9 to 1

'Madame Alfred Carrière' 16 ft.; double pale pink flowers mature to white; fragrant; cold-hardy in USDA zone 6 to 9; heat-tolerant in AHS zones 9 to 1

'Royal Sunset' 16 ft.; double pale orange to gold; strong fragrance; cold-hardy in USDA zones 6 to 9; heat-tolerant in AHS zones 9 to 1

Graham Thomas

PHOTO: Courtesy of David Austin Roses® (Graham Thomas)

www.GardenGateMagazine.com *the* YEAR IN GARDENING 21

'Sally Holmes' (right), 'Climbing Iceberg' (left)

GARDEN DESIGN: Shellene Mueller/Designs by Shellene

Southwest There's a lot of heat in the Southwest but not a lot of water, so drought-tolerant roses like the ones at right are your best bet. But even these tough beauties need more moisture than rainfall can provide in a climate this dry. To save on watering, apply a 3- to 4-in. layer of organic mulch and water even established roses deeply every seven to 10 days. Use a soaker hose or drip irrigation to cut down on evaporation.

The afternoon sun here can get a little too hot in summer, even for roses. So plant them where they'll get at least six hours of morning light and some shade in the afternoon.

FIVE GREAT ROSES

'American Pillar' rambler; 12 to 20 ft.; single salmon-pink with a white center; fragrant; cold-hardy in USDA zones 6 to 9; heat-tolerant in AHS zones 9 to 1

PHOTO **'Climbing Iceberg'** 8 to 10 ft.; double white; fragrant; cold-hardy in USDA zones 6 to 9; heat-tolerant in AHS zones 9 to 1

'Climbing Pinkie' 9 to 10 ft.; semidouble pink; fragrant; cold-hardy in USDA zones 6 to 9; heat-tolerant in AHS zones 9 to 1

'Crépuscule' 8 ft.; double copper to buff; fragrant; cold-hardy in USDA zones 7 to 9; heat-tolerant in AHS zones 7 to 1

PHOTO **'Sally Holmes'** 6 to 13 ft.; creamy flowers change to white as they age; fragrant; cold-hardy in USDA zones 5 to 9; heat-tolerant in AHS zones 9 to 1

Southeast Gardening in the Southeast is great. The growing season is long and the winters are mild. But summers can be very humid, and fungal diseases, such as blackspot and powdery mildew, can be a real problem. Look for disease-resistant roses that will keep their attractive foliage all through the growing season. The roses you'll find in the list at right are all outstanding performers that can take the challenges the Southeast has to offer and still look good.

FIVE GREAT ROSES

America ('JACclam') 10 to 12 ft.; double salmon-pink; fragrant; cold-hardy in USDA zones 6 to 9; heat-tolerant in AHS zones 9 to 1

Lady Banks (*Rosa banksiae*) rambler; 12 to 18 ft.; double white; fragrant; cold-hardy in USDA zones 8 to 10; heat-tolerant in AHS zones 9 to 1

PHOTO **'Old Blush' (*Rosa odorata* 'Pallida')** 12 to 20 ft.; double pink; fragrant; cold-hardy in USDA zones 7 to 9; heat-tolerant in AHS zones 9 to 1

'Rhonda' 7 to 10 ft.; large double pink; fragrant; cold-hardy in USDA zones 5 to 9; heat-tolerant in AHS zones 9 to 1

'Sombreuil' 6 to 10 ft.; double white; fragrant; cold-hardy in USDA zones 6 to 9; heat-tolerant in AHS zones 12 to 1

'Old Blush'

KEEP YOUR CLIMBER BLOOMING

A big tangle of thorny rose canes can seem complicated, not to mention dangerous, to prune. But it's not as difficult as you might think. A little attention about three times a year is all you need to get the best blooms.

Late spring The rose in the illustration at right is looking great. There are still a lot of blooms but some are past. Now it's time to start removing those spent blossoms. You've probably heard complicated instructions about pruning back to outward-facing buds and so on. But research by the Royal Horticulture Society in Great Britain has found a simpler way to get this job done: Just use pruners or your hands to pinch spent flowers anywhere from 1 to 4 in. below the base of the bloom. If it's a rose that has clusters, like the one in the photo at right, cut individual flowers as they fade or wait and remove the whole spray when it's done flowering.

Spring As temperatures warm in spring, new canes start growing, and they'll need to be trained to the structure the rose is growing on. Gently bend (or wrestle, as the case may be) the cane toward the support structure. If you can fan the canes out a bit, you'll get more blooms. If the stem in the small illustration at right were growing straight up and down, it would have flowers only at the tip. But because this cane is growing at about a 45-degree angle, it's loaded with buds all along the stem.

Use twine or a piece of old stocking — something soft that won't dig into the stem — to tie the canes in a figure eight to the lattice. See in the photo how the figure eight holds the cane away from the wood? That way the cane doesn't rub against the structure and create a wound where insects or disease can enter.

Late winter If you live where winters are mild, gentle pruning the second year will keep your rose from getting away from you. But if you live where it's colder, don't prune your climbing rose the first two years so it can get established. Wait until late winter of the third year. Notice how all the foliage is gone in the lower part of this illustration at right? That makes it easier to see the shape of the rose. First, remove any dead branches. They'll be brown or gray in color, not green. Now step back and evaluate the whole plant. Get rid of branches that are growing the wrong direction or detract from the shape of the shrub. As the plant matures, cut out older, woodier-looking canes like the one in the photo. This will encourage new canes (the bright green ones), which in turn produce more flowers.

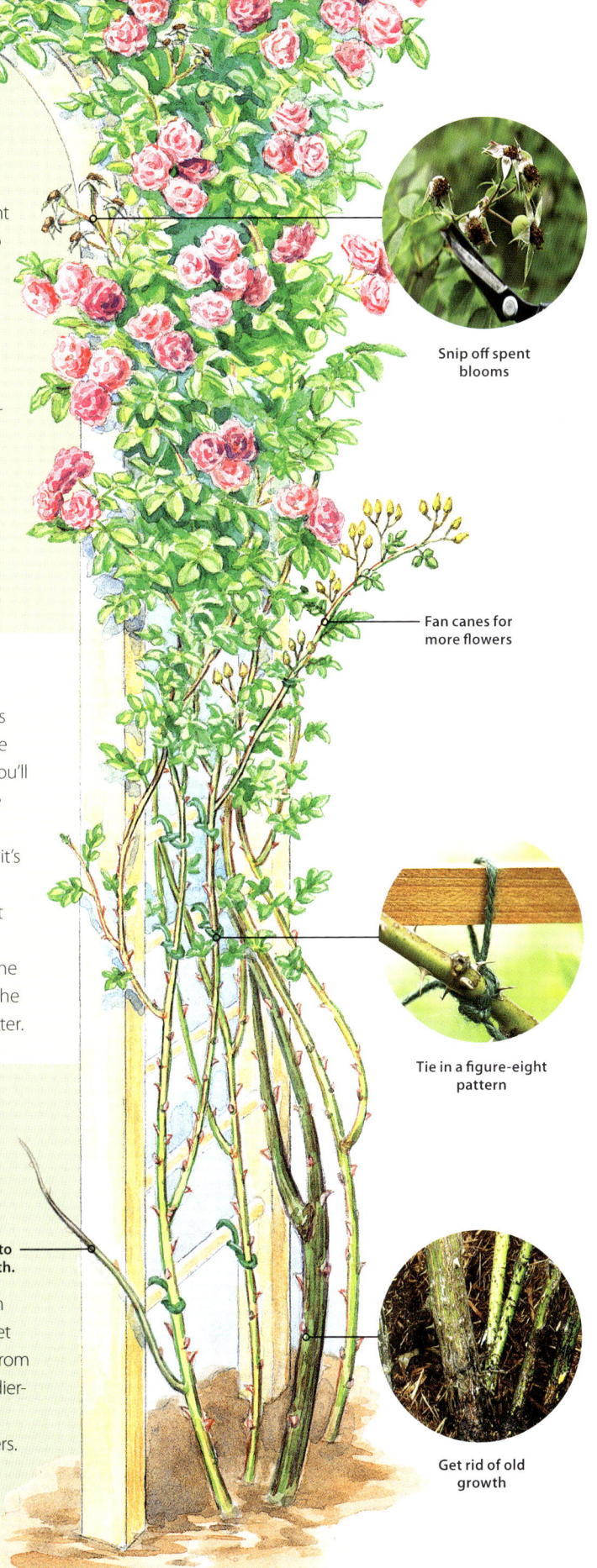

Snip off spent blooms

Fan canes for more flowers

Tie in a figure-eight pattern

Cut dead canes back to green growth.

Get rid of old growth

www.GardenGateMagazine.com — the YEAR IN GARDENING — 23

PLANTS | SHADE PERENNIAL

Bring on the color — even in the shade!
Corydalis

Corydalis lutea

CORYDALIS
Corydalis spp.

4 to 18 in. tall,
6 to 12 in. wide

Flowers in shades of
yellow, white, blue
and purple

Part sun to shade

Well-drained soil

Cold-hardy in
USDA zones 4 to 8

Heat-tolerant in
AHS zones 8 to 1

Botanical Names

Blue corydalis
  Corydalis flexuosa
Hakonechloa
  Hakonechloa spp.
Hellebore *Helleborus* spp.
Hosta *Hosta* hybrids
Impatiens *Impatiens* hybrids
Old-fashioned bleeding heart
  Dicentra spectabilis
Strawberry begonia
  Saxifraga stolonifera
White corydalis
  Corydalis ochroleuca
Yellow corydalis
  Corydalis lutea

PHOTOS: Courtesy of www.TerraNovaNurseries.com ('Berry Exciting' and 'Blue Panda')

If you have shade, you've probably already grown hostas and impatiens. But what if I told you there's a perennial that grows happily in the shade, is covered in blooms all spring and has pretty foliage the rest of the time? Sound good to you? Try corydalis!

There are a lot of corydalis species and hybrids out there. Some species are better suited to rock gardens, but three species and their hybrids are easy to find and grow in perennial borders. Whether you shop at a nursery or from catalogs, you'll find these plants listed by their botanical names. But you can also tell them apart by flower color. Yellow corydalis, in photo 1, is the most common and doesn't die back in summer as quickly as other corydalis do. 'Pere David', 'Purple Leaf' and 'Blue Panda' in the first inset at right are all good choices for blue corydalis. White-flowered corydalis, in the center, can be a little harder to find but is just as easy to grow. If you're looking for something new, try a hybrid: 'Berry Exciting' in the last inset has golden yellow leaves and purple flowers. 'Canary Feathers' has especially large flowers.

GET GROWING If you're heading to the garden center, check out "Don't pass me by" below before you go. With corydalis, first impressions can be deceiving.

You can grow corydalis in part sun if there's plenty of moisture in that spot. Where corydalis really shows its stuff, though, is in the shade. Good drainage and regular watering are important to keep this perennial looking its best. Plants growing in clay soil generally don't survive winter because they rot.

Corydalis is a temperature-sensitive plant. When summers get hot, humid and dry, don't be surprised if it goes dormant, as old-fashioned bleeding heart does. For this reason, corydalis doesn't usually do well in Southeastern gardens. If the foliage gets tattered in the heat, just cut it back to within a few inches of the ground. When temperatures cool off again in fall, the foliage will return and maybe a few flowers, too. Blue-flowering types can look even brighter when mornings and evenings stay cool.

To get more corydalis, your best bet is to buy plants or replant seedlings. Corydalis doesn't divide well. In fact, where it's happy, it can reseed so much it becomes a bit of a pest, but the seedlings are easy to pull. Hybrids don't usually self seed.

LOOKING GOOD With its low-growing mounded habit, corydalis is a natural near the front of the border, next to a patio or along a path. I think you'll find that most shade-tolerant plants are good companions for this tough perennial. Go ahead, tuck a few into your hosta border to add a splash of color. Or combine corydalis with impatiens for some shocking yellow and orange or pink combos. And don't forget

---

DON'T PASS ME BY

Corydalis can look a little puny in the garden center. Often, it's because it's been watered *too* much. But don't let plants like the one in the photo at left fool you. Planted in well-drained soil, even a plant that looks like this one will soon be the star of your garden.

the YEAR IN GARDENING

(1) Keep shade colorful with yellow-flowered corydalis. When the blooms are done you can enjoy the pretty blue-green foliage.

Blue Panda

White corydalis

'Berry Exciting'

to choose companions with contrasting foliage. The combination in photo 1 is a good example of how to contrast corydalis foliage with perennials that have different leaf shapes and colors. Lacy corydalis leaves really stand out near the long, elegant chartreuse leaves of hakonechloa, the round, red-green strawberry begonia down near the stone and the large hellebore leaves above it.

I especially like to take advantage of the plant's tendency to self-seed. I love the surprise of finding a little plant in an unexpected place. It's just one of the many great things about this tough perennial. ☐

— *Sherri Ribbey*

Mail-order sources

Forestfarm
www.forestfarm.com
541-846-7269. Catalog free

Digging Dog Nursery
www.diggingdog.com
707-937-1130. Catalog $4

PLANTS | SUMMER PERENNIAL

What if you could have one daylily with three months of color?

Marathon BLOOMS

'Stella de Oro'

DAYLILY
Hemerocallis hybrids

1 to 3 ft. tall,
 9 to 24 in. wide

Flowers in every
 color but blue in
 early summer
 through fall

Full sun to part shade

Moist, well-drained soil

Daylily rust and deer
 are occasional
 problems

Cold-hardy in
 USDA zones 3 to 9

Heat-tolerant in
 AHS zones 9 to 1

Gardeners love daylilies because they produce loads of flowers with little care. Wouldn't it be great if they also bloomed for months? Believe it or not, some do. Traditionally, the most reliable reblooming daylilies had small yellow or orange flowers that opened in midsummer — think 'Stella de Oro'. But hybridizers have been expanding the range of color and size of flowers and plants. Doubles and fragrant blooms are available, too. Many of these marathon-bloomers start earlier in summer and last longer into fall. Let me show you seven of the best long-blooming (75 days or longer) daylilies. Most are heat-tolerant in AHS zones 9 to 1, but cold-hardiness varies a bit, so I'll list this for each one. I've included the heights for each as well, but you can space all these daylilies 18 to 24 inches apart.

1 'VARIETY IS THE SPICE' This rebloomer flowers almost nonstop for 75 days. For each plant sold, $1 is donated to Variety — The Children's Charity. Go to www.charityplants.com to find a nursery near you. Midsummer to fall; 4-inch, double coral-red flowers; 26 inches tall; USDA zones 4 to 8

2 'MISS AMELIA' If you're looking for a prolific long-bloomer, this is your daylily. Each plant has loads of fragrant blooms for more than three months! In addition, 'Miss Amelia' multiplies quickly, so you'll have a beautiful mass in no time. Early to late summer; 3½-inch pale yellow flowers; 30 inches tall; USDA zones 3 to 9

3 'MATT'S GIFT' Add a cheery yellow dash to any border with the nicely ruffled blooms of 'Matt's Gift', a 2005 introduction. A soft fragrance makes them even nicer to have in the garden. Mid- to late summer; 7-inch bright lemon-yellow blooms; 36 inches tall; USDA zones 3 to 10

4 'QUEEN CAROLINE' You need to wait until a little later in summer for the beautiful blooms and light fragrance of 'Queen Caroline'. But this 2008 introduction is worth the wait. Midsummer to midfall; 6-inch gold-ruffled pastel peach flowers; 24 inches tall; USDA zones 3 to 10

5 'ELEGANT CANDY' The bright blooms of 'Elegant Candy' hold their color well and have an added bonus of being strongly perfumed. The red eye and green throat, along with the heavily ruffled edges, add even more splash to the garden. Early to midsummer; 4¼-inch pink blooms; 25 inches tall; USDA zones 3 to 9

6 'INWOOD' NEW '09 Fragrance and a dramatic purple-plum eye highlight the flowers of this brand-new 2009 introduction. The flowers sport plum-picoteed edges that look like tightly compressed pie crust. Each branch holds 25 buds. Early to midsummer; 6½-inch peach-cream flowers; 25 inches tall; USDA zones 3 to 9

7 'LADY SCARLET' 'Lady Scarlet' offers loads of buds on vigorous plants. Eye-popping color and velvety texture make this one of the best red rebloomers. Early to midsummer; 6-inch scarlet red blooms; 24 inches tall; USDA zones 4 to 10

As you can see, some of these daylilies are recent introductions, while others have been around a while. One might become your new favorite. Give them a try! □

— *Deborah Gruca*

Mail-order

Garden Crossings
www.gardencrossings.com
616-875-6355. *Online catalog only*

Klehm's Song Sparrow Farm and Nursery
www.songsparrow.com
800-553-3715. *Catalog free*

Oakes Daylilies
www.oakesdaylilies.com
800-532-9545. *Catalog free*

the YEAR IN GARDENING   27

.ANTS | EDITOR'S CHOICE

Frosty Kiss Mix Gazania

Gazania rigens

Size	8 in. tall, 7 to 8 in. wide
Type	Annual
Bloom	Pink, yellow, orange and white daisy-shaped flowers from spring to fall
Soil	Well-drained
Light	Full sun
Pests	None serious
Hardiness	Cold: USDA zones 10 to 11 Heat: AHS zones 12 to 1

Sometimes gaudy is good! These showy flowers will certainly liven up your garden.

And they're not just perky. These little plants are tough, too. They'll take hot, dry conditions without a whimper, and they don't need much care to bloom all summer. Let's take a look at where to plant them and how to make them look their best.

CREATIVE COLORS They're bright and showy, but gazanias aren't very tall. So put them close to a path or patio, where you'll be able to see them easily. Or plant a mass of gazanias together. As you can see in the photo, you can't help but notice that splash of color.

Another way to show off gazanias is in a container, like the one in "A can't-miss combo" below. That gets the gazanias up where you can admire all the gorgeous detail.

You can buy gazania plants in just about any garden center. Look for the Frosty Kiss Mix in the photo — they have more silvery hairs on their leaves than most gazanias. Color mixes are easy to find, but what if you want a bunch of one color? Buy seed packets instead to get more single-color choices. Keep reading to find out how to grow them from seed or plants.

GROW GAZANIAS! The most important thing about gazanias is that they don't mind a little drought. In fact, they prefer things on the dry side. Like many plants with fuzzy leaves, summer rain or humidity can collect on the foliage and cause the plant to rot. Gazanias don't even like cloudy days — the flowers close up if it's not sunny!

That susceptibility to humidity means that sometimes gazanias crash by midsummer in humid parts of the South. If that's the case for you, grow them as cool-weather annuals and replace them for the summer. Gazanias often flower all summer in cooler Northern gardens.

So when do you plant gazanias? You can buy plants for early spring planting. But if you buy seeds, count on blooms about 12 weeks after sowing. You'll want to start them inside, just as you would vegetable seeds. Plant the seeds about ⅛ inch deep, and keep them at a temperature of 65 to 75 degrees. As you might guess, don't overwater the seedlings! Once the weather warms up and there's no chance of frost, plant them outside and prepare to enjoy the colorful show. ☐

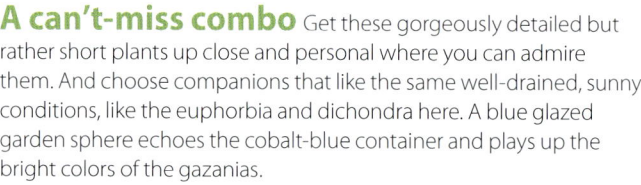

A can't-miss combo Get these gorgeously detailed but rather short plants up close and personal where you can admire them. And choose companions that like the same well-drained, sunny conditions, like the euphorbia and dichondra here. A blue glazed garden sphere echoes the cobalt-blue container and plays up the bright colors of the gazanias.

A **Euphorbia** *Euphorbia hypericifolia* Diamond Frost® 12 to 18 in. tall, 12 in. wide; cold-hardy in USDA zones 10 to 11; heat-tolerant in AHS zones 12 to 1

B **Gazania** *Gazania* Frosty Kiss Mix 8 in. tall, 7 to 8 in. wide; cold-hardy in USDA zones 10 to 11; heat-tolerant in AHS zones 12 to 1

C **Dichondra** *Dichondra argentea* Silver Falls™ 3 to 4 in. tall, 16 to 24 in. wide; cold-hardy in USDA zones 9 to 11; heat-tolerant in AHS zones 12 to 1

Mail-order source

Harris Seeds
www.harrisseeds.com
800-544-7938. *Catalog free*

PLANTS | SHADE PERENNIAL

Plant Japanese painted fern in a tough spot and watch it shine!

Shimmer in the Shade

PHOTO: Deborah Gruca

JAPANESE PAINTED FERN
Athyrium niponicum pictum

12 to 18 in. tall, spreading
Moist, humus-rich,
   well-drained soil
Part shade to shade
No serious pests or diseases
Cold-hardy in
   USDA zones 4 to 9
Heat-tolerant in
   AHS zones 9 to 1

Botanical Names

Bugleweed
   Ajuga reptans
Coleus
   Solenostemon hybrids
Coral bells
   Heuchera spp.
Hosta *Hosta* spp.
Wood sorrel *Oxalis* spp.

Mail-order sources

Whitney Gardens & Nursery
www.whitneygardens.com
800-952-2404. Catalog $4

Dayton Nurseries
www.daytonnursery.com
866-500-6605. Catalog free

There are plenty of great shade plants for perennial gardens. But for an outstanding plant with fascinating texture, it's hard to do better than Japanese painted fern.

Sure, its airy, beautifully subtle fronds give it an unmistakable elegance. And watching those fiddleheads unfurl from a bed of ground covers in early spring is always fascinating. However, this tough fern has more going for it than a pretty face. Great cold- and heat-tolerance and the ability to spread into a lovely drift are other features that make it well worth a spot in your shade garden. Because it's small and so fine-textured, it can be a little tricky to showcase in the border. Check out three great ideas for combos at right.

SIMPLE TO GROW Japanese painted fern prefers moist, compost-rich soil. But it will grow in acid, wet or dry conditions. It'll even tolerate heavy clay soil if you make sure to add a couple inches of compost around the plant each spring.

For a gorgeous ground cover, space your young plants 12 inches apart. This might be closer than you'd think, but Japanese painted ferns don't take off very quickly. (This makes them good in containers — they won't crowd out their companions.) It may be a year or longer before you notice any difference in size at all. Give them a couple of years before they grow dense enough to shade out weeds.

As I mentioned, they're tolerant of dry soil, but even moisture is really best. Your plants will grow faster, bigger and look better overall. If plants dry out, the fronds often turn brown, and the plants will just sit there, not putting on new growth.

Because they're slow to get going, you won't need to divide your plants very often. Every four or five years is about right, if the plants form a colony that's larger than the space you've allotted for it. Dividing is easy to do: Just dig the plants around the edge of your clump in early spring when you see the new fiddleheads start to emerge from the ground. Replant the divisions at the same depth they were growing or share some with gardening friends. They'll be happy to get them and you'll be adding a little bit of elegance and shimmer to *their* shade, too. □

— *Deborah Gruca*

(1) Bring out the color Rosy 'Caramel' coral bells makes a natural companion, as it brings out the colors of the Japanese painted fern's stems and leaf centers. Fern cultivars here are (clockwise from the top) 'Ghost', 'Wildwood Twist' and 'Pewter Lace'.

(2) Size it up It's easy to make Japanese painted fern shine when you grow it in a pot with smaller plants. The airy fronds burst from this basket next to bright green wood sorrel, purple bugleweed and red coleus. And the fern will stay a manageable, compact size when grown in a container. Take all but the coleus out and plant them in the garden in fall. Want the plan for this container? Check out our Web extra.

(3) Contrast in texture Enhance the fine fronds of Japanese painted fern by planting it near partners with large bold leaves. Here, foliage of hosta and coral bells add a different texture to the mix.

PLANTS | EDITOR'S CHOICE

'Elizabeth' Magnolia

Magnolia 'Elizabeth'

Size	20 to 35 ft. tall, 20 to 25 ft. wide
Habit	Upright oval tree
Bloom	Creamy yellow in spring
Soil	Moist, well-drained, slightly acid
Light	Full sun to part shade
Pests	None serious
Hardiness	Cold: USDA zones 4 to 8 Heat: AHS zones 8 to 1

I've always liked magnolias, or, as some folks call them, tulip or cucumber trees. However, where I live in northern zone 5, the buds of many magnolias sometimes turn black, ruined by a late freeze. But not 'Elizabeth'. Just a couple of weeks' tardiness makes a big difference in the blossoms.

Catalogs list 'Elizabeth' as yellow, and the pointed buds are a rich yellow. But as you see in the photo, they open the color of cream. No matter what color the flowers are, they have a lovely, sweet fragrance.

Compared to many magnolias, 'Elizabeth' is moderate- to fast-growing — sometimes putting on 2 feet of growth a year. And even a young, 3-foot-tall sapling will bloom with full-size, 6-inch-wide flowers.

THE BEST SPOT Want to show the pale flowers to perfection? Plant 'Elizabeth' in front of a dark or solid-colored backdrop, such as evergreens.

If you garden around and under 'Elizabeth', be gentle. The roots are shallow and fleshy so it's easy to damage them as you dig. Carefully tuck a few spreading plants under the tree while it's young. Ground covers, such as vinca, lily of the valley or the bluebells you see in our illustration below, work well.

OFF TO A GOOD START Magnolias resent transplanting as they get older, so purchase a young plant, one that's smaller than 6 or 8 feet tall, either balled and burlapped or in a container. And when you plant, make sure the crown, where the trunk and roots meet, is set level with the surrounding soil. If in doubt, it's always better to plant the tree on a bit of a mound.

'Elizabeth' isn't one of those trees that's spectacular for just one season and then goes into hiding. Big glossy leaves look good all summer. And peek between the leaves in early autumn to see the cucumber-shaped pods as they begin to turn pink. Later, the leaves often change to a warm, golden brown just before they fall. This ornamental tree definitely deserves a spot in your garden. ◻

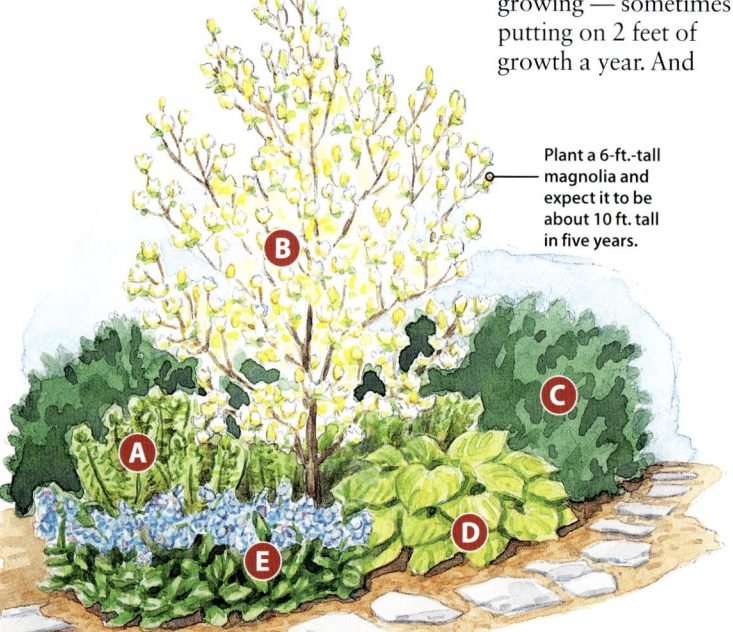

Plant a 6-ft.-tall magnolia and expect it to be about 10 ft. tall in five years.

Spring beauty Capitalize on the pale-yellow magnolia flowers by contrasting them with a few spring Virginia bluebells. Later, enjoy the contrast between the bold foliage of 'Elizabeth' and the fine-textured yews and ostrich ferns.

A **Ostrich fern** *Matteuccia struthiopteris*; 3 to 5 ft. tall, 3 ft. wide; cold-hardy in USDA zones 3 to 8; heat-tolerant in AHS zones 8 to 1

B **Magnolia** *Magnolia* 'Elizabeth'; 20 to 35 ft. tall, 20 to 25 ft. wide; cold-hardy in USDA zones 4 to 8; heat-tolerant in AHS zones 8 to 1

C **Yew** *Taxus xmedia* 'Brownii'; 5 ft. tall and wide; cold-hardy in USDA zones 4 to 7; heat-tolerant in AHS zones 7 to 1

D **Hosta** *Hosta* 'Sum and Substance'; 30 in. tall, 5 ft. wide; cold-hardy in USDA zones 3 to 8; heat-tolerant in AHS zones 8 to 1

E **Virginia bluebells** *Mertensia virginica*; 12 to 24 in. tall, spreading; cold-hardy in USDA zones 3 to 7; heat-tolerant in AHS zones 7 to 1

Mail-order sources

ForestFarm
www.forestfarm.com
541-846-7269
Catalog free, $5 in Canada

Klehm's Song Sparrow Perennial Farm and Nursery
www.songsparrow.com
800-553-3715. Catalog free

PLANTS | SPRING PERENNIAL

Sure Sign of Spring

Moss phlox is better than ever!

'Emerald Pink'

MOSS PHLOX
Phlox subulata

4 to 6 in. tall, 12 to 24 in. wide
Flowers in shades of red, pink, violet, blue and white in early spring
Full sun to part shade
Well-drained soil, slightly alkaline
No serious pests
Cold-hardy in USDA zones 3 to 9
Heat-tolerant in AHS zones 9 to 1

Botanical Names

Daffodil
Narcissus hybrid
Tulip *Tulipa* hybrid

Moss phlox is one of those tried-and-true perennials that we often neglect in lieu of newer flowers. But wouldn't you like to have a perennial that insects leave alone? Or one that comes through the coldest winters and the hottest summers without extra care?

You may know this spring bloomer as moss pink, mountain phlox, ground pink, creeping phlox or flowering moss. No matter what you call it, this perennial is easily recognized by the low, dense mounds of bright color you see at right.

DRY IS GOOD While you can plant moss phlox and forget it, choosing the right spot and doing a little bit of maintenance will reap bigger rewards. The first thing to keep in mind is that this plant grows best with good drainage. Now, I don't mean pure sand or gravel, but a spot where water drains away quickly is ideal. A rock wall like the one in this photo is a good place. If you're planting in a garden, squeeze a handful of your soil when it's moist. If it forms into a tight ball, it's not fast-draining. The roots will rot and the plant will die.

To protect moss phlox from crown rot in heavy soils, plant the crown, the spot where the roots and stems meet, an inch or two higher than the surrounding area. This slight mound of soil won't show later, since each plant forms a broad mat that will cover it.

SHOW IT OFF Plant moss phlox along a path where you can enjoy the flowers in spring and the semi-evergreen foliage later in the year. Since this is a plant that tolerates heat, it'll even take that sunny spot along your sidewalk or driveway. Most spring bulbs need well-drained soil while they're dormant, so moss phlox is a great companion. Tuck tulips or daffodils around the plant so they'll poke through the mat of flowers.

Wherever you grow moss phlox, it'll look best if you plant several in a group. Use all one variety or create a tapestry of color by letting several colors grow together. After the flowers fade, you have a mat of clean, fine, needlelike foliage. In "Shear beauty," below at right, I'll show you how to keep it looking fresh.

PROPAGATION TIPS When you want more moss phlox, you *can* divide old clumps after they flower. But to be honest, the spot where the roots and stems meet is small and woody, making it difficult to split.

Layering takes a little longer, but I've had better luck with it. In mid- to late spring, dig two or three shallow holes underneath the mat of stems, about halfway between the crown and the stem tips. The hole only needs to be a couple of inches wide and an inch or two deep. Push several stems into each hole and spread the soil back on top of them. Set a rock over the stems to hold them in place. The stems will form roots where they come into contact with the soil. Next spring, after the flowers fade, go ahead and cut the new plants from the parent and move them.

As you can see, this charming and easy-to-grow perennial has as much to offer as its taller, summer-blooming phlox cousins. It's ready, and able, to take its place front and center in the very best perennial gardens. □

— *Jim Childs*

There are several great named cultivars, but this perennial's been around so long that often it's just sold by color. To get the best habits and colors, try to find named cultivars like the 'White Delight' and 'Atropurpurea' in this rock wall, or the ones shown in the insets below.

'Red Wing'

'Emerald Blue'

Candy Stripe ('Tamaongalei')

SHEAR BEAUTY

Lightly shear the top growth after the flowers fade.

Cut back the diameter by about half to keep a full and dense plant.

If your moss phlox is beginning to get a bald spot in the center or looks tired and ragged, it's easy to remedy. Every year or two, right after it blooms, remove any dead stems that have built up underneath. Next trim all of the stems back so you reduce the mat to roughly half its original diameter. Then lightly shear the top just to even it out, no more than an inch. This may sound severe, but new growth will sprout from the center and the remaining stems. In a few weeks you'll have a dense mat of fresh new foliage. And next spring will bring a lush carpet of flowers.

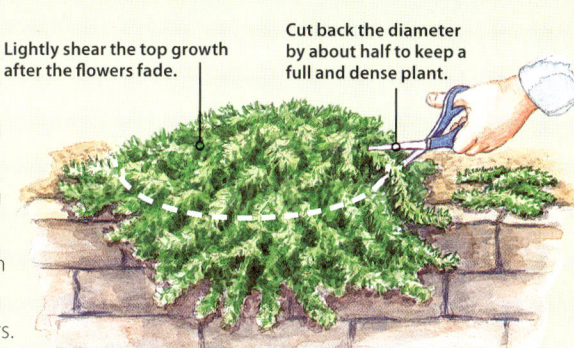

PLANTS | EDITOR'S CHOICE

Naked Ladies

Lycoris squamigera

Size	18 to 24 in. tall, 6 to 18 in. wide
Type	Bulb
Bloom	Pink flowers on bare stalks in late summer
Soil	Rich, well-drained soil
Light	Sun to part sun
Pests	None serious
Hardiness	Cold: USDA zones 5 to 9 Heat: AHS zones 9 to 1

An elderly neighbor once asked me what these pretty pink flowers were called. I said they were surprise lilies. She laughed, "When I was a girl, we called those naked ladies!" Well, so had I, but I hadn't wanted to say that to her!

This is a plant with a lot of common names. You might also hear it called "magic lily" or "resurrection lily." But whatever you call it, it's a late-summer star. In spring, strappy leaves emerge. They stick around for about a month, then wither. And then … nothing happens for a couple of months. Finally, up comes a cluster of bare stalks (that explains those common names), practically overnight. Each stalk has three to eight fragrant flowers that last for a couple of weeks before they fade.

CAREFREE CHARM
What do you have to do to grow naked ladies? Not much!

Pick the right spot, because these plants take a couple of years to get established and they don't like to be moved. An area with full to part sun and rich, well-drained soil is perfect. They don't need much water after the foliage dies down. A little all-purpose fertilizer around the foliage is fine, but it's not crucial.

When you're planting bulbs, usually in early to midsummer when they're dormant, tuck them in 5 to 6 inches deep and 6 inches apart. (In USDA zones 8 and 9, where winters are warmer, you can plant them just 2 or 3 inches deep.)

Naked ladies will spread into clumps that can be divided, but they don't set seed. You can divide an established clump just as the foliage goes down. But be warned: They may not do anything, even put out leaves, for two or three years after being divided. So don't forget to mark where you planted them!

SET THE SCENE
These pink beauties are a welcome splash of color at a slow time in the garden. Tuck them behind something that'll hide the fading foliage, like the barberry at right. In "Late-summer sensation" below, they pop out from behind perennial geraniums. But don't try to combine them with annuals — like most bulbs, naked ladies don't like to be watered when they're dormant. So pair them with tough perennials or shrubs, then wait to be surprised! ☐

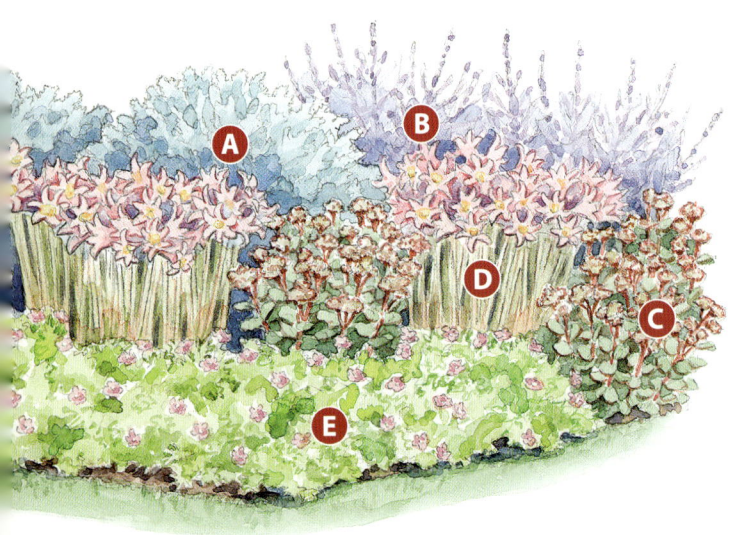

Late-summer sensation Shades of blue, purple and pink will make even the hottest late-summer day feel a few degrees cooler.

- **A** **Dwarf blue spruce** *Picea pungens* 'Globosa' 3 to 4 ft. tall, 4 ft. wide; cold-hardy in USDA zones 2 to 8; heat-tolerant in AHS zones 8 to 1
- **B** **Russian sage** *Perovskia atriplicifolia* 3 to 5 ft. tall, 2 to 4 ft. wide; cold-hardy in USDA zones 3 to 9; heat-tolerant in AHS zones 9 to 1
- **C** **Sedum** *Sedum* 'Matrona' 18 to 24 in. tall and wide; cold-hardy in USDA zones 3 to 8; heat-tolerant in AHS zones 9 to 1
- **D** **Naked ladies** *Lycoris squamigera* 18 to 24 in. tall, 6 to 18 in. wide; cold-hardy in USDA zones 5 to 9; heat-tolerant in AHS zones 9 to 1
- **E** **Geranium** *Geranium* 'Tiny Monster' 12 to 15 in. tall, 24 to 36 in. wide; cold-hardy in USDA zones 4 to 8; heat-tolerant in AHS zones 8 to 1

Mail-order sources

Brent and Becky's Bulbs
www.brentandbeckysbulbs.com
877-661-2852. *Catalog free*

Old House Gardens
www.oldhousegardens.com
734-995-1486. *Catalog $2*

PLANTS | EDITOR'S CHOICE

Red Barrenwort

Epimedium xrubrum

Size	6 to 12 in. tall, spreading
Bloom	Red with creamy yellow centers in early spring
Soil	Moist, humus-rich, well-drained soil
Light	Part shade to shade
Pests	None serious
Hardiness	Cold: USDA zones 5 to 9 Heat: AHS zones 9 to 1

Flowering ground covers for sun are a dime a dozen. But what about ones that grow in shade and are also drought-tolerant? They do exist — let me tell you about my favorite.

LOTS TO LOVE Red barrenwort is a great plant for lots of reasons. First, this deer-resistant ground cover spreads a bit faster than most barrenworts, though not aggressively so. And the plant won't die out in the center, like a lot of other spreaders do. In fact, you can grow red barrenwort in one place, such as in the dry shade beneath trees and shrubs, for many years before it needs dividing. Though it prefers moist, well-drained soil, established plants are also quite drought-tolerant. And the dense leaves discourage weeds from sprouting nearby.

About the same time the daffodils finish blooming in spring, the intricate ¾-inch flowers you see at right open on wiry stems and last for several weeks. They eventually fall away on their own, so you don't even need to deadhead.

As the flowers fade, the emerging foliage stretches to cover the bare flower stems. In spring, the heart-shaped leaves are framed by a thin red margin. The center of the leaf is blushed with a beautiful red mottled pattern that turns a bright green by summer. Then in fall, the leaves have a bronze-red tinge.

DOWN IN FRONT Because the plant and flowers are small, you might walk right by them without noticing, so place the plants at the front of the border where you'll see them. An ideal place is right next to an often-used path, as in "A shade better," below.

EASY CARE As you can see, red barrenwort is a cinch to grow. I already mentioned that you don't have to deadhead, water or divide it often. Just plant it in a spot that gets morning sun. And work 2 inches of compost or rotted manure into the soil before you plant.

In USDA cold-hardiness zone 7 and warmer, the leaves stay on the plant through the winter, though heavy snow may flatten them to the ground. About the only thing you need to do is cut off the old foliage with scissors as you see the new growth emerge in early spring. (If you do it early, you won't risk cutting off the new growth, too.)

Even cutting back isn't necessary. The plant won't mind if you don't do it, but it'll look tidier. And it's certainly not too much work for such a great plant! □

Plant bugleweed 12 in. apart; they'll quickly form a dense mat.

A shade better Add color to a shady spot from early spring to summer with plants that thrive in moist or even dry soil. The dainty bell-shaped blue flowers of the lungwort open at the same time as the red and cream blooms of barrenwort. And by late spring into summer, bugleweed opens its beautiful blue flowers.

A Japanese painted fern *Athyrium niponicum pictum* 12 to 18 in. tall, 18 in. wide; cold-hardy in USDA zones 4 to 9; heat-tolerant in AHS zones 9 to 1

B Red barrenwort *Epimedium xrubrum* 6 to 12 in. tall, spreading; cold-hardy in USDA zones 4 to 9; heat-tolerant in AHS zones 9 to 1

C Lungwort *Pulmonaria* 'Roy Davidson' 14 in. tall, 18 in. wide; cold-hardy in USDA zones 4 to 8; heat-tolerant in AHS zones 8 to 1

D Bugleweed *Ajuga reptans* 'Bronze Beauty' 6 in. tall, spreading; cold-hardy in USDA zones 3 to 9; heat-tolerant in AHS zones 9 to 1

Mail-order sources

Forestfarm
www.forestfarm.com
541-846-7269. *Catalog free*

Deer-Resistant Landscape Nursery
www.deerresistantplants.com
800-595-3650. *Catalog $3.85, refunded with purchase*

Big Dipper Farm
www.bigdipperfarm.com
360-886-8133. *Online catalog only*

'Becky'

'Fluffy'

'Fiona Coghill'

'Sunny Side Up'

'Crazy Daisy'

(1) For fantastic flowers that open from mid- to late summer, grow 'Becky' Shasta daisies in a sunny, well-drained spot.

PHOTOS: Deborah Gruca ('Sunny Side Up', 'Crazy Daisy', 'Fluffy', 'Fiona Coghill')

40 the YEAR IN GARDENING www.GardenGateMagazine.com

PLANTS | SUMMER PERENNIAL

Light up your garden with Shasta daisies' summer-long blooms.

Raising Daisies

'Becky'

SHASTA DAISY
Leucanthemum ×*superbum*

10 to 40 in. tall,
24 in. wide
White or pale yellow
 flowers from mid-
 to late summer
Full sun to part shade
Well-drained soil,
 slightly alkaline
No serious pests
Cold-hardy in
 USDA zones 4 to 9
Heat-tolerant in
 AHS zones 9 to 1

Botanical Names

Ox-eye daisy
Leucanthemum vulgare

Shasta daisies have long been sunny garden favorites, both in beds and, with their long, stiff stems, as cut flowers. They're a cinch to grow, they bloom for a long time and they attract butterflies, but not deer.

You may be familiar with 'Becky', a heavy-bloomer with an upright habit. That's it, paired with hydrangeas, in photo 1 at left. Growing Shastas in a drift like this is a terrific way to show off the uniform habit and those gorgeous 3½-inch flowers on their sturdy 3-foot stems. 'Becky' starts to flower in July and keeps it up straight through to September. And it's true that 'Becky' is great, but let's take a look at a few of the many other cultivars that you'll find at nurseries and garden centers now.

IMPRESSIVE PETALS Plenty of the new cultivars sport larger flowers, with more eye-catching petals than the older Shastas. Check out the aptly named 'Fluffy', with its fully double flowers sprouting threadlike petals. My favorite double is 'Fiona Coghill', with its audacious pompon flowers. The stout stems are strong enough to hold those heavy 3½-inch blooms, even when they're wet after watering or rain.

If you go for a little more traditional daisy-shaped flowers, try 'Sunny Side Up'. It has a yellow center that's larger than those on other cultivars and the petals, described as "crested," are shorter and more rounded. 'Crazy Daisy' is a 30-inch-tall Shasta that adds a playful attitude to the garden and the haphazard arrangement of petals is as endearing as its name.

A SIZE FOR EVERYONE You will find that Shasta cultivars range in height from 10 to 40 inches and flower size from 2 to almost 5 inches across. Both 'Fluffy' and 'Fiona Coghill' grow to around 27 inches tall, shorter than some but bigger than 16-inch 'Tinkerbelle', with its petite 2-inch blooms. At the other end of the scale, 'Amelia' reaches a good 40 inches tall with 5-inch flowers.

WHITE IS ALRIGHT For the most part, white is the color of Shasta daisies, though there are a few that claim yellow petals. 'Sunshine' ('Sonnenschein') is really a pale yellow, while 'Cobham Gold' is closer to a soft butter-cream.

By now, you probably want lots of Shastas. Just don't accidentally pick up the weedy lookalike I'll show you in "Wild relative," below.

Then turn the page and I'll share some design ideas for the other long-blooming charmers.

WILD RELATIVE

Ox-eye daisy is a Shasta relative with smaller flowers that bloom earlier on thinner, more arching stems. It's considered a weed in some areas because it spreads so quickly and can be hard to get rid of.

Ox-eyes produce tons of seeds that remain viable for years, even after being eaten and digested by animals. And if you dig out the plants, they readily resprout from even small parts of the rhizomes left in the soil.

Ox-eye daisy

GREAT DAISY DESIGN

Botanical Names

Bee balm
Monarda spp.
Catmint *Nepeta* spp.
Lantana
Lantana camara
Shasta daisy
Leucanthemum ×*superbum*
Veronica
Veronica spicata
Yarrow *Achillea* spp.

Because of their inherently rugged nature and the range of plant sizes, there are many different uses for Shasta daisies.

I mix in the shorter cultivars with other plants near the front of borders, where the faded blooms are easy to reach. The ironically named 'Snowcap', at a petite 18 inches tall, looks great among 'Tickled Pink' veronica and 'Confetti' lantana in photo 2. I like how their tidy, upright habit keeps them from sprawling out of the bed. (This is particularly useful where you want to avoid tripping anyone walking along a much-used path or around steps.)

The more common 2- to 3-foot Shastas mingle well with similar-sized plants at the center or back of the bed. Contrasting flowers and leaves make yarrow, bee balm and catmint great companions. Keep in mind that daisy-shaped flowers evoke a calm feeling — probably because of their flat top and familiar shape. Mix them with flowers of other shapes to add some excitement. But go easy on spikes — a few go a long way in any setting. I especially like Shastas combined with the arching stems of large grasses. And the white color of the Shastas shows up well and has the advantage of complementing all other flower hues. For a coordinated, pulled-together look, repeat several clumps of three to five Shastas around the bed.

In addition to mixed borders, Shastas are often planted in classic drifts or mass plantings. A large grouping of the fresh white flowers makes a big impact, even when you view it from a distance. If you're not crazy about deadheading all those

(2) Contrast simple Shasta flowers with those of other shapes, like the spikes of light pink veronica and the rounded domes of pink and orange lantanas.

42 *the* YEAR IN GARDENING   www.GardenGateMagazine.com

flowers, place the bed at the far end of the yard where a few faded blooms aren't as noticeable.

Another place to grow Shastas is in containers. Give them full sun and even moisture, but make sure the potting mix is well drained, so the roots don't rot. Plant a larger size plant, though, at least a 4-inch pot or bigger, so it doesn't get overwhelmed right away by more-vigorous pot mates. I snipped the faded blooms of 'White Knight' in the glazed pot in photo 3 every other day and it bloomed for me nearly all summer long.

So try a few Shastas — you'll soon be hooked. Because however you use them, Shastas add a touch of magic to your garden, along with tons of fresh white blooms, from simple to simply splendid!

— *Deborah Gruca*

(3) Keep the flowers flowing in containers by regularly removing faded blooms. Cut or pinch the stem below the bloom and just above a set of leaves.

GROWING SHOWY SHASTAS

When you grow Shastas in well-drained soil in full sun to part shade, these plants don't need a lot of care. A single feeding with an all-purpose fertilizer in spring and regular deadheading are about it. Most don't require staking, but occasionally taller cultivars get knocked down by heavy rains and strong wind.

Shastas take a couple of years to reach their full size and some folks find that they're short-lived (3 or 4 years). But if you amend the soil with plenty of well-rotted manure and compost before you plant, this doesn't have to be the case. Remove faded blooms by cutting the stems just above a pair of leaves with sharp scissors. Doing this also makes the plants look better and the bloom period last considerably longer, so it's well worth the effort.

Flowering is finished by late summer, and you can cut the plant back for a tidier look. Remove the brown stems just above the mound of green foliage, as I'm doing in the photo. You may get a very light rebloom. If, after several years, blooming starts to decline, divide the plants in early spring or early fall to revive them.

Good drainage is as crucial while the plants are dormant as when they're actively growing. Wet soil during the winter can kill them. That's one reason you shouldn't mulch Shastas heavily in winter, not even in northern zones — a light covering of pine needles or chopped leaves is enough. And be sure to remove the mulch and any other debris as the plants emerge in the spring.

PLANTS | EDITOR'S CHOICE

Soapwort

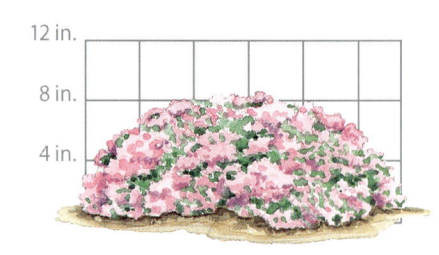

Saponaria ocymoides

Size	6 to 12 in. tall, 24 to 36 in. wide
Type	Perennial
Bloom	Pink flowers in late spring
Soil	Well-drained to dry
Light	Full sun
Pests	None serious
Hardiness	Cold: USDA zones 3 to 8 Heat: AHS zones 8 to 1

Yes, the name is funny, but the plant is certainly pretty! And for a perennial that looks so dainty, it's surprisingly rugged.

This plant was once grown for the soap-like compounds in its leaves and roots. That's not the case now, but you'll still want to grow soapwort. Let's find out how!

EVER SO EASY This easy-care charmer only needs well-drained soil and full sun to perform like crazy. Good drainage is especially important in the winter, when wet soil will cause the roots to rot, killing the plant. In the photo, you'll see it growing on top of a retaining wall. That's a perfect location for soapwort because of the good drainage.

What else do you need to do? Not much! Soapwort is semi-evergreen, meaning that in the southern part of its range, the leaves stay green. But in Northern gardens, it goes dormant for the winter. In early spring, cut back the stems to an inch or two high to leave room for new growth.

You may find that soapwort reseeds if it's in a spot it likes. Seedlings' roots are shallow, so you can easily pull strays. Or shear the plant back by half after it finishes blooming. This will cut down on reseeding and encourage fresh new growth and a nice plant shape.

Soapwort likes a little all-purpose granulated fertilizer in the spring, along with the rest of your perennials. But if you forget, that's fine. Just be sure to avoid over-fertilizing, which causes weak, spindly plants.

OK, it's easy to take care of. So how do you make it look great?

A GARDEN STAR
At no more than a foot tall, soapwort belongs in the front of your garden. Its favorite places, rock gardens and retaining walls, are a great way to show off the mounding, trailing habit. Or let it spill onto a sidewalk or down the side of a raised bed. Those pink blooms show up in late spring and stay for a long time, as long as two or three weeks. Combine it with other perennials, as we have in "Pink and fluffy" below. Or let it fill in around spring-blooming bulbs — it enjoys the same well-drained areas that most bulbs prefer, and it'll be the basis of a gorgeous spring-time show, too!

Pink and fluffy No one would deny that this little planting is as pink and fluffy as cotton candy. But it's also as tough as nails. These plants all like full sun and well-drained, even dry, soil, so they'll be happy companions.

A **Soapwort** *Saponaria ocymoides* See botanical box, above left

B **Geranium** *Geranium* x*cantabrigiense* 'Biokovo' Perennial; 8 to 12 in. tall, 18 to 24 in. wide; cold-hardy in USDA zones 5 to 8, heat-tolerant in AHS zones 8 to 1

C **Sedum** *Sedum telephium* 'Purple Emperor' Perennial; 12 to 15 in. tall and wide; cold-hardy in USDA zones 3 to 9, heat-tolerant in AHS zones 9 to 1

D **Gaura** *Gaura lindheimeri* 'Siskiyou Pink' Perennial; 30 to 36 in. tall and wide; cold-hardy in USDA zones 5 to 8, heat-tolerant in AHS zones 8 to 1

Mail-order sources

Busse Gardens
www.bussegardens.com
800-544-3192. *Catalog $3*

High Country Gardens
www.highcountrygardens.com
800-925-9387. *Catalog free*

PLANTS | SUMMER ANNUAL

ZINNIAS are HOT!

'Scarlet Flame' — a traditional zinnia

ZINNIA
Zinnia elegans

1 to 4 ft. tall, 1 ft. wide

Flowers in all colors except blue

Full sun

Moist, well-drained soil

Powdery mildew can disfigure foliage and occasionally flowers

Annual

Heat-tolerant in AHS zones 12 to 1

Botanical Names

Black-eyed Susan
   Rudbeckia spp.
Petunia
   Petunia hybrids
Sweet alyssum
   Lobularia maritima
Yarrow
   Achillea spp.

Sometimes simple is the way to go: Food that's easy to prepare, clothing that's comfortable and doesn't go out of style quickly. And simple flowers, like zinnias, are the best. Give me a fast-growing, easy-to-take-care-of plant that adds lots of color to my garden and I'll be happy.

Not only easy to grow, zinnias are the most cheerful flowers you can plant. I think it's all of those vivid colors that give them their personality. These days you'll find traditional types, like the ones you see in the photos at right, as well as lots of new hybrids, too. I'll show you those on the next pages. Whether you sow the seeds directly or pick up cell packs at the garden center, it's time to bring you up to date on what's been happening with zinnias.

TRADITIONAL OLD FRIENDS It used to be that most of us grew zinnias in rows. You still can, but why not toss a few seeds around in your border, like the gardener did in the photo at right? What a colorful, and economical, way to fill out a flower bed. Plus, just imagine how many bouquets you could pick from this border!

It's a true testament to the durability of this annual that many of the cultivars grown 50 or more years ago are still available. For example, 'Envy', in the inset at right, was a big hit in the 1950s. And today it's still coveted by both gardeners and flower arrangers. But if you wonder what color to pair with these green flowers, it's been made much easier for you today. Check out "What's new" in the box below right.

Like 'Envy', many of these tall zinnias have large blooms, some 6 inches or more across. Too big for your bouquets? Grow 'Cut and Come Again' zinnias, with 2- to 3-inch flowers. Visiting butterflies will still have plenty of room to stand as they sip nectar from the center of the flower.

Butterflies also like the vivid, easy-to-spot colors. While most zinnias are just one color, you'll also find bicolors — each bloom has a mix of colors on each petal, like the two insets at right. Cheery 'Candy Cane' has petals streaked or splashed with red and white. 'Zowie! Yellow Flame' glows with orange-red petals that look as if the tips have been dipped in gold. Both of these look best if you pair them with solid color flowers that won't compete for attention.

The blooms in most of these photos are called "dahlia-flowered" because of the layers of petals. However, 'Cactus Mix' in the lower right corner, or 'Raggedy Ann', have shaggy petals. They're perfect in a casual garden or an informal bouquet.

We could spend more time reminiscing about these wonderful traditional zinnias. But turn the page and let's take a look at some newer, updated family members.

the YEAR IN GARDENING   www.GardenGateMagazine.com

(1) Butterflies love zinnias, as well as the black-eyed Susans, gold yarrow, purple petunias and white sweet alyssum in this garden. Bright colors also make it easy for butterflies to spot a bed when they're hungry.

'Envy'

'Candy Cane'

'Zowie! Yellow Flame'

'Cactus Mix'

What's new? Tall zinnias are great when you want lots of color. It used to be you bought packets of mixed colors. Then came individual cultivars. These days you'll find color blends, like this chartreuse and apricot 'Décor'. It's available from Renee's Garden Seeds at www.reneesgarden.com. All you have to do is sow the seeds, sit back and enjoy the color!

DESIGN: April and Dallas Janes (1)

www.GardenGateMagazine.com   *the* YEAR IN GARDENING   47

EASY-GOING ZINNIAS

'Profusion Cherry' — a modern zinnia

ZINNIA
Zinnia hybrids

12 to 18 in. tall, 8 to 24 in. wide
Flowers in all colors except blue
Full sun
Moist, well-drained soil
Extremely disease resistant
Annual
Heat-tolerant in AHS zones 12 to 1

Botanical Names

Ageratum
Ageratum houstonianum
Butterfly bush
Buddleja davidii
Coleus
Solenostemon hybrids
Coreopsis
Coreopsis spp.
Heliotrope
Heliotropium arborescens
Mealycup sage
Salvia farinacea
Napier grass
Pennisetum purpureum
Sweet potato vine
Ipomoea batatas

Look around gardens these days and you just might spot zinnias popping up in some new, and sometimes unusual, spots. But you may have to look twice to recognize these new forms.

ZINNIAS ON THE EDGE 'Crystal White', in photo 2, looks more like small daisies than a zinnia. This is a great example of how to use these newer, smaller and densely branched cultivars. They're perfect for landscaping because they don't need staking or even deadheading to look great. Plus, zinnias can take the heat, especially along a south-facing sidewalk like this one. Instead of starting with a packet of seed, pick up a cell pack or two of seedlings at the garden center, pop them in the ground and you have instant color. But if you want lots of them, they're as easy to grow from seeds as the traditional types.

GROW THEM IN A CONTAINER Take a look at 'Profusion Orange' in photo 3. I like the way it "knit" itself into this container combo, peeking out under the coleus and between the blades of grass. Go ahead and crowd zinnias like this in containers. With old cultivars, this would have meant a bad case of powdery mildew on the foliage. But these newer hybrids are extremely resistant to foliage disease. And their compact form means they're easy to take care of, too. You don't have to worry about pinching to keep their size in bounds. If some of the flowers start to look tired, snip them off and you're done — except for watering, of course.

THE NONTRADITIONAL TRADITIONALS
Don't get the idea that all of these new zinnias only have small, 2-inch-diameter flowers. Some of the large-flowered traditional types now come in shorter, stockier forms, too. Check out 12- to 14-inch-tall 'Magellan Coral' in photo 4. This combo is sure to be a butterfly magnet. While the flowers may not be as prolific as the smaller-flowered cultivars, you still get lots of color with the Magellan series. And that's really what zinnias are all about — giving you as much color as possible until frost. But that's OK. Next year, if you like, you can try a completely new color scheme of zinnias. And believe me, there are lots to try! □

— *Jim Childs*

What's next? Don't let their easy-going character fool you — zinnias are tough! But breeders are working to make them even tougher. So what can you expect in the future? Look for larger flowers in stronger, even more long-lasting colors. There's hope there will even be double flowers, instead of mostly singles like the Profusion series in this photo. And since these newer zinnias are so versatile in the landscape, expect to see plants with more branches and spreading habits so you can fill up a large bed with fewer plants.

(2) 'Crystal White' zinnias can take the summer heat, even against a south-facing sidewalk. And since these newer types of zinnias have more branches, you'll get lots of flowers from just a few plants. You won't need to plant masses of them to get a big impact!

(3) 'Profusion' series zinnias are extremely disease resistant. No worries about powdery mildew ruining the foliage in this tightly packed combo of zinnias, variegated coleus, bronze sweet potato vine, spiky 'Princess' napier grass and blue ageratum.

(4) 'Magellan Coral' zinnia is a perfect choice for this butterfly-attracting combo of purple heliotrope, white mealycup sage, magenta butterfly bush and bright yellow coreopsis.

GROWING ZINNIAS

Remember, zinnias are easy to grow. But like most plants, an extra bit of care will yield more, and healthier, flowers.

GET THEM OFF TO A GOOD START Choose a location with good air circulation and full sun — zinnias will be floppy and sickly in shade. And while these annuals tolerate a wide range of soil types, they'll bloom best in a moist, well-drained soil that has lots of compost worked into it. In good soil there's really no need for extra fertilizer, but if you want, a light sprinkling of a low-nitrogen, slow-release food will keep them blooming all summer.

Zinnias will languish in cold weather — they really do like the heat. Sow the seeds directly on tilled soil; and lightly cover them, or set out seedlings you buy in cell packs when the soil is thoroughly warm (about the same time you'd put out tomato plants).

Dry conditions translate to healthier zinnias, so don't overwater. And by all means keep moisture off their leaves to prevent powdery mildew. If you have to water, apply it only at the base of the plant so the foliage stays dry. Add a couple of inches of organic mulch, such as compost, around the plants to keep the soil moist and you won't have to do as much watering.

GROW STRAIGHT STEMS Most of the short cultivars do fine on their own, but tall, traditional types can be top heavy. A "corset" of stakes and twine is ideal. Put it in place while the seedlings are only a few inches tall, as I've done in the illustration below. Zinnia foliage is raspy and rough, so even if you don't weave twine across the circle, the plants will grasp each other and help hold up their neighbors.

KEEP PICKING One of the best things you can do to keep more flowers coming is to deadhead. But why wait for the flowers to fade or turn brown? Pick lots of bouquets, cutting just above a set of healthy leaves. In a week or two, you'll find two new stems sprouting from that spot — and that means more flowers!

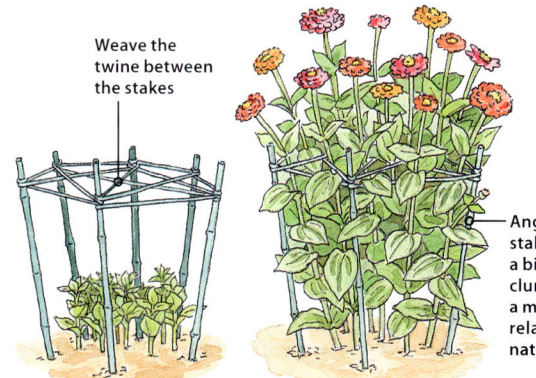

Weave the twine between the stakes

Angle the stakes out a bit so the clump has a more relaxed, natural look

did you know...

Overwintering gerberas
Jane Goodrell, Washington

Q *I have two gerbera daisies. How can I overwinter them?*
A Actually, there are a couple of ways to keep brightly colored gerbera daisies (*Gerbera jamesonii*) over the winter. If your plants are growing in pots, simply bring them, pot and all, into a frost-free space, like a basement or garage, and let the plant go dormant. Don't worry about giving it any light. Check the plant a few times during the winter and give it just enough water to keep the soil barely moist.

Another way to overwinter your gerbera is to bring the plant into the house and keep it growing there. Give it bright light but not direct sunlight. It won't flower much indoors, so cut back on watering and don't feed it until it goes back outside when the weather warms into the 60s in spring.

If your plant has grown quite large by the end of summer, you can also cut it into two or more pieces before bringing it inside. Cut through the crown with a sharp knife and replant the divisions in separate 6-inch containers of well-drained potting mix. Gerberas are susceptible to crown rot, so plant them with the crown just at the soil level and water them in.

Not seeing double
Diane Varrelman, New York

Q *Last year I bought a 'Doubledecker' coneflower, but still haven't seen the double flowers. Why is that?*
A This unusual-looking double coneflower cultivar (*Echinacea purpurea* 'Doubledecker') was developed from a mutant form of the plant. It usually blooms with the standard single flower for the first season after transplanting. The second year, it'll start producing the weird two-tiered flowers that you see at right. Even then, the doubles may be sporadic or look quite different from this one. Sometimes the top layer of the flower looks more upright and irregular. (Both of these flowers were photographed on the same plant in our test garden!)

So be patient and give your coneflower at least one more growing season to develop those unique blooms.

Pop Quiz: Which of these is 'Doubledecker' purple coneflower? (Answer: Both!)

---

in the news

The right rose for you
All-America Rose Selections has a new addition to its Web site that helps you choose the right rose for your region. Visit www.rose.org/regions-choice and you'll find a link for the area where you live. There you'll see a list of the past AARS winners that are best for your region. Click on the photo of the rose you like for more information on growing that variety.

How to prune a crabapple
Marilyn Yost, Minnesota

Q When and how do I prune my flowering crabapple tree (*Malus* hybrid)?

A Late winter to early spring while the tree is dormant is the best time. You want branches to grow from the main stem at a wide angle so they will withstand ice, snow and wind. Remove dead or damaged branches or suckers growing straight up from branches or the base. Cut the branch close to the trunk so you don't leave ugly stubs where diseases can enter. Also, cut out any crossing or rubbing branches for the same reason. And never remove more than a third of the tree's growth at one time.

Resize overgrown burning bush
Chris Schultz, New Jersey

Q I have 4-foot-tall burning bushes (*Euonymus alatus*). Can I prune them down to 2 feet tall?

A Depending on what look you like, you have two options for resizing overgrown burning bushes. For a tightly clipped look, shear the entire shrub back to 18 inches in late winter. As the illustration below shows, the shrub will start growing in spring and fill in to be 2 feet tall. Maintain that height by shearing only the new growth back to the 2-foot size.

The other option, for a more informal look, is to use pruners to cut the bush back in stages over two years. Cut it back to 30 inches high the first year. The next year, cut it back to 18 inches. Make these cuts at branching points to maintain the natural habit. Then you'll have a 2-foot-tall plant.

Shady shrubs
D.A. Fichtl, Georgia

Q What evergreen shrubs can I grow in part shade?

A Gardening in any amount of shade can be tricky. But the good news is, there are options for you. First watch your garden to determine how many hours of direct sun it gets each day. Then match your numbers with the plants listed in the chart below.

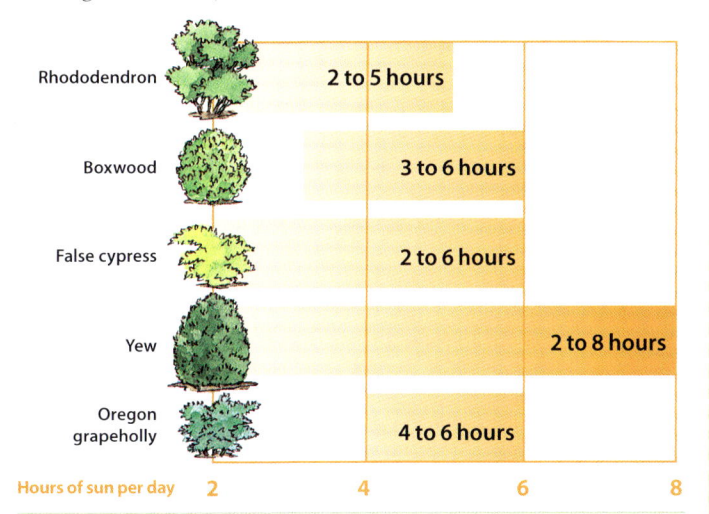

Shrub	Hours of sun per day
Rhododendron	2 to 5 hours
Boxwood	3 to 6 hours
False cypress	2 to 6 hours
Yew	2 to 8 hours
Oregon grapeholly	4 to 6 hours

Rhododendron *Rhododendron* spp. Broadleaf evergreen; flowers in shades of pink, white, purple, red; grows 2 to 10 ft. tall and 5 to 8 ft. wide; cold-hardy in USDA zones 4 to 9; heat-tolerant in AHS zones 9 to 1

Boxwood *Buxus* spp. Broadleaf evergreen; wrap with burlap to protect from drying winter winds; tolerates shearing; grows 3 to 6 ft. tall and wide; cold-hardy in USDA zones 5 to 9; heat-tolerant in AHS zones 9 to 1

False cypress *Chamaecyparis* spp. Needled evergreen; variegated types need more shade so they don't scorch; grows slowly to 6 to 10 ft. tall and wide; cold-hardy in USDA zones 4 to 9; heat-tolerant in AHS zones 9 to 1

Yew *Taxus* spp. Needled evergreen; tolerates shearing; needs well-drained soil; grows 2 to 20 ft. depending on species and cultivar; cold-hardy in USDA zones 4 to 8; heat-tolerant in AHS zones 8 to 1

Oregon grapeholly *Mahonia aquifolium* Broadleaf evergreen; glossy, hollylike leaves; yellow flowers and grapelike fruit; grows 3 to 6 ft. tall and wide; cold-hardy in USDA zones 5 to 9; heat-tolerant in AHS zones 9 to 1

When pruning or shearing shrubs to a particular height, it's best to cut them about 6 in. too short so they'll grow into the final size in spring.

did you know... (CONTINUED)

Cool clematis
June Cole, New York

Q *I've heard that clematis vines need to have shaded roots. How do I do that?*

A The old saying is, "Head in the sun, feet in the shade," and it's partially true. Clematis don't actually need shade on their roots so much as they need cool, moist soil for their roots to grow in.

Spreading a 4-inch-thick layer of bark mulch around the base of the vine will not only keep the soil cool, but will also help conserve moisture. Keep the mulch about 2 inches from the stems to prevent them from developing decay.

Another option is to select planting companions that will shade the soil as they grow. Bearded irises, like those in the illustration at left, are great because they have shallow roots that won't compete with those of the clematis. And in spring you'll enjoy their colorful blooms, too. Roses (*Rosa* spp.) and sea holly (*Eryngium planum*) are two more perennials that make good clematis neighbors. Whatever plant you choose, make sure it likes sun and fertile, moist, well-drained soil too.

If your garden is tight on space, place a container or decorative rock in front of the clematis to shade the soil.

Keep clematis roots cool and moist with mulch or shade-giving plants, such as iris.

Mind your mockorange
Mark Gould, Texas

Q *My five-year-old mockorange has never bloomed. Can you tell me the reason?*

A There are a few possible reasons. First, it's not unusual for a mockorange (*Philadelphus* hybrids) to be slow to start blooming. Small plants take up to two years to start producing a few flowers. But it could be a matter of light. Full sun to part shade is needed for blooms. You might also check to see if it's growing where it receives lawn fertilizer, which is high in nitrogen. This promotes good foliage growth, but not flowers.

In spring, cut out the oldest stems close to the ground.

If neither of these is true for you, try cutting the plant back by a third to half in early spring. Remove the oldest wood as shown above. This should make the plant bloom the following year. If not, try a hard pruning where you cut all the stems back to the ground. After a couple of years it should regrow and start to bloom. Don't want to wait that long? Just remove it and plant another blooming shrub in its place.

Coleus control
Patti Love, Iowa

Q *I put one 'Pineapple' coleus in each of my whiskey barrels. The crazy things got huge and overpowered my other flowers. What can I do?*

A You can easily keep coleus to a manageable size by pinching it back every week. Pinch the growing tips back to just above a pair of leaves. But even then, you may find that a healthy coleus can quickly become large enough to crowd out smaller, less vigorous plants. Luckily, coleus come in a huge range of colors and sizes. If you're looking for a more compact chartreuse coleus, you might want to try one of the smaller ones, such as 'Life Lime', 'Gay's Delight' or 'Freckles'.

For info, photos and suppliers of hundreds of coleus cultivars, see www.coleusfinder.org.

in the news

Fishy plants
Ginnie Heath, North Carolina

Q *I'm looking for plants to grow around my new pond. Are there plants that are bad for the fish?*

A Plants and trees provide welcome shade for the fish in your pond. But when leaves and other plant debris fall into the water, they break down and foul the water. The decomposition uses up the oxygen that the fish need to survive. In addition, the leaves, fruit or bark of some plants have toxic chemicals that poison the fish, so plant choices are very important. Check out the box below for a list of plants you don't want next to your pond.

So rather than growing plants that hang over the water, plant them well away from the edge. Or grow floating water plants, such as water lilies or water lettuce, in the pond to keep your fish cool.

Plants toxic to fish

- **Bleeding heart** *Dicentra* spp.
- **Castor bean** *Ricinus communis*
- **Horse chestnut** *Aesculus* spp.
- **Lily-of-the-valley** *Convallaria majalis*
- **Red maple** *Acer rubrum*
- **White snake root** *Eupatorium rugosum*
- **Yew** *Taxus* spp.

Web extra: See a larger **list** of plants toxic to fish.

Invasive pear trees
Callery pears (*Pyrus calleryana*) have been a staple in urban gardens for years. Varieties 'Bradford', 'Chanticleer' and 'Aristocrat' have graced city streets and back yards with their beautiful spring flowers and fall foliage. Unfortunately, in natural areas, a wild hybrid that sets more fruit and has numerous sharp, thornlike spurs has taken root. The sharp spurs make it difficult to get rid of a tree once it has become established.

Thanks to genetic testing by Dr. Theresa Culley, a professor at the University of Cincinnati, we now know that this invasive pear occurs when 'Bradford' hybridizes with one of the many other cultivars available. The trees have taken hold along roadways, park edges and railroads. So far, the biggest problem is in the South, and some states, such as Maryland, are no longer allowing Callery pears to be planted on city properties. You may want to think twice before planting one in your yard.

Hardy bellflower evaluation results
The Chicago Botanic Garden has its latest plant evaluation out — this time on bellflowers (*Campanula* spp.). After an 8-year trial in its USDA zone 5 gardens, researchers have found some standouts. 'Sarastro' received the top rating of "Excellent," and 31 others were rated "Good." Here are just a few of those: 'Caroline' clustered bellflower (*C. glomerata*), 'Blue Waterfall' Serbian bellflower (*C. poscharskyana*) and 'Wedding Bells' spotted bellflower (*C. punctata*). For the complete study, visit www.chicagobotanic.org/research/plant_evaluation/.

Annuals changes
Scientists at the University of Ghent in Belgium have found a way to change annual thale cress (*Arabidopsis thaliana*) into a perennial. Annuals use a lot of their energy producing that big display of flowers we enjoy in the garden. This, of course, leads to a multitude of seeds that ensures another generation of plants the following year. The scientists found that if they "deactivated" two of the genes associated with flowering, thale cress started acting like a perennial. In addition, there were fewer later flowers and the plant developed a woodier base. With continued research, maybe someday we'll have perennial marigolds and zinnias.

Slowing down sudden oak death
Sudden oak death, caused by the bacterial fungus *Phytophthora ramorum*, is a problem affecting many plant species. Spores are spread by wind and rainwater, and symptoms vary depending on the plant. Not all those infected die — some just carry the disease. This has resulted in reports of infected plants in more than 20 states and a few nurseries in Canada.

Scientists with the Agricultural Research Station in Colorado, the USDA Forest Service and Oregon State University have taken a big step toward preventing the spread of sudden oak death. Working with compounds made from heartwood, the oldest wood found at the center of a tree, researchers have created a fungicide. It limits the growth and reproduction of *P. ramorum* in the lab. Though further study is needed, the heartwood of western red cedar and incense cedar has shown promise.

did you know... (CONTINUED)

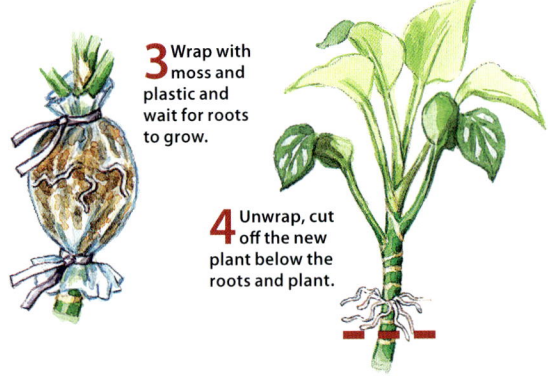

1 Make a cut along the stem where you'll get a reasonably sized plant.

2 Dust with rooting hormone powder and prop open with a toothpick.

3 Wrap with moss and plastic and wait for roots to grow.

4 Unwrap, cut off the new plant below the roots and plant.

Double your dieffenbachia
Susan Fischer, Georgia

Q How do I propagate my dumb cane (Dieffenbachia spp.)?

A A technique called air-layering is a good way to propagate plants that don't easily root from stem cuttings. Besides dumb cane, you can use it on croton, rubber tree and fiddle-leaf fig.

First, wound the plant so new roots will start. A few inches below a tuft of leaves, make an upward slanting cut with a knife a quarter to a third of the way through the stem. You may need to stake the stem so it doesn't break off too early, especially if it's top heavy.

Next, use a small paintbrush to dust the cut with rooting hormone, available from the garden center. The toothpick in illustration 2 is holding the cut open so it doesn't heal closed. Squeeze a fist-sized ball of presoaked sphagnum moss to remove excess water and place it around the wound. Use clear plastic wrap and two twist ties, as in illustration 3, to hold the moss in place.

Every 7 to 10 days, check to see if the moss is wet. If it needs water, undo the top twist tie, pour a little in and seal it back up. It may take two months or more for roots to develop. But when you see roots in the moss, it's time to pot your new plant. The red line in illustration 4 shows where to cut off the new plant. Plant it in well-drained potting mix and water well. The old stem will sprout new leaves and stems below the cut.

Shrinking hosta
James Thomas, Massachusetts

Q This year, all the leaves on my hostas are smaller than when I planted them last year. Why did they shrink?

A First, make sure your hostas are planted in conditions they like: Morning sun and afternoon shade. They do well in moist, well-drained soil with lots of organic material mixed in, but not in heavy clay soils. Double check that they weren't planted too deeply or that they're not being overfed or bothered by pests, such as slugs.

If none of these is true of your situation, the plants are probably just suffering a little transplant shock. Strug- gling plants often have smaller leaves, little or no new growth and may not flower.

Remember to keep newly installed plants moist, but not over-watered, since that can also stunt their growth. Then be patient — it might take them several years to reach full size.

Rusty rudbeckias
Donna Albertson, Michigan

Look for the bright orange, yellow or brown pustules of rust on the leaves and stems.

Q My rudbeckias have a red-brown substance on the leaves. Will this kill the plants or spread to other plants?

A Your rudbeckias have rust (*Puccinia*, *Uromyces* or *Aecidium* spp.), which is caused by a fungus. The disease creates rust-colored spores or orange, yellow or brown pustules on the stems and tops and bottoms of leaves. When you touch them the color comes off on your fingers.

Rust is worse in cool, humid weather. It affects plants that are crowded or have poor air circulation. Though rust often yellows leaves or stunts growth, it rarely kills rudbeckias or spreads to other plants.

Prevent rust by buying resistant varieties (check the plant tag before you buy) and providing plenty of room around plants. For existing plants, water early in the day and don't wet the leaves, as this is how the fungus spreads. Remove affected leaves or, if all of them are affected, the plants. Dispose of all the debris on the soil around plants, where rust overwinters. And apply a fungicide, such as Ortho® Max™ Garden Disease Control, as soon as you first notice the symptoms.

Just leave those lilies alone
Marion Smith, Washington

Q I planted 'Stargazer' lilies in 20-inch pots. Do I have to dig them up before winter?

A Your lilies will be fine outdoors in your area, where winter temperatures don't drop below 15 degrees. The biggest danger is that they might get waterlogged if there's lots of winter rain or snow. Simply move your container under an overhang, roof or deck that will keep out any precipitation.

For folks in colder zones, cut the brown stems back to the soil and move the pot into an unheated garage or basement for the winter. Hold off on water and light and let the bulbs go dormant.

When the weather warms in spring, bring the pot back outdoors, place in a sunny spot, water and feed with a 10-10-10 fertilizer.

product pick

When Perennials Bloom

Whether you're planning a new flower garden or just buying a few perennials at the garden center, one question you're sure to ask is, "When do these plants bloom?" The answers will be at your fingertips with this new book by Tomasz Anisko, curator of plants at Longwood Gardens in Pennsylvania. Drawing on years of experience, he profiles 450 perennials, including photographs and charts showing which months you can expect to see flowers. With this book you're sure to have a garden in bloom from spring to fall.

Bottom line A great reference to use while planning your garden.
Source Local and online bookstores and www.GardenGateStore.com
Price $59.95; hardcover; 510 pages

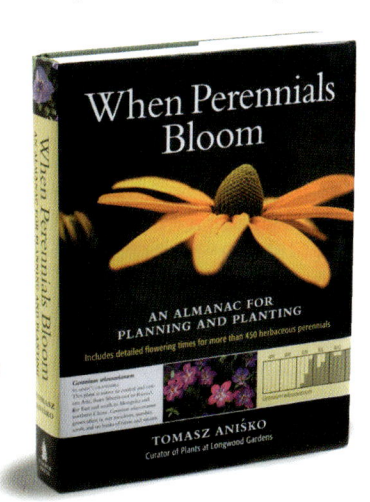

did you know... (CONTINUED)

Bagworms attach bits of leaves of the tree they are feeding onto a cocoon of spun silk.

What are these?
D.R. Shelty, Ohio

Q *What are the weird brown conelike things hanging on my arborvitae shrub?*

A They're cocoons made by bagworm caterpillars. After hatching in late spring, the caterpillars start to feed on the leaves. As they grow, they build the cocoons and, in winter, hibernate inside them.

Usually, bagworms won't hurt the tree they're feeding on. But severe infestations can strip foliage from branches or even entire trees and kill them. Common on arborvitae and cedars, bagworms will also eat other species of trees, including deciduous ones.

Before the caterpillars start to pupate in their cocoons in fall, simply pluck the cocoons off the branches and destroy them. For larger infestations, contact a tree care professional.

Say "no" to gnawing
Ed Gonia, Wisconsin

Q *How do I keep rabbits from chewing on my young Japanese tree lilac?*

A During winter, hungry rabbits can gnaw on and seriously damage the bark of young shrubs and trees, like your Japanese tree lilac (*Syringa reticulata*).

Your best bet is to protect the trunk with a wire cylinder that's 2 to 3 inches out from the tree trunk. Use ¼-inch hardware cloth or chicken wire with holes less than an inch across. Get a roll that's at least 36 inches wide so it will be tall enough to keep the rabbits out. With snow on the ground, rabbits can reach higher than they do in summer. It's not unusual to see winter damage 2 to 3 feet up a tree. Hardware cloth is stiff enough to stand without posts, but it's still a good idea to have just one to keep it extra sturdy. More flexible chicken wire needs two or three sturdy stakes put in the ground around the trunk.

Secure the bottom of the mesh to the ground with landscape staples. That way rabbits can't squeeze in underneath, either. Using hardware cloth will also protect your tree lilac from smaller pests, such as mice and voles.

If you get more snow than you expected, attach another cage to the top of the first one to protect the bark farther up the trunk.

The same method works for multistemmed trees. You just have to make the fence further out to include all the trunks. Once the tree matures, the bark will get rougher and less appealing to rabbits.

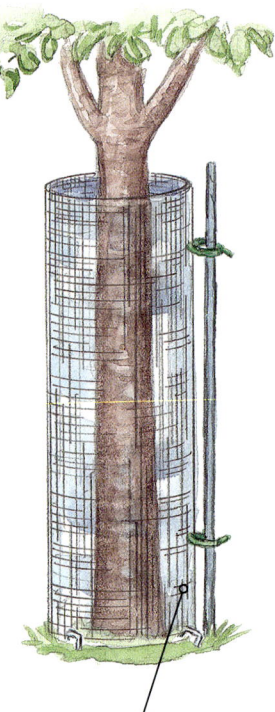

Attach the hardware cloth cage to stakes and pin the bottom to the ground with landscape staples so rabbits can't squeeze underneath.

Russian sage advice
Diane Morris, MI

Q *I have a 3-year-old Russian sage that has outgrown its space. Can it be transplanted?*

A Yes, and here's how: In early spring, if you haven't already done this, cut your Russian sage back by half. Dig carefully down around the plant. The woody crown is very brittle, so some of it will probably break off. The key is getting all of the long, brittle taproot. Replant your Russian sage at its original depth, and water in well. When new growth appears, prune out any dead branches.

For a new Russian sage in that small space, try 'Little Spire'. It only grows 25 inches tall and wide. 'Little Spire' may be available locally, but if not, try Bluestone Perennials at www.bluestoneperennials.com or call 800-852-5243 to order your plant.

Help for hibiscus
Vira Doughton, Pennsylvania

Q *The leaves of my hardy hibiscus are turning yellow and dying. Any suggestions?*

A A few yellow leaves is nothing to be concerned about, but a lot of yellow could mean your plant is stressed.

Hardy hibiscus (*Hibiscus moscheutos*) prefers consistent moisture but doesn't tolerate wet feet. Make sure the soil is well-drained, whether it's growing in a pot or in the ground. Water the plant deeply and let the soil dry out before watering again.

If your hibiscus is getting enough water, your plant may be stressed from too much fertilizer, rapid changes in temperature or extreme wind. But most likely, the culprit is a pest like spider mites. They can be especially bad on plants that have been dried out repeatedly. Look for tiny webs on the tips of shoots or under the leaves, then blast all plant surfaces with a stream of water. For a bigger infestation, spray the plant weekly for two to three weeks with insecticidal soap to take care of the problem.

"Bulbs" are actually thickened sections of roots that help hold moisture.

The facts on foxtail "bulbs"
Yolanda Beverly, Alabama

Q *Can I propagate my foxtail fern from the round white bulbs on the roots?*

A No, those round structures you see on the roots of the foxtail fern (*Asparagus densiflorus* 'Myersii') in the photo above are not actually bulbs. They're swollen sections of the tuberous root that help hold water and form as the plant ages.

If you want more plants, you can divide an older one in spring. You'll know it's time to divide when roots start to show at the top of the soil and the plant gets spindly and yellow.

The foliage can be thick and tangled, so to make dividing easier, cut the top growth back to 4 to 6 inches tall and knock the plant out of its container. With a sharp knife, cut the root ball into sections. The size of each new plant doesn't really matter, as long as each one contains a portion of the crown.

Replant the divisions in fresh potting mix or set them out in the garden. Water well and you'll soon have more of these lush green plants.

Stick it to slugs
Nettie Sullivan, Indiana

Nettie's clematis was beautiful last summer — until big holes started showing up on the flower petals! Taking a closer look, she noticed several shiny slime trails, a tell-tale sign that slugs had been to dinner. Nellie remembered she had some double-sided carpet tape on hand so she decided to give it a try as a deterrent.

She cut a piece of tape long enough to wrap around each trellis leg. Slugs don't seem to like the sticky tape, and there were no more slimy trails or holes in the clematis flowers. (For extra protection, sprinkle diatomaceous earth around the stem so they can't get up that way, either.)

Tulips bring in spring with a splash. Meet more of our favorite spring flowers on page 68.

top picks

your favorite shade flowers, *our* favorite bulbs and more!

LET US TELL YOU WHAT WE THINK are great plants. The best reseeding annuals. The easiest clematis. Bulbs that show off in spring, summer and fall. Finally, enough about us — what are *your* favorites? We asked our readers about their favorite shade flowers, and they told us. Find out if yours made the cut!

New Plants for 2009	**60**
Spring-Blooming Flowers	**68**
Flowers that Plant Themselves	**74**
Readers' Favorite Shade Flowers	**80**
Bulbs for Three Seasons of Color	**88**
Easiest Clematis Ever	**96**

top new annuals

new plants 2009

You told us and we listened. Stories about new plants are our readers' favorites. So we've packed as many of 2009's best new plants into this story as we could. And you'll find even more scattered throughout this book. Just look for this icon: **NEW '09**

You know how hard it is choosing which plants to take home from the garden center. It's the same when it comes to choosing plants for this story. But this time, because there were so many excellent choices, I've squeezed in six additional staff favorites on p. 67. And if you still can't get enough, check out our Web extra for 10 more.

Remember, because these plants are new, some of them may be hard to get your hands on. But be patient — there are sure to be larger quantities available next year. Growing information can be a little uneven, too. For example, the growers of the perennial verbena think it may be even more cold-hardy than listed but are still testing, and heat zones on many of our new introductions haven't yet been determined.

So what's going on with new plants this year? Unusual flowers, for one thing. Take a look at the cosmos, coneflowers and bleeding heart if you want to add some spice to your flower garden. The foliage of the sedum and honeysuckle isn't anything to sneeze at, either. But one thing that stands out with this group is drought tolerance. With water conservation being a concern in more places these days, you need plants that are tough, and we've got you covered. Take a look at the annuals, coneflowers, sedum, sea holly, false indigo, beardtongue and honeysuckle.

Now let's find out more about these great new plants for 2009! □

— *Sherri Ribbey*

Web extra Check out our **slide show** of 10 more new plants!

'Double Click Rose Bonbon' cosmos
Cosmos bipinnatus

Flower gardeners are always looking for pretty flowers. This new cosmos really delivers. Just take a look at the big 3- to 4-inch fully double pink flowers. Wow! To make it even better, 'Double Click Rose Bonbon' is easy to grow, too. Direct-sow the seed in any sunny spot in your garden after all threat of frost has passed. As long as the soil is well-drained, cosmos will grow well, even in poor soils. By early summer, you'll have flowers just like the ones above. With deadheading, they'll keep coming until frost. Since they come true from seed, stop deadheading in fall and you'll have more of these beauties next spring.

Type Annual
Size 24 to 36 in. tall, 20 in. wide
Bloom Summer to fall
Soil Well-drained, poor soil
Light Full sun
Hardiness
  Cold: Annual
  Heat: AHS zones 12 to 1
Introducer/Source
  Select Seeds
  www.selectseeds.com
  800-684-0395
What's new?
  Large, double pink flowers

'TigerEye Gold' rudbeckia
Rudbeckia hirta

Everyone here at *Garden Gate* commented on the bright golden-yellow blooms of 'TigerEye Gold' rudbeckia. We grew it in containers, with lantana and flowering tobacco. Multi-branched stems were full of blooms that lasted so long, they didn't seem real. Eventually, the blooms did fade but with deadheading, more kept coming all summer.

The foliage was nice, too, with no signs of powdery mildew on the leaves.

Rudbeckia hirta is a variable species and 'TigerEye Gold' is more tender than others in this group. It's only cold-hardy in zone 10 and warmer, so most gardeners will treat it as an annual.

Type Tender perennial
Size 16 to 24 in. tall and wide
Bloom Spring to fall
Soil Well-drained
Light Full sun
Hardiness
 Cold: USDA zone 10 to 12
 Heat: AHS zones 12 to 1
Introducer
 Goldsmith Seeds
Source Local garden centers
What's new?
 Big flowers on compact, well-branched plants

Begonia BIG™ series
Begonia hybrid

The Big series is kind of like wax begonias on steroids. It's the same easy care plant, it's just bigger. From the glossy foliage, to the clusters of large flowers that weigh down the long stems from summer to fall. Its graceful habit makes an impressive mass planting. Or grow it in a container like we did here.

Many begonias prefer shade, but this one does well in full sun, too. No crispy foliage or drooping plants. However, we found that a little protection from the afternoon sun kept the foliage color deeper and the flowers brighter. The Big series comes in three colors: Red with Green Leaf (shown), Rose with Bronze Leaf or Red with Bronze Leaf.

Type Annual
Size 12 to 18 in. tall and wide
Bloom Spring to fall
Soil Well-drained
Light Sun to shade
Hardiness
 Cold: Annual
 Heat: AHS zones 12 to 1
Introducer
 Benary®
Source Local garden centers
What's new?
 Big flowers and big foliage that can thrive in sun or shade

top new perennials

'Mac 'n' Cheese' and 'Tomato Soup' coneflowers
***Echinacea* hybrids**

You've probably noticed that coneflowers aren't necessarily purple anymore. These two new colors will fill out the rainbow of flower colors quite nicely. Besides being pretty, these plants have the same hardy constitution that coneflowers are known for. Both varieties have upright habits with good branching, which means there will be plenty of those 4- to 5-inch flowers for you to enjoy. And you're not the only one who will be excited about these new introductions. Butterflies love coneflowers while they're in bloom, and goldfinches feast on the seedheads that are left in fall.

Type Perennials
Size 'Mac 'n' Cheese': 26 in. tall, 18 to 24 in. wide
'Tomato Soup': 32 in. tall and wide
Bloom Summer
Soil Well-drained soil
Light Full sun
Hardiness
Cold: USDA zones 4 to 9
Heat: Not available
Introducer Terra Nova Nurseries
Source Lazy S's Farm Nursery
www.lazyssfarm.com
What's new?
Cool new colors

'Sweet Joanne' beardtongue
***Penstemon* hybrid**

There are 250 species of beardtongue in North America but not many that are really cold-hardy. Here's a new one that can take the cold as well as the heat. 'Sweet Joanne' also has bigger flowers than other cold-hardy beardtongues, and blooms from late spring to early summer. Remove the spent stems for more flowers by fall. Its upright habit and glossy green foliage stay good-looking because it's very disease-resistant. Insects don't seem to have a taste for this beardtongue, either.

Try growing 'Sweet Joanne' with other sun-loving companions, such as blue fescue or dianthus.

Type Perennial
Size 24 in. tall and wide
Bloom Late spring to early summer
Soil Well-drained
Light Full sun
Hardiness
Cold: USDA zones 5 to 9
Heat: AHS zones 9 to 1
Introducer Blooms of Bressingham
Source Big Dipper Farm
www.bigdipperfarm.com
360-886-8133
What's new?
Hardy beardtongue with larger flowers

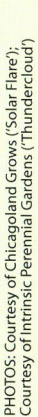

'Solar Flare' false indigo
Baptisia hybrid

False indigo is one of the prettiest and toughest plants you'll find. It's drought-, deer-, rabbit-, and disease-resistant. This new hybrid is all that *and* comes in an exciting new color. 'Solar Flare' flowers open lemon-yellow and gradually fade to rusty orange. Flower stalks, 12 to 18 inches long, cover the plant in early summer. Stems change to purple when nighttime temperatures are cool. Butterflies love the flowers, and you will, too. Cut a few and bring them inside to enjoy.

Once you have false indigo planted, think twice before moving this slow grower. Because of the deep fleshy root system, it doesn't move well.

Type Perennial
Size 3 to 4 ft. tall, 4 to 4½ ft. wide
Bloom Early summer
Soil Well-drained
Light Full sun
Hardiness
  Cold: USDA zones 4 to 8
  Heat: Not available
Introducer
  Chicagoland Grows®, Inc.
Source Avant Gardens
  www.avantgardensne.com
  508-998-8819
What's new?
  Unusual flower color

'Thundercloud' sedum
Sedum hybrid

There have been a lot of tall sedums introduced in the past few years. But this one is really different. 'Thundercloud' is the same drought-tolerant and easy-care plant as other varieties, but its gray-green scalloped leaves make it stand out from the crowd. White flowers with a hint of pink show up in late summer, providing a much-needed treat for butterflies and bees. Because of its compact size the stems don't flop like some varieties do. They even stay standing well into winter, which adds interest and structure to the garden even when the snow flies.

Type Perennial
Size 12 in. tall and wide
Bloom Mid- to late summer
Soil Well-drained
Light Full sun to light shade
Hardiness
  Cold: USDA 4 to 9
  Heat: Not available
Introducer
  Intrinsic Perennial Gardens
Source Busse Gardens
  www.bussegardens.com
  800-544-3192
What's new?
  Scalloped foliage

top new perennials *continued*

'Big Blue' sea holly
Eryngium hybrid

If you haven't tried growing sea holly yet, try this one. Like other sea hollies, 'Big Blue' is easy to grow and quite drought-tolerant, once established. It's not picky about soil, either. It does best in lean, dry soil but will tolerate moist situations, too. Lots of organic matter causes flower stems to flop, and you won't want the flowers of 'Big Blue' in the mud. These 4-inch spiky flowers are almost iridescent, and the color really glows in areas with cool evenings. The low rosette of foliage sends up many multi-branched stems, so there will be plenty of flowers to enjoy.

Type Perennial
Size 24 to 30 in. tall and wide
Bloom Summer
Soil Average to dry
Light Full sun
Hardiness
  Cold: USDA zones 4 to 9
  Heat: Not available
Introducer
  North Creek Nurseries, Inc.
Source Forestfarm
  www.forestfarm.com
  541-846-7269

What's new?
  Big iridescent blue flowers

PHOTOS: Courtesy of North Creek Nurseries, Inc. ('Big Blue'); Courtesy of Walters Gardens, Inc. ('Golden Sunrise')

'Golden Sunrise' Winter Jewels series Lenten rose
Helleborus hybrid

After a long winter, Lenten rose is a welcome sight, sometimes blooming even through snow. 'Golden Sunrise' is the first in the Winter Jewels™ series, which has large flowers in true color strains. That means the flowers will be the same color, instead of a mix, like many other Lenten rose hybrids.

'Golden Sunrise' has 2- to 3-inch, downward-facing yellow flowers. Each has red in the center. Some have a blush, some are solid and others are spotted like the one above. All have red veining on the petal backs so you get a colorful view from above, too.

Type Perennial
Size 18 to 22 in. tall, 24 in. wide
Bloom Late winter to early spring
Soil Moist, well-drained
Light Part shade
Hardiness
  Cold: USDA zones 4 to 9
  Heat: Not available
Introducer
  Walters Gardens, Inc.
Source Garden Crossings
  www.gardencrossings.com
  616-875-6355

What's new?
  Consistently yellow flowers with red centers

64 *the* YEAR IN GARDENING   www.GardenGateMagazine.com

top new vine

'Burning Hearts' bleeding heart
Dicentra hybrid

There were a lot of offers to take this new plant home when it came through the door at *Garden Gate*. Those deep red flowers trimmed with white are stunning set against the soft blue-gray foliage. 'Burning Hearts' has a mounded habit and blooms from spring to fall. Fernleaf bleeding hearts tend to be more drought-tolerant than other species, but you'll still want to give it a little extra water during a dry spell. Without it, the plant goes dormant, which means the foliage disappears. But don't worry if it does: This hardy plant will show up again the following spring.

Type Perennial
Size 10 to 12 in. tall, 12 in. wide
Bloom Early spring to fall
Soil Moist, well-drained
Light Part sun to shade
Hardiness
Cold: USDA zones 3 to 8
Heat: Not available
Introducer
Skagit Gardens
Source Great Garden Plants
www.greatgardenplants.com
877-447-4769

What's new?
Unusual deep red flowers

Rebecca clematis
Clematis 'Evipo016'

Want to attract attention? Get Rebecca™ clematis. Its huge 6- to 7-inch red flowers are real show-stoppers. And you'll have these beauties from early to late summer. Like most clematis, Rebecca is easy to grow. At 6 to 8 feet tall, the vines are good-sized but aren't overpowering. So it's perfect for small gardens.

Rebecca is a member of pruning group 2 or B. The only pruning it needs is removing any broken, dead or weak stems in spring before it leafs out. Cut stems back to where two leaves were growing the previous year. If you haven't cut in just the right place it's not a big deal — this hardy vine will grow back with ease.

Type Vine
Size 6 to 8 ft. tall
Bloom Early to late summer
Soil Well-drained
Light Full sun
Hardiness
Cold: USDA zones 4 to 9
Heat: Not available
Introducer/Source
Klehm's Song Sparrow Farm and Nursery
www.songsparrow.com
800-553-3715

What's new?
Big red flowers on a compact vine

PHOTO: Courtesy of Raymond Evison (Rebecca)

top new shrubs

Port Sunlight rose
Rosa 'Auslofty'

Roses with an old-fashioned look are hard to resist, but sometimes they aren't so easy to grow. Not so with Port Sunlight. This hardy, disease-resistant shrub rose has lush flowers full of petals that remind me of English country gardens. The strong tea rose fragrance and repeat flowering make this a good rose to grow near a patio or path so you can enjoy the flowers up close. To encourage a quicker rebloom, you can deadhead spent flowers 1 to 4 inches below the base of the bloom.

In areas where winters don't get below freezing, Port Sunlight will grow tall enough that you can treat it as a small climber.

Type Shrub
Size 5 ft. tall, 3 ft. wide
8 ft. as a climber
Bloom Summer to fall
Soil Well-drained
Light Full sun
Hardiness
Cold: USDA zones 5 to 9
Heat: Not available
Introducer/Source
David Austin Roses
www.davidaustinroses.com
800-328-8893
What's new?
New apricot-colored flowers all season

PHOTO: Courtesy of David Austin Roses (Port Sunlight)

Edmee Gold boxleaf honeysuckle
Lonicera nitida 'Briloni'

Not all honeysuckles are big shrubs or vines. This one has a shrubby habit and even better — chartreuse foliage. The flowers are quite small. It's the boxwoodlike leaves and cascading habit that help big hostas, such as 'Krossa Regal' or 'Paul's Glory', look so good. Once established, honeysuckles like this one don't need much care or extra watering.

Where Edmee Gold™ isn't hardy, grow it in containers, as we did. Watch out for too much sun, though, as it can burn the foliage. If that does happen, just move the plant to a shadier spot and trim out the damaged foliage. The new growth will fill in in a few weeks.

Type Shrub
Size 24 to 36 in. tall, 18 to 24 in. wide
Bloom NA
Soil Humus rich, well-drained
Light Shade
Hardiness
Cold: USDA zones 6 to 9
Heat: Not available
Introducer Novalis
Source White Flower Farm
www.whiteflowerfarm.com
800-503-9624
What's new?
Bright chartreuse foliage for shade

the YEAR IN GARDENING www.GardenGateMagazine.com

6 bonus new plants

Verbena *Verbena* hybrid 'Annie'

WHAT IT LOOKS LIKE Lavender flowers with a light fragrance; blooms spring to frost; 6 in. tall, 24 to 30 in. wide

HOW TO GROW IT Full sun; well-drained soil; cold-hardy in USDA zones 4 to 8; heat zones not available

INTRODUCER/SOURCE High Country Gardens, www.highcountrygardens.com, 800-925-9387

Echeveria *Echeveria rudofhii* Metallica

WHAT IT LOOKS LIKE Rosette of metallic-looking foliage; long-lasting peachy-pink Dr.-Seusslike flowers in summer; 6 to 12 in. tall, 8 to 10 in. wide

HOW TO GROW IT Part shade; well-drained soil; great in containers; cold-hardy in USDA zones 9 to 10; heat-tolerant in AHS zones 12 to 1

INTRODUCER Proven Selections® from Proven Winners®

SOURCE Local garden centers

Hydrangea *Hydrangea macrophylla* Forever & Ever® White Out

WHAT IT LOOKS LIKE Large 8-in. white mophead flowers summer to frost; deep-green foliage; 28 in. tall, 25 in. wide

HOW TO GROW IT Part shade; moist, well-drained soil; cold-hardy in USDA zones 4 to 8; heat zones not available

INTRODUCER Zelenka Nursery®

SOURCE Sooner Plant Farm, www.soonerplantfarm.com, 918-453-0771

American bittersweet *Celastrus scandens* Autumn Revolution™ ('Bailumn')

WHAT IT LOOKS LIKE More fruit than the species; not invasive like Oriental bittersweet (*Celastrus orbiculatus*); 15 to 25 ft. long

HOW TO GROW IT Full sun; well-drained soil; cold-hardy in USDA zones 2 to 8; heat zones not available

INTRODUCER Bailey Nurseries

SOURCE Busse Gardens, www.bussegardens.com, 800-544-3192

Blanket flower *Gaillardia* Commotion™ Tizzy

WHAT IT LOOKS LIKE Fluted red petals with more petals on each flower than other similar varieties; 18 to 24 in. tall, 24 in. wide

HOW TO GROW IT Full sun; well-drained soil; deadhead for more blooms; cold-hardy in USDA zones 6 to 9; heat zones not available

INTRODUCER Skagit Gardens

SOURCE Forestfarm, www.forestfarm.com, 541-846-7269

Coleus *Solenostemon* hybrid Henna ('Balcenna')

WHAT IT LOOKS LIKE Copper and chartreuse leaves with burgundy undersides; serrated edges; 18 to 24 in. tall, 14 to 16 in. wide

HOW TO GROW IT Full sun to shade; well-drained soil; Annual, heat-tolerant in AHS zones 12 to 1

INTRODUCER Ball® Horticulture

SOURCE Local garden centers

PHOTOS: Courtesy of High Country Gardens (Annie'); Courtesy of Bailey Nurseries (Autumn Revolution)

Spring-Blooming Flowers

Learn how to layer bulbs with our exclusive *video*.

Spring is a colorful time of year. Your garden is announcing that it has survived the winter and is anxious to get growing again. And what better way than with lots of vibrant flowers? We've selected a few of our favorites to share with you. Our picks start in late winter and progress into late spring. Some are tiny, like winter aconite, our earliest herald of the season. (Speaking of bulbs, check out our Web extra to learn how to "layer" them for extra effect.) Others, such as redbuds and flowering crabapples, are ornamental trees. There's something here for every size garden. And with each profile we've included a handy growing tip, other good cultivars or a few great companion plants.

GREAT LOCATIONS Whether you garden in sun or shade, you can add color to your spring. Bloodroot has a strange name, but it's perfect among shade-loving ferns and hostas. Have a spot that stays moist? Grow cowslips. Dry, sunny areas are great for irises and candytuft.

Many spring flowers have more than one season of interest, too. For example, crabapples have spring blooms *and* colorful fruits that hang on into winter. And don't forget old standbys like tulips and daffodils. Let's get to know these spring showoffs better, as well as some great companions. □

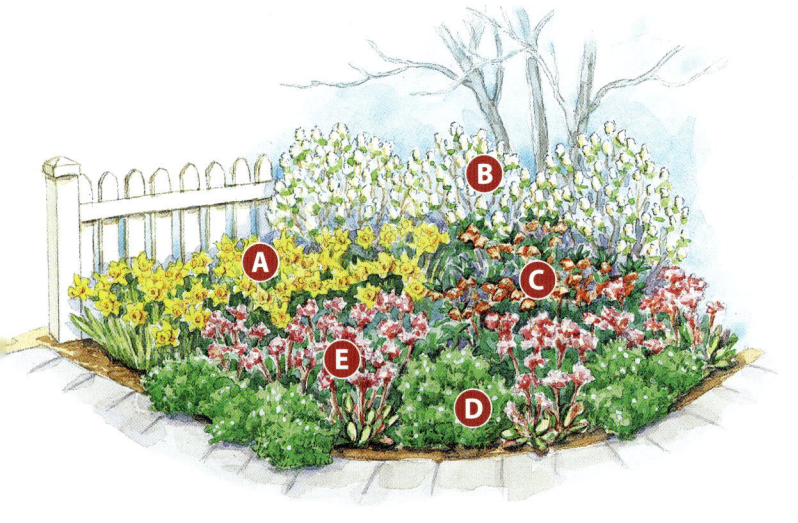

Spring stroll There is absolutely nothing better than spotting that first bulb "nose" poking through the soil. It's a sure sign that spring is on its way. We've designed this small vignette to be planted along a path or sidewalk where it'll be easy to spot signs of growth on that first warm, and wishful, late-winter day.

A **Daffodil** *Narcissus* 'Pay Day' See profile, p. 71
B **Fothergilla** *Fothergilla gardenii* 3 ft. tall and wide; cold-hardy in USDA zones 5 to 8; heat-tolerant in AHS zones 8 to 1
C **Hellebore** *Helleborus orientalis* 18 in. tall and wide; cold-hardy in USDA zones 4 to 8; heat-tolerant in AHS zones 8 to 1
D **Evergreen candytuft** *Iberis sempervirens* See profile, p. 71
E **Bergenia** *Bergenia* 'Firefly' See profile, p. 72

This tough little flower blooms even before the snow melts!

Winter aconite
Eranthis hyemalis

This is one of the first bulbs to appear, often before the snow melts. The small flowers open on sunny days and close at night when temperatures dip below freezing.

Plant the tubers in moist ground in early fall, even before annuals are knocked down by frost — they need time to get established before winter. And plant them in tight clumps — nearly touching each other — of at least 10 or 20 tubers near a path, where you'll spot them as they bloom.

After the flowers finish, let the foliage die down naturally. That'll give the seed heads time to ripen so you'll have even more blooms in years to come.

Type Perennial tuber
Size 2 to 3 in. tall and wide
Bloom Yellow in late winter
Light Full sun to part shade
Hardiness
Cold: USDA zones 4 to 7
Heat: AHS zones 7 to 1
Source Old House Gardens
www.oldhousegardens.com
734-995-1486
Catalog $2

handy **tip**
Tubers shriveled and dry when they arrive? Before you plant, soak them overnight in warm water to plump them up.

Bloodroot
Sanguinaria canadensis

Start looking for bloodroot's white flowers to poke through the soil in late March or early April, about the same time blue squill, like the one in this photo, bloom. The fragile flowers only last a few days, but the interesting lobed foliage will stick around into summer.

This native wildflower likes a rich, humusy soil. And don't bother raking the leaves away in fall: Bloodroot will appreciate the natural mulch.

Plant small potted starts or bare rhizomes in spring. Be patient: Bloodroot can be slow to take off. However, given time it'll spread into colonies that make a great ground cover on a shady slope.

Type Perennial
Size 6 to 14 in. tall, 12 in. wide
Bloom White in early spring
Light Part shade to shade
Hardiness
Cold: USDA zones 3 to 9
Heat: AHS zones 9 to 1
Source Well-Sweep Herb Farm
www.wellsweep.com
908-852-5390
Catalog $3

looks **great with**
Pair bloodroot with other native woodland plants like Solomon's seal (*Polygonatum biflorum*) for a fresh spring look.

top spring-blooming flowers *continued*

Cowslip
Primula veris

As you can see in the photo of yellow 'Prinic' (sometimes also sold as 'Katy McSparron'), above, cowslips have a lot to offer the early spring garden. Colorful flowers, either single or double, open atop sturdy stems and bloom for several weeks. And attractive, leathery bright-green leaves form a lovely mound at the plant's base.

Cowslips prefer part shade and moist, well-drained soil with lots of organic matter. They'll tolerate full sun if the soil is kept moist, but tend to go dormant with the arrival of hot summer temperatures. Extra mulch will help them through the winter in the coldest part of their growing range.

Type Perennial
Size 6 to 12 in. tall by 16 in. wide
Bloom Many colors
Light Part to full shade
Hardiness
  Cold: USDA zones 4 to 8
  Heat: AHS zones 8 to 1
Source Plant Delights Nursery, Inc.
  www.plantdelights.com
  919-772-4794
  Catalog free

handy tip
Polymer moisture crystals (available in most garden centers) will keep cowslips happy. Sprinkle them sparingly into the planting hole before you set the plant in it.

Rock garden iris
Iris reticulata

This diminutive member of the iris family is also one of the earliest irises to bloom in spring. Fragrant, 2½-inch flowers, held on leafless stems, start to open about the same time as snowdrops and early crocuses. 'Clairette', in the photo, has blue flowers with white marks, but you'll find white, yellow and purple blooms, too. The grasslike foliage dies back by late spring.

If you plant the bulbs in small groups, the low-growing blooms can be hard to see. So, for the most bang for the buck, plant these little beauties in drifts. Choose sites with well-drained soil that stays dry during summer — that way, the bulbs won't rot.

Type Bulb
Size 3 to 6 in. tall by 3 in. wide
Bloom White, yellow, blue or purple in early spring
Light Sun to part shade
Hardiness
  Cold: USDA zones 5 to 9
  Heat: AHS zones 9 to 1
Source John Scheepers, Inc.
  www.johnscheepers.com
  860-567-0838
  Catalog free

looks great with
Rock garden irises are great companions for glory-of-the-snow (*Chionodoxa luciliae*) or snowdrops (*Galanthus* spp.).

Daffodil
***Narcissus* hybrids**

Daffodils are a sure sign of spring! Early bloomers, like yellow 'Rijnveld's Early Sensation' above, will sometimes open even with snow on the ground. Later daffs, like 'High Society' in the inset, keep the show going for weeks.

Daffodils grow best in well-drained soil. Mix coarse sand and lots of organic material, such as peat moss or well-rotted compost, into the hole for excellent drainage.

Plant daffodil bulbs three times deeper than their height in early autumn to give them time to establish roots while the ground is warm. If you have to plant right before the ground freezes, mulch the soil to keep it warm later into fall.

Type Bulb
Size Up to 20 in. tall by 12 in. wide
Bloom White, pink, pale salmon, yellow or orange in spring
Light Sun to part shade
Hardiness
  Cold: USDA zones 3 to 8
  Heat: AHS zones 9 to 1
Source Brent & Becky's Bulbs
  www.brentandbeckys bulbs.com
  877-661-2852
  Catalog free

try these
Classic yellow daffodil
'Dutch Master'
Midspring white flowers 'Thalia'

Evergreen candytuft
Iberis sempervirens

The tiny, fresh white flowers of this well-known perennial blanket rock gardens and tumble beautifully over retaining walls. This low-growing ground cover is also perfect at the edge of a path or the front of a border of spring-blooming shrubs.

But even after summer heat causes the blooms to fade, the attractive, fine-textured foliage persists right up to a heavy frost.

Candytuft does best in well-drained soil; planting in soggy areas leads to crown rot, which quickly kills the plant.

In USDA zone 4 and colder, protect the foliage from desiccation and sun scorch by laying evergreen boughs over the plants in early winter.

Type Perennial
Size 12 in. tall, 18 in. wide
Bloom White in late spring
Light Sun
Hardiness
  Cold: USDA zones 3 to 9
  Heat: AHS zones 9 to 1
Source Bluestone Perennials, Inc.
  www.bluestone perennials.com
  800-852-5243
  Catalog free

handy tip
Shear plants back by half after flowering is done to encourage new growth and keep plants neat and compact.

top spring-blooming flowers *continued*

Redbud
Cercis canadensis

There's nothing more stunning in spring than a redbud in full bloom! Those clusters of shocking purple-pink flowers on bare branches really stand out. (Prefer white flowers? You'll find them on *C. canadensis alba*, in the inset.) And the pretty round leaves, when they appear after the flowers fade, look great through summer, often turning bright yellow in fall.

These are natural understory trees, so they're fine at the edge of a wooded area. But they'll be just as happy in full sun out in your yard. Plant them in spring — sometimes redbuds have difficulty getting established if you plant them in the fall.

Type Tree
Size 15 to 30 ft. tall, 20 to 30 ft. wide
Bloom Pink or white in midspring
Light Full sun to part shade
Hardiness
Cold: USDA zones 4 to 8
Heat: AHS zones 8 to 1
Source Greer Gardens
www.greergardens.com
800-548-0111
Catalog free

try **these**
Burgundy foliage 'Forest Pansy'
Weeping, twisted habit 'Covey'

Bergenia
Bergenia cordifolia

In spring, you can enjoy wands of purple, pink or white flowers, often on red stems. Then the foliage takes over — those big leaves stay glossy all summer. Cool fall weather often turns the leaves bronze or red.

Speaking of foliage, bergenia looks best in part shade and consistently moist, slightly acid soil. More sun produces more flowers, but you'll need to be careful to keep the ground moist, or the leaf edges will scorch.

In Southern gardens, bergenia is evergreen. But if you live in USDA zone 6 or colder, cover it with a 2- or 3-inch layer of light mulch, like pine needles, to protect it.

Type Perennial
Size 8 to 24 in. tall, 1 to 2 ft. wide
Bloom White, pink or purple in mid- to late spring
Light Part shade
Hardiness
Cold: USDA zones 4 to 9
Heat: AHS zones 9 to 1
Source Fieldstone Gardens
www.fieldstonegardens.com
207-923-3836
Online catalog only

looks great **with**
Ferns, hostas and hellebores offer lots of foliage contrast.

Tulip
Tulipa hybrids

There are some plants that just stand for a certain season, and nothing says "spring" as loud and clear as tulips!

There's a tulip out there for everyone. You'll find nearly any color except blue, and some flowers are streaked with two or three colors. Some are that classic tulip shape, like 'Barcelona' above, while others have fringed or ruffled edges, double blooms or elegant, pointed, lily-shaped flowers.

Like most bulbs, tulips like a spot that's sunny in the spring, but they're perfectly content under big shade trees that leaf out later. Just make sure they're in well-drained soil, or the bulbs can rot.

Type Bulb
Size 4 to 24 in. tall by 3 to 5 in. wide
Bloom Wide range of colors from early to late spring
Light Sun to part shade
Hardiness
Cold: USDA zones 3 to 8
Heat: AHS zones 8 to 1
Source Van Bourgondien
www.dutchbulbs.com
800-622-9997
Catalog free

handy tip
The best way to feed bulbs is to scratch a specific bulb fertilizer (available at garden centers) into the ground around them in fall.

Crabapple
Malus hybrids

Another spring classic — and one that looks great in other seasons, too! Crabapples, with their foam of spring flowers in white, pink, red or purple, often have red or yellow fruits to keep the tree colorful in fall and winter.

These trees are the perfect fit for any yard, too, since most of them don't get too big. Some, like red-fruited 'David', above, are rounded in shape, while others are more upright. And a few are weeping, for an unusual, dramatic look in any garden.

As with any spring-flowering tree or shrub, try to do any necessary pruning right after the flowers fade so you don't minimize next year's show.

Type Tree
Size 10 to 30 ft. tall, 10 to 20 ft. wide
Bloom White, pink, red or purple in midspring
Light Full to part sun
Hardiness
Cold: USDA zones 4 to 8
Heat: AHS zones 8 to 1
Source Local garden centers

try these
Dark foliage, pink flowers, red fruit 'Prairie Fire'

Unusual leaf shape, white flowers, yellow fruit 'Golden Raindrops'

Flowers That Plant Themselves

Free plants! There — did I get your attention? Well, that's what reseeding annuals are. You buy them once, and for years after you get new plants for free! Let me introduce you to 10 of my favorite reseeders. They're great for creating a cottage garden or filling in areas around perennials or shrubs. (Strictly speaking, some of these plants are perennials, but they're so tender that gardeners in most of North America treat them as annuals.)

Most seed packets tell you to sow after threat of frost is past so seedlings don't get zapped by the cold. It's interesting that for many reseeders, later generations are more vigorous than the earlier plants and can handle more cold.

That said, not all reseeders will come back for you — different gardens have different conditions. But the 10 plants I'm sharing here are both pretty *and* known as reliable reseeders.

To give plants the best start that first year, till lots of organic material into the soil and smooth it out with the back of a rake. Plant the seeds at the depth and spacing the package tells you and water them carefully. Mark the location so you can keep the area free of weeds. Many packets have an illustration of the seedling, so you know what *not* to pull now or in future years. When the seedlings are up a few inches, thin them to the correct spacing. This reduces competition for water and nutrients and gives plants good air circulation to prevent fungal diseases. If they're very close together, snip a few off with scissors so you don't damage the roots of the ones you leave in place. Or dig the extras and move them. Many reseeders transplant easily, while others, like larkspur and Indian paintbrush, resent it. When in doubt, sow the seeds right where you want them so you won't be disappointed.

Most named cultivars don't reseed, or if they do, don't look like the parent plant. On the other hand, some species can be aggressive in certain areas. I've included a few tips for curbing their spread in "Control the madness!" at left. But don't worry, these 10 aren't invasive in most areas. So feel free to let them spread their color and charm all through your garden!

— *Deborah Gruca*

Control the madness!

Reseeders are great, but you *can* get too much of a good thing. Here are tips to keep them under control:

- Deadhead at least half the plants.
- Cover the soil with a preemergent herbicide, such as corn gluten, where you don't want the seedlings to sprout.
- Plant seeds in dry areas, where most are less prone to be aggressive.
- Avoid plants considered invasive for your area. For a list of invasives, go to www.usna.usda.gov/Gardens/invasives.html.

Mail-order sources

Annie's Annuals & Perennials
www.anniesannuals.com
888-266-4370. *Catalog free*

Native American Seed
www.seedsource.com
800-728-4043. *Catalog free*
(Indian paintbrush)

Balsam
Impatiens balsamina

Your grandmother may have known this old-fashioned annual as touch-me-not. The name refers to the way the ripe seeds burst from the pods at a touch — as far as 20 feet!

Balsam seed, usually available in a mix of colors, germinates quickly. The plant handles heat and humidity with ease, as long as the soil doesn't dry out. It produces a good root system right away and lots of 1½- to 2-inch flowers in many colors. For the healthiest plants, thin the seedlings to a foot apart; either toss the extras or move them to another spot.

Reseeded seedlings come up anytime from early summer to early fall and are easy to pull, if needed.

Size 12 to 36 in. tall, 12 to 14 in. wide
Bloom Pink, purple, red, white in summer to early fall
Soil Moist, well-drained
Light Sun to part shade
Hardiness
　Cold: Annual
　Heat: AHS 12 to 1

getting **started**
Direct sow seed outdoors or start seeds indoors eight weeks before last frost.

Morning glory
Ipomoea purpurea

Morning glory's lush green foliage and large flowers in many shades can quickly envelop a structure by the middle of summer. And the blooms, which open in morning and last just one day, keep coming until a frost knocks them out. That's 'Heavenly Blue' above.

The classic trumpet-shaped flowers of morning glories come back each year, though you may see a variety of flower colors. (But 'Grandpa Otts' keeps its rich purple year after year.) Once the seedlings get a few inches high, thin them to about a foot apart. The plants will be healthier and you'll get that full, lush growth morning glory enthusiasts rave about.

Size 6 to 10 ft. tall
Bloom Pink, blue, white, lavender, red or purple in mid- to late summer
Soil Moist, fertile, well-drained
Light Sun
Hardiness
　Cold: Annual
　Heat: AHS 12 to 1

getting **started**
Before you plant in spring, nick the seed coat or soak the seeds in warm water overnight to speed germination. Hard to transplant — direct sow in garden.

top reseeding annuals *continued*

Love-lies-bleeding
Amaranthus caudatus

Love-lies-bleeding is not a plant you can ignore. The long narrow leaves are handsome, but the plant produces scores of dramatic, drooping, foot-long (or longer!) tassels of tiny blood-red flowers. These striking blooms make great cut flowers for fresh or dried arrangements.

The seeds need warm soil temps to germinate, so in zones 9 and colder, you may want to buy small starts the first year. You'll see flowers sooner and for a longer period of time before frost hits. Plants *will* reseed. But, with a shorter summer, you'll get fewer of these stunning plants the second year (and probably none in following years) than farther south, where it reseeds heavily.

Size 2 to 4 ft. tall, 2 ft. wide
Bloom Red, green or cream from summer to frost
Soil Average to lean, well-drained
Light Sun to part shade
Hardiness
　　Cold: USDA 10 to 11
　　Heat: AHS 12 to 1

getting **started**
Buy small starts, as seeds can take three months until bloom.

LOCATION: Chicago Botanic Garden (loves-lies-bleeding)

Larkspur
Consolida ajacis

If you've ever seen a large drift of larkspur, you know how pretty this delphinium relative is. Each of the many flower stems holds a panicle, or spike, of spurred flowers in early summer for an exuberant cottage garden look.

Not fond of hot, humid weather, larkspur does best in most areas if you seed it in fall. When the young plants emerge in spring, thin them to about a foot apart to keep powdery mildew at bay. Larkspur doesn't transplant well, so simply toss the extra plants.

Reseeded seedlings come up thickly all over the garden in early to midsummer. Those from named cultivars retain the same colors as the parent.

Size 18 to 24 in. tall, 9 to 12 in. wide
Bloom Pink, blue, purple or white in early summer
Soil Moist, well-drained
Light Sun
Hardiness
　　Cold: Annual
　　Heat: AHS 12 to 1

getting **started**
Sow in fall on top of loosened, well-drained soil and tamp the seeds down lightly.

Indian paintbrush
Castilleja indivisa

Its resemblance to paint-dipped brushes gives this plant its common name. Those small white-green structures you see in the photo are the actual flowers. The red-orange bracts and flowers together create up to 8-inch-long spikes atop unbranched stems.

This plant is *hemi-parasitic*, meaning it can get part of its nutrients from other plants. As the roots of Indian paintbrush grow, they penetrate the roots of nearby plants. This doesn't harm the other plants but helps paintbrush to compete and survive.

Sow the seed in fall for colorful spring flowers and Indian paintbrush will reseed for years to come.

Size	6 to 16 in. tall, 9 to 12 in. wide
Bloom	Red-orange in spring to early summer
Soil	Dry, sandy
Light	Full sun
Hardiness	Cold: USDA 8 to 10 Heat: AHS 12 to 1

getting **started**
Direct sow outdoors in late summer to fall.

California poppy
Eschscholzia californica

The bright, cup-shaped flowers of this annual love sun — exactly what you'd expect of the state flower of California!

In areas with mild winters and very hot summers, California poppy is a perennial that goes dormant in midsummer. In cold-winter areas, the plant acts like an annual — it reseeds and sprouts when weather warms up in spring. A deep taproot makes it drought-tolerant but also hard to transplant.

Often the reseeded seedlings emerge and bloom just as the parent plants flag. Thin ruthlessly so they don't take over the whole garden. They require very little other effort in exchange for plenty of pretty blooms.

Size	12 to 18 in. tall, 6 in. wide
Bloom	Orange, red, yellow, cream or pink in summer
Soil	Sandy
Light	Full sun (flowers close on cloudy days and at night)
Hardiness	Cold: USDA 6 to 11 Heat: AHS 12 to 1

getting **started**
Direct sow in the garden ¼ in. deep.

top reseeding annuals *continued*

Moss rose
Portulaca grandiflora

Moss rose is one of the few reseeding succulent plants. The thick, fleshy leaves and stems of this ground cover make it very drought-tolerant. Indeed, it often reseeds in poor, dry or rocky soil, such as in rock gardens and crevices in walks. Because of its height and trailing habit, moss rose makes a great front-of-the-border plant. Flowing over the edges of hanging baskets or scattered among steppers are two other good uses. But if it's a path you use much, watch your step — the plant doesn't take kindly to foot traffic.

Moss rose is a moderate reseeder. The seedlings emerge the next spring very close to the parent plant.

Size 6 to 9 in. tall, 12 to 15 in. wide
Bloom Pink, red, orange, yellow, or white from late spring to fall
Soil Prefers sandy, well-drained soil
Light Sun (flowers close by midafternoon and on cloudy days)
Hardiness
　Cold: Annual
　Heat: AHS 12 to 1

getting **started**
Mix the tiny seed with sand for easier planting or buy plants.

Spider flower
Cleome hassleriana

Opening atop 4-foot-tall stems, the fantastic white to pink blooms of spider flower are real conversation-starters. They begin blooming in early summer when the plants reach about 2 feet tall and keep up the show as the stems keep rising. I often take scissors and snip off the seed pods in bunches to prevent too much reseeding. Otherwise, you'll get lots of new plants the next year.

By summer's end, the plant loses many of its lower leaves, but this isn't a problem. Shorter plants hide the bare knees of this back-of-the-border plant.

Spider flower is pretty carefree. Most pests don't bother it, but it's often visited by hungry butterflies and hummingbirds.

Size 18 to 48 in. tall, 12 to 36 in. wide
Bloom Pink, purple, white or bicolors from early summer to frost
Soil Moist, well-drained
Light Sun
Hardiness
　Cold: Annual
　Heat: AHS 12 to 1

getting **started**
Sow in garden in spring after danger of frost is past. Needs light to germinate, so cover lightly.

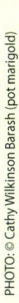

Sweet alyssum
Lobularia maritima

This diminutive reseeder creates mounds of fragrant, densely packed, tiny white or purple flowers. Sweet alyssum starts easily when sown directly in the garden but is also available as starter plants.

Either way, the soft mass of flowers continues for most of the summer in northern areas. For gardens farther south, sweet alyssum benefits from a little shade during the hottest part of the day, otherwise it flags by midsummer. Revive the plants by shearing them back by up to half.

Place this gentle reseeder around spring-blooming bulbs where each year the seedlings will help hide the fading bulb foliage.

Size   3 to 9 in. tall, 6 to 12 in. wide
Bloom   White or purple from spring to midsummer
Soil   Moist, well-drained
Light   Sun to part shade
Hardiness
          Cold: Annual
          Heat: AHS 12 to 1

getting **started**
Sow in garden in late spring or in late summer in hot-summer areas for fall bloom.

Pot marigold
Calendula officinalis

Bright, cheery 2- to 4-inch flowers of this reseeder reappear in your garden each year and attract colorful butterflies, as well.

If the heat of midsummer slows the plants down a bit, cut them back by about half. By fall, the plants will revive and flower again, just as vigorously as in the spring. Pot marigolds grow and bloom best in cool weather; in fact, they easily shrug off a light frost in fall. Leave the faded blooms on the plant and it'll reseed modestly in the same spot next spring.

In gardens in zones 7 to 10, where summers are long and very hot, sow the seeds in the garden in late summer to get late-winter to early spring blooms.

Size   12 to 30 in. tall, 12 to 18 in. wide
Bloom   Yellow or orange; bloom times vary
Soil   Moist, well-drained
Light   Sun to part shade
Hardiness
          Cold: Annual
          Heat: AHS 12 to 1

getting **started**
Seed needs dark to germinate, so cover with ¼ in. of soil; they'll germinate in eight to 10 days.

Readers' Favorite

Shade Flowers

Quick, think about shade. OK, what comes to your mind? Is it cool, lush and green? Maybe you don't visualize lots of beautiful flowers in a rainbow of colors, but really, you could, because there are plenty of colorful flowering shade plants.

Recently, we asked our readers for their favorite shade-loving plants, and they responded with dozens of great annuals and perennials that thrive in light to full shade. I'll share 10 of the most popular flowering ones with you here. Plus I'll help you figure out how much shade you have in your garden so you'll know which ones will thrive in your situation. Then on p. 86, you'll find three garden plans that include some of these plants.

HOW MUCH SHADE? As I've said, there are lots of good plants that grow and bloom in shade. But, as with most things, there are different degrees of shade. And the secret to having a great-looking shade garden is to choose the right plants for the conditions and the amount of sunlight you have. So, to make it easier to do this, along with the growing information, I'll tell you how much shade each plant will tolerate. But first, let's talk about those terms you see in the catalogs and what they mean.

Light shade Two to four hours of shade during the day is considered light shade. Many plants that prefer full sun can handle, or may even appreciate, a couple hours of shade, especially during the hottest hours and in the South.

Part shade Most sun-lovers might survive in four to five hours of shade per day, but they won't bloom as well as they would in full sun. For areas such as these, look for plants described as part shade.

Filtered shade A similar situation to part shade is filtered shade, such as a place shaded by trees like birch or ash with foliage that's not too dense. Some sunlight gets through the leaves all during the day.

Full shade There are spots in shade all day that never get any direct sun. These would be places on the north side of buildings or under trees with thick canopies. In these cases, use plants that can handle full shade.

Now that you know about levels of shade, watch your garden and figure out how long it's shaded and where. Or use a shade meter, available at nurseries or garden centers, to find out what you have. That information is key to finding the right plants to fit your bed and create a flowery place out of the sun!

Astilbe
Astilbe spp.

The colorful, feathery plumes of astilbe are attention-grabbers in any garden. But this pretty perennial is also easy to grow and not bothered by many pests or diseases.

Though astilbe prefers part shade in most zones, it'll tolerate full sun in USDA zone 4 gardens, unless the soil dries out. Without consistent moisture the leaves will turn brown and the plant will go dormant for the rest of the season.

'Rheinland', above, blooms in early summer, but other cultivars bloom later, so you can plan to have flowers most of the summer. Feed with a 10-10-10 fertilizer in early spring and again in mid-fall to keep plants healthy.

Type Perennial
Size 1 to 4 ft. tall, 1 to 3 ft. wide
Bloom White, pink, lavender, purple and red in summer
Light Part shade to sun
Soil Moist, well-drained
Hardiness
 Cold: USDA zones 4 to 8
 Heat: AHS zones 8 to 1

quick **fact**
Fascinating blooms last a long time and look good even as they dry on the plant.

Hosta
Hosta spp.

This popular shade-lover is usually grown for its wide range of colorful streaked and patterned foliage. But many hostas, like 'Blue Angel' in the photo, also sport beautiful flowers. Its trumpet-shaped blooms start out pale lavender and change to almost white.

'Blue Angel' isn't the only hosta with showy flowers. 'Aphrodite' boasts fragrant, double white flowers. And 'Honeybells', as you might guess from the name, also has fragrant flowers, white but lightly tinged with purple.

Give hostas an inch of water each week and plant them in rich soil to help them grow and bloom their best.

Type Perennial
Size 4 to 48 in. tall, 10 to 60 in. wide
Bloom White, lavender, purple in summer
Light Light to full shade
Soil Moist, well-drained
Hardiness
 Cold: USDA zones 3 to 9
 Heat: AHS zones 9 to 1

handy **tip**
If your hostas suffer slug damage, sprinkle a product with iron phosphate, such as Sluggo®, around plants to prevent future problems.

top shade flowers *continued*

Old-fashioned bleeding heart
Dicentra spectabilis

It's a joy to look forward to the flowers of old-fashioned bleeding heart in spring. The interesting heart-shaped pink and white flowers dangle from arching stems. Or grow 'Alba' for those delicate white flowers you see in the inset above.

Each year this perennial makes a bigger impact as it comes back taller (up to 3 feet or more) and wider, with even more flowers. Plant it where it has plenty of elbow room. It can be a challenge to transplant, thanks to its brittle roots.

Preferring moist soil, old-fashioned bleeding heart doesn't tolerate heat or drought well, however. By midsummer, the plant sometimes goes dormant.

Type Perennial
Size 2 to 3 ft. tall, 18 to 30 in. wide
Bloom Pink or white in spring
Light Part to full shade
Soil Moist, humus-rich, well-drained
Hardiness
Cold: USDA zones 3 to 8
Heat: AHS zones 8 to 1

looks good with
Plant among hostas or coral bells that will fill in and disguise the fading bleeding heart foliage.

Lily-of-the-valley
Convallaria majalis

As a shade-loving ground cover, lily-of-the-valley can't be beat. Not only is it cold-hardy to USDA zone 2, but this tough little plant grows and blooms in full shade. And speaking of blooms, its waxy, diminutive pink or white bell-shaped flowers have a surprisingly strong fragrance when they open in late spring. Even a small planting of lily-of-the-valley can create a wonderful wave of perfume that washes over the area.

Top-dress the soil with a little compost each fall, give plants a couple of years and they'll spread into a nice mass. They're easy to divide anytime from summer to fall by digging them and cutting apart the rhizomes.

Type Perennial
Size 8 in. tall, spreading
Bloom White or pink in late spring
Light Part to full shade
Soil Moist, well-drained
Hardiness
Cold: USDA zones 2 to 7
Heat: AHS zones 7 to 1

try these
Pink-flowered 'Rosea'
Double-flowered 'Flore Pleno'
Cream and green variegated leaves 'Albostriata'

Impatiens
Impatiens hybrids

What's the most popular bedding annual sold? It's impatiens, hands down! Breeders have developed sturdy cultivars that are covered with colorful single or double flowers, such as the double pink shown here.

Their small size makes them easy to fit into any shady spot in a container, at the front of a border, along a walk or any place you'd like a splash of season-long color.

Pinch the growing tips of young starts as you plant them to encourage them to branch. Once they're planted, care is simple — just give them consistent moisture. You don't even have to deadhead the faded blooms, as they're self-cleaning.

Type Grown as an annual
Size 6 to 18 in. tall and wide
Bloom Orange, red, pink, purple, rose, white and bicolors from summer to frost
Light Light to full shade
Soil Moist, well-drained
Hardiness
Annual
Heat: AHS zones 12 to 1

handy tip
If the seeds or seedlings of your favorites are difficult to find, overwinter a cutting or a plant indoors. Keep it in bright light and reduce watering until spring.

White trillium
Trillium grandiflorum

If you've spent much time walking in the woods in early spring, you may have come across a large mass of white trillium. Whorls of deep green leaves are topped with 3-inch single or double white flowers, which turn a light pink. In damp areas, the leaves will stay green all summer, but in dry summer weather, the plants may go dormant.

White trillium grows best in light shade and moist, slightly acid to neutral, well-drained soil. Once the plant is established, it doesn't like to be moved. But you can help it flourish by applying a little granular 12-12-12 fertilizer to the soil near the plant before it emerges early in the season.

Type Perennial
Size 12 to 18 in. tall, 12 in. wide
Bloom White in early spring
Light Light to part shade
Soil Moist, humus-rich, well-drained
Hardiness
Cold: USDA zones 5 to 8
Heat: AHS zones 8 to 1

quick fact
Buy your plants at a garden center or nursery. Never pick or dig white trillium found in the wild — it's endangered in some areas.

top shade flowers continued

Toad lily
Tricyrtis hirta

In early fall, the spotted, orchidlike flowers of toad lily start to open, lasting for up to five weeks. The stems of 'Miyazaki', in the photo, are arching, with the plant topping out at around 2 feet tall. It's covered with slightly hairy, medium-green leaves.

Though the flowers are intriguing, at 1 inch long, they're not terribly showy. So grow the plant near the front of a border or where you can see them up close.

Toad lily blooms best with a little morning sun and consistent moisture. Where winters are cold, grow the plant in a sheltered spot. Be sure to mulch the soil in late fall with a couple inches of composted leaves to protect the roots.

Type Perennial
Size 2 to 3 ft. tall, 1 to 2 ft. wide
Bloom Purple, lavender, fuchsia, white in early to late fall
Light Light to part shade
Soil Acid, moist, fertile
Hardiness
Cold: USDA zones 5 to 9
Heat: AHS zones 9 to 1

try these
Upright habit; 3 ft. tall 'Amethystina'
Solid lavender and white flowers; 2 ft. tall 'Tojen'

Hellebore
Helleborus spp.

Do you long for spring even when snow's still on the ground? Meet hellebore. This early season beauty often emerges and blooms right through the snow. And you'll get to enjoy the pretty flowers, like 'HGC Jacob', above, for as long as a few months. In areas with mild winters or where the plant gets a protective snow cover, the foliage is evergreen.

These tough perennials can grow in the same spot for many years without needing to be divided. But many types reseed, making them quite prolific. If they start to get crowded, in Northern zones divide them after the flowers finish in spring. Farther south, any time is fine.

Type Perennial
Size 1 to 3 ft. tall and wide
Bloom White, pink, green, red, yellow or purple in late winter to early spring
Light Part to full shade
Soil Well-drained, tolerates dry soil
Hardiness
Cold: USDA zones 5 to 9
Heat: AHS zones 9 to 1

quick fact
Few pests bother hellebores, but remove plant debris in late winter to discourage fungal problems.

Brunnera
Brunnera macrophylla

With its large, bristly, heart-shaped leaves and clouds of tiny blue flowers, brunnera is a study in contrasts. Mature plants form large clumps, but brunnera grows so slowly that you won't need to divide the plant often. And when you grow it in humus-rich soil, there's no need to fertilize, either.

Brunnera is content in any full or part-shade spot. But moist soil is crucial or the edges of the leaves will get crispy. Grow the plant, like 'Variegata' above, in full shade where summers are hot and dry, to prevent the plant from dying back for the rest of the season. Mulch around it with 2 to 3 inches of chopped leaves to conserve moisture.

Type Perennial
Size 1 to 2 ft. tall and wide
Bloom Blue in early spring
Light Part to full shade
Soil Moist, humus-rich, tolerates poor soil
Hardiness
Cold: USDA zones 3 to 7
Heat: AHS zones 7 to 1

handy tip
Cut back the brown leaves after flowering is finished for a tidier mound of foliage.

Coral bells
Heuchera hybrids

It's true they're known for their easy care and heat- and humidity-tolerance. And coral bells come in nearly every foliage color, from chartreuse to almost black, including rose, caramel, pink and mahogany.

But coral bells also offer lots of gorgeous flower power. 'Raspberry Regal', in the photo, produces 30-inch-tall dense spikes of hummingbird-attracting red flowers.

When your older plants die out in the middle, dig them up in spring, remove and discard the woody centers and replant the small divisions.

Mulch around the plants after the ground freezes to keep them from heaving out of the ground during changing winter temps.

Type Perennial
Size 6 to 18 in. tall, 10 to 24 in. wide
Bloom Red, pink or white in late spring
Light Part shade to full sun
Soil Moist, well-drained
Hardiness
Cold: USDA zones 3 to 9
Heat: AHS zones 9 to 1

try these
Heavy-blooming, with masses of deep-pink flowers 'Rave On'
Blood-red flowers with light fragrance 'Ruby Bells'

top shade flowers *continued*

shades of brilliance

There's a long-held notion that it's hard to have a great-looking garden in the shade. Nothing could be further from the truth. Just take a look at the shady designs on these pages and you can see that it's easy to create beautiful, colorful shade borders, whether it's in light or deep shade, in soil that's damp or even on the dry side. The right plants make all the difference.

To help you find the right ones for your particular situation, here are three shade garden designs. They use many of the plants we've talked about on the previous pages, plus a few more tough and easy-care shade-loving beauties to give you even more options for your gorgeous garden in the shade. ☐

— *Deborah Gruca*

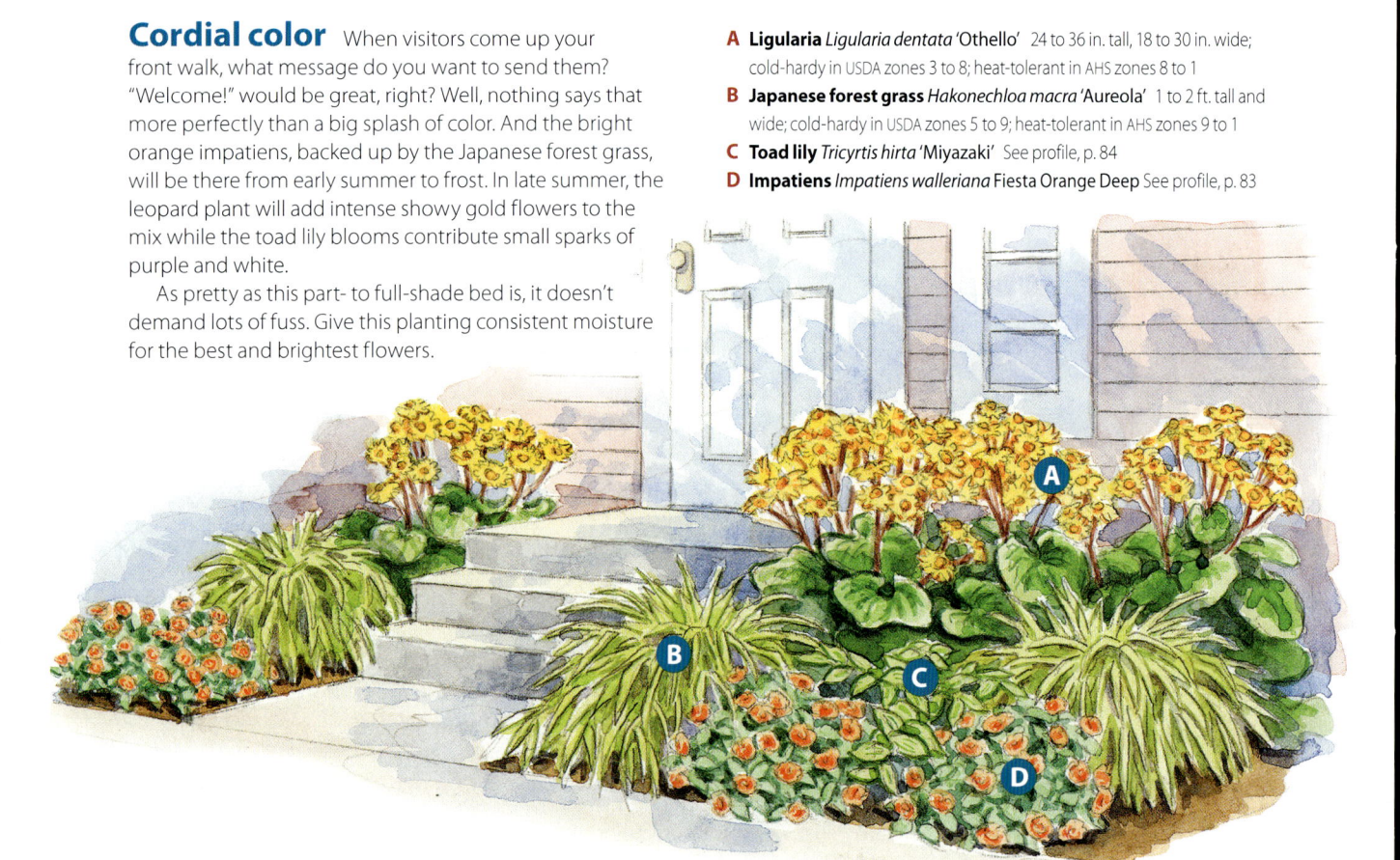

Cordial color When visitors come up your front walk, what message do you want to send them? "Welcome!" would be great, right? Well, nothing says that more perfectly than a big splash of color. And the bright orange impatiens, backed up by the Japanese forest grass, will be there from early summer to frost. In late summer, the leopard plant will add intense showy gold flowers to the mix while the toad lily blooms contribute small sparks of purple and white.

As pretty as this part- to full-shade bed is, it doesn't demand lots of fuss. Give this planting consistent moisture for the best and brightest flowers.

A Ligularia *Ligularia dentata* 'Othello' 24 to 36 in. tall, 18 to 30 in. wide; cold-hardy in USDA zones 3 to 8; heat-tolerant in AHS zones 8 to 1

B Japanese forest grass *Hakonechloa macra* 'Aureola' 1 to 2 ft. tall and wide; cold-hardy in USDA zones 5 to 9; heat-tolerant in AHS zones 9 to 1

C Toad lily *Tricyrtis hirta* 'Miyazaki' See profile, p. 84

D Impatiens *Impatiens walleriana* Fiesta Orange Deep See profile, p. 83

Dry shade delight There are plenty of pretty plants that love shade. But *dry* shade can be more of a challenge. Luckily, there are some great plants out there that are tough enough for this situation.

When you set new plants in the garden, be sure to water them deeply to encourage them to develop deep roots. And keep the soil moist for the first year, until the plants are well-established. A 2-in.-thick layer of organic mulch will also help to conserve soil moisture.

'Red Lady' and 'Mrs. Betty Ranicar' Lenten roses start the show in very early spring in this full-shade bed, followed by the delicate blooms of red barrenwort and the purple flowers of the deadnettle. The gorgeous variegated foliage of the deadnettle will keep this planting looking good all summer long.

A Hellebore *Helleborus* 'Mrs. Betty Ranicar' See profile, p. 84

B Deadnettle *Lamium maculatum* 'Purple Dragon' 4 to 8 in. tall, spreading; cold-hardy in USDA zones 3 to 9; heat-tolerant in AHS zones 9 to 1

C Red barrenwort *Epimedium* x*rubrum* 6 to 12 in. tall, spreading; cold-hardy in USDA zones 5 to 9; heat-tolerant in AHS zones 9 to 1

D Hellebore *Helleborus* 'Red Lady' See profile, p. 84

Moist and cool Do you have one of those places that never seems to get very dried out? This little part-shade bed, located on the north side of a house, is almost always moist and cool. Consistent moisture like this means that even after the brunnera and the bleeding heart bloom in spring, they'll continue to look good all summer. And the lady fern will thrive in these conditions, too. You won't see scorched leaves or plants going dormant, like they can in hotter, drier spots.

The 'Moonlight' coral bells will stay lush and fresh in this spot, but you'll want to keep an eye out for slugs. And be sure to tuck in some chopped leaves or wood chips around the plants after the ground freezes to keep them from heaving out of the ground. Check plants regularly in winter and if you find any that are heaving, gently press them back into the soil with your toe.

A Lady fern *Athyrium filix-femina* 2 to 3 ft. tall, 24 to 30 in. wide; cold-hardy in USDA zones 4 to 8; heat-tolerant in AHS zones 8 to 1

B Brunnera *Brunnera macrophylla* 'Looking Glass' See profile, p. 85

C Fernleaf bleeding heart *Dicentra* 'King of Hearts' 1 to 2 ft. tall and wide; cold-hardy in USDA zones 3 to 8; heat-tolerant in AHS zones 8 to 1

D Coral bells *Heuchera* 'Moonlight' See profile, p. 85

top fall bulbs

Bulbs for Three Seasons of Color

If you grow bulbs, you know how fascinating they are on their own, as well as mixed in borders with other plants. If you haven't grown them, you'll find there are lots that provide a colorful show for up to several weeks with little or no care. Choose right and you can have bulbs bursting into bloom in nearly every season and returning for years.

On the next pages, I'll introduce you to 11 great easy-to-grow bulbs. We'll start with fall-bloomers that you'll be seeing soon, then move on to spring- and summer-bloomers. Now, when I say "bulbs" I'm including not only true bulbs but also tubers, rhizomes, corms and tuberous roots. I'll let you know what each one is as we move through the story.

For the widest selection, order from mail-order companies that specialize in bulbs — I've included some sources below. It's a good way to go if you're looking for hard-to-find cultivars. When they arrive, check them over carefully and plant them as soon as possible so your plants will have a good start.

Finally, I'll share some tips on buying and planting bulbs. And with our plan mixing some of these great bloomers with other plants, you can grow a border that looks beautiful for a full three seasons.

Mail-order sources

Brent and Becky's Bulbs
www.brentandbeckysbulbs.com, 877-661-2852. *Catalog free*

Digging Dog Nursery
www.diggingdog.com, 707-937-1130. *Catalog $4*

Old House Gardens
www.oldhousegardens.com, 734-995-1486. *Catalog $2*

Cyclamen
Cyclamen hederifolium

It's hard to say which is more appealing about hardy cyclamen: The perky fall flowers or the charming round to heart-shaped leaves. Colorful blooms push up through fall leaves first. They're followed by foliage that sports zones of silver or patterns of lighter or darker colors on the surface with red or purple undersides.

After a few seasons, a tuber in the garden can grow into a clump that reaches 12 inches across. So even though they're small, plant them with plenty of elbow room — 6 to 8 inches apart.

Cyclamen tubers can take two to three years to start growing. Buy young plants for a quicker start.

Type Tuber
Size 4 to 6 in. tall and wide
Bloom Pink or white in late summer to late fall
How to plant In early fall, just below the soil's surface
Soil Well-drained
Light Filtered shade
Hardiness
Cold: USDA zones 5 to 8
Heat: AHS zones 8 to 1

did you **know?**
Not sure which side is up? Plant it with the flattest side down. Both the leaves *and* the roots emerge from the more rounded side, which you want to be on top.

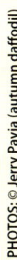

Autumn daffodil
Sternbergia lutea

The goblet-shaped yellow blooms of autumn daffodil bring a welcome splash of color to the fall garden, when most perennials are dying down. Opening on sturdy stalks, the flowers are quickly followed by narrow deep- green leaves.

These tough little bloomers love slightly alkaline and sharply drained — even rocky — soil. In these conditions, they'll form a nice clump in a few years. (If blooming declines after several years, dig the bulbs in spring and replant them 6 inches apart.)

Plant bulbs in late summer and mark the area so you'll know where they are until they emerge in the fall.

Type Bulb
Size 6 to 10 in. tall, 6 in. wide
Bloom White or yellow in autumn
How to plant In summer, 5 in. deep
Soil Sharply drained, slightly alkaline
Light Full sun
Hardiness
  Cold: USDA zones 6 to 11
  Heat: AHS zones 11 to 1

did you **know?**
Try fall crocus (*Crocus speciosus*). This fall-bloomer is cold-hardy to USDA zone 3.

Kaffir lily
Schizostylis coccinea

Extend the bloom season in your garden with dozens of small star-shaped red, pink or white flowers on 2-foot-tall stems. Kaffir lily blooms for a few weeks in the cool weather of the fall garden, or for more than a week when cut and enjoyed indoors. Handsome, narrow straplike leaves add to Kaffir lily's graceful and elegant appearance.

If you want to divide a clump, dig and separate the rhizomes in spring so there are five or six shoots each. Replant divisions 2 inches deep in moist soil.

NOT HARDY FOR YOU?
Grow Kaffir lily in containers, or dig the rhizomes in fall and store them in peat in a dry, cool (45 degrees) place.

Type Rhizome
Size 18 to 24 in. tall, 12 in. wide
Bloom Red, pink or white in late fall
How to plant In spring, 2 in. deep
Soil Moist
Light Full sun
Hardiness
  Cold: USDA zones 7 to 9
  Heat: AHS zones 9 to 1

did you **know?**
Unlike most bulbs, Kaffir lily tolerates year-round moisture, and thrives in boggy areas around ponds.

top spring bulbs

Glory-of-the-snow
Chionodoxa luciliae

Glory-of-the-snow is aptly named, as it's one of the earliest spring flowers to bloom, occasionally even in the snow. An established clump can create a colorful carpet lasting for up to a month, a sure sign of spring for the winter-weary gardener. White-eyed 'Pink Giant', in the photo above, is slightly taller, at 8 inches, than the blue species.

This delicate-looking but rugged plant is a good naturalizer. It spreads by bulb offsets and by self-seeding — so don't bother to deadhead it.

Plant glory-of-the-snow in rock gardens or beneath deciduous trees or shrubs where it'll soon cover the ground in large drifts of flowers.

Type Bulb
Size 6 in. tall, 3 in. wide
Bloom Blue, pink or white in early spring
How to plant In fall, 2 in. deep
Soil Well-drained
Light Full sun to light shade
Hardiness
Cold: USDA zones 3 to 9
Heat: AHS zones 9 to 1

did you know?
It looks great growing with crocus *Crocus* spp. or hellebore *Helleborus orientalis*.

Species tulip
Tulipa spp.

Species tulips are true workhorse bulbs of the spring garden. Diminutive flowers open on plants that, for the most part, reach no more than 12 inches tall. They're less affected by wind and rain and are tougher and longer-lived than many of their cultivated cousins. Many naturalize easily, spreading into beautiful drifts in just a few years.

There are dozens of different species tulips (that's *Tulipa tarda* in the photo). Cold winters and hot summers are necessary, though the dormant bulbs don't need to stay quite as dry in summer as those of hybrids. This makes them easier to tuck in around shrubs and perennials in mixed borders.

Type Bulb
Size 4 to 12 in. tall, 3 to 6 in. wide
Bloom Spring
How to plant In fall, three times the height of the bulb
Soil Moist, well-drained
Light Full sun
Hardiness
Cold: USDA zones 3 to 8
Heat: AHS zones 8 to 1

did you know?
Species tulips thrive in raised beds and rock gardens where they get sharp drainage.

Chinese ground orchid
Bletilla striata

Beautiful, nodding, bell-shaped flowers of Chinese ground orchid dangle above pleated, pale-green leaves for about a month in spring. This part-shade-lover is as pretty as true orchids, but easier to grow.

Loose, well-drained soil in dappled shade, such as at the edge of a woodland garden, is a perfect place for Chinese ground orchid. (You can also buy it in pots as a perennial.) After several years, it forms a large clump and the longer you leave it, the prettier and larger the flowers get. The rhizome doesn't go dormant until late fall, so it appreciates regular moisture during the spring and summer.

Type Tuberous rhizome
Size 12 to 18 in. tall, 6 to 12 in. wide
Bloom Magenta, white or yellow in mid- to late spring
How to plant In fall, 4 in. deep
Soil Well-drained
Light Part shade
Hardiness
Cold: USDA zones 5 to 9
Heat: AHS zones 9 to 1

did you know?
Unlike most bulbs, after the flowers fade in summer, the foliage remains all season.

Allium
Allium **spp. and hybrids**

Growing eye-catching globe-shaped flowers is a sure way to create excitement in your borders. Alliums often bloom for three weeks or more in spring, summer or fall. After the blooms fade and dry, leave the dried seed heads in place or even spritz them with spray paint for enduring color.

Plant and flower sizes vary greatly depending on the allium you choose, but all do best in very well-drained soil — they're prone to rot in wet soil.

Also, for the biggest and brightest flowers, feed the plants a 7-10-5 bulb food three times a year, in spring as the leaves emerge, in summer as the blooms fade and again in late fall.

Type Bulb
Size 8 to 60 in. tall, 6 to 24 in. wide
Bloom Violet, purple, white or yellow in spring (some species in summer and fall)
How to plant In fall, three times the height of the bulb
Soil Well-drained
Light Full sun
Hardiness
Cold: USDA zones 3 to 9, depending on the species
Heat: AHS zones 9 to 1

did you know?
To get the biggest flowers, buy the largest bulbs you can afford.

top summer bulbs

Byzantine gladiola
Gladiolus communis byzantinus

If you love the bright, showy flowers of glads, but don't care for their sometimes top-heavy look, try Byzantine glads. Flower spikes bear up to 20 or more dainty, 2-inch tubular blooms. In summer they open from the bottom of the spike up and the stalks stay upright even without staking. Bladelike leaves give the whole plant a graceful look that fits nicely into any informal border or cottage garden.

Byzantine glads do best in moist soils and are grateful for a little shade during the hottest part of the day in warmer areas. The corms naturalize easily into beautiful clumps in just a few years.

Type Corm
Size 2 to 3 ft. tall, 3 to 6 in. wide
Bloom Deep magenta or white in late spring to midsummer
How to plant In spring, 3 to 5 in. deep
Soil Moist, well-drained
Light Full sun to part shade
Hardiness
Cold: USDA zones 5 to 9
Heat: AHS zones 9 to 1

did you **know?**
This glad will draw lots of attention, but not from deer — they don't care for it.

Society garlic
Tulbaghia violacea

Society garlic has a lot to recommend it for the summer garden. First are the clusters of long-lasting lavender-pink or white flowers that blend well with any color palette. Add to this its easy-to-grow nature and drought-tolerance. Also, the rhizomes aren't picky about soil, growing in sand, clay or even standing water for a few weeks at a time!

You'll sometimes find society garlic sold as plants. No matter how you buy it, it gradually spreads into nice-sized clumps, but not aggressively so.

NOT HARDY FOR YOU?
Overwinter society garlic in a pot indoors in a bright, cool (40 to 50 degrees) room with little watering.

Type Rhizome
Size 12 to 24 in. tall, 9 to 12 in. wide
Bloom Lavender-pink or white in early summer to early fall
How to plant In spring, 2 in. deep
Soil Humus-rich, moist, well-drained
Light Full sun
Hardiness
Cold: USDA zones 7 to 10
Heat: AHS zones 10 to 1

did you **know?**
Its garlic scent makes it a poor cut flower, but isn't noticeable out in the garden.

Pineapple lily
Eucomis bicolor

Every border needs something to spice it up, and this plant is a great choice! Pineapple lily gets its name from the long clusters of flowers topped by a jaunty green cap, making it look a lot like the fruit of the same name. The species, above, has green blooms with maroon markings, but some cultivars have maroon or white blossoms. Combine this summer-bloomer with low-growing flowers, like the heliotrope and fan-flower in the photo, so it really stands out.

NOT HARDY FOR YOU? Plant bulbs in spring. Dig them in fall and let them dry for a couple of days. Store them in dry peat moss in a dark place at 45 to 60 degrees.

Type   Bulb
Size   18 to 24 in. tall, 6 in. wide
Bloom   Green, white or maroon in midsummer
How to plant   In fall, 6 in. deep
Soil   Well-drained
Light   Full sun
Hardiness
   Cold: USDA zones 8 to 11
   Heat: AHS zones 11 to 1

did you **know?**
In a container, plant the bulb so the pointed tip is just barely sticking up through the soil.

Crocosmia
***Crocosmia* spp. and hybrids**

Bold, bright funnel-shaped flowers on branched stems make crocosmia a great accent in any summer border. Each 4-foot stem, loaded with up to 40 hummingbird-attracting blooms, arches horizontally, like scarlet-flowered 'Lucifer', above. Lance-shaped leaves add to the tropical feel.

Keep crocosmia blooming its best by dividing it every few years. In fall, dig the clump and pull or cut the corms apart. Replant the sections immediately at the same depth they were growing.

NOT HARDY FOR YOU? Crocosmia won't have time to spread in a single season. Lift and store the bulbs in fall and replant them in spring.

Type   Corm
Size   2 to 4 ft. tall, 12 to 15 in. wide
Bloom   Red, orange or yellow in mid- to late summer
How to plant   In spring, 2 to 3 in. deep
Soil   Humus-rich, moist, well-drained
Light   Sun
Hardiness
   Cold: USDA zones 6 to 9
   Heat: AHS zones 9 to 1

did you **know?**
Crocosmia is virtually pest- and disease-free and makes long-lasting cut flowers.

PHOTOS: © Jerry Pavia (Byzantine gladiola, society garlic)

Bring in the color with bulbs!

Tuck a few bulbs in with your perennials and shrubs to keep the color in your garden going all year long. I've included some easy-care choices here, as well as some basic bulb tips on the next page, to get them off to a great start. As the seasons come and go, the bulbs appear and disappear, adding another interesting dimension to your garden. □

— *Deborah Gruca*

Let Kaffir lily get a bit root-bound for the best blooms.

▲ **Bright fall flair** In fall, bright yellow autumn daffodils emerge all along the edge of the thyme growing among the pavers. To one side shine the soft pink flowers of 'Xenox' sedum. A little farther back in the bed, pink Kaffir lily blooms in its container. Peach daylilies and pink roses still bloom sporadically until frost, backed by the deep red-purple viburnum foliage.

THE GARDEN'S PALETTE

Code	Plant Name	No. to Plant	Blooms	Type	Cold/Heat Zones	Height/Width	Special Features
A	Arrowwood viburnum *Viburnum dentatum* Blue Blaze™ ('Blubzam')	4	White; spring	Shrub	3-8/8-1	4-5 ft./ 5-6 ft.	Maintains compact, tidy habit; large clusters of blue berries in summer; red-purple fall foliage; attracts birds
B	Shrub rose *Rosa* Easy Elegance® Little Mischief ('BAlief')	4	Deep-pink; summer to frost	Shrub	4-9/9-1	2-3 ft./ 2-3 ft.	Ever-blooming deep-pink flowers age to light pink; glossy green foliage is disease-resistant
C	Allium *Allium hollandicum* 'Purple Sensation'	12	Purple; late spring	Bulb	3-8/8-1	20-30 in./ 12 in.	Baseball-sized flowers look attractive dried on plant; light fragrance; resistant to deer and rabbits
D	Purple coneflower *Echinacea purpurea* 'Magnus'	2	Pink; summer to frost	Perennial	3-8/8-1	3 ft./3 ft.	Large, 7-in. flowers bloom and bring in butterflies from early summer through fall; birds eat dried seed heads
E	Bleeding heart *Dicentra spectabilis* 'Alba'	1	White; spring	Perennial	3-8/8-1	24-36 in./ 18-30 in.	Nodding white flowers hang from arching stems in spring; foliage often goes dormant by midsummer
F	Daylily *Hemerocallis* 'Spanish Glow'	3	Peach; summer to fall	Perennial	3-9/9-1	18-26 in./ 15-24 in.	Ruffled blooms rebloom off and on all summer long; tolerates poor or dry soils
G	Kaffir lily (in container) *Schizostylis coccinea*	1	Red, pink or white; late summer to fall	Bulb	7-9/9-1	18-24 in./ 12 in.	Blooms best when slightly root-bound; long-lasting cut flower; tolerant of wet soil
H	Chinese ground orchid *Bletilla striata*	6	Pink-purple; spring	Bulb	5-9/9-1	12-18 in./ 6-12 in.	Foliage remains attractive all through summer with even moisture; provide winter mulch in zone 5
I	Pineapple lily *Eucomis bicolor*	3	Green, white or maroon; early to midsummer	Bulb	8-11/12-1	18-24 in./ 6 in.	Single stem bears bottlebrushlike flower in midsummer; let soil dry when bulbs are dormant in late summer
J	Tall sedum *Sedum telephium* 'Xenox'	2	Soft pink; fall	Perennial	3-10/9-1	10-14 in./ 12-24 in.	Burgundy-purple leaves with scalloped edges are green and mauve in spring; compact habit; attracts butterflies
K	Autumn daffodil *Sternbergia lutea*	23	Yellow; fall	Bulb	6-11/11-1	6-10 in./ 6 in.	Bright yellow flowers in autumn; tolerates rocky soil; good naturalizer; protect from harsh winter cold
L	Common thyme *Thymus vulgaris*	10	Light purple to white; spring	Perennial	5-9/9-1	6-12 in./ 16-18 in.	Gray-green fragrant foliage; spreads in sandy and rocky soils; drought-tolerant; attracts butterflies

Midspring medley ▶

'Purple Sensation' alliums flower among the foliage of the roses, which are heavily budded and nearly ready to burst into bloom themselves. Tiny magenta Chinese ground orchids open on their arching stems, separated from the alliums by the white flowers of bleeding heart. Meanwhile, sedums, coneflowers and daylilies are just emerging from the soil as the arrowwood viburnums, covered in their flat-topped white flower clusters, provide a background.

Gently pull the allium blooms when they fade or leave them for their interesting texture.

Clusters of brilliant blue viburnum berries follow the white spring flowers.

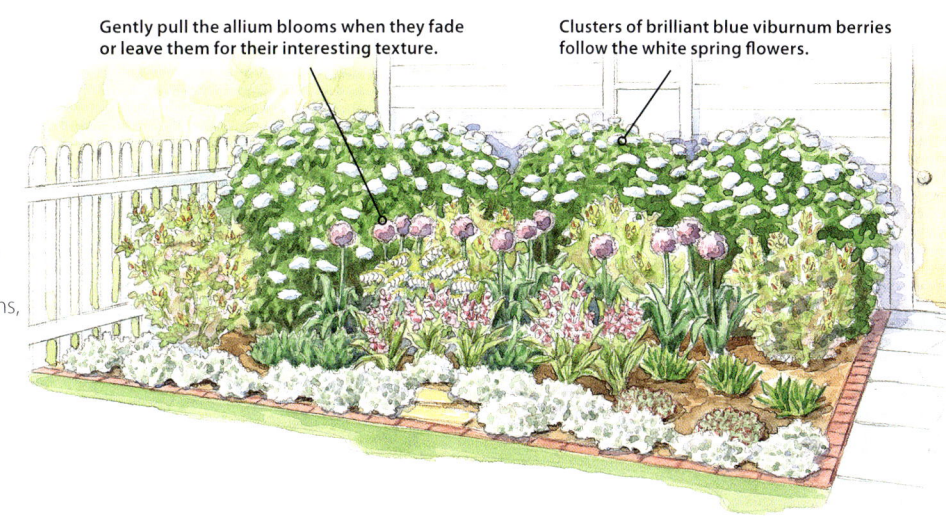

Place a container on bricks over the gap left by the dormant bleeding heart.

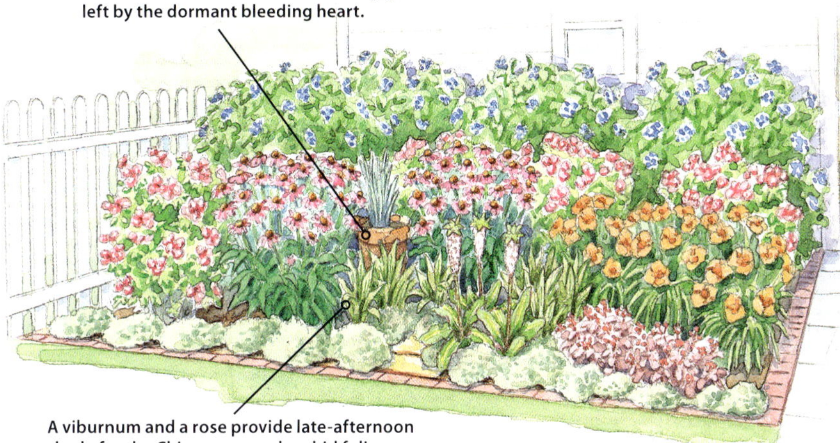

◀ Summer flurry of color

The Little Mischief roses are covered in pink blooms behind the stately white pineapple lily spikes. Coneflowers bloom on one side of the bed and on the other, warm peach daylilies. The still fresh-looking Chinese ground orchid foliage flanks the stepping stones. The steppers provide easy access for both adding the container of Kaffir lily in summer and lifting the pineapple lilies in the fall.

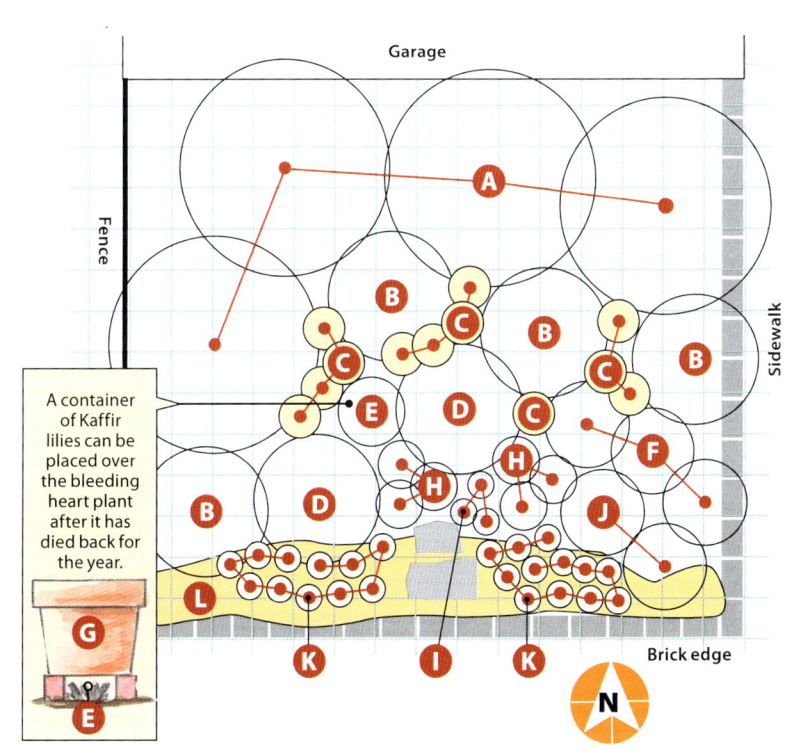

A viburnum and a rose provide late-afternoon shade for the Chinese ground orchid foliage.

A container of Kaffir lilies can be placed over the bleeding heart plant after it has died back for the year.

Scale: 1 square = 1 square ft.

Bulb-growing basics

Most bulb plants are easy to grow and have similar cultural needs. Here are a few tips:

- **Choose well** Buy only the largest, firmest and heaviest bulbs.
- **Save money** Buy bulb mixes if you aren't particular about getting specific colors.
- **Provide good drainage** Work in 3 to 4 in. of compost or leaf mold into the soil to improve texture and drainage.
- **Plant at the right depth** Dig holes three times the height of the bulb. So, for a 2-in.-tall allium bulb, dig a hole 6 in. deep. Dig holes a little shallower in zones 6 or warmer or in heavy clay soil.
- **Feed as you plant** Using a trowel, mix some bulb fertilizer, such as 5-5-5 or 5-10-10 into the soil at the bottom of the hole.
- **Stake early** For tall plants, place the stake next to the bulb in the hole when planting so you don't damage the bulb or roots.
- **Mark the spot** Prevent accidentally digging into them later by using tags or labels.

www.GardenGateMagazine.com   *the* YEAR IN GARDENING   95

Easiest Clematis Ever!

Clematis xdurandii

Mail-order sources

Donahue's Clematis Specialists
www.donahuesclematis.com
507-334-8404. *Catalog free*

Garden Crossings
www.gardencrossings.com
616-875-6355. *Online catalog only*

Klehm's Song Sparrow Farm and Nursery
www.songsparrow.com
800-553-3715. *Catalog free*

Heronswood Nursery
www.heronswood.com
877-674-4714. *Catalog free*

Everyone loves clematis — or at least it seems that way to anyone who's ever grown one. This huge family of climbers has flowers in colors from white to red or purple and even yellow. Flower shape varies widely also, including everything from nodding or upfacing bells to flat single or double flowers with large fluffy centers in contrasting colors. The fact that plants range from 4 to 30 feet tall adds to their versatility. It means that you can use them in the garden in a plethora of different ways, from scrambling along the ground to climbing up a pergola. If that's not enough, most of these vines have fascinating fluffy seed heads to finish the season with style.

PRETTY AND EASY I'd like to introduce you to 10 clematis that are smothered in colorful blooms every year. But these 10 are also very resistant to mildew and wilt, which can be problems for other clematis. I'll talk more about this later. And, because these flower on the current season's stems, they are even easy to prune. Just cut back all of these plants almost to the ground every spring. You don't have to decide what to cut and what to leave!

ONES TO LOOK FOR Because the blooms take time to form every year, they don't show up until at least midsummer. While these 10 are certainly beautiful and easy care, they're not the only ones out there. Late-season clematis include several species, such as *viticella, texensis, tangutica, integrifolia* and *durandii* and their hybrids. If this article has you interested in finding more great clematis, look for plants with one of these in their name.

I'll show these plants in order from smallest to biggest, and give you some great plant companions. Also, you'll get tips on lots of ways to design with these versatile vines and how to choose the right supports. Finally, on p. 102 I'll give some pointers on how to care for these easy-care, colorful climbers.

'Fascination'

This plant really lives up to its name as its intricate 2-inch violet bells, edged in silver, capture your attention. The pointed petals curve back to reveal a tight cluster of yellow anthers — great for cutting or in the garden. This newer Dutch hybrid produces a profusion of pretty blooms for a long time starting in midsummer. As you draw near, you'll detect their light, sweet fragrance. And even when the flower show ends, 'Fascination' is festooned with the silky silver seedheads for which some clematis are so famous.

Grow this diminutive plant on a short 4- to 5-foot trellis on or near a patio. That way, you'll have the flowers right at eye-level where they can captivate the imagination of anyone who happens to be nearby.

Size 4 to 6 ft. tall
Bloom Purple with silver edges in mid- to late summer
Light Full sun to part shade
Hardiness
Cold: USDA 4 to 9
Heat: AHS 9 to 1

Perfect partners

'Fascination' grows well and looks great in containers, especially near companions with gray or gray-green foliage:
Bluebeard *Caryopteris* ×*clandonensis*
Rose campion *Lychnis coronaria*
Artemisia *Artemisia* spp.

'Romantika'

Here's a clematis that has some of the deepest purple flowers out there. The 4- to 5-inch-diameter blooms are accented with a center of bright-gold stamens. 'Romantika' starts blooming in summer, easily handling the heat of the season, straight through to fall. To get a close-up view of the deep-hued flowers, let this vine climb up a pretty obelisk in front of a light-colored background like a wall or fence. Or train it into the branches of a shrub or small tree by placing bamboo canes from the ground up to the lower branches where it can grab on. In early spring, it's easy to cut the vine near the ground and pull the stems from the branches. Pruning it back hard assures you the plant will be covered with beautiful blooms by summer.

Size 5 to 8 ft. tall
Bloom 4- to 5-in. dark purple-black flowers in summer to early fall
Light Full sun
Hardiness
Cold: USDA 4 to 9
Heat: AHS 9 to 1

Perfect partners

Grow this small clematis over sturdy evergreens with yellow or gold foliage to contrast with the deep purple blooms:
Golden dwarf cypress *Chamaecyparis obtusa* 'Nana Lutea'
Juniper *Juniperus* ×*pfitzeriana* 'Daub's Frosted'

easiest clematis continued

Durand's clematis
C. xdurandii

Handsome indigo-blue 4- to 5-inch flowers adorn the stems of Durand's clematis. Several prominent ribs run down the center of each petal. The white ball-shaped center, made up of a tuft of stamens, is blue-tinged at its base. When cut, the blooms show well in a mixed bouquet and last a long time in a vase.

Clematis species that have been grown for a long time demand a place of respect in the gardening world. And this one has been popular for more than a century in gardens around Europe and North America. The deep, rich flower color looks dramatic with gold or silver-variegated plants like spotted deadnettle (*Lamium maculatum*) or winter creeper (*Euonymus fortunei*), which set off the clematis' simple dark-green leaves.

This clematis doesn't twine, so you'll need to tie it to supports, or use it as a colorful, flowery ground cover.

Size 5 to 8 ft. tall
Bloom Indigo-blue in midsummer to early fall
Light Full sun to part shade
Hardiness
Cold: USDA 4 to 9
Heat: AHS 9 to 1

Did you know?
Have a large boulder or interesting sculpture in your garden? Let this colorful non-twiner scramble along the ground and call attention to these features.

Passion flower clematis
C. florida sieboldiana

Talk about drama! The white summer petals of this clematis change to a creamy green by fall. But that eye-popping mass of purple stamens in the center creates a bold look not many other clematis can match. Though it's not quite as cold-hardy or vigorous a grower as some other clematis, the unusual flowers make it worth a little effort to have it in the garden. If you live in zone 5 or colder, grow this vine in a container, surrounded by shorter white or blue-flowered companions to play up the striking purple center. Then you can move it and the container into an unheated garage or shed to give it some protection from the cold. In spring, cut back the old stems to 4 to 6 inches, replace the top 2 inches of soil in the pot with fresh potting mix and roll the container back out into the spring sun.

Size 6 to 10 ft. tall
Bloom Cream-white petals with deep purple centers in midsummer to early fall
Light Full sun to part shade
Hardiness
Cold: USDA 6 to 9
Heat: AHS 9 to 1

Perfect partners
Burgundy- or purple-foliaged shrubs or perennials highlight the purple center:
Bugleweed *Ajuga reptans*
Purple smokebush *Cotinus coggygria* 'Royal Purple'

'Duchess of Albany'

Each 2- to 3-inch 'Duchess of Albany' flower resembles a small pink tulip. Deeper pink bands run up the centers of the petals, which fade to pale pink and curve back slightly at the tips. Thick flower stems hold the blooms upright on the plant and make 'Duchess of Albany' a good, long-lasting cut flower.

This charming climber is one of the most heat-tolerant clematis. So it's a great choice for Southern gardeners, handling the hot, sultry summers without any trouble. If you garden where mildew is a problem, prevent it by spraying your clematis with a fungicide each month, starting in late spring.

Though not one of the taller clematis, its vigorous growth needs a sturdy support. The blooms show especially well growing along a deck railing or a low fence.

Size 6 to 12 ft. tall
Bloom Pink upfacing miniature tulips in mid- to late summer
Light Full sun to part shade
Hardiness
Cold: USDA 4 to 9
Heat: AHS 9 to 1

Also try

Other tulip-shaped clematis to grow:
Red-flowered 'Lady Bird Johnson'
Deep-pink 'Princess Diana'
Scarlet 'Sir Trevor Lawrence'

'Comtesse de Bouchaud'

This beautiful large-flowered late-bloomer is so trouble-free and easy to grow, it's often recommended for novice gardeners. But I know clematis fanatics who always have at least one growing in their gardens as well.

Starting in midsummer, the plant is covered with 5-inch-wide pink blooms that make it hard to see the clean foliage. Crepe-paper-textured petals that curve back slightly at the tips surround a center of cream-colored stamens. The soft color tends to fade or sunburn a bit in very hot sun, so give the plant some shade during the hottest part of the day to keep the flowers looking fresh.

Though not particularly tall, 'Comtesse de Bouchaud' is a dense, heavy vine. Be sure to give it sturdy support, such as a wooden arbor or pergola. A lightweight trellis won't work for this plant.

Size 6 to 12 ft. tall
Bloom Rose-pink from mid-summer to early fall
Light Full sun to part shade
Hardiness
Cold: USDA 4 to 9
Heat: AHS 9 to 1

Did you know?

To extend the bloom time, prune in late winter as usual. Then, in April, prune just the tips of one-third to one-half of the stems to prevent them from blooming until later in the summer.

easiest clematis continued

'Purpurea Plena Elegans'

This old cultivar produces voluptuous red-purple blooms. The velvety petals, which are grayish on the back, curve slightly toward the tips. Often the outer petals are tinged with green as the bud starts to unfurl. Later, these outer petals may fall off, leaving the smaller, darker-colored inner rosette of petals to open gradually and finish the show. The elegant, slightly nodding flowers hang from extra long stems, making them perfect for adding to mixed arrangements. Picture them arching out of a large formal bouquet in a footed vase.

'Purpurea Plena Elegans' looks beautiful with a background of gray foliage or bark, so growing it up into trees and shrubs is a natural design use. Up the side of a house or garden wall is also a good idea, as the plant is a vigorous grower when it's established.

Size 10 to 12 ft. tall
Bloom 2½-in. double red-purple from midsummer to fall
Light Full sun to part shade
Hardiness
Cold: USDA 3 to 9
Heat: AHS 9 to 1

Also try

These doubles also have fluffy centers. (The cultivar names come from the breeders, Evison and Poulsen.):
Blue Crystal Fountain ('Evipo038')
Red and pink Avant-Garde ('Evipo033')

Golden clematis
C. tangutica

Loads of bright-yellow flowers, about 1¼-inch long, set this clematis apart from its relatives. And this vigorous plant is extremely resistant to mildew and clematis wilt, so it's a very care-free, as well as pretty, addition to your garden.

The blooms start out as tight little golden globes. Opening gradually, the tips of the petals curve outward until the flowers look like tiny bells or lanterns covering the entire plant. Though the flower show is impressive, it's improved by the addition of the eye-catching seedheads. They form while the flowers are still blooming so that both flowers and seedheads appear on the plant at the same time. Resembling exploding balls of silver threads, the seedheads glimmer in the sun, extending the show into late autumn. And left in the garden, plant and seedheads even provide winter interest.

Size 10 to 15 ft. tall
Bloom Small, yellow bells in summer to early fall
Light Full sun to light shade
Hardiness
Cold: USDA 4 to 9
Heat: AHS 9 to 1

Did you know?

Grow this vine up and over a pergola so you'll get a good view of the fluffy, showy seedheads on this hefty plant.

'Gravetye Beauty'

The deep red blooms of 'Gravetye Beauty' stand out from the mostly purple-to-pink clematis crowd. The undersides of the petals show a more muted shade of red. Starting out looking like small tulips, the flowers open gradually until they are nearly flat and star-shaped. A profusion of flowers covers the wilt-resistant blue-green foliage from the middle of summer and lasts for several weeks. The stems of this vine are a little on the brittle side. Handle them gently if you train the plant onto a structure like an obelisk.

Because the flowers are upward-facing, 'Gravetye Beauty' looks great when allowed to grow down close to the ground. Let it scramble over the top of low walls, hedges or around a water feature. Or plant it in a large container in a border and let it tumble down over the sides and along the ground.

Size	10 to 12 ft. tall
Bloom	4 to 6 in. tuliplike deep red in summer to early fall
Light	Full sun to part shade
Hardiness	Cold: USDA 4 to 9 Heat: AHS 9 to 1

Did you know?
'Gravetye Beauty' takes three to four years to get established and then blooms profusely, especially when grown in its favored gritty or even gravelly soil.

Sweet autumn clematis
C. terniflora

Have a very small garden? If yes, then this clematis is probably *not* for you. This jumbo-size climber will easily swallow up even an 8-foot trellis and can take over a small space in no time. (In fact, because of reseeding, it's considered an aggressive weed in some areas, so check with your local extension service before you plant it.)

But in the right space, sweet autumn clematis is a joy to have in the garden. In fall, as the name implies, it erupts in huge billows of tiny star-shaped white flowers that exude a wonderful fragrance. Winged visitors of all sorts are attracted to the flowers.

Give this exuberant vine a sturdy structure to clamber up — a pergola is great. You can also let it climb a tall tree, but pulling the dead growth out of the branches in early spring can be a challenge.

Size	15 to 30 ft. tall
Bloom	Clusters of scented starlike white in late summer to midfall
Light	Full sun
Hardiness	Cold: USDA 4 to 9 Heat: AHS 9 to 1

Did you know?
Sweet autumn clematis provides a late-season nectar source for honeybees and other pollinators. When feeding, bees rarely bother people, but site the plant away from seating areas just to be careful.

PHOTOS: Deborah Gruca (sweet autumn clematis)

easiest clematis continued

Different twists on clematis

Want to build your own clematis-friendly trellis? Download our easy weekend **plan** at www.GardenGateStore.com.

A wide range of sizes makes clematis very versatile in the garden. To simplify the design uses, I've divided the plants into short ones (under about 10 feet tall) and tall ones (10 feet and taller). I'll share design uses and, next to the illustrations, give some clematis that work especially well for each one.

Designing with short clematis

Short clematis are a good fit for any size garden, even small ones or container gardens on a patio.

ON OBELISKS OR TRELLISES This is a classic clematis use. You'll find ready-made supports at garden and home centers in vinyl, wood and metal in a range of sizes. The right size structure is at least two-thirds to three-fourths the height of the vine. So for an 8-foot vine, use a 5- to 6-foot or taller support and let the rest of the vine drape down from the top a bit.

IN CONTAINERS When growing a clematis in a container, use a pot that's at least 18 inches in diameter and has drainage holes. Clematis dislike having "wet feet." They do like their roots to stay cool, though, so avoid plastic or metal containers, which don't insulate well. Pair the clematis with shallow-rooted plants (like most annuals) that will shade the clematis roots.

AS GROUND COVERS Clematis easily clambers over tree stumps, rocks and perennials. Non-twining clematis or ones with upfacing- and tulip-shaped flowers are naturals for these situations. And you'll get the very best view of the blooms.

Designing with tall clematis

The majority of late-season clematis are large, vigorous plants that work well as focal points. Here are some ideas for using them in your landscape.

THROUGH TREES AND SHRUBS Any medium to tall clematis looks elegant twining up through the branches of shrubs or trees. You can train them not only on open-branched trees like apples or pears, but also on more dense evergreens, such as English holly.

ON ARBORS OR PERGOLAS Clematis larger than 10 or 12 feet tall are perfect choices for arbors or pergolas. Ones with nodding flowers are especially nice — you can see the flowers easily as you pass beneath. Another bonus? As you look up, they're framed attractively against a blue-sky background.

ON FENCES OR WALLS The really tall ones look at home scaling walls of buildings — perhaps screening that unsightly garden shed! Give them something to grasp, whether it's rough twine or lattice panels, and they'll rise to impressive heights.

I've already told you these plants are easy to grow. Take a look at the next page to see just how simple it is to care for them. □

— *Deborah Gruca*

As ground covers
- 'Princess Diana'
- 'Sir Trevor Lawrence'

In containers
- Pistachio ('Evirida')
- Passion flower clematis

On obelisks or trellises
- 'Black Prince'
- 'Madame Julia Correvon'

HOW VINES TWINE

Clematis grasp with their petioles, or leaf stalks, so choose supports that are no bigger around than about ¾ in.

Train a clematis up sturdy fishing line by attaching steel sinkers to the monofilament every foot so the vine won't slip. The fishing line nearly disappears!

Sinker on fishing line

On fences or walls
- Sweet autumn clematis
- 'Bill MacKenzie' golden clematis

Through trees or shrubs
- 'Purpurea Plena Elegans'
- Clematis flammula

On arbors or pergolas
- 'Lambton Park'
- 'Étoile Rose'

6 EASY TIPS FOR BEAUTIFUL CLEMATIS

1 LIGHT Full sun to part shade is best for clematis. White, deep blue, purple and red hold their colors well in full sun. Pale blues, pinks and mauves tend to fade in too much light, so give those plants some afternoon shade.

2 MOISTURE Clematis like consistent moisture, so topdress with 3 to 4 in. of mulch, keeping the mulch 2 in. away from the stems.

3 PRUNING The 10 plants in this story are group 3 clematis, which are a cinch to prune! Even if there's new growth sprouting higher on the stems, just cut all the stems back to 4 to 6 in. from the ground in late winter or early spring.

4 PESTS These clematis are very resistant to wilt, but your plant may still get it. Caused by a soil-borne fungus, it affects the plant almost overnight. It attacks the tip growth and youngest foliage first, and then the stem or the entire plant quickly turns black. Cut the affected growth back, remove all the plant debris and drench the soil once a month for several months with a copper-based fungicide. Wilt won't kill your clematis; the plant will sprout again from leaf nodes below the soil.

5 FEEDING Apply all-purpose, granular 10-10-10 fertilizer once a year after pruning or topdress with 2 in. of compost in spring.

6 PLANTING In USDA zones 7 and colder, plant in early spring. In warmer zones, fall planting is best. Hydrate the root ball of either bare-root or container plants by soaking it for 20 minutes before planting. Dig a hole at least 18 in. deep and wide and set the plant, whether bare-root or container grown, so two sets of leaf nodes are below soil level. Clematis prefer moist, well-drained, slightly alkaline soil with some compost worked into it.

Find out how one gardener created this drought-tolerant front yard on page 116.

before & after

transform *your* garden, we show you how

READY FOR A CHANGE?

Get inspiration and know-how here. In these six garden makeovers you'll find smart tips for easier upkeep, how to design for more color, how to deal with a difficult slope and more. Check it out.

How to Work Less!	**106**
Three-Season Color	**110**
Season-Long Color	**112**
Water-Wise Beauty	**116**
A Whole New Level to Your Garden	**120**
Quick and Easy Update	**124**

BEFORE & AFTER | BACK YARD

how to work less!
even in a garden packed with plants

Botanical Names

Barberry
Berberis thunbergii
Boxwood
Buxus sempervirens
Hosta
Hosta fortunei
Magnolia
Magnolia hybrid
White pine
Pinus strobus

The space behind my new garage in the "before" photo was looking pretty bare. I really wanted a casual area where I could experiment with new plants and combinations. But I still needed to give it enough structure that it would fit in with the rest of my garden, which leans toward formal. Sound impossible? It's not. I'll show you how to create a structured framework so the casual mix of plants in it is simple to change around.

FORMAL ATTIRE Just because a garden is formal doesn't mean it has to be stuffy. Generally, formal gardens have straight lines, simple curves, a focal point and a limited palette. But you don't have to follow style "rules" to the letter. Bending the rules gives a garden personality.

This garden has formal "bones" that give it season-long interest and a sense of balance. The tightly laid brick and simple line of the path lead you directly to the focal point of the magnolia in the center.

Symmetrically planted boxwoods are planted at the top of the steps and again where the path meets the circle. Upright 'Helmond Pillar' barberries are in containers next to the steps. They're similar in texture to the boxwoods but have contrasting form and color to provide added interest to the entrance of this garden.

The planting beds around the perimeter of the path are where this garden diverges from formal style. Here is where I try out my planting ideas. A more relaxed layout means plants are easy to slip in and out if something isn't working.

CHANGE IS GOOD You'll notice in the before photo that the original layout was a rectangle. Early on, I wanted to get an idea of what shape fit the space best. But after starting to lay it out, I decided a circle provided better traffic flow to the

(1) Don't be afraid to make changes. I planned a rectangular bed but it just didn't look right. So I changed it to a circle.

area. It's also a nice change from all the straight lines and 90-degree angles in the rest of the garden. In addition, the space sloped down from the garage and needed a retaining wall to keep the soil in place. A straight wall would have worked with the style, but it seemed too confining for the space. The circle felt more welcoming. When you're planning your garden, don't be afraid to try several bed shapes.

MIXED MEDIA Combine hardscaping materials to make a more interesting and sophisticated look. Bricks are a common material in formal gardens. Their straight lines and regular shape fit in perfectly with the straight path and symmetrical plantings. Pale limestone blocks have a rough weathered look that adds interest along the way. Nestled in next to these simple lines, lush plantings shelter the area and provide a sense of privacy.

You might think a formal garden like this one is hard to maintain, but surprisingly, it isn't. On the next page I'll tell you how easy it is to have a formal, yet low-maintenance, garden.

(2) Like this magnolia? Find out how to grow the unusually hardy 'Elizabeth' magnolia in our Editor's Choice on p. 32.

PHOTOS: Craig Anderson; Courtesy of Jim Childs (before)

106 *the* YEAR IN GARDENING www.GardenGateMagazine.com

The blooms and large foliage of this 'Elizabeth' magnolia contrast with the fine-textured white pines behind it.

Can you believe these hostas are only three years old? 'Albomarginata' is one of the fastest-growing cultivars you'll find.

Turn the page for tips on a low-maintenance formal garden.

easy upkeep tips for any garden

Botanical Names

Allium
Allium spp.
Hydrangea
Hydrangea spp.
Impatiens
Impatiens walleriana

This is one formal garden you won't have to spend a lot of time maintaining. For one thing, as you'll notice in the illustration, there aren't many symmetrical plantings to worry about. If you had a line of shrubs carefully placed around the circular path and one of them died or lost a few branches in an ice storm, it would take a long time to fill in again. With this more casual approach, if a plant doesn't work out or there's damage to a tree or shrub, it's no big deal. There are plenty of interesting plants in different shapes, sizes and colors to take up the slack. Here are a few more easy-care ideas to keep any formal garden low-maintenance.

SQUEEZE OUT WEEDS Working on the "you can always find room for a few more plants" theory, I squeeze a lot of annuals, perennials and shrubs into this garden. Because I tend to grow my plants close together, the weeds don't stand a chance. And any that do take hold are spindly and easy to pull.

Bricks set tightly together in a path or patio make it hard for weed seeds to grow, too. But when a weed pokes through the cracks, it's sometimes tough to pull. Check out "Five tips for a weed-free path" below to see some easy strategies.

NO MORE DEADHEADING Flowers are beautiful, but they do take work. Deadheading to keep plants reblooming and to prevent reseeding is a chore. Fewer flowers means less time spent cutting and pinching or removing unwanted seedlings. If you take a look at the small photos at right you'll notice that most of the plants have a variety of foliage colors and shapes that keep the garden interesting. See those spots of pale pink impatiens around the path? They brighten the shade but they're not much work — the spent flowers fall off on their own. Those big potted hydrangeas and alliums in the top left photo won't drop their flowers. But you can just leave the spent ones on the plant. They'll look great through most of the winter. Or cut the dried, brown blossoms and add them to a seasonal flower arrangement.

Now with all the time you've saved, you can sit down, relax and enjoy a quiet moment or two in the shade. □

— *Jim Childs*

FIVE TIPS for a WEED-FREE path

No matter how tightly bricks are packed together, weeds seem to find their way between the crevices. Here are five tips to keep them from taking over.

1 SKIP THE FABRIC When installing a path, save yourself the cost of landscape fabric. Most of the weeds that grow between bricks are the result of seeds taking root at the surface, not roots coming up from below.

2 PUT DOWN A BARRIER Keep seeds from germinating with a corn gluten meal pre-emergent herbicide. Follow label directions and sprinkle it on the pavers. Work it into the crevices with a broom because corn gluten needs to be in contact with soil to work. Then water it in. Corn gluten can stain some surfaces if you let it sit, so test a small area first before putting it down.

3 USE THE RIGHT TOOL You don't need to buy any special tools. Use what you already have around the house to make weeding easier. A pair of needlenose pliers and an old paring knife are great for getting weeds out of tight places. See how the pliers in the photo keep your knuckles from getting skinned up on the rough brick? Use the knife to loosen stubborn weeds in narrow spaces.

4 SPRAY SOME VINEGAR Did you ever think that weeding could be as easy as a few squirts of vinegar? It's true. The USDA has studied various concentrations of vinegar for use in organic farming, and found that even the stuff you have in your cupboard works to kill small weeds. Be careful using it around ornamental plants, though, as it will burn the foliage. If the weed happens to pop up again, get out your spray bottle. Another application should do the trick.

5 GET OUT THE TARP To avoid spreading seeds as you weed the garden, lay a tarp down on the bricks first. Then pull it along with you as you get rid of unwanted plants.

Most formal gardens have a very symmetrical plan. This one is balanced, too, just not with identical plants or hardscape. This heavy stone bench, along with a colorful planter, visually balances out the stone wall on the opposite side.

This New Zealand flax looks great in the garden but it isn't hardy here. I dig a hole the size of the pot and sink it in the ground for summer. A little mulch hides the pot edge. In fall, I lift the plant out and overwinter it inside.

Framing the stairs with these classically shaped urns keeps the formal feel going even as you exit this area of the garden.

A stone retaining wall made of the same material as the edging continues the line of the path and keeps the slope in place. Plus, it doubles as seating for parties.

www.GardenGateMagazine.com *the* YEAR IN GARDENING 109

BEFORE & AFTER | BACK YARD

simple, sophisticated look, three-season color

(1) Change is good. These annuals were pretty, but after a few years it was time to freshen up the look.

There was no garden in the back yard when Jack Systema first moved into his Michigan home. Nothing would grow beneath the two large trees there. So he had them removed and started the garden in photo 1 above. It was full of color, from dahlias, zinnias, phlox and other flowers. Now the cutting garden has evolved into the sophisticated mixed border in photo 2 with low-maintenance shrubs, colorful annuals and three-season color.

EASY-CARE SHRUBS Adding the arborvitae really changed the look of the garden. Their blocky, dense form provides structure, and the foliage color is different than the other plants. And their height is a real attention grabber. Plus, the repeated shape and size along the back of the bed helps your eyes move through the garden easily. When the arborvitae were first planted, Jack left space for them to grow together. But it seemed so bare that he decided to add color by tucking in a few large containers filled with begonias. It looked great! Now he prunes the arborvitae every spring to keep them this size and he adds the containers as in photo 3 below.

Botanical Names

Arborvitae *Thuja* spp.
Begonia *Begonia* hybrid
Dahlia *Dahlia* hybrid
Impatiens *Impatiens* spp.
Phlox *Phlox paniculata*
Zinnia *Zinnia* hybrid

Because these arborvitae are kept smaller than they would normally grow, they won't overshadow any plants growing in front of them. Plus, the relaxed shape given by a light pruning fits in better with this casual garden than a more formal-looking square hedge would.

SMART SHOPPING If big shrubs are too pricey for your pocketbook or if you need a lot of them, look for smaller plants at end-of-season sales. But don't plant them directly into the border if you have other, vigorous plants nearby. Established plants can crowd out new transplants, causing them to grow more slowly. They also shade the new plant's foliage, causing it to drop or turn brown. These arborvitae were grown in containers for a few years before they went into the garden so they grew more quickly and had a nice full habit. If you need something tall in the garden bed while you're waiting for the shrubs to grow, plant a pretty annual vine on a trellis.

NEW ADDITIONS The arborvitae aren't the only improvements in this garden bed. Now, each season has a colorful show. Take a look at the insets at right for tips on keeping the flowers in this border looking good. When perennials take a little down time, annuals are there to brighten things up.

More shrubs and perennials means less room for annuals in the garden. But they're not out of the picture completely. Besides the large containers of begonias, there are small pots of impatiens sitting on the windowsill and hanging in wall planters on the garage, bringing the color to new levels.

Containers need more frequent watering than the perennials in the ground. But at 6 to 7 feet, the depth of this bed is very manageable so it's easy to reach everything with a watering wand. If your bed is deeper, leave space for a few stepping stones so you can get in and attend to watering or maintenance chores without crushing the plants.

No matter how old or new your garden bed may be, it can always benefit from a few new ideas (and plants!). □

(3) Containers not tall enough? No problem. Even though these pots are tall, they still need the 3-in.-thick concrete base below to be seen above the peonies.

— *Sherri Ribbey*

(2) Repeat shapes, like these upright arborvitae, to help lead your eye through the garden.

Late spring's double pink peonies are beautiful but hard to appreciate when the heavy blooms flop on the ground. Keep the blooms upright with a wire hoop placed around the plant. Put the hoop in place as new growth emerges in spring. Later, foliage will cover it.

In early summer, vibrant-red bee balm brightens the border. To get a second, smaller rebloom, cut plants back by half after the first flush of blooms is done. Choose a mildew-resistant variety, such as 'Jacob Cline'.

Heat up the border in late summer with orange dahlias. If they're not hardy where you live, dig the tubers and bring them inside for winter. Let the tubers dry out for a few days. Then store them in a box of peat moss in a cool, dry place. In spring, replant the tubers for more blooms.

BEFORE & AFTER | BACK YARD

plan a garden for season-long color

(1) No rows Instead of planting annual seeds in rows, mark the area where you want them and sprinkle the seeds evenly.

The best thing about annuals is the constant supply of color they provide for a garden. Well, almost constant. Annual beds may start out empty and lifeless like photo 1 in spring. But that bare earth is filled with potential. Take a look at the same raised bed in photo 2 a couple months after it was planted with long-blooming annuals.

WHAT'S SO GREAT ABOUT ANNUALS? Lots of variety, for one thing. There are hundreds of different annuals from which to choose. Some plants, such as zinnias, are true annuals. They grow, set seed and die the same year. Others, such as coleus, are tender perennials. These plants are hardy in areas where winters stay above freezing, but gardeners in colder zones can still grow them — they just treat them as annuals.

Stroll through any garden center and you'll notice a huge variety of flower and foliage colors, shapes and sizes. You can change the look of your garden every year if you want to! Try a cottage garden packed with old-fashioned favorites, such as flowering tobacco, love-in-a-mist and larkspur one season. The next year, grow a tropical oasis of coleus, cannas and jewel-toned nasturtiums.

Do you have a place where a perennial or shrub has died out? Annuals make great fill-in plants, as you wait for a small transplant to grow larger. Or maybe you're just not sure which flower color will look good with a group of perennials — annuals to the rescue again. If you don't like the color combo, it's easy to pull the plants out and try something different.

MAXIMIZE COLOR Want to make the most of the colorful flowers you've chosen? Plant large groups, or drifts, for eye-catching results. Take a look at all those small red salvia flowers. They don't have much pizzazz by themselves. But plant five or six plants close together in a big group and they'll really stop traffic.

Make that bare garden plot look good quickly by planting some cool-season annuals. The white Cape daisy here gets going earlier in spring than other choices. And it thrives in fall's cooler temperatures. If summer weather gets really hot and dry, cool-season annuals tend to fade, and you may even need to replace them.

SIMPLIFY CARE A garden bed full of annuals is actually simple to care for. As long as you choose plants that need similar growing conditions, you can water and fertilize them all at the same time. Most annuals do best with a weekly dose of a liquid fertilizer, such as Miracle Gro®, to produce plenty of big, beautiful flowers. Speaking of maintenance, planting in masses also makes deadheading a lot easier. Just grab a handful of stems and cut off the spent flowers.

If you like the garden on this page, check out the plant list below. You'll find just what you need to know to plant a great-looking annual garden in the sun. Most of the plants are easy and economical to start from seed. But you're more likely to find the Cape daisy and kale as plants in the garden center. And if you don't see anything you like here, there are three more annual gardens to choose from on the next page.

Botanical Names

Canna
Canna hybrids

Coleus
Solenostemon hybrids

Flowering tobacco
Nicotiana alata

Larkspur
Consolida ambigua

Love-in-a-mist
Nigella damascena

Nasturtium
Tropaeolum hybrids

Keep the color coming

A Texas sage *Salvia coccinea* 'Lady in Red' Red flowers summer to fall; 24 to 36 in. tall, 12 in. wide; cold-hardy in USDA zones 9 to10, heat-tolerant in AHS zones 12 to 1

B Cape daisy *Osteospermum* Asti™ White White blooms with purple centers in spring and fall; 17 to 20 in. tall and wide; cold-hardy in USDA zones 10 to 11, heat-tolerant in AHS zones 12 to 1

C Zinnia *Zinnia* Profusion™ Knee High Red Red blooms summer to fall; 15 to 20 in. tall, 18 to 24 in. wide; annual, heat-tolerant in AHS zones 12 to 1

D Cosmos *Cosmos bipinnatus* 'Sonata Mix' Pink, white or lavender flowers all season; 18 to 24 in. tall, 15 in. wide; annual, heat-tolerant in AHS zones 12 to 1

E Spider flower *Cleome* Senorita Rosalita® Pink and white blooms from summer to fall; 24 to 48 in. tall, 18 to 24 in. wide; annual, heat-tolerant in AHS zones 12 to 1

F Ornamental kale *Brassica oleracea* Grown for foliage shape and color; 6 to 12 in. tall, 18 to 24 in. wide; cold-hardy in USDA zones 7 to 11, heat-tolerant in AHS zones 12 to 1

(2) Deadhead spent salvia, cosmos and spider flowers. In a week or so side branches will grow large enough to bloom.

Turn the page for more great annual gardens.

BEFORE & AFTER | BACK YARD

3 colorful annual gardens

Annuals are a great source of color for the garden, and these three plans are packed with them! The plants should be easy to find but if you can't find the exact cultivar, don't worry — just choose a similar variety. Check out "Packets or pots?" below right to help you decide whether to buy seeds or plants. For seeds, be sure to sow and thin according to the directions on the packet.

Each garden has a different color scheme but the same rectangular shape, 9 feet long and 7 feet deep. For a large area, you can repeat the plan end to end to fill the space. With a smaller garden, cut back on the number of plants.

Whichever plan you choose, these annuals will give you a colorful garden from spring to fall. □

— Sherri Ribbey

Bodacious blue and orange

Bright and cheerful, this garden is a mix of energetic orange and peaceful blue for full sun.

Mexican sunflower is easy to start from seed. Sow it directly into the soil when all danger of frost is past in spring. Once the plants are blooming, cut some to enjoy inside. Be careful, though, as the stems are hollow and bend easily. The dahlias here are usually sold in the annuals section of the garden center. And while you *can* overwinter the tubers inside, they often don't survive.

A **Mexican sunflower** *Tithonia rotundifolia* Orange flowers summer to fall; 2 to 6 ft. tall, 2 to 4 ft. wide; annual, heat-tolerant in AHS zones 12 to 1

B **Dahlia** *Dahlia* Mystic Spirit ('BestBett') Peach-orange flowers summer to fall; 24 to 36 in. tall, 12 in. wide; cold-hardy in USDA zones 7 to 11, heat-tolerant in AHS zones 12 to 1

C **Floss flower** *Ageratum* High Tide™ Lavender-blue flowers all season; 14 to 16 in. tall, 12 in. wide; annual, heat-tolerant in AHS zones 12 to 1

D **Orange New Zealand sedge** *Carex testacea* Foliage emerges green and develops orange tint later; 18 to 24 in. tall and wide; cold-hardy in USDA zones 6 to 10, heat-tolerant in AHS zones 12 to 1

E **Dahlia** *Dahlia* Mystic Desire ('Scarlet Fern') Orange-red flowers summer to fall; 18 to 24 in. tall, 12 to 16 in. wide; cold-hardy in USDA zones 7 to 11, heat-tolerant in AHS zones 12 to 1

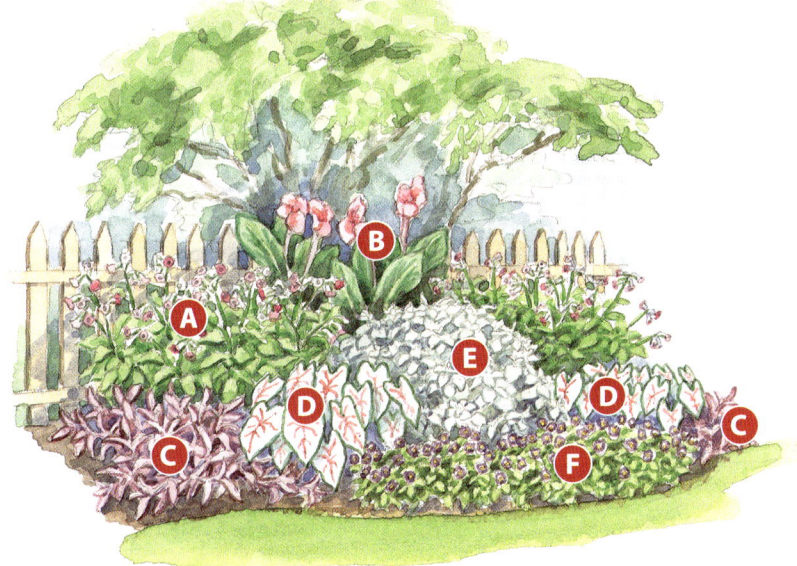

Pastels in part shade

Soft pastel colors are peaceful and relaxing. They're a great way to brighten up an area that gets four hours or less of sun a day. Pastel colors are lighter because they have more white in them, which means they'll show up better in the shadows. Plant this garden near a comfortable seating area and you'll have a wonderful view as you unwind from the day.

No need to worry about deadheading the flowers in this garden. They're self-cleaning, which means they fall off easily when they're done blooming. The flowering tobacco is fragrant, so don't forget to stop and smell its blooms once in a while. Overwinter the canna and caladium tubers to use again next year. And the tradescantia makes a great house plant when temperatures get chilly.

A Flowering tobacco *Nicotiana mutabilis* 'Marshmallow' Flowers in shades of pink and white in summer; 36 to 48 in. tall, 15 to 18 in. wide; cold-hardy in USDA zones 7 to 11, heat-tolerant in AHS zones 12 to 1

B Canna *Canna* 'Pink Perfection' Pink flowers in summer; 36 to 60 in. tall, 18 to 24 in. wide; cold-hardy in USDA zones 10 to 11, heat-tolerant in AHS zones 12 to 1

C Purpleheart tradescantia *Tradescantia pallida* 'Purpurea' Deep purple foliage all season; 6 to 12 in. tall, 12 to 18 in. wide; cold-hardy in USDA zones 10 to 11, heat-tolerant in AHS zones 12 to 1

D Caladium *Caladium* 'White Queen' White leaves with green edges and red veins; 12 to 18 in. tall, 9 to 12 in wide; cold-hardy in USDA zones 9 to 11, heat-tolerant in AHS zones 12 to 1

E Plectranthus *Plectranthus argentatus* 'Silver Shield' Silvery foliage; 24 to 30 in. tall and wide; annual, heat-tolerant in AHS zones 12 to 1

F Wishbone flower *Torenia* Clown™ Violet Violet flowers all summer; 8 to 10 in. tall, 10 to 12 in. wide; annual, heat-tolerant in AHS zones 12 to 1

Sizzlin' hot combo

The hot colors used in this garden won't go unnoticed! Red, orange and yellow are all considered "warm" colors and these bright tones will attract attention to any sunny spot.

All these plants are easy to care for. Get your elephant ear bulb early and start it inside. This bulb prefers warm temperatures and you'll get a larger plant for that season if you don't have to wait for soil temperatures to warm up. Or buy ones already started a little later. The pot marigold and cosmos reseed easily, so if you don't want them there next year, keep them deadheaded. On the other hand, you'll save a little money if you let some go to seed.

A Cosmos *Cosmos sulphureus* Orange flowers summer to fall; 1 to 3 ft. tall, 1 to 2 ft. wide; annual, heat-tolerant in AHS zones 12 to 1

B Elephant ear *Colocasia esculenta* Large green leaves all summer; 2 to 5 ft. tall, 2 to 3 ft. wide; cold-hardy in USDA zones 8 to 10, heat-tolerant in AHS zones 10 to 1

C Zinnia *Zinnia elegans* 'Red Cap' Small red flowers summer to fall; 18 to 24 in. tall, 12 in. wide; annual, heat-tolerant in AHS zones 12 to 1

D Celosia *Celosia* Glow Series Pink flowers all season; 10 to 12 in. tall, 8 to 10 in. wide; annual, heat-tolerant in AHS zones 12 to 1

E Pot marigold *Calendula officinalis* 'Bon Bon Yellow' Yellow, summer to fall; 12 in. tall, 12 in. wide; annual, heat-tolerant in AHS zones 12 to 1

Packets or pots?

Is a packet of seed you buy in early spring a better deal than buying small plants a month or two later? It can be, depending on the plant and your specific needs. If you have a lot of space to fill, direct-sown seeds are a cheaper alternative than plants. Direct sown means you sow the seed directly into the soil when temperatures get warm enough in spring, instead of starting seeds indoors. Some varieties, mostly old-fashioned ones, will even self-sow or are easy to save seed from each year, which will save you more money. However, if you only need a few plants, or if it's something that's hard to start from seed, plants are a better bet. Here's a list of several favorite annuals and my favorite way to buy them.

Buy seeds
Cosmos *Cosmos* spp.
Flowering tobacco
 Nicotiana alata
Four o'clock
 Mirabilis jalapa
Marigold *Tagetes* spp.
Pot marigold
 Calendula officinalis
Spider flower *Cleome* spp.
Zinnia *Zinnia* spp.

Buy plants
Calibrachoa
 Calibrachoa hybrids
Cape daisy
 Osteospermum hybrids
Gazania *Gazania rigens*
Geranium
 Pelargonium hybrids
Impatiens
 Impatiens hybrids
Lantana *Lantana* hybrids

BEFORE & AFTER | FRONT YARD

water-wise beauty
grow a gorgeous garden with less water

Would you guess that the gorgeous garden in photo 1 doesn't need a lot of water? It sure doesn't look like a typical drought-tolerant garden. At first glance, it looks more like something from the English countryside. The earlier garden plan, which you see in the inset at right, had that same plant-packed feel with a different cast of characters. But times change, and Patty Christianson wanted to simplify the garden and cut down on the amount of watering needed in her Southern California garden. The plants she has now, once established, don't need additional watering, except during a long dry spell.

HOT, DRY DRIVE Dry weather isn't the only difficulty for this garden. Reflected heat from the driveway adds to the problem. Fortunately, some plants, like the snow-in-summer and creeping thyme, actually thrive in the heat. So they can grow close to the pavement and still look good, instead of scorching as some other plants would.

Driveways may be utilitarian, but they don't have to be unattractive. With a drive that comes right up to the front door like this one does, you really want it to look nice. After all, it's where visitors get their first impression of your home. The exposed aggregate concrete and brick of the drive are good choices because they blend well with the brick and stone of the house. Dark pavement or bright white concrete would be a stark contrast. But the driveway is not Patty's only hardscaping challenge here.

(1) Color and variety are what made this garden near the house so interesting early on. But now simplicity makes the garden really pop!

BIG AND BEAUTIFUL Those huge rocks in photo 2, below, are too big to move. And who would want to? They're a wonderful natural feature. The only problem with something that large is that it can overwhelm the surrounding garden. Fortunately, this climbing rose is big enough to compete. Smaller tea or shrub roses would be dwarfed by comparison. Some years the rose gets a hard pruning to keep it from looking too leggy, and the rocks play a bigger role in the design of this garden. If you don't like roses, try growing a clematis on a trellis or a large shrub, such as lilac or beauty bush.

SIMPLE COLOR Along with narrowing down the plant list, cutting back on color simplifies other things, too. This particular garden is predominantly white with touches of lavender from the sweet pea shrub and creeping thyme flowers. If you think about it, two colors are much easier to shop for than five or six. The white flowers echo the porch railing and house trim. In addition, they absolutely glow in the twilight.

Are you wondering how you can create your own beautiful, water-wise garden like this one? Let's turn the page and find out.

Botanical Names

Beauty bush
Kolkwitzia amabilis
Creeping thyme
Thymus serpyllum
Lilac *Syringa* spp.
Rose *Rosa* spp.
Snow-in-summer
Cerastium tomentosum
Sweet pea shrub
Polygala dalmaisiana

(2) Big boulders like these are overwhelming when plants are small. Fortunately, with time, plants grow. Just look at how large the 'Climbing Iceberg' rose is now. You can't even see the stones.

Turn the page to learn how to grow this garden.

www.GardenGateMagazine.com *the* YEAR IN GARDENING 117

low water plants: regional best bets

Water conservation is an important concern, but that doesn't mean you're limited to cactus and yucca. Many plants, once established, grow well without much supplemental watering. The plants in this garden only need extra watering during extended dry spells. The key is choosing plants that are adapted to your region. Patty lives where winters are mild but summers get hot and the soil is lean. She deals with this by bringing in organic topsoil every year. Top that off with 3 inches of organic mulch and she has a recipe for success.

You'll find the plan for this garden below, along with a list of how many plants you'll need. A spot that gets full sun to part shade and has well-drained soil is best. And if you live outside the Southwest, there are alternate regional plant lists to your right. Now you can grow your own beautiful, water-wise garden!

— *Sherri Ribbey*

Southwest
USDA cold-hardiness zones 6 to 10

A Sweet pea shrub *Polygala dalmaisiana* Shrub; 3 to 4 ft. tall and wide; purple flowers all season; cold-hardy in USDA zones 9 to 10; heat-tolerant in AHS zones 10 to 1

B Boston ivy *Parthenocissus tricuspidata* Vine; 30 to 50 ft. tall, 5 to 10 ft. wide; green foliage turns red to red-purple in fall; cold-hardy in USDA zones 3 to 9; heat-tolerant in AHS zones 9 to 1

C Holly *Ilex xmeserveae* 'Blue Girl' Shrub; 6 to 8 ft. tall, 3 to 6 ft. wide; need male cultivar for berries; evergreen; cold-hardy in USDA zones 4 to 9; heat-tolerant in AHS zones 9 to 1

D Snow-in-summer *Cerastium tomentosum* Perennial; 6 to 12 in. tall, 9 to 12 in. wide; reseeds vigorously; white flowers in spring; silver-gray foliage; cold-hardy in USDA zones 3 to 10; heat-tolerant in AHS zones 10 to 1

E Creeping thyme *Thymus serpyllum* Perennial; 3 in. tall, 6 to 12 in. wide; lavender flowers in summer; cold-hardy in USDA zones 4 to 9; heat-tolerant in AHS zones 9 to 1

F Boxwood *Buxus microphylla* 'Winter Gem' Shrub; 4 to 6 ft. tall and wide; evergreen foliage; cold-hardy in USDA zones 5 to 9; heat-tolerant in AHS zones 9 to 1

G Fringe flower *Loropetalum chinense* Razzleberri® ('Monraz') Shrub; 4 to 6 ft. tall, 4 to 5 ft. wide; bright pink flowers all season; cold-hardy in USDA zones 7 to 9; heat-tolerant in AHS zones 9 to 1

H Climbing rose *Rosa* 'Climbing Iceberg' 12 to 20 ft. tall; fragrant double white flowers; reblooms; cold-hardy in USDA zones 5 to 9; heat-tolerant in AHS zones 9 to 1

I Rose *Rosa* 'The Fairy' Shrub; 2 to 3 ft. tall and wide; double pink flowers; reblooms; disease-resistant foliage; cold-hardy in USDA zones 5 to 9; heat-tolerant in AHS zones 9 to 1

J Climbing rose *Rosa* Eden Climber® ('Meiviolin') 12 to 15 ft. tall; double pink flowers in spring; reblooms; cold-hardy in USDA zones 5 to 10; heat-tolerant in AHS zones 10 to 1

Plant a male holly, such as 'Blue Boy', in an inconspicuous place to ensure berries on the females, such as 'Blue Girl'.

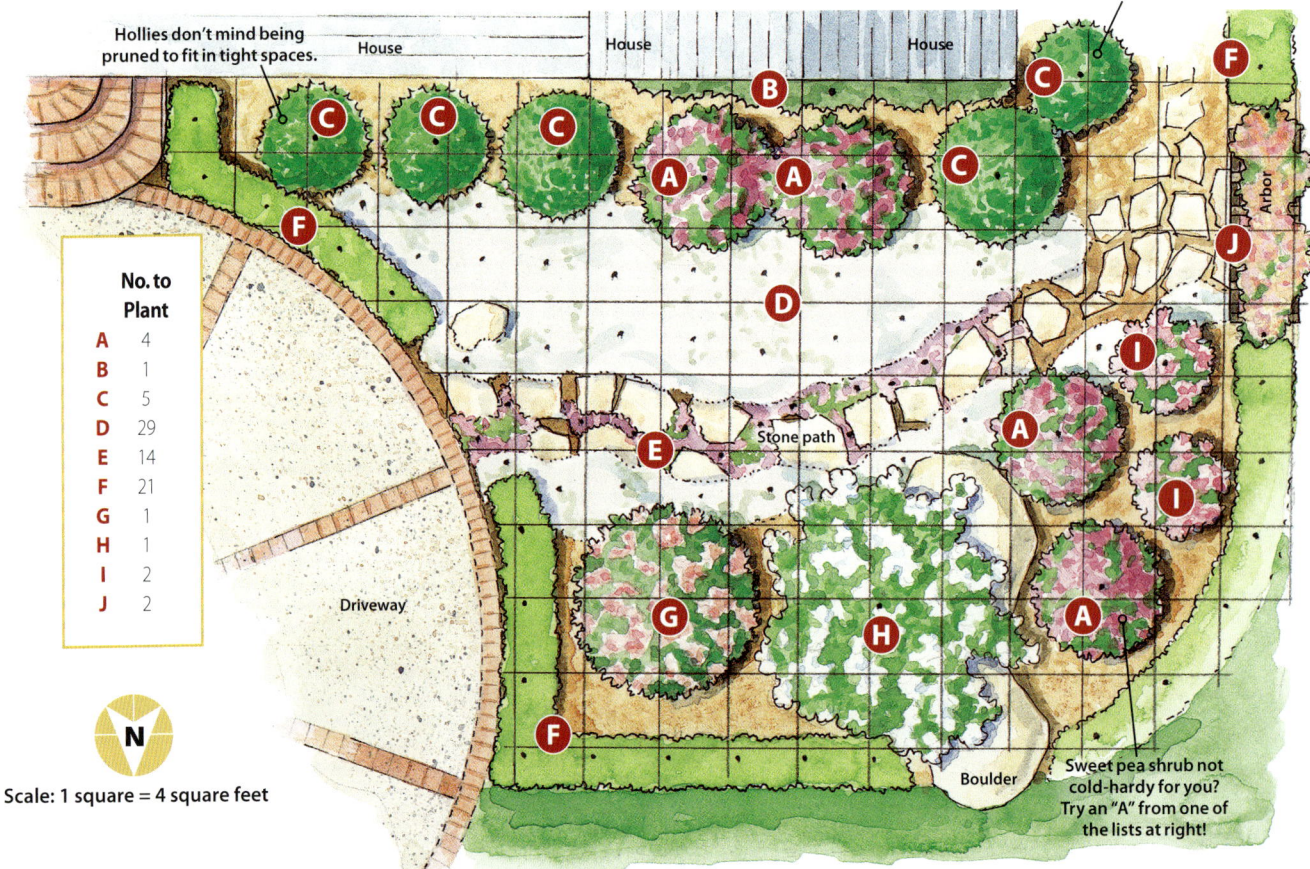

Hollies don't mind being pruned to fit in tight spaces.

	No. to Plant
A	4
B	1
C	5
D	29
E	14
F	21
G	1
H	1
I	2
J	2

Scale: 1 square = 4 square feet

Sweet pea shrub not cold-hardy for you? Try an "A" from one of the lists at right!

Northwest
USDA cold-hardiness zones 6 to 9

A Hydrangea *Hydrangea macrophylla* 'Mini Penny' Shrub; 3 to 4 ft. tall and wide; pink or blue flowers summer to frost; cold-hardy in USDA zones 5 to 9; heat-tolerant in AHS zones 9 to 1

B Boston ivy *Parthenocissus tricuspidata* Vine; 30 to 50 ft. tall, 5 to 10 ft. wide; green foliage turns red-purple in fall; cold-hardy in USDA zones 3 to 9; heat-tolerant in AHS zones 9 to 1

C Holly *Ilex xmeserveae* 'Blue Girl' Shrub; 6 to 8 ft. tall, 3 to 6 ft. wide; need male cultivar for berries; evergreen; cold-hardy in USDA zones 4 to 9; heat-tolerant in AHS zones 9 to 1

D Roman chamomile *Chamaemelum nobile* Perennial; 3 in. tall, 12 in. wide; white flowers summer to fall; cold-hardy in USDA zones 4 to 9; heat-tolerant in AHS zones 9 to 1

E Bellflower *Campanula xpulloides* 'Jelly Bells' Perennial; 3 to 6 in. tall, 14 in. wide; purple flowers in spring; cold-hardy in USDA zones 5 to 8; heat-tolerant in AHS zones 8 to 1 **NEW '09**

F Boxwood *Buxus microphylla* 'Winter Gem' Shrub; 4 to 6 ft. tall and wide; evergreen foliage; cold-hardy in USDA zones 5 to 9; heat-tolerant in AHS zones 9 to 1

G Oregon grapeholly *Mahonia aquifolium* Shrub; 3 to 6 ft. tall, 2 to 5 ft. wide; bright yellow flowers in spring; blue-black fruit in fall; cold-hardy in USDA zones 5 to 9; heat-tolerant in AHS zones 9 to 1

H Climbing rose *Rosa* 'Climbing Cécile Brunner' 26 ft. tall; fragrant double pink flowers; reblooms; cold-hardy in USDA zones 4 to 11; heat-tolerant in AHS zones 12 to 1

I Rose *Rosa* 'The Fairy' Shrub; 2 to 3 ft. tall and wide; double pink flowers; reblooms; cold-hardy in USDA zones 5 to 9; heat-tolerant in AHS zones 9 to 1

J Climbing rose *Rosa* 'Compassion' 10 ft. tall; fragrant double salmon-pink flowers; reblooms; disease resistant; cold-hardy in USDA zones 5 to 9; heat-tolerant in AHS zones 9 to 1

Mountain west
USDA cold-hardiness zones 3 to 5

A Smooth hydrangea *Hydrangea arborescens* Shrub; 3 to 5 ft. tall and wide; white flowers in summer; cold-hardy in USDA zones 3 to 9; heat-tolerant in AHS zones 9 to 1

B Boston ivy *Parthenocissus tricuspidata* 'Lowii' Vine; 30 to 50 ft. tall, 5 to 10 ft. wide; green foliage turns red-purple in fall; cold-hardy in USDA zones 3 to 9; heat-tolerant in AHS zones 9 to 1

C Chokeberry *Aronia melanocarpa* 'Autumn Magic' Shrub; 3 to 6 ft. tall, 4 to 7 ft. wide; white flowers in spring followed by purple berries; cold-hardy in USDA zones 3 to 8; heat-tolerant in AHS zones 8 to 1

D Deadnettle *Lamium maculatum* Pink Chablis ('Checkin') Perennial; 6 to 12 in. tall, 12 to 18 in. wide; pink flowers in spring; green and white foliage; cold-hardy in USDA zones 3 to 9; heat-tolerant in AHS zones 8 to 1

E Moss phlox *Phlox subulata* Candy Stripe Perennial; 4 in. tall, 16 to 24 in. wide; pink and white striped flowers in summer; cold-hardy in USDA zones 3 to 9; heat-tolerant in AHS zones 9 to 1

F Spirea *Spiraea nipponica* 'Snowmound' Shrub; 2 to 4 ft. tall and wide; snow-white flowers in spring; cold-hardy in USDA zones 3 to 8; heat-tolerant in AHS zones 8 to 1

G Alpine currant *Ribes alpinum* Shrub; 3 to 6 ft. tall and wide; bright green leaves change to yellow in fall; cold-hardy in USDA zones 2 to 6; heat-tolerant in AHS zones 6 to 1

H Climbing rose *Rosa* 'Alba Suaveolens' 10 to 14 ft. tall; fragrant semidouble white flowers in spring; cold-hardy in USDA zones 3 to 9; heat-tolerant in AHS zones 9 to 1

I Rose *Rosa* 'Morden Blush' Shrub; 2 to 3 ft. tall and wide; fragrant double ivory to pink flowers; reblooms; cold-hardy in USDA zones 3 to 7; heat-tolerant in AHS zones 7 to 1

J Climbing rose *Rosa* 'William Baffin' 10 ft. tall; fragrant double pink flowers; reblooms; cold-hardy in USDA zones 3 to 7; heat-tolerant in AHS zones 7 to 1

Midwest/ Northeast
USDA cold-hardiness zones 4 to 7

A Hydrangea *Hydrangea macrophylla* Endless Summer® ('Bailmer') Shrub; 3 to 4 ft. tall and wide; pink or blue flowers; reblooms; cold-hardy in USDA zones 4 to 9; heat-tolerant in AHS zones 9 to 1

B Boston ivy *Parthenocissus tricuspidata* Vine; 30 to 50 ft. tall, 5 to 10 ft. wide; green foliage turns red-purple in fall; cold-hardy in USDA zones 3 to 9; heat-tolerant in AHS zones 9 to 1

C Koreanspice viburnum *Viburnum carlesii* Shrub; 4 to 6 ft. tall and wide; fragrant pink to white flowers; cold-hardy in USDA zones 4 to 8; heat-tolerant in AHS zones 8 to 1

D Candytuft *Iberis sempervirens* Perennial; 6 to 12 in. tall, 6 to 18 in. wide; white flowers in spring; cold-hardy in USDA zones 3 to 8; heat-tolerant in AHS zones 8 to 1

E Pink *Dianthus* Firewitch ('Feuerhexe') Perennial; 3 to 6 in. tall, 12 in. wide; pink flowers summer to fall; blue-gray foliage; cold-hardy in USDA zones 3 to 9; heat-tolerant in AHS zones 9 to 1

F Spreading yew *Taxus xmedia* 'Densiformis' Shrub; 3 to 4 ft. tall, 4 to 6 ft. wide; keep clipped for size; red berries in winter; evergreen foliage; cold-hardy in USDA zones 4 to 7; heat-tolerant in AHS zones 7 to 1

G Summersweet *Clethra alnifolia* Vanilla Spice® ('Caleb') Shrub; 3 to 6 ft. tall and wide; fragrant white flowers that are larger than other varieties; cold-hardy in USDA zones 4 to 8; heat-tolerant in AHS zones 8 to 1 **NEW '09**

H Climbing rose *Rosa* 'Lillian Gibson' 8 to 10 ft. tall; fragrant double pink flowers in spring; cold-hardy in USDA zones 4 to 9; heat-tolerant in AHS zones 9 to 1

I Rose *Rosa* 'Henry Hudson' Shrub; 3 ft. tall and wide; fragrant double white flowers; reblooms; cold-hardy in USDA zones 2 to 7; heat-tolerant in AHS zones 7 to 1

J Climbing rose *Rosa* 'John Davis' 6 to 8 ft. tall; double pink flowers; reblooms; cold-hardy in USDA zones 3 to 7; heat-tolerant in AHS zones 7 to 1

Southeast
USDA cold-hardiness zones 7 to 9

A Hydrangea *Hydrangea* Edgy™ Hearts Shrub; 2 to 4 ft. tall and wide; pink flowers edged in white in summer; cold-hardy in USDA zones 5 to 9; heat-tolerant in AHS zones 9 to 1 **NEW '09**

B Boston ivy *Parthenocissus tricuspidata* Vine; 30 to 50 ft. tall, 5 to 10 ft. wide; green foliage turns red-purple in fall; cold-hardy in USDA zones 3 to 9; heat-tolerant in AHS zones 9 to 1

C Holly *Ilex xmeserveae* 'Blue Girl' Shrub; 6 to 8 ft. tall, 3 to 6 ft. wide; need male cultivar for berries; evergreen; cold-hardy in USDA zones 4 to 9; heat-tolerant in AHS zones 9 to 1

D Meadow moss campion *Silene alpestris* Perennial; 3 to 6 in. tall, 12 in. wide; white flowers in spring; cold-hardy in USDA zones 5 to 9; heat-tolerant in AHS zones 9 to 1

E Thyme *Thymus praecox* Perennial; 8 in. tall, 6 to 12 in. wide; pink flowers in summer; cold-hardy in USDA zones 5 to 9; heat-tolerant in AHS zones 9 to 1

F Boxwood *Buxus microphylla* 'Winter Gem' Shrub; 4 to 6 ft. tall and wide; evergreen foliage; cold-hardy in USDA zones 5 to 9; heat-tolerant in AHS zones 9 to 1

G Rhododendron *Rhododendron* 'Vulcan's Flame' Shrub; 5 ft. tall and wide; red flowers in spring; very heat-tolerant; cold-hardy in USDA zones 5 to 9; heat-tolerant in AHS zones 9 to 1

H Climbing rose *Rosa odorata* Old Blush ('Pallida') 12 to 20 ft. tall; fragrant double pink flowers; reblooms; cold-hardy in USDA zones 7 to 9; heat-tolerant in AHS zones 9 to 1

I Rose *Rosa* 'Nearly Wild' Shrub; 2 to 3 ft. tall and wide; fragrant single pink flowers; reblooms; disease-resistant foliage; cold-hardy in USDA zones 4 to 9; heat-tolerant in AHS zones 9 to 1

J Climbing rose *Rosa* 'Sombreuil' 12 ft. tall; fragrant double creamy-white flowers; reblooms; cold-hardy in USDA zones 6 to 9; heat-tolerant in AHS zones 9 to 1

NEW '09 Newly available variety. See p. 60 for 19 more of our favorite new plants this year.

BEFORE & AFTER | FRONT YARD

how to add
a whole new level to your garden

(1) Adding a second retaining wall to this front yard created another garden space.

Botanical Names

Coral bells
Heuchera spp.
Hardy geranium
Geranium spp.
Hosta *Hosta* hybrid
Jacob's ladder
Polemonium caeruleum

PHOTO: Courtesy of Kim Gravestock (before)

Nothing says "Welcome!" better than a beautiful garden. But if you've got a sloping front yard, it can be hard to maintain. Retaining walls are a great solution. Originally, Kim Gravestock's Colorado yard sloped from the gray limestone wall you see in photo 1 down to the curb. It was covered in chunky rock mulch so when visitors got out of their cars, the footing was unstable and rocks scraped their doors. The first things Kim did were get rid of the mulch and build a low timber retaining wall. Once the wall was 18 inches back from the curb, visitors could disembark without worry. There's a bonus, too: An up-close view of the lovely garden you see in photo 2.

TWO FOR ONE Now there are two distinct garden situations: One in shade and one in sun. Up by the house are two mature trees. The filtered light in this area is perfect for growing coral bells, hostas, Jacob's ladder and other shade lovers. But the sun-filled terrace, created when the retaining wall went in, provides a whole new set of plant possibilities from which to choose.

Leveling out a slope and adding a garden full of flowers creates a lot of curb appeal. Building a small retaining wall isn't as complicated as you might think. Check out "Wall how-to" below for some building basics.

FENCED IN A fence on top of a retaining wall might seem like it would loom over visitors climbing the stairs. But here, the added height is actually a plus. The fence creates a friendly looking boundary and a nice backdrop. With widely spaced pickets, you get a glimpse of what's beyond, and a few plants can still peek through in an inviting way. Its neatly painted appearance has a casual cottage-garden feel that provides a structural background for the mass of colorful plants below. The soft sage green paint makes the fence noticeable, but not as much as when it was bright white.

EASY ACCESS With the lower slope leveled out and filled with plants, it's important to be able to get in there and take care of things from time to time. Although you can't see it in the photo, there's a path on either side of the landing for access to the garden. The path makes it easy to reach plants to weed, deadhead or to just stroll between the pretty flowers.

Take a close look at photo 1 and you'll see that originally the path was the only area covered with pea gravel. But the gravel kept spilling and spreading out into the garden. Sensing she was fighting a losing battle, Kim decided to make things easier on herself and mulch the whole area with the gravel. As it turns out, the plants in this drought-tolerant garden did a lot better with gravel mulch anyway. But if that type of mulch doesn't work well for your situation, use bark chips or pine needles for your path and mulch instead.

Once all the hardscaping was taken care of, it was time for some fun: Choosing the plants. Find out just what they are in the plan on p. 122.

Wall how-to Retaining walls under 3 ft. tall can be simple to build. While railroad ties used to be the material of choice, these days it's landscape blocks. And installation is even easier with the small lip on the back of the blocks, which makes positioning them a no-brainer. For a stable foundation, place the first row of block just below soil level on a base of crushed limestone. The limestone is small, and tamping it down compacts the stone, which prevents shifting. As you add each row of blocks, fill in behind it with larger gravel to help water drain. Tamp each layer as you go to prevent settling. Then top it off with 10 to 12 in. of soil for your garden.

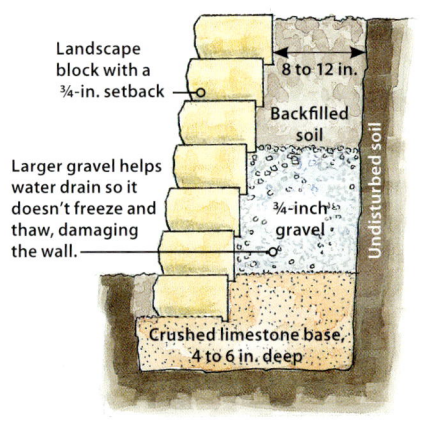

- Landscape block with a ¾-in. setback
- 8 to 12 in.
- Backfilled soil
- Larger gravel helps water drain so it doesn't freeze and thaw, damaging the wall.
- ¾-inch gravel
- Undisturbed soil
- Crushed limestone base, 4 to 6 in. deep

the YEAR IN GARDENING — www.GardenGateMagazine.com

(2) Bright colors from a multitude of flowers provide plenty of curb appeal all summer in this terraced garden. Notice the path next to the curb in the small photo? That gives visitors room to open the car door and provides a nice level path to the steps.

(3) Secret access You won't notice this path as you face the garden. It's not apparent until you get to the landing and see that it just might be a good idea to take a detour and enjoy the view.

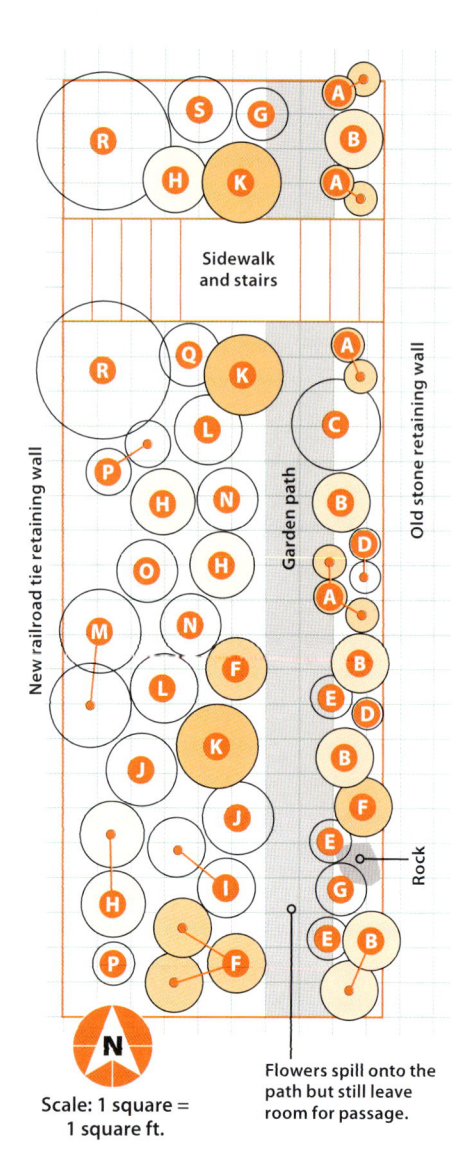

Scale: 1 square = 1 square ft.

Flowers spill onto the path but still leave room for passage.

easy-care flowers

Every garden needs a little maintenance from time to time. And this colorful garden filled with tough, sun-loving plants is no exception. An access path is just what you need for occasional deadheading, weeding and pruning. Notice the path in photo 3 above? That's the access path for this garden. But these helpful walkways can take many forms. Check out "Easy access" at right for tips on working a path like this into your garden design.

FLOWERS GALORE Are you wondering what this garden looked like a few weeks after this photo was taken? It looked just as good. That's because of long-blooming plants, such as the potentilla, which blooms from early summer to frost, and the pineleaf penstemon, which blooms for 6 to 8 weeks. Deadheading encourages reblooming for most of these plants, but it's not a requirement. They'll just send out new blooms more quickly if you do cut them back.

The other thing that keeps these plants healthy and blooming is well-drained soil. To get this, Kim worked a 1- to 1½-inch layer of compost into the garden. This is a good solution for any type of soil: Additional compost loosens clay and holds moisture in sand. The bonus is that as this organic matter breaks down, it turns to minerals, moisture and carbon dioxide, which all help the plant grow better, too!

RESEEDERS TO THE RESCUE Take a look at the bright orange flowers above. Those are horned poppies. With plenty of warmth and good drainage, they happily reseed along with several others here. So you may see them in places in the photo that don't show up on the plan. Start with plants in the designated areas and they'll soon make themselves at home throughout the garden.

Keep these easy-care flowers happy and you'll have a garden that blooms all summer! □

— *Sherri Ribbey*

A COLORFUL SUNNY PATH

Code	Plant Name	No. to Plant	Cold/Heat Zones	Height/Width	Special Features
A	Larkspur *Consolida regalis* 'Blue Cloud'	9	Annual/12-1	18-30 in. /10-12 in.	Blue flowers from spring to summer; reseeds easily
B	Horned poppy *Glaucium grandiflorum*	6	6-9/ 9-1	12-18 in. /15-18 in.	Bright orange flowers; 4-in.-long seed pods are ornamental
C	Soapweed yucca *Yucca glauca*	1	4-8/8-1	36 in. (flower) /24-36 in.	White flowers in summer; foliage is sharp, handle carefully
D	Snapdragon *Antirrhinum majus* 'Black Prince'	3	5-11/12-1	12-18 in. /12 in.	Deep red flowers all season; reseeds; deadhead for more blooms
E	Blue flax *Linum perenne*	3	4-8/8-1	12-24 in./6-18 in.	Blue flowers from spring to summer; reseeds easily
F	Pincushion flower *Scabiosa columbaria ochroleuca*	5	4-8/8-1	24-36 in. /18-24 in.	Pale yellow flowers all summer; pest free; good cut flower
G	Desert marigold *Baileya multiradiata*	2	7-10/12-1	12-18 in./18 in.	Yellow flowers all summer; reseeds; needs sharp drainage
H	Rocky mountain penstemon *Penstemon strictus*	5	4-9/9–1	24-36 in./18-24 in.	Long-lasting purple flowers; tolerates heavier soils than other penstemons; spreads by long stolons; forms large clumps
I	Silky thread grass *Stipa tenuissima*	2	7-10/12-1	18-36 in. /15-18 in.	Cream flowers in summer; reseeds easily; good in dry conditions
J	Artemesia *Artemisia ludoviciana* 'Valerie Finnis'	2	4-9/9-1	18-24 in. /18-24 in.	Grown for its silvery foliage and compact habit
K	Lavender cotton *Santolina chamaecyparissus*	3	5-9/9-1	12-18 in./24-36 in.	Yellow flowers in summer; foliage fragrant when brushed
L	Sage *Salvia officinalis* 'Purpurascens'	2	6-9/9-1	12-24 in./ 12-18 in.	Grown for fragrant and flavorful foliage; new growth is purple
M	Verbena *Verbena* 'Homestead Purple'	2	7-10/12-1	6-18 in. /24-36 in.	Purple flowers all summer; mildew-resistant foliage
N	Twinspur *Diascia integerrima* Coral Canyon®	2	5-8/12-1	12-18 in. /15-18 in.	Coral-pink flowers all summer; hardier than other twinspurs
O	Bearded iris *Iris* hybrid	1	3-9/ 9-1	8-40 in. /18 in.	Colorful flowers in late spring; architectural foliage all season
P	Silver thyme *Thymus citriodorus* 'Argenteus'	3	5-8/8-1	8 in. /12-18 in.	Pink flowers in summer; lemon-scented foliage
Q	Pineleaf penstemon *Penstemon pinifolius*	1	4-9/9-1	15 in. /18 in.	Orange-red flowers in summer; great for hummingbirds
R	Shrubby cinquefoil *Potentilla fruticosa*	2	3-9/9-1	2-4 ft./2-4 ft.	Flowers of yellow or orange from early summer to fall; pest free
S	Jupiter's beard *Centranthus ruber*	1	5-8/8–1	18-36 in. /24-30 in.	Dusty pink flowers in spring; great for butterflies

EASY ACCESS

Whether your garden is large or small, you need to be able to get into it without crushing plants, compacting soil and stepping on dormant bulbs or new transplants. Here are some ideas for working an access path into your garden design.

SMALL STEPS In a small cutting garden like the one at right, a few strategically placed steppers do the trick. Because they're visible, choose something colorful or with a pattern that complements your garden style. Then they'll not only be practical, they'll be pretty, too.

BIG AND BEAUTIFUL Large gardens give you more options. One option is to make the path go through the garden. But if you have the room, why not place it in back like the one in the illustration? That way, you're not walking on the soil in the growing area as much. And a path hidden by plants doesn't have to look as good as the garden around it. Cover the soil with bark mulch, a few concrete steppers or even a board — whatever keeps your feet dry and doesn't cost a lot.

Placing the entrance to the side like the path in this garden makes it less conspicuous. A width of 2 to 3 ft. should provide enough room to work. After all, you might want to bring a load of compost in or haul a bunch of clippings out so you want your wheelbarrow to fit easily down the path, too.

Small steps

Place steppers near plants you need to deadhead or prune.

Big and beautiful

Entrance

Plants spill into the entrance, camouflaging it a bit.

Place a few steppers near the path to get further into the garden.

BEFORE & AFTER | FRONT YARD

quick and easy update
for your garden

(1) No privacy here. Just one glance and you can see through the fence into this back yard.

Botanical Names

Arborvitae
Thuja occidentalis
Daylily
Hemerocallis spp.
Morning glory
Ipomoea spp.
Climbing rose
Rosa spp.

Rita Ward wasn't satisfied with the entry area to her Minnesota garden but she couldn't quite put her finger on what was wrong. So she took photo 1 above to help give her a new perspective. The most obvious problem here is the lack of privacy. You can see right through the fence into the back yard. Besides that, the fence and arbor don't work with the house style very well. Let's take a look and see how she took care of these problems and got a great-looking garden as a result.

QUICK FIX Want privacy fast? Buy large plants. These arborvitae were 8 feet tall when Rita purchased them, so they're an instant screen. And they'll get taller with time. Better still, arborvitae are evergreen so they provide color, structure and privacy all year.

For a privacy hedge, set plants close together — 6 to 12 inches closer than their full-grown diameter. For example, these arborvitae grow 3 feet wide. If you plant them 2½ feet apart they'll grow together so you can't see between them. For an immediate fix, plant the shrubs even closer together.

Since you can't see through the fence anymore, these shrubs help frame the view to the back yard. The open gate invites you to come in and see more of this beautiful garden.

ARBOR REDO Originally the arbor was a dark metal Mission-style model. Though attractive, it was hard to see against a green background of foliage. So Rita's husband built the wooden frame you see in photo 1 to fit around it. The new frame was an improvement, but they decided the arbor would look even better if the pitch of the top more closely matched the pitch of the nearby house roof. That meant building the new top you see in photo 2 and painting the whole thing the same color as the house trim. Now, the added height and hefty wood provide visual weight so the arbor isn't dwarfed by the house.

PATH PERFECTION Even low-maintenance plants need some care to look their best. And getting into a big bed like the one to the right of the arbor is much easier with a path. You may have noticed the bricks in front of the hydrangea at right. Those are part of a simple path that cuts across the center. Now deadheading, weeding and pruning are a snap. The path is also a quick shortcut from the front yard to the garden entrance. It's not very noticeable because some of the plants lean or grow part way into the walkway. Want to see the plan for this garden? Turn the page.

(2) Place brightly colored flowers like these daylilies just inside a garden's entrance to invite visitors to come in.

(3) Morning glory and climbing rose are good vines to grow on the side of an arbor. The flowers are pretty and the foliage helps make the arbor a part of the garden.

tip Build up perennial beds with compost and soil to add extra height. Plants will stand taller and partially block the view, creating a little mystery.

Turn the page to learn how to grow this garden.

www.GardenGateMagazine.com · the YEAR IN GARDENING · 125

simple plants, lots of impact

Sometimes all a garden needs is a little reworking to get it just right. With the addition of evergreen shrubs and tweaks to the arbor design, the backdrop for this garden was set. So what's the best way to set off the new additions? Colorful, long-blooming flowers. Even better, make sure they won't drain your time or pocketbook.

TOUGH CUSTOMERS Nothing makes gardening easier than choosing tough, reliable plants for your garden. Take the purple salvias in the photo at right, for example. Talk about tough — these plants actually sat out on the ground for a couple of days after they were divided. We don't recommend that, but a plant that easy-going is bound to thrive in your garden. And would you believe this photograph shows the *second* flush of blooms? After you remove the first spent blossoms, the side branches can take off and should bloom in a couple of weeks. The pale-pink yarrow, white phlox and red bee balm here will all bloom again if you keep them deadheaded, too. (And they're just about as tough as the salvias, as well!)

DIVIDE AND CONQUER A big garden needs a lot of plants to fill it up. Here's an easy and inexpensive way to do that: Divide your established plants and spread them around the garden. Easy-care plants like the salvia, bee balm and yarrow take division in stride. With regular watering and a sunny place to grow, the new transplants will get established quickly and may even bloom a little the first year. After all, you've always heard that repeating a plant or color throughout the garden creates unity. Division is an easy way to save money and make your garden look good, too.

Another great way to get and share new plants is to hold a plant swap party with friends. However, some plants can be a little too enthusiastic — you may not want to bring just anything home. Take a look at "Know before you go" so you don't plant a thug that will take over.

MIX IT UP Don't just stick to perennials in your border — put some shrubs in the mix, too. Shrubs are usually fairly

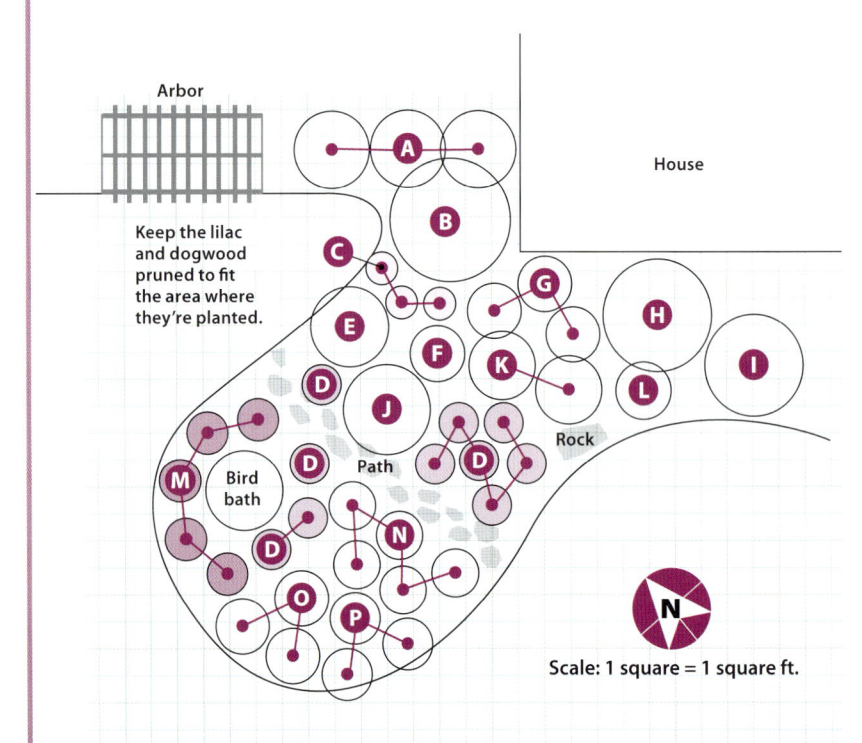

Know before you go

When you're looking over your options at a plant sale, keep one thing in mind: Sometimes the reason that someone has a lot of divisions to share is because the plant spreads quickly or aggressively. That's not always a problem — if you have an area where you can keep these plants under control, you may find that they're a great asset to your garden. But it's a good idea to check out a plant's habits before you grow it. Here are a few common perennials that you might want to think twice about picking up unless you can give them room to run.

Artemisia *Artemisia vulgaris* 'Oriental Limelight' ('Janlim') Also known as wormwood; cold-hardy in USDA zones 4 to 8, heat-tolerant in AHS zones 8 to 1

Chameleon plant *Houttuynia cordata* 'Chameleon' Cold-hardy in USDA zones 3 to 9, heat-tolerant in AHS zones 9 to 1

Gooseneck loosestrife *Lysimachia clethroides* Cold-hardy in USDA zones 3 to 8, heat-tolerant in AHS zones 8 to 1

Obedient plant *Physostegia virginiana* Also known as false dragonhead; cold-hardy in USDA zones 3 to 9, heat-tolerant in AHS zones 9 to 1

Lily-of-the-valley *Convallaria majalis* Cold-hardy in USDA zones 2 to 7, heat-tolerant in AHS zones 7 to 1

Bugleweed *Ajuga reptans* Cold-hardy in USDA zones 3 to 9, heat-tolerant in AHS zones 9 to 1

Keep the lilac and dogwood pruned to fit the area where they're planted.

Scale: 1 square = 1 square ft.

(4) Small to tall is the way to go. These plant sizes rise up gently to meet the arbor, so the structure feels like part of the garden.

low-maintenance and provide structure year-round, even those that don't have foliage in winter. Many have flowers, colorful foliage or stems, berries or fruit. Some hydrangeas, like the Endless Summer® in this garden, bloom on both old and new wood, so you'll get flowers, even with winter dieback. In addition, the flowers dry nicely and look good well into fall. Along with the arborvitae, the boxwoods stay green all winter. And redtwig dogwoods add a little winter excitement, too. Young stems are red, so cut the oldest stems back to the ground each year in early spring to keep those bright red stems coming.

Combine tough perennials, good-looking shrubs and a little planning — it all adds up to a gorgeous garden! □

— *Sherri Ribbey*

tip Plant masses of color. It will be attractive to you and the neighborhood butterflies.

EASY-CARE GARDEN

Code	Plant Name	No. to Plant	Blooms	Type	Cold/Heat Zones	Height/Width	Special Features
A	Arborvitae *Thuja occidentalis* 'Holmstrup'	3	NA	Shrub	3-7/7-1	10-15 ft./3 ft.	Soft, bright-green evergreen foliage
B	Dwarf Korean lilac *Syringa meyeri* 'Palibin'	1	Lavender; spring	Shrub	3-7/7-1	4-5 ft./5-7 ft.	Keep pruned to fit the space
C	Swamp milkweed *Asclepias* 'Cinderella'	3	Pale pink; mid- to late summer	Perennial	3-9/9-1	3-4 ft./1-3 ft.	Plant sap can irritate skin
D	Salvia *Salvia ×sylvestris* 'May Night' ('Mainacht')	10	Purple; summer to fall	Perennial	4-9/9-1	18-24 in./15-18 in.	Reblooms
E	Bee balm *Monarda* 'Jacob Cline'	1	Red; early summer to fall	Perennial	4-9/9-1	3-4 ft./3 ft.	Reblooms with deadheading
F	Turtlehead *Chelone lyonii* 'Hot Lips'	1	Pink; late summer	Perennial	3-9/9-1	24-36 in./12-24 in.	Needs consistent moisture
G	Garden phlox *Phlox paniculata* 'David'	3	White; summer	Perennial	3-9/9-1	2-4 ft./2 ft.	Reblooms; fragrant
H	Redtwig dogwood *Cornus alba*	1	White; spring	Shrub	2-8/8-1	8-10 ft./8-10 ft.	Keep pruned to fit the space
I	Juniper *Juniperus ×pfitzeriana* 'Armstrongii'	1	NA	Shrub	3-9/9-1	3-4 ft./3-4 ft.	Gray-green needled foliage
J	Hydrangea *Hydrangea macrophylla* Endless Summer® ('Bailmer')	1	Pink or blue; midsummer	Shrub	4-9/9-1	3-4 ft./3-4 ft.	Flower color depends on soil
K	Boxwood *Buxus* 'Green Gem'	2	NA	Shrub	4-9/9-1	2-4 ft./2-4 ft.	Slow-growing evergreen
L	Shrub rose *Rosa* 'Nearly Wild'	1	Single pink; summer to fall	Shrub	4-9/9-1	2-3 ft./2-3 ft.	Reblooms
M	Lamb's ear *Stachys byzantina* 'Big Ears'	5	NA	Perennial	4-8/8-1	8-12 in./12-18 in.	Velvety gray foliage
N	Yarrow *Achillea* 'Pretty Belinda'	5	Pink; midsummer	Perennial	3-9/9-1	24-36 in./18-24 in.	Less floppy than some yarrow
O	Bee balm *Monarda fistulosa* 'Claire Grace'	3	Pink; summer to fall	Perennial	3-9/9-1	2-3 ft./2-3 ft.	Mildew-resistant; reblooms
P	Penstemon *Penstemon digitalis* 'Husker Red'	3	White; summer to fall	Perennial	3-9/9-1	24-36 in./12-24 in.	Foliage is darker in more sun

We'll share tips for filling up a big garden without wearing yourself out on page 152.

garden design

great *ideas* you can use!

SOLID DESIGN ADVICE FOR A BEAUTIFUL YARD... Let's start at the beginning, with measuring your property and dreaming big. Then let's walk through the whole process of developing a design. When we're done, you'll be able to design your yard like a pro. Finally, we'll share design tips from lots of other gardens... back yards, front yards, colorful beds and those that bring in the birds and butterflies. Prepare to be inspired!

Start from Scratch	130	Nature's Masterpiece	160
Set the Style	134	Color	164
Welcome Change	138	4 Fabulous Fall Combos	168
Think Outside the Trellis	142	Warm, Winged Welcome	172
Triangles Make a Point	144	Butterflies Welcome	174
Rain Gardens	148	Bird-Friendly Garden	178
The Big Picture	152	Did You Know	182
Time to Relax	158		

design your dream garden: the master plan

Assess your needs and the rest is easy!

Start from Scratch

Assess what you have

Here are 10 things you'll want to keep in mind as you make your site analysis.

- ☐ Size and shape of your lot
- ☐ Size and location of the house and all other buildings
- ☐ Location and sizes of sidewalks, paths, driveway — any permanent features you plan to keep
- ☐ Overhead and underground utility lines; in the United States contact One Call at 811 to mark your property
- ☐ Location and general sizes of doors, windows, meters, dryer vents and AC units
- ☐ Trees and shrubs you intend to keep
- ☐ North, so you know sun and shade patterns
- ☐ Desirable, as well as objectionable, views
- ☐ Drainage issues that will influence your design
- ☐ Service areas for compost, trash and recycling

On any journey, the first step is often the hardest. Designing your own landscape can be an overwhelming proposition. But it doesn't have to be. I'll start by sharing tips on evaluating your existing landscape in a site analysis. Then you'll learn how to make a base map, similar to a blueprint. Once you have that, you'll be able to refer to it any time you might want to make changes to your landscape.

So grab a pencil, some paper and your tape measure. Let's get started!

ANALYZE YOUR SITE Before you head outdoors, roughly sketch the shape of your lot, house, garage, driveway and deck or patio on a sheet of paper as I've done in the illustration at right. Any elements that'll influence your final design need to be on there. For example, I've included the shape of the house, as well as placement of the driveway and sidewalks. Once you get outdoors, it'll be much easier to simply add the measurements to your sketch.

MEASURE EVERYTHING If you have a friend to hold one end of the measuring tape, your job will go quickly. If not, you may need a stake to hold the end of the tape. Or check out your local tool rental store. It may have a measuring wheel that makes measuring large areas easy.

In the box "Assess what you have," at left, I've listed many of the elements you need to include on your site analysis. You'll see that lots of them are on my site analysis at right, where I've started to add in some of the measurements.

TAKE A LOOK AROUND Once you have all the utilities, measurements and locations added to your site analysis, it's time to sit down. However, you're not ready to rest yet. Take some time to look around.

While there's nothing really wrong with the landscape we're working with, it's become outdated and bland. The vegetable garden's important but as the back yard tree has grown, it's become more shaded. And the compost pile isn't much to look at. More space for shrubs and perennials would be nice, especially to improve the veiws from the family room windows. There's a wooden deck outside the family room. For now I'll consider keeping it, but it's really too small for entertaining.

Before you finish, check out the views in your garden. Are there objectionable ones you want to block? For example, there's a view from the deck area just outside the family room door that looks directly at the neighbor's trash cans. I'll want to block that. However, from the family room and

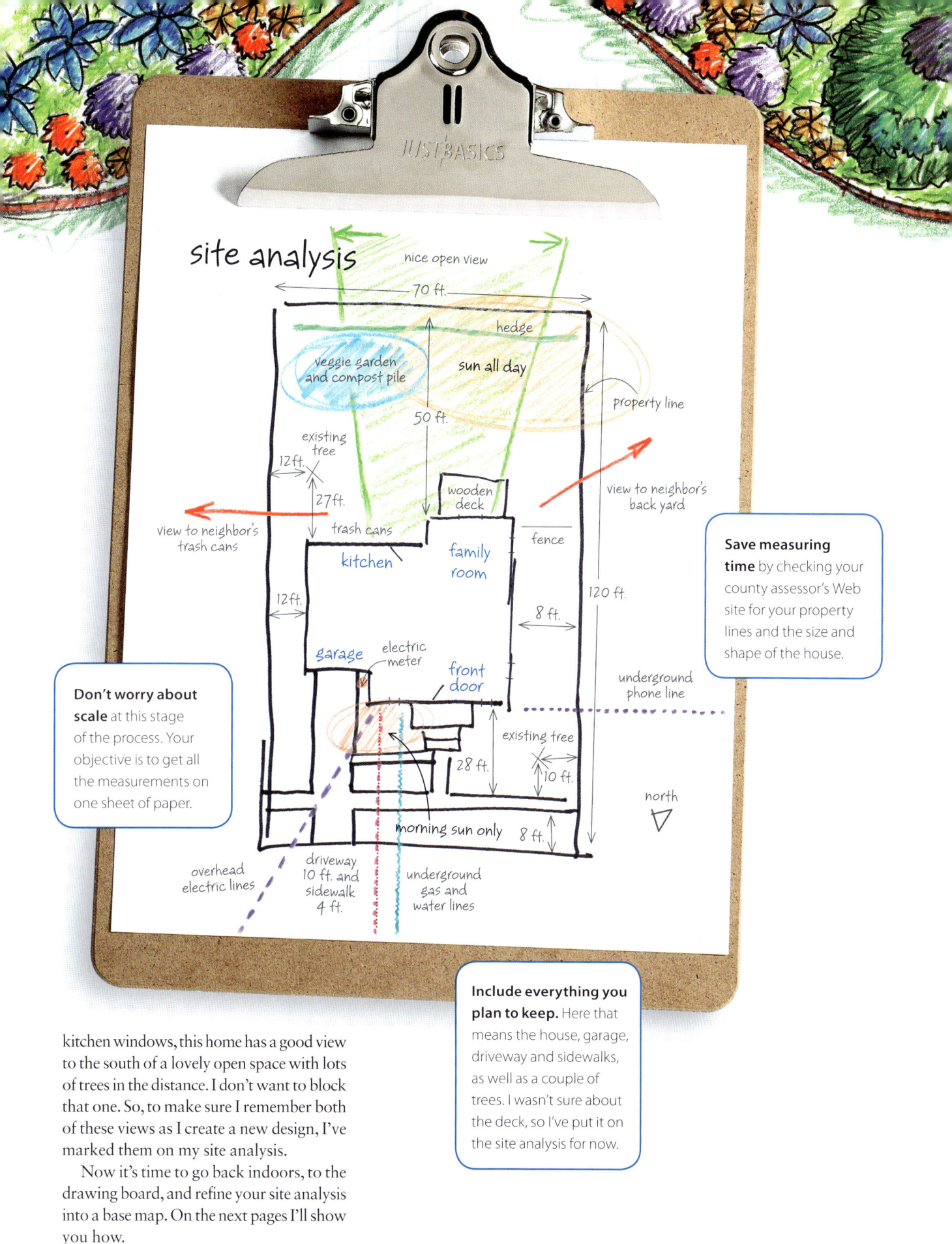

site analysis

nice open view
70 ft.
hedge
veggie garden and compost pile
sun all day
property line
50 ft.
existing tree
12 ft.
27 ft.
view to neighbor's trash cans
trash cans
wooden deck
view to neighbor's back yard
fence
kitchen
family room
120 ft.
12 ft.
8 ft.
garage
electric meter
front door
underground phone line
existing tree
28 ft.
10 ft.
north
morning sun only
8 ft.
overhead electric lines
driveway 10 ft. and sidewalk 4 ft.
underground gas and water lines

> **Don't worry about scale** at this stage of the process. Your objective is to get all the measurements on one sheet of paper.

> **Save measuring time** by checking your county assessor's Web site for your property lines and the size and shape of the house.

> **Include everything you plan to keep.** Here that means the house, garage, driveway and sidewalks, as well as a couple of trees. I wasn't sure about the deck, so I've put it on the site analysis for now.

kitchen windows, this home has a good view to the south of a lovely open space with lots of trees in the distance. I don't want to block that one. So, to make sure I remember both of these views as I create a new design, I've marked them on my site analysis.

Now it's time to go back indoors, to the drawing board, and refine your site analysis into a base map. On the next pages I'll show you how.

design your dream garden: the master plan (continued)

CREATE YOUR
BASE MAP

What do you want?

Here's a list of things you may want to work into a new design. I've checked the priorities for this plan.

- ☑ Colorful flower beds and borders
- ☑ Private garden hideaway
- ☑ Welcoming front garden
- ☐ Play structure for children
- ☐ Water feature
- ☐ Fire pit
- ☑ Screen views
- ☐ Greenhouse
- ☐ Rose garden
- ☑ Foundation plantings with year-round interest
- ☑ Pergola, arbor or other structure
- ☑ Garden shed for potting and storage
- ☐ Hot tub
- ☑ Path from front area to back
- ☐ Swimming pool
- ☐ Rain garden
- ☑ Good-looking vegetable garden
- ☐ Room for a clothesline
- ☐ Off-street parking
- ☐ Tennis court
- ☐ Dog kennel
- ☐ Screened porch
- ☑ Deck or patio

Once you complete the site analysis, it's time to refine that information into a base map, like the one below. This map needs to be in scale, so I find it's easiest to work with graph paper and a ruler. I decided on a scale where each quarter inch equals a distance of 5 feet. So, one square equals 25 square feet.

You're going to draw and write your ideas on the base map. Since it's something you'll want to save for future reference, make several photocopies and keep the original clean. Or, if you prefer, lay tracing paper over the original and draw on that. I like copies because they stand up to erasers better. Whether you use a color or black and white copier, select a dark setting so the pale grid will show.

ANY QUESTIONS? In this phase, think about what you'd like and how you'll use the new garden. And of course, consider how much time you want to spend on maintenance. Be sure to ask other members of your family what they'd like, too. You may have to cut items later because of space or budget, but for now, dream. To help you get started, I've pulled together a list of possibilities in "What do you want?" at left. The checked items are the ones I want to try to include in this garden.

base map

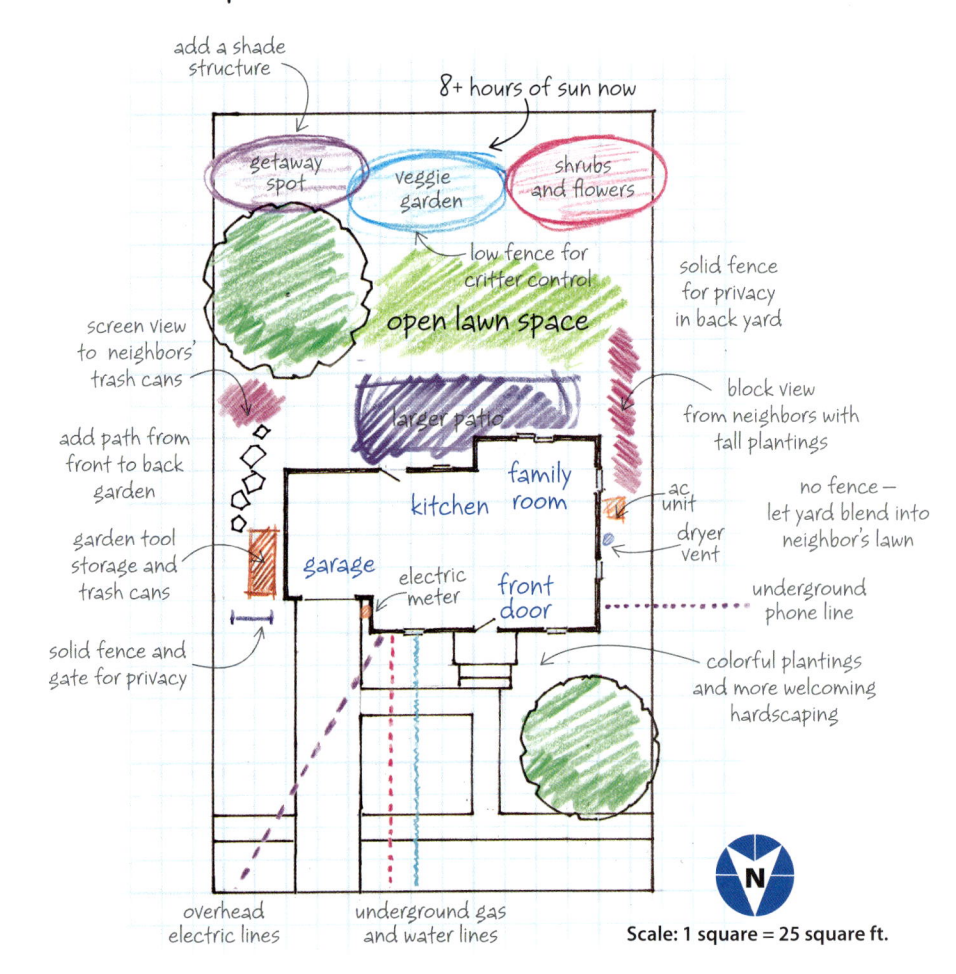

Scale: 1 square = 25 square ft.

132 the YEAR IN GARDENING www.GardenGateMagazine.com

Dealing with unique lot shapes

BACK TO THE DRAWING BOARD Now you've begun to figure out what you really need and what's negotiable. Take a copy of your base map and begin to place the elements from your list where they might work best. On my early maps I tried to leave the veggie garden where it was and just spruce it up. But that corner was the furthest from the house and seemed the natural spot for a secluded hideaway. So, on the final base map at left, I put the getaway in the corner and moved the vegetable garden over.

Mark up several base map copies with ideas. You don't need defined shapes and sizes, just circle the location. Then take your base map and walk around the garden, envisioning where the elements you want might best be located. Remember that old deck I mentioned? I've decided to remove it and include something larger, so I'll mark the location. Later, I can determine how big, what style and what materials I'll use.

It's a good idea to set your notes aside for a day or two. Many of your best ideas may come to you when the base map isn't staring you in the face. Write these ideas down, fit them in and tour your garden again. When you have the best fit, go back inside and, on a clean copy of your base map, sketch them in.

Not all lots are the same shape or size. What if you don't have room for a private area away from your house? In "Dealing with unique lot shapes" at right, I'll show you three challenging scenarios and how to deal with them.

Whew! That's a lot to think about as you get ready to design your new garden. But arranging your landscape on paper is much easier and cheaper than having to adjust it once you start installation. ☐

— *Jim Childs*

L-shaped L-shaped lots can give you extra space, but they can also be hard to manage. Often there are narrow sideyards with paths that are used only as passageways. Here, I've decided to add a hard-surfaced patio screened by a tall fence for privacy.

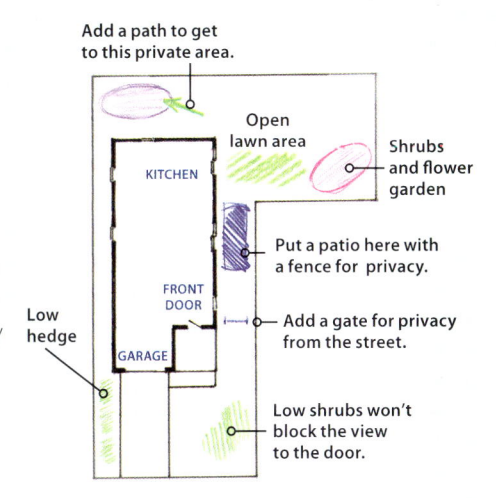

- Add a path to get to this private area.
- Open lawn area
- Shrubs and flower garden
- Put a patio here with a fence for privacy.
- Add a gate for privacy from the street.
- Low hedge
- Low shrubs won't block the view to the door.

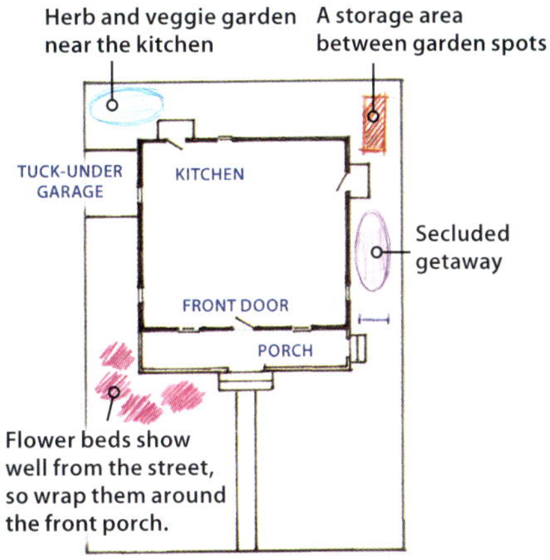

No back yard You have a tiny lot and no back yard. Everything is out front. You want to garden, but how? A small veggie garden is a good fit on the sunny corner near the kitchen. And a hideaway can easily be tucked in the narrow side yard, leaving a small spot for storage in between.

- Herb and veggie garden near the kitchen
- A storage area between garden spots
- Tuck-under garage
- Secluded getaway
- Flower beds show well from the street, so wrap them around the front porch.

Pie-shaped Tight corners are not easy to mow. Ease them into more manageable shapes with plantings. On the other hand, for the illusion of more space, leave the front yard open to blend into the neighbor's lawn.

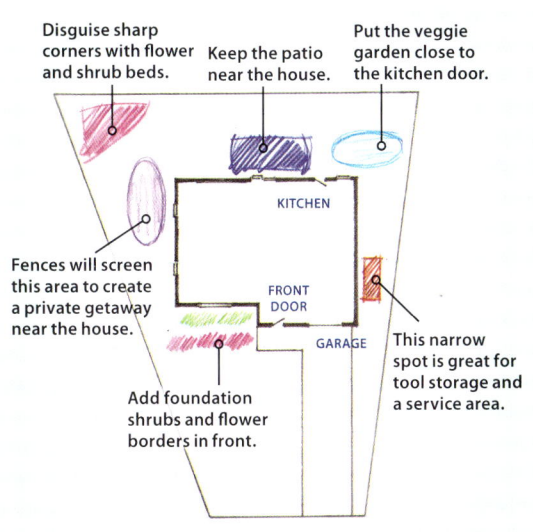

- Disguise sharp corners with flower and shrub beds.
- Keep the patio near the house.
- Put the veggie garden close to the kitchen door.
- Fences will screen this area to create a private getaway near the house.
- This narrow spot is great for tool storage and a service area.
- Add foundation shrubs and flower borders in front.

design your dream garden: part 2 — define the shapes

It's time to give your design some shape.
Set the Style

Do you dream of having a beautiful new garden? Like building a house, creating the garden of your dreams takes planning. We started with a site analysis on page 130. Check out "The story up 'til now" below for a recap. Now it's time to start defining the shapes of the beds and other key elements.

TAKE A CUE FROM THE HOUSE Garden style ties the shapes of borders, structures and all the other elements together. The biggest structure in your garden will most likely be the house, so that's where to start. Many houses are a mix of styles, giving you lots of latitude when it comes to garden design. But if your house is well-defined, perhaps an English Tudor or a Colonial saltbox, you'll want to keep the garden a similar style. A dramatic contrast, such as putting a Southwestern xeric landscape with that Tudor, may look out of place. However, choosing a style simply comes down to deciding what you like and what looks good.

KEEP YOUR OPTIONS OPEN It's time to take several copies of the base map you've made and draw in the elements you chose. Before you sketch, ask yourself the "Questions of style," at right to help you set the look of your new garden.

Do more than one sketch so you can see how different shapes will fit together. Even though you have several base maps, be sure to keep an eraser handy — you'll probably use it frequently!

You can see six options for the yard I'm planning at right. I started with three sketches that have curved forms. Then I did three with straight edges. With each sketch you can see what I like and some of the problems.

When I sketched ideas, I started with the patio area because it's the largest element in the yard. Then I moved to the border around the back yard, fitting in the focal-point vegetable garden and the hideaway area in the far left corner. Next, I looked at the path along the side of the house. Since it'll be used a lot, I want to make sure it looks good and is easy to navigate. And I sketched ideas for the front area last.

Keep practical considerations in mind as you start. For example, the new patio needs to connect the kitchen and living areas. I don't want to carry food through the house or navigate a narrow zigzag path, especially if I have my hands full on the way to the patio table.

Don't worry about perfect lines, or even exact measurements at this point; just draw in shapes and rough sizes to see how they look. Once you have several sketches put together, take them outside and walk through the garden. If it helps, drag out the hose or some twine and stakes to outline areas to picture your ideas better.

On the next pages I've refined the ideas you see here to come up with two designs — one with curves and one with straight lines. Let's take a look at the process.

The story up 'til now
On page 130 I showed how to make a site analysis. First, you evaluate the permanent elements in your garden, such as the house, the driveway and existing trees. That information becomes a base map — a scale drawing you can use as you plan. Next, make a list of things you would like in your new garden. Then take those elements and organize them on the base map. This is the base map we settled on and are working from now.

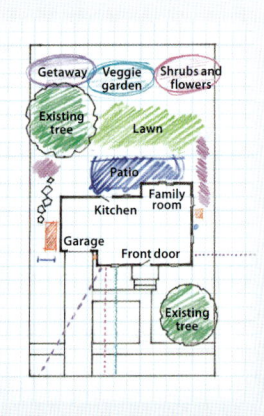

Experiment with lines and shapes

Designing on the curve

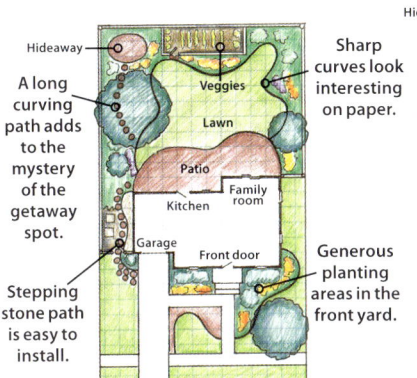

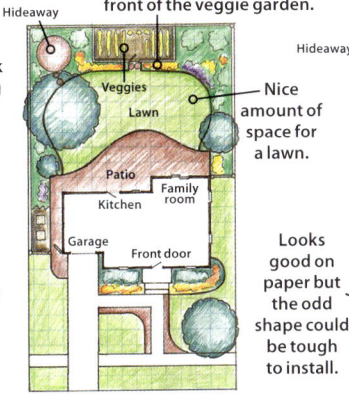

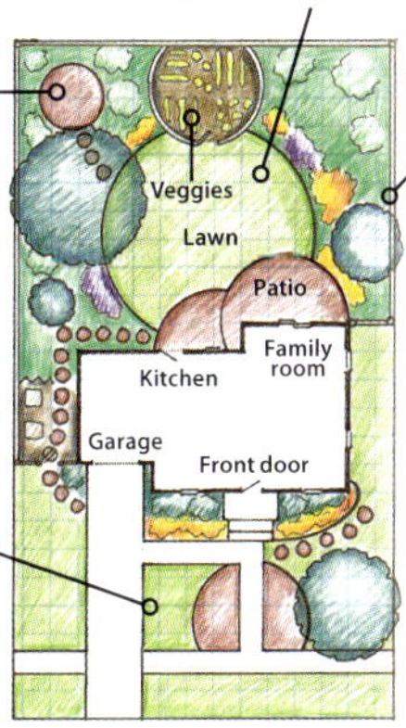

DRAMATIC CURVES These curves give the garden a natural feel. And traveling the long path through the border to the hideaway will give the impression of a journey away from the house.

- A long curving path adds to the mystery of the getaway spot.
- Sharp curves look interesting on paper.
- Stepping stone path is easy to install.
- Generous planting areas in the front yard.

GENTLE FLOW Broad curves are easy to maneuver with the mower. I really like the curves where I want to expand the existing front sidewalk, too. They'll make the area look and feel much more welcoming to visitors.

- Lots of space for more flowers in front of the veggie garden.
- Nice amount of space for a lawn.
- Looks good on paper but the odd shape could be tough to install.

CLASSIC CIRCLES A circular lawn gives lots of open space around the beds. The stepping stone path from the patio would be easy to install, but may not be as easy to navigate as a solid surface. The round vegetable garden is intriguing — is it practical?

- This lawn is smaller so there's more room for shrubs and flowers.
- Privacy fence screens the back yard and patio.

Questions of style

- ☐ Does your house have a definite style, such as Victorian or Georgian?
- ☐ Do you prefer straight lines, geometric forms and well-defined corners, or natural, gently curving lines with no sharp angles?
- ☐ When you visit other gardens, do you like symmetrical balance where two or more elements match exactly, like a mirror image? Or is asymmetrical balance, where items in the garden relate to each other but are not identical, more appealing to you?
- ☐ Are you drawn to gardens where the style is loose and natural, with masses of plants and very few hard surfaces?
- ☐ Do you like to see individual, well-spaced specimen plants?
- ☐ When you think about structures in your garden, are they painted and ornate or left to weather naturally?
- ☐ Do you mow with a riding mower or a walk behind? Tight curves and angles may mean you need to go back and trim by hand.

Straightforward lines

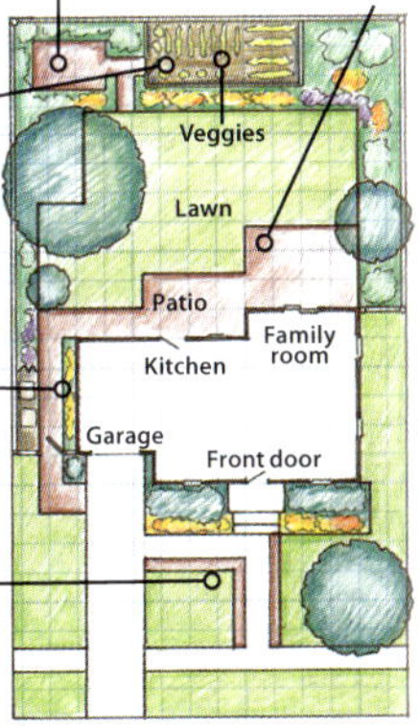

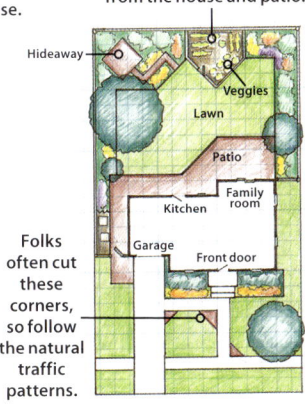

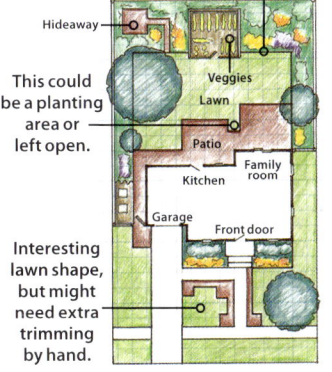

SIMPLE LINES The veggie garden is a good fit and has room in front to add a border of flowers or low shrubs. This plan would be quick to lay out, build and plant, especially for a do-it-yourself project.

- Patio shape follows lines of the house.
- Setting the vegetable garden into the border makes it less noticeable.
- Space for plants, but it's too narrow to grow much.
- Simple solution to widen the sidewalk, but just looks boring.

DRAMATIC DIAGONAL Turning things on a diagonal adds excitement. The diagonals make for a unique vegetable garden and front sidewalk. And the simple lines of this patio would be easy to live with.

- Unique garden shape makes a good focal point viewed from the house and patio.
- Folks often cut these corners, so follow the natural traffic patterns.

A TRADITIONAL LOOK An open space gives the patio the feeling of two separate areas. The veggie garden is a traditional shape. There's lots of planting space in the borders, and the edges are easy to maintain.

- Straight edges are easy to keep neat and tidy.
- This could be a planting area or left open.
- Interesting lawn shape, but might need extra trimming by hand.

Scale: 1 square = 25 square ft.

design your dream garden: part 2 — define the shapes (continued)

Once I've made sketches, I usually find that I like elements from several of them. So I'll work them into my final designs. That's just what I've done here. I've adjusted the shapes and sizes to create two designs — one with curving lines and one with mostly straight lines and sharp angles. Check out the options — I bet there are some tips you can use in your own garden, too!

— *Jim Childs*

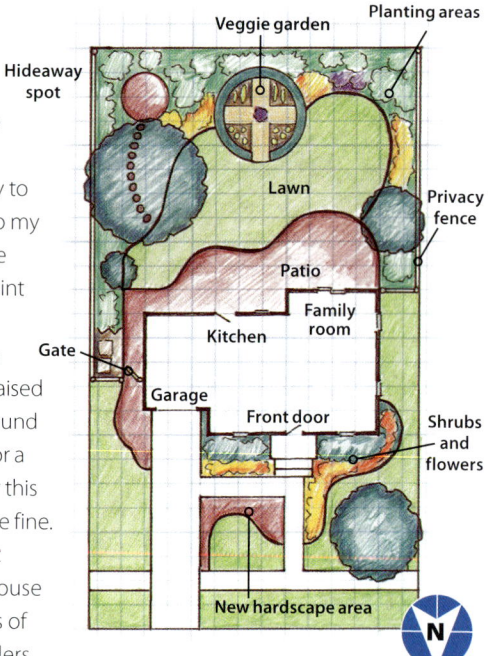

Curved lines I liked the circles you saw on one of my early sketches, so I found a way to integrate a couple of them into my final plan. The round vegetable garden will be a good focal point when viewed from the house and patio. I'll plant it in wedges separated by paths and put a raised bed of flowers in the center. Round may not be a practical shape for a large vegetable garden, but for this 20-ft.-diameter spot it would be fine.

This patio design lets traffic move across the back of the house efficiently, too. And there's lots of space for plantings in the borders around the back yard. There's even enough depth to the bed in the upper left hand corner to make the hideaway feel really secluded.

In the front garden, flowing curves widen the sidewalk and add a welcoming look. Plus, all of these gently curving edges, in the front and back garden, will be easy to mow without going back to trim.

Labels on plan: Veggie garden, Planting areas, Hideaway spot, Lawn, Privacy fence, Patio, Family room, Kitchen, Gate, Garage, Front door, Shrubs and flowers, New hardscape area. Scale: 1 square = 25 square ft.

Front yard view

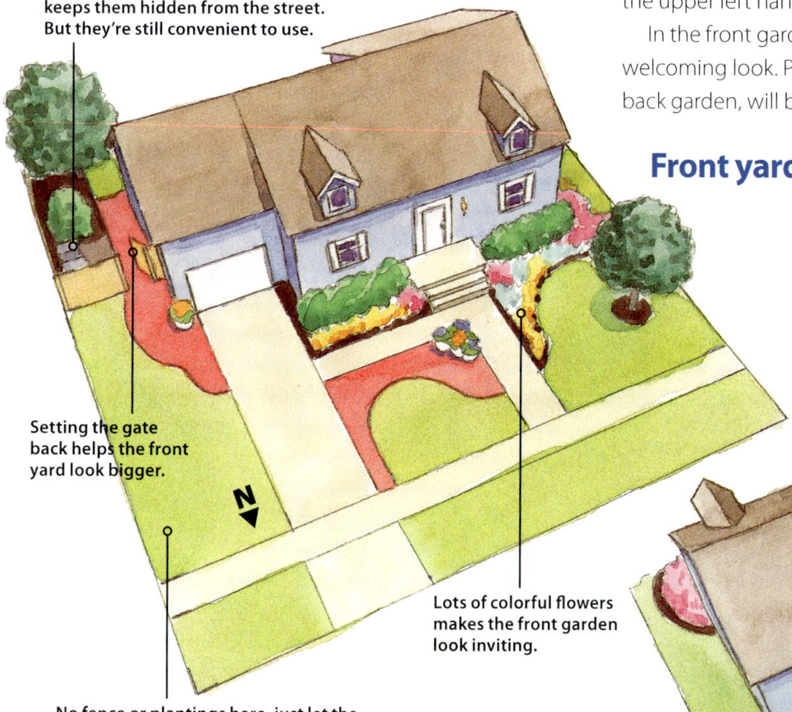

- Tucking tool storage, compost and potting bench behind this fence keeps them hidden from the street. But they're still convenient to use.
- Setting the gate back helps the front yard look bigger.
- No fence or plantings here, just let the lawn blend into the neighbor's lawn. It'll make the front yard seem bigger and make the neighborhood look friendlier.
- Lots of colorful flowers makes the front garden look inviting.

Back yard view

- The generous size of the patio ties the kitchen and family room areas together.
- This circular hideaway is 10 ft. in diameter, a good size for two chairs and a small table.
- This ornamental tree casts some shade on the southwest corner of the patio, blocks the view of the neighbor's trash cans and provides privacy for the patio from the second story of the house next door.
- Keep this south side of the yard open with no privacy fence or large hedge. This offers an unobstructed view of the open space beyond from the house and patio.
- A formal veggie garden? Divide the beds with paths for easy access into each section.

136   *the* YEAR IN GARDENING   www.GardenGateMagazine.com

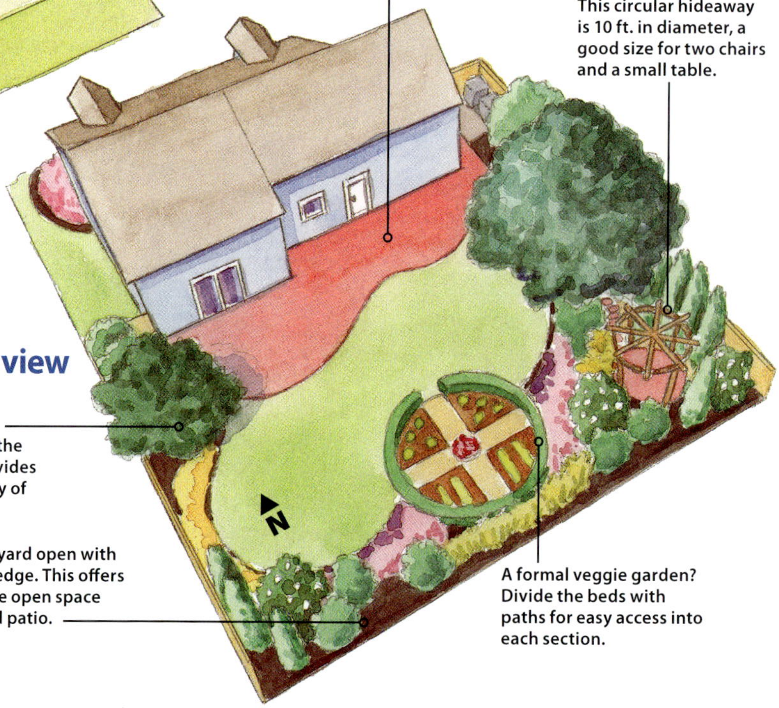

Straight lines The generous sizes of the borders in this layout are perfect for plenty of shrubs and flowers. And see the large patio across the back of the house? Not only will it offer lots of space for entertaining, but it's efficient. Notice how it connects both doors on the back of the house? That means serving a meal will be easy. Plus, the patio ties into the path that leads around the house to the front yard so guests won't have to go through the house to get to the back yard.

Adding just a small bit of hard surface around the existing sidewalk is an easy way to give your entry a unique look and distinguish it from similar homes on the street. Plus, it's less expensive than taking out all of the concrete. Not only is the look unique, the wider sidewalk helps make the front yard feel more spacious and welcoming, too. These hard surface areas in the angles of the sidewalk give visitors more areas where they can stand and chat. And they provide spots for a few containers to change the look of the entrance without a lot of work.

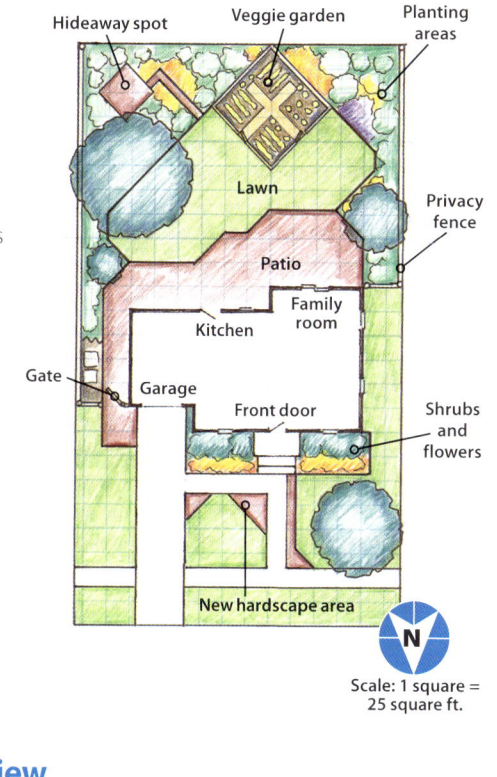

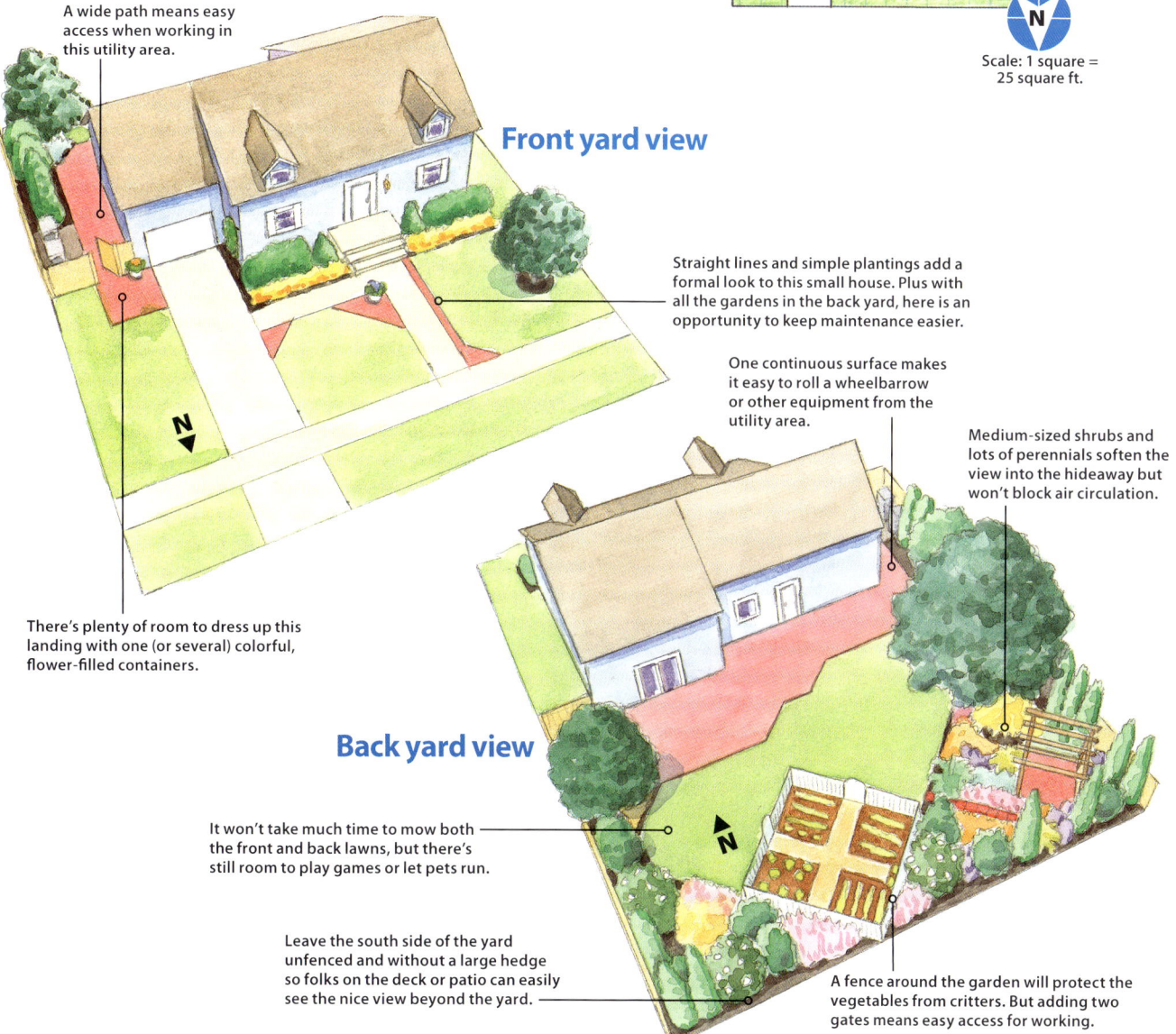

Labels on plan: Hideaway spot · Veggie garden · Planting areas · Lawn · Privacy fence · Patio · Family room · Kitchen · Gate · Garage · Front door · Shrubs and flowers · New hardscape area

Scale: 1 square = 25 square ft.

Front yard view

- A wide path means easy access when working in this utility area.
- Straight lines and simple plantings add a formal look to this small house. Plus with all the gardens in the back yard, here is an opportunity to keep maintenance easier.
- There's plenty of room to dress up this landing with one (or several) colorful, flower-filled containers.

Back yard view

- One continuous surface makes it easy to roll a wheelbarrow or other equipment from the utility area.
- Medium-sized shrubs and lots of perennials soften the view into the hideaway but won't block air circulation.
- It won't take much time to mow both the front and back lawns, but there's still room to play games or let pets run.
- Leave the south side of the yard unfenced and without a large hedge so folks on the deck or patio can easily see the nice view beyond the yard.
- A fence around the garden will protect the vegetables from critters. But adding two gates means easy access for working.

DESIGN | ALL AROUND THE YARD

(1) Close a large gate like this and you have very little idea what's on the other side. Leave it open and it frames your view to the garden inside.

Welcome Change!

Create the right mood for every transition in your garden.

As soon as you step into any room in your house, you get a different vibe. The kitchen is all about convenience and comfort. The bedroom is probably soothing and private, and since the dining room is where you gather, you want it to feel welcoming. The entrance into a room needs to work with the decor to set the tone. You probably wouldn't put a set of casual sliding glass doors into an elegant formal dining room. The mood would be all wrong.

Along those same lines, you have many rooms in your garden: your foundation planting, the patio where you gather with friends, the private little getaway behind the garage. And when you design a transition to match the room, you can help set a mood for the space and direct traffic effortlessly. In the garden, you have all sorts of tools available to create transitions: gates, arbors, steps, pathways and more. Let's take a look at how some of these could work in your garden.

IMPORTANT AND DRAMATIC A transition can be obvious. The big gate and fence in photo 1 provide security and privacy for our test garden. That is, they do until the gate opens, what lies beyond is revealed and your curiosity is satisfied. But there's more going on here. Notice how the fence and gate frame a view? The small glimpse of the lush plantings and charming gazebo entices you to move into the garden. Your eyes focus on them, at least until you pass through the gate. Then you see more of the garden and have many options about which way to go. That's why there is a large circle of flagstone just inside the gate. It gives you a spot to stop and look around before you move further into the garden.

SIMPLE AND SUBTLE Our next entrance, in photo 2, is more subtle. This garden would be fine without the simple posts and picket fence. But they do a good job of separating the garden from the driveway, adding some structure and lending a more intimate feeling to the garden. Understated transitions like this are good where you want to define an edge but not block the view or detract from the garden itself.

You see the neutral-colored fence, but your eye quickly moves to the house and entrance beyond. If the fence were painted white or a bright color, it would slow, or even stop your eyes. And while the driveway is mostly concrete, trimming it with the same brick used in the path unifies this transition.

Getting the idea? Garden passages can be simple or elaborate. Let's make the transition to the next page and look at several more.

(2) An open entrance helps make the transition from the drive to the front door a pleasant journey. And the neutral fence color lets the garden and the door be the stars of this scene.

LEADING TRANSITIONS

Transitions all have one thing in common — they lead you along. Some can speed you up, making you curious about what lies beyond. Others slow you down, inviting you to take time and look at them and their surroundings. They can be so bold that they're a major focal point in the entire garden, or they can be subtle, barely noticed. Here are some examples of what I mean.

RELAX WITH YOUR TRANSITION How about a transition that can also be used as a wayside stop? The pergola in photo 3 links two portions of this casual garden. Plus, the built-in benches give you a comfortable place to pause and really look at the garden before you continue down this path. With a solid roof overhead, you're protected from the elements on either a sunny *or* a rainy day. Being at the bend in a path, no matter which way you're traveling, you're only able to see glimpses of the garden beyond. But sitting inside, you can look both directions to enjoy the whole area.

The vine and a hanging basket help soften some of the hard angles of this structure and blend it into the informal setting. But it still stands out as a focal point for much of the garden surrounding it.

Don't have a spot for a structure, but like the idea of a passage where you can sit and relax? Create a similar nook by matching several tall, narrow shrubs on each side of a path. Set the shrubs back far enough to lay a few pieces of flagstone in front of them. Place a pair of comfortable benches on the stone, and you have a "natural" transition.

MAKE IT FUNCTIONAL A passage from one area to the next doesn't have to block or control a view or even be an ornamental structure. The bold flight of stone steps in the retaining wall in photo 4 is a necessity. It's the perfect solution to get people up the hillside. And its rugged look helps set a style for the rest of the garden. Even though you can't see much of it in the photograph, I bet you can guess that this garden has a casual, almost rustic, feeling. There are no tightly clipped or sheared plants to be found.

Bold slabs of stone set against fine-textured plants create a strong contrast and draw your attention. While the steps can be a focal point from the lower level, they pretty much disappear once you reach the top and you've made a transition into a completely different part of the garden. If you don't have a grade change like this one in your garden, you can still create a similar passage — build a bridge over a stream, a man-made water feature or even a dry stream bed.

(3) A destination transition gives you a place to relax and enjoy the garden. While this pergola definitely separates two garden rooms, you can sit and enjoy views in both directions.

(4) Steps make a dramatic passage. Even though they're a necessity in this retaining wall, these bold, rustic steps create a transition. They signal that you're leaving one area, the driveway, and entering the garden.

PACE-SETTING PASSAGE Like an elegant or colorful front door on your home, some transitions are meant to really draw your attention. Take this painted arbor, for example. It's more of an ornament than a structure, yet it separates two areas. But before you really notice what it does, it asks you to stop and take a closer look at it. Even though it's a simple design, the white is a strong contrast to the foliage around it.

This path and colorful garden would be fine without the arbor. Because the structure attracts so much attention as a focal point, you pause for a moment to focus on it. Once you look it over, you move on and notice the garden beyond. A transition like this one causes you to slow down rather than rush down the path. Same with the gentle curve in the path — it slows your pace much more than a straight path would.

Got the idea? Adding a transition, whether it's simple or imposing, can make your garden, no matter the size, a much more interesting place. However, before you design one, you'll want to check out "Transition no-nos" at right for a few more design tips. ◻

— *Jim Childs*

(5) Add emphasis to a transition. A neutral color, such as gray or brown, would make this arbor blend in. But white gives it added importance so you see it before you look at the surrounding garden.

TRANSITION NO-NOS

No matter what style passage you decide on, you'll want it to be "user-friendly." To that end, here are some points to keep in mind as you plan a new transition.

- ☐ **Avoid thorns** Plants with thorns might reach out and snag folks as they pass by.
- ☐ **Bee free** Flowers are nice, but if you're allergic to bees, plants that will attract lots of them might be a problem.
- ☐ **High maintenance** Skip plants that need lots of care. Since they'll be noticed frequently, and up close, you want plants that look good most of the time.
- ☐ **Easy to navigate** Don't make passages too narrow, or uncomfortable to walk on. They should be wide enough for at least one person to pass through easily. And the path surface should be durable and secure.

DESIGN | ALL AROUND THE YARD

think outside the trellis
try something new with vines

Give a gardener a vine, and odds are he or she will plant it next to a trellis or an arbor. But do vines really have to be grown only on a structure? No! I recently spoke with Linda Beutler, garden writer, educator and author of "Gardening with Clematis," about landscaping with vines. She shared three creative, and sometimes surprising, ways you can put versatile vines to work in your garden.

KEEP THOSE WEEDS DOWN Vines can make excellent ground covers. See how they visually unify the group of trees in the illustration below? Or plant them to cover a bed of spring-flowering bulbs.

You'll want to choose a vine with dense foliage so it will completely shade the ground and choke out weeds. And if it's a flowering vine, varieties with blossoms that face up show best. Keep in mind that woody types, such as wisteria, won't make a dense cover. Plus, if you have to cut a woody vine back for any reason, it'll take longer to fill in again. You'll find a list of good ground cover vines at left.

In a small space, some vines may grow too quickly and will creep out into the lawn or onto a driveway. Keep a pair of shears handy and snip stems that start to sprawl too far or twine into a neighboring plant. The snipping will also stimulate more side branches so you get a denser cover. And more branches often means more blooms.

Another word of caution: Vine stems that touch the soil may take root. That can be good if you want more plants. But in a small bed, these extra vines can get out of hand and create a dense tangle that's hard to keep tidy. You'll want to remove some of the new starts.

PLANT UP A CONTAINER Grow a vine in a container as a single specimen or as part of a colorful combo. You'll find a list of good container choices at right. Just keep the pot size in balance with the size of the vine so your plant's not falling over all the time. If in doubt, go with a larger pot — a bigger mass of roots will reward you with a healthier, and more stable, plant. Provide a frame for the vine to climb, such as a spiral or obelisk, as we've done for the yellow mandevilla in the illustration at right. Train the plant to the support and keep it tidy by clipping. But don't overlook vines as the "spiller" at the edge of the pot. They're perfect in containers set up high on a wall, like the bougainvillea in our illustration.

To keep your potted vine growing happily, every year remove several inches of potting soil, down to where you find roots. Refill the container with fresh potting mix that has a handful of bone meal or slow-release fertilizer mixed into it. And after a vine has been in the same pot for four or five years, remove it, wash off all the soil and trim the roots so they're not spiraling in the container. Then use fresh potting mix to replant your vine into the same pot.

Great ground covers

Clematis *Clematis* hybrids 6 to 12 ft. tall, 3 to 6 ft. wide; blooms in spring and summer; cold-hardy in USDA zones 4 to 8; heat-tolerant in AHS zones 8 to 1; good cultivars whose up-facing flowers show well are 'The President', 'Will Goodwin' and 'Doctor Ruppel'

Five-leaf akebia *Akebia quinata* 20 to 40 ft. tall, 6 to 12 ft. wide; blooms in spring; cold-hardy in USDA zones 4 to 8; heat-tolerant in AHS zones 8 to 1

Silver lace vine *Fallopia baldschuanica* 15 to 25 ft. tall and wide; blooms in late summer; cold-hardy in USDA zones 4 to 7; heat-tolerant in AHS zones 7 to 1

Trumpet honeysuckle *Lonicera sempervirens* 6 to 12 ft. tall, 3 to 5 ft. wide; blooms in summer; cold-hardy in USDA zones 4 to 9; heat-tolerant in AHS zones 9 to 1

PHOTO: Loma Smith, courtesy of Linda Beutler

Make sure the vine will get the amount of sunlight it needs to bloom.

Clip the tips of vines, like this clematis, to keep the bed tidy.

This mockorange is the star in spring.

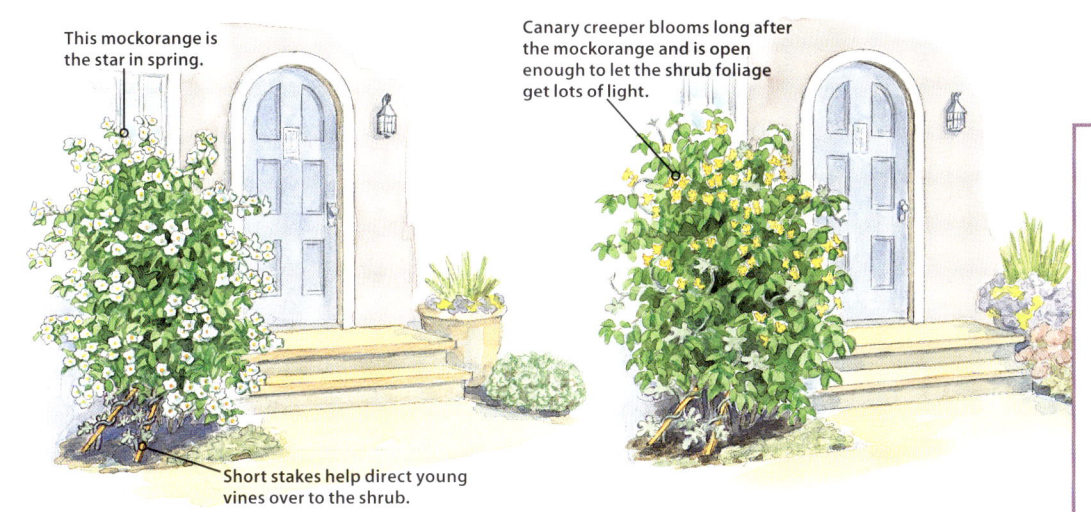

Canary creeper blooms long after the mockorange and is open enough to let the shrub foliage get lots of light.

Short stakes help direct young vines over to the shrub.

Right at home with shrubs

Canary creeper *Tropaeolum peregrinum* 4 to 10 ft. tall, 2 to 4 ft. wide; cold-hardy in USDA zones 9 to 10; heat-tolerant in AHS zones 12 to 1

Clematis *Clematis* hybrids 6 to 12 ft. tall, 3 to 6 ft. wide; blooms in spring and summer; cold-hardy in USDA zones 4 to 8; heat-tolerant in AHS zones 8 to 1

Cup and saucer vine *Cobaea scandens* 10 to 20 ft. tall, 3 to 6 ft. wide; blooms in summer; cold-hardy in USDA zones 9 to 11; heat-tolerant in AHS zones 12 to 1

Cypress vine *Ipomoea quamoclit* 6 to 20 ft. tall, 3 to 6 ft. wide; blooms all summer; annual; heat-tolerant in AHS zones 12 to 1

Sweet pea *Lathyrus odoratus* 3 to 8 ft. tall, 2 to 3 ft. wide; blooms in spring; annual; heat-tolerant in AHS zones 8 to 1

DOUBLE-DUTY PLANTING Before there were man-made supports, vines grew up into other plants, such as shrubs. And they still can. But, to avoid a messy look, choose a vine with an open and wispy habit, like the canary creeper in the illustration above. That allows the shrub to show through a bit. You'll find a list of vines that work well with shrubs at right. Just as you would on a trellis, choose a vine that's a similar height to the shrub. And annual vines, or ones that can be cut back hard each year while they're dormant, let you remove the dead stems. That way you won't end up with lots of dead stuff tangled in the branches of the shrub.

Don't combine vines with shrubs that require lots of maintenance, such as spraying for diseases or insects, constant shearing or regular deadheading. The vine will only get in the way. It's better to choose a large, open shrub, such as a mockorange, that'll age gracefully without a lot of help from you. And keep in mind that most needled evergreens don't like their foliage shaded or they'll brown out, possibly even die back.

Who doesn't love the colorful flowers and lush foliage vines have to offer? Now you have at least three more places where they can shine! □

— *Jim Childs*

Container choices

Bougainvillea *Bougainvillea* hybrid 2 to 40 ft. tall, 2 to 10 ft. wide; blooms in late spring; cold-hardy in USDA zones 9 to 12; heat-tolerant in AHS zones 12 to 1

Carolina yellow jessamine *Gelsemium sempervirens* 12 to 20 ft. tall, 3 to 6 ft. wide; blooms in spring and summer; cold-hardy in USDA zones 7 to 10; heat-tolerant in AHS zones 10 to 1

Purple bell vine *Rhodochiton atrosanguineus* 4 to 10 ft. tall, 2 to 3 ft. wide; blooms in late summer; cold-hardy in USDA zones 11 to 12; heat-tolerant in AHS zones 12 to 1

Yellow mandevilla *Pentalinon luteum* 6 to 8 ft. tall, 2 to 4 ft. wide; blooms in summer; cold-hardy in USDA zones 10 to 12; heat-tolerant in AHS zones 12 to 1

Set the containers high enough to let the vines cascade.

Set an obelisk or small trellis securely into the container if you want the vine to climb.

Botanical Names

Mockorange *Philadelphus* hybrids
Wisteria *Wisteria* spp.

DESIGN | ALL AROUND THE YARD

Make a Point

Draw attention to your garden with triangles.

Botanical Names

Boxwood *Buxus* spp.
Carolina jessamine *Gelsemium sempervirens*
Fuchsia *Fuchsia* spp.
Spruce *Picea* spp.

Have you ever simply stood and surveyed your garden? No, not looking for weeds, but just letting your eyes wander over the area? Your eyes always stop on certain things, don't they? For example, if you spot something with a point at the top, like the pyramidal topiaries in photo 1, your eye will focus on that point every time. Ever wonder why, and why this may be important to garden design? Let me explain.

Rounded and spreading plant forms are so common that they blend together and are considered neutral patterns — your eye moves easily and quickly over them. But toss a pointy pyramid, like a spruce, into the mix and your eye is drawn immediately to its contrasting shape. This contrast is what makes this pointy shape I'll call a triangle so useful in design. Let me show you five spots in your garden where triangles might come in handy. And I'll share the tips you need to know to use them successfully. We'll start at the front door.

1 MAKE IT EASY TO FIND If you've ever visited the home of a new friend and weren't quite sure where to knock, triangles could have helped. Granted, the door in photo 1 is near the center of this photo. But the pyramids framing it help draw you to it. Imagine the placement of the gracefully rounded boxwoods and the yellow Carolina jessamine topiaries reversed. You can see what I mean in the illustrations below the photo. With the pyramidal topiaries at the door, you quickly look past the rounded boxwoods. What if there's a step up from your driveway to the path? Reverse the shapes and visitors will stop at the topiaries and see the step before heading for the door. That's because shapes that meet in a point are more noticeable in a landscape than gently rounded forms are.

2 SET THE SPEED LIMIT While your eye may rest on the colorful fuchsia for a moment in photo 2, it's the bright-green triangular conifer in the distance that you focus on. Placement of a triangle can influence how quickly you move down the path. Let me show you in the illustrations below the photo how you can use triangles to pull visitors into your garden. In the first illustration, visitors look down the path and see the triangle. They'll easily and quickly move toward it, probably even passing the bench without pausing. Set the triangle at a slight bend in the path and folks will still head for it, but they'll slow down as they reach it. They might even stop to sit on the bench as they look around for the next focal point.

USE TRIANGLES TO DIRECT THE VIEW

Triangles by the door help draw visitors' attention to the door quickly.

Bring those same plants forward so visitors notice the step in the path.

LET TRIANGLES SET THE PACE ALONG A PATH

Set at a distance, a triangle or a pyramid becomes a focal point or destination, and visually draws you to it.

At the bend, a triangle set among contrasting shapes slows you down, even though you can see that the path continues.

PLAY UP TRIANGLES

Botanical Names

Boxwood *Buxus* spp.
Colorado spruce
 Picea pungens
Hydrangea
 Hydrangea paniculata
Petunia
 Petunia hybrids

Now that you've seen how the placement of a triangle can affect your garden, it's time to see more ways you can put this shape to work.

3 SHAPE UP YOUR BEDS Triangles don't have to be standing upright; they can be on a horizontal plane, too. Notice how the lines of the ground cover bed lead you to a path? And so you really don't miss the path, pyramidal boxwoods add extra emphasis to this entry spot.

Working with a limited area? Use triangular beds to make it appear larger. Plan the broad base of a triangle near where you will view the garden the most. As the lines along the sides point into the distance, your eye follows them, looking for the spot where they come together. Visually you focus on where the point might be, not the area directly in front of you, so your mind translates that to distance.

Now, you may be saying that triangles like these tend to look a bit formal, and I'd agree with you. But check out how triangle bed shapes can be either formal or informal in the two illustrations below photo 3.

4 TRIANGLE COMBINATIONS There's nothing that says pyramids can be used only as specimens. Unless triangles are the most common shape in the entire garden, they'll still draw your attention. So go ahead and group several together, like the planting in photo 4. Here three distinct triangle shapes and sizes — the broad Colorado spruce, the tightly clipped spiral topiary and the smaller hydrangea flowers — work together to create one pleasing focal point. Since the shapes and sizes are varied, your eyes slowly travel around them, looking at all of the points. But like all good combos, this one has a contrasting shape to keep it balanced. Can you spot it? It's the bold horizontal mass of petunias.

POINT FOLKS IN THE RIGHT DIRECTION

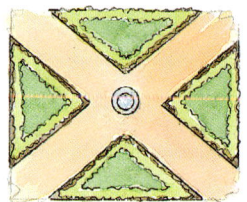

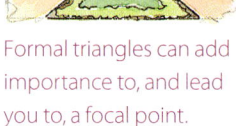

Formal triangles can add importance to, and lead you to, a focal point.

Beds seem larger when the broadest side of the triangle is closest to you.

5 ENLARGE A SMALL SPACE Vertical triangles can make a small garden feel spacious. Plant a triangle with a sharp point and your eye is drawn to the top and then past it. When you look up, you're less likely to notice how close the boundaries of the garden really are. Repeating narrow pyramids in a small space, like the Irish yews in photo 5, doesn't take up much area. But they do make an excellent contrast to the rounded perennials and shrubs as well as the horizontal line of the top of the fence. As you look up you'll forget about being enclosed in this courtyard. Like the idea? Learn about 5 more "pointers" in "5 slender choices" to the far right.

So, will your garden be fine without a triangle? Sure. But if you want to set your garden a "point" above the rest, try a triangle or two. □

— *Jim Childs*

MAKE INTERESTING GROUPS

Vary the shape, size and direction of the triangles when they're in a grouping like this. Lots of similar shapes and sizes together can look monotonous. But here a mass of various sizes of the same shape becomes a large focal point framed by a horizontal mass of petunias.

5 SLENDER CHOICES

There are many great triangular evergreens. However, in a small space, you want height but not much width. Check out these narrow triangles for your garden.

Arborvitae *Thuja occidentalis* 'Emerald' ('Smaragd'); evergreen; 15 ft. tall and 3 to 4 ft. wide; cold-hardy in USDA zones 4 to 8; heat-tolerant in AHS zones 8 to 1

Dwarf Alberta spruce *Picea glauca albertiana* 'Conica'; evergreen; grows slowly to 8 ft. tall and 5 ft. wide; cold-hardy in USDA zones 2 to 8; heat-tolerant in AHS zones 8 to 1

Irish yew *Taxus baccata* 'Fastigiata Robusta'; in photo; evergreen; up to 30 ft. tall and less than 8 ft. wide; cold-hardy in USDA zones 6 to 9; heat-tolerant in AHS zones 9 to 1

Japanese holly *Ilex crenata* 'Sky Pencil'; broadleaf evergreen; 6 to 8 ft. tall and 2 to 3 ft. wide; cold-hardy in USDA zones 5 to 9; heat-tolerant in AHS zones 9 to 1

Juniper *Juniperus scopulorum* 'Skyrocket'; evergreen; up to 20 ft. tall and less than 5 ft. wide; cold-hardy in USDA zones 5 to 9; heat-tolerant in AHS zones 9 to 1

DESIGN | ALL AROUND THE YARD

rain gardens
filter rain water *and* beautify your yard!

Have you ever watched the sheets of water flowing down your driveway during a rainstorm and wondered where it goes? That water goes into storm sewers, often carrying surface pollutants with it. Eventually the water ends up in lakes, streams and rivers. What if I told you that you could keep more of that water on your property and filter it at the same time? It's easier than you think!

All you need is a rain garden, a shallow, plant-filled depression that catches and holds water. As the water percolates through the root-filled soil, pollutants are filtered out. And the rain soaks deep into the ground, helping replenish local underground water supplies.

Plus, a rain garden will attract birds, butterflies and lots of compliments, too. To figure out how to make a rain garden, I spoke with Lisa Reas. As the owner of LJ Reas Environmental Consulting Corporation in Green Lake, Wisconsin, she has designed and installed many rain gardens. She shared these helpful tips.

SIZE IT UP Start by looking at the water draining from your house through your downspouts. In the best case scenario, the size of the rain garden should match the size of the roof area that feeds into it. As an example, the house in this illustration has a footprint of about 1800 square feet. We estimate that a sixth of the roof, or 300 square feet, drains to the downspout just off the driveway. To handle the runoff, the rain garden in the foreground of the illustration ideally should be 300 square feet, too.

You could make one big rain garden if you could direct several downspouts into it. However, it's often easier to build a separate one near each downspout. That way you won't have to run long extensions to carry the water. So, to handle water from another part of this roof there's a second rain garden near the back of the house in the upper right hand corner of the illustration. You'll find a detailed plan, including plant choices, for this garden on the next pages.

Rain gardens can be any size you wish. Bottom line: Any size rain garden is better than none. Even if they can't hold all of the water, the excess will flow out onto the lawn. Just make sure it won't flow onto a neighbor's property.

FIND THE BEST SPOT To keep water from seeping into your basement, rain gardens should be at least 10 feet down-slope from your foundation. The house above has underground tile to route the water directly into the front garden, and a dry stream bed sends water to the back garden. Downspout extensions would also work for this.

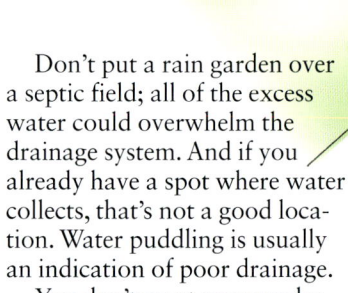

Don't put a rain garden over a septic field; all of the excess water could overwhelm the drainage system. And if you already have a spot where water collects, that's not a good location. Water puddling is usually an indication of poor drainage.

You don't want your garden to breed mosquitoes, either. They need seven to 12 days to lay and hatch eggs, so make sure your water drains within 24 hours and you'll be fine. Before you install, find out if your soil drains quickly enough: Dig a hole 6 to 8 inches deep and fill it with water. If the water doesn't drain away in a day, try another spot.

THEY'RE EVEN EASY CARE
Depending on how much rain you receive, you may need to do some extra watering the first two years to get the garden established. When you water, soak the soil deeply to encourage plant roots to grow down into the soil.

Now that you have the basics, it's time to dig the basin. Check out "You can dig it!" at right. Then, on the next pages I'll share a rain garden design, along with some moisture-loving plants.

PHOTO: Courtesy of Ginnie Judd   ILLUSTRATIONS: Travis Rice

148 *the* YEAR IN GARDENING   www.GardenGateMagazine.com

A rain garden doesn't have to stand out in the middle of your lawn. Check out our plan on the next pages for this one integrated into a border.

Calculate how much of your roof drains to the downspout to help you determine how big to make your rain garden.

You don't want a wet basement, so place your rain garden at least 10 ft. from your foundation.

Buried drain tile

Instead of washing into the street, roof runoff is directed to a rain garden.

Even if your rain garden can't hold all the runoff from your roof, it's better than having no rain garden at all.

YOU CAN DIG IT!

The average rain garden should be set in a 6- to 8-in. basin with a level bottom, so water flows evenly into all parts of it. However, if you plan to add mulch, dig the garden about 2 in. deeper.

TAKE TWO STAKES After you test for drainage, locate your utilities and have the best location, you want to stake out the area. As you see in the illustration below, you'll need at least two stakes. Drive one into the ground at the highest point where you're putting your rain garden, and the second one down-slope. Tie a string as low as you can on the upper stake. Attach a string level on it (you can pick one up at your local hardware store) and stretch the string to the lower stake. Adjust the string until it's level and then tie it to the stake. This is your guide as you dig.

START DIGGING You want the bottom to be level, so starting at the lowest stake, remove just a thin layer of soil. As you continue digging toward the upper stake, dig deeper and toss the soil just outside the lowest stake to build a berm.

CHECK THAT LEVEL As you dig, frequently check the distance from the string to the bottom of the basin to make sure the bottom is level. For a large garden, pound in extra stakes around the low side and run strings to the highest stake so you have more spots where you can check the level.

ADD THE FINISHING TOUCHES To give your plants the best start, till the basin and rake it level before planting. Then gently slope the edges so they won't collapse when the soil's saturated. After you finish planting, spread 2 in. of mulch to keep the garden moist between rains, free of weeds and looking good.

Gently slope the edges of the basin.

DOWN-SLOPE

Soil dug from the bottom of the basin is piled on the low side to form a berm that is as high, or higher, than the edge on the up-slope side.

Lower stakes

String and string level

Upper stake

UP-SLOPE

This basin is 8 in. deep.

Water ways

You'll need to guide water down any degree of slope and into the garden. Where the water enters the garden, break the flow with a large rock or let the water spill out onto a piece of flagstone to help prevent erosion.

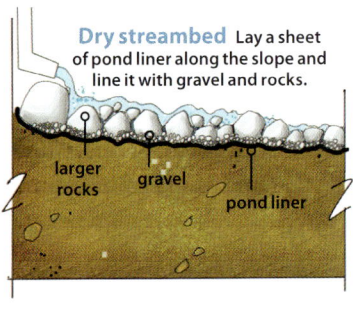

Dry streambed Lay a sheet of pond liner along the slope and line it with gravel and rocks.

larger rocks · gravel · pond liner

Underground tile Attach field drain tile to your downspout and bury it at least 4 to 6 in. under the sod.

plastic drain tile

control runoff *and* enjoy a beautiful rain garden

Can you have a beautiful garden and improve the environment at the same time? We think so. Rain gardens can look like any other part of your garden, just specifically designed to collect runoff. So, the plants will need to tolerate periods of wet soil. However, since the soil will dry out between rains, you don't want aquatics, or plants that need constant or standing water. Your selections will have to survive dry periods, too.

In a rain garden 200 square feet or larger, you can add structure with a few shrubs, as I've done here. Even a small tree or two is fine. But don't overdo them. Large trees and shrubs can be water hogs that rob smaller plants of moisture. Go for just a few specimens and choose small or dwarf varieties — they'll look more in scale with the size of most rain gardens.

Water for this garden is carried in a dry streambed from the downspout to the basin. You can see how to build a streambed like this one, as well as an invisible routing option, in "Water ways" at left.

The two flagstone terraces support the wooden bridge, which is held 6 inches above the bottom of the rain garden. A couple of concrete blocks support the center of the bridge yet still let rain water flow into the entire garden.

What could be better? You get to enjoy a beautiful garden and protect your local water source, too. □

— *Jim Childs*

8 GREAT PLANTS for a rain garden

Plant list (Number to plant)

A **Winterberry holly** *Ilex verticillata*
Red Sprite ('Nana') (2) and 'Jim Dandy' (1)
3 to 5 ft. tall and wide; deciduous holly; female Red Sprite has bright red winter fruit; need male 'Jim Dandy' to pollinate; cold-hardy in USDA zones 4 to 8; heat-tolerant in AHS zones 8 to 1

B **Gray sedge** *Carex grayi* (23)
24 to 30 in. tall and 18 in. wide; bright green grasslike foliage; spiked seed heads; cold-hardy in USDA zones 5 to 9; heat-tolerant in AHS zones 9 to 1

C **Tatarian aster** *Aster tataricus* 'Jindai' (5)
4 to 6 ft. tall and 2 ft. wide; tall, stiff spires of lavender flowers in late fall; cold-hardy in USDA zones 4 to 8; heat-tolerant in AHS zones 8 to 1

D **Sweet coneflower** *Rudbeckia subtomentosa* 'Henry Eilers' (4)
4 to 5 ft. tall and 18 to 24 in. wide; bright yellow flowers with quilled petals from summer into fall; cold-hardy in USDA zones 4 to 8; heat-tolerant in AHS zones 8 to 1

E **Blue lobelia** *Lobelia siphilitica* (20)
3 ft. tall and 12 to 18 in. wide; long-blooming true-blue flowers in mid- to late summer; cold-hardy in USDA zones 5 to 9; heat-tolerant in AHS zones 9 to 1

F **Spiderwort** *Tradescantia virginiana* (11)
18 to 24 in. tall and 18 in. wide; grassy foliage and long-blooming clusters of lavender-blue flowers in summer; cold-hardy in USDA zones 4 to 9; heat-tolerant in AHS zones 9 to 1

G **Little bluestem** *Schizachyrium scoparium* (11)
2 to 4 ft. tall and 18 to 24 in. wide; native grass with blue-tinted foliage that turns shades of orange and red in fall; cold-hardy in USDA zones 4 to 9; heat-tolerant in AHS zones 9 to 1

H **Bee balm** *Monarda* 'Gardenview Scarlet' (6)
2 to 3 ft. tall and 1 to 2 ft. wide; bright red flowers in summer; cold-hardy in USDA zones 3 to 9; heat-tolerant in AHS zones 9 to 1

Scale: 1 square = 1 square foot

DESIGN | BACK YARD

Make any garden more manageable with smart design tips.

The Big Picture

Botanical Names

Azalea
Rhododendron spp.
Hosta *Hosta* hybrid
Rhododendron
Rhododendron spp.
Yucca *Yucca filamentosa*

PHOTO: Rob Cardillo

Have you ever heard the expression, "your eyes were bigger than your stomach"? Well, sometimes you end up with more garden space than you can easily manage. So how can you make the big garden dramatic without being a slave to its upkeep?

CURB YOUR IMPULSES Your first impulse may be to buy lots of perennials to fill it up. But in a big space, that can be expensive, not to mention high maintenance, with all the deadheading, dividing and such. The key is to use plants that will grow larger, like trees and shrubs, to make a frame for the garden. And structures can come in handy to fill up a large space, too. Then fill in with perennials and annuals.

That's just what Inta Krombolz from Pennsylvania did in her 75-by-150-foot border garden. To start, she chose shrubs and trees with a variety of forms, colors and textures. But there are still plenty of flowers. The season kicks off with some spring bulbs and several early flowering shrubs, such as azaleas and rhododendrons. Mixed in among all of the shrubs are a few low-maintenance perennials, such as grasses, yuccas and hostas, to keep the area ever-changing. You could even tuck in a few summer-blooming annuals if you like.

The rustic arbor on the left side of this photo is a visual element rather than a protective structure. It never needs painting and makes a great focal point. A large container in front of it adds interest, and can be filled with different plants as the seasons progress. Last but not least, several small, colorful metal ornaments add even more interest to the area. You still notice them, however, they don't steal the show.

But let's not get ahead of ourselves — we've only looked at a piece of this garden so far. There's a lot more to see and tips to be shared, so let's examine more of this lovely border.

(1) Want to draw attention to a path? This stone apron juts into the lawn to let you know there's a path among the plants.

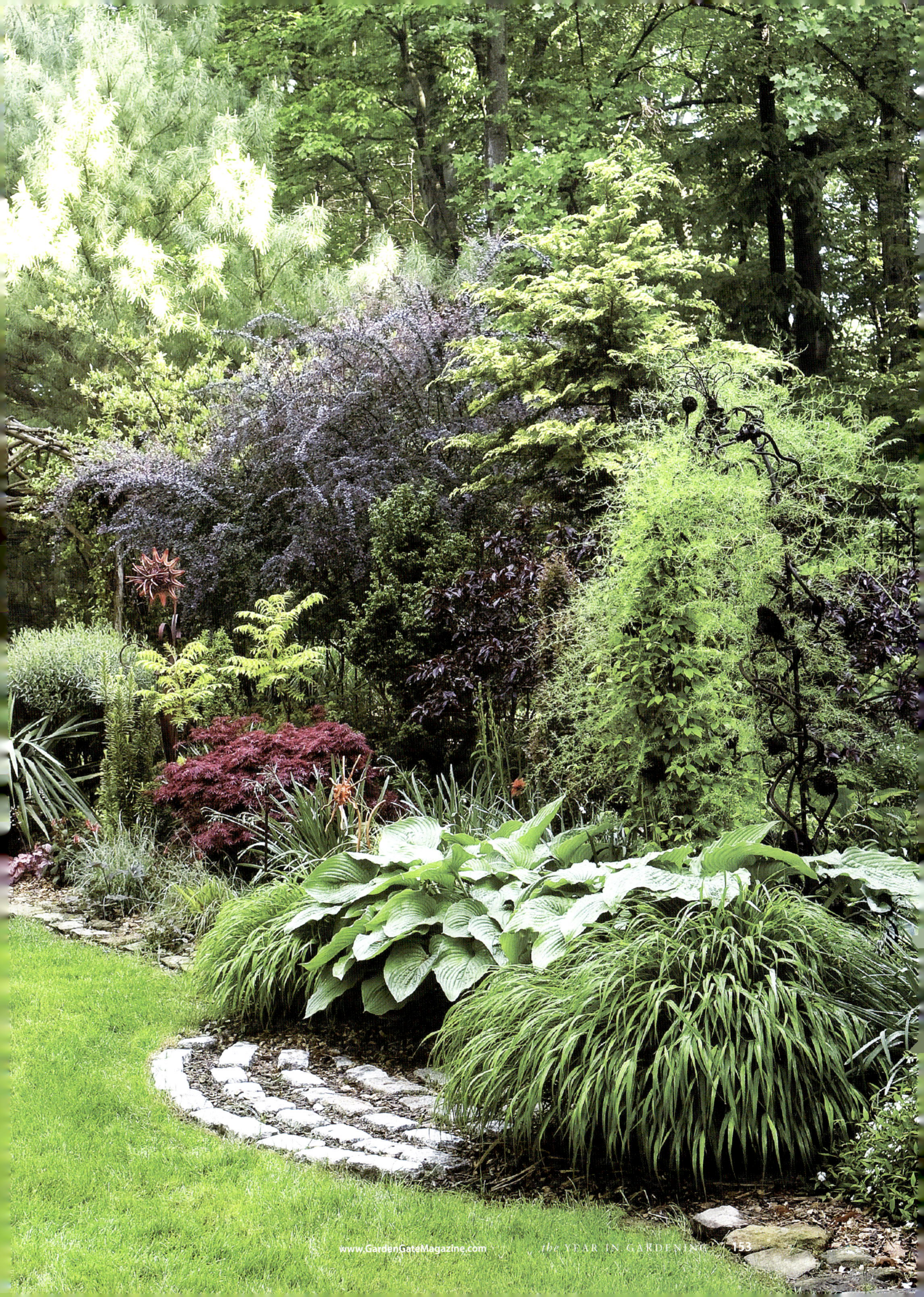

DESIGNING A BIG GARDEN

Step into the garden, and this is what you'll see. It's late summer, so the red salvia, orange impatiens and other annuals in front of the arbor are at their peak. Some of the trees and shrubs are beginning to take on the tints of fall. It's a great time to be in the garden, and there's lots to look at in this one.

MIX IT UP A BIT This part of the garden has a neutral backdrop of large trees that stops your eye. These trees make this area feel more enclosed. To fill the bed in front of them, there's a creative mix of plants. For example, shrubs don't have to be relegated to just the background. Go ahead and bring a few down near the front edge of the border. Take a look at the very vertical 'Helmond Pillar' barberries used here. They seem perfectly natural scattered through the center and front of the garden. Two fine-textured dwarf arctic blue willows frame the arbor. They obscure part of the structure, as well as the garden, creating curiosity about what might be tucked behind them.

But don't go overboard with too many shrubs near the front. After all, you still want to see the rest of the garden behind them. Choose shrubs that have a unique shape, colorful foliage or a fine texture, like the ones just mentioned. Want something

White pine
'Helmond Pillar' barberry
Dwarf arctic blue willow

Give it an edge Nothing adds a finished look to any garden more than a crisp, clean, well-defined edge. These large, rough stones are in scale with the size of this big garden. In a smaller garden you'd want to use smaller stones or paving bricks.

Scale matters Your border will look best if the plants are in scale with their surroundings. Grow plants whose heights are 1½ times the width of your border. For example, if your bed is 12 ft. wide, the tallest plants can be around 18 ft. tall.

A "small" tip
Don't have room for a full-size tree? Look for a shrub that has a similar appearance. The white pines in the background have a very fine texture. But if you don't have room for a 50-ft. tree, grow a dwarf white pine that stays less than 8 ft. tall.

larger? Go with shrubs, such as lilacs, that have a loose or open branching habit. They'll add some interest, as well as mystery about what's behind them, but won't completely block your view or stop your eye from looking at the rest of the garden.

REPEAT AGAIN As you look at the rustic arbor, you'll notice that several of the plants, such as the red salvias, the two gold-tipped false cypresses and the upright barberries, have been repeated. They all help balance the scene, especially when the garden is seen from a distance. Repetition like this helps avoid a hodgepodge and gives any garden a well-planned look.

Using a much more noticeable formal balance, like the two spiky yuccas in front of the arbor, can be helpful, too. Compared to the rest of the garden, matched specimens like these really stand out. Why? Because the foliage texture contrast draws your eye to them, adding emphasis to the area around the arbor.

You'll need paths to get into the beds. Some you'll want hidden, for maintenance purposes only. But a simple concrete ball draws attention to the path and shed.

And the concrete bench provides a perfect spot to sit and relax. But our tour's not over, so don't sit down yet.

Botanical Names

Arctic blue willow *Salix purpurea* 'Nana'
Barberry *Berberis thunbergii*
Daylily *Hemerocallis* hybrid
Elephant ear *Colocasia esculenta*
False cypress *Chamaecyparis* spp.
Hakonechloa *Hakonechloa macra*
Impatiens *Impatiens* hybrid
Lilac *Syringa vulgaris*
Peony *Paeonia* spp.
Salvia *Salvia splendens*
White pine *Pinus strobus*
Yucca *Yucca filamentosa*

False cypress

Go with low maintenance
If a perennial needs to be babied, this is probably not the garden where you want to plant it. You'll enjoy the garden more if you make selections, such as peonies and daylilies, that don't require lots of extra watering, feeding, deadheading or dividing.

Add year-round appeal
Combine plants that look great at different times, or have interesting foliage or structure. This hakonechloa looks good most of the year, while the giant leaves of 'Black Magic' elephant ear behind it add interesting contrast during the summer growing season.

(2) Broad steps on the left are gentle enough to drive a lawn tractor up or down for yard work.

STRUCTURES AND SURROUNDINGS

Botanical Names

Hakonechloa
Hakonechloa macra
Hosta
Hosta hybrid
Impatiens
Impatiens hybrid
Giant dogwood
Cornus controversa

The garden you've been touring is in front of the house, just off the driveway. As you walk toward the garden, you're drawn forward by glimpses of white. Variegated foliage stands out dramatically against all of the dark green leaves and attracts your attention. Two large specimens of variegated giant dogwood in photo 2, above, create that curiosity. Walk down the broad, sloped steps and you get the full effect of these stunning trees. But once you enter the garden and step past them, your focus moves on to other plants and objects. Since the two trees are near the entrance of this garden, they don't compete with the rest of the border, allowing other focal points to lead you further into this large garden.

INVESTIGATE MICROCLIMATES Much of this garden is sunny, but look underneath the trees and you'll discover a collection of hostas, as well as other shade-loving plants. In any size garden, it's nice to create pockets, or microclimates, like these. You'll be able to grow shade-loving plants under trees or on the north and east side of tall, dense shrubs.

ADD FUNCTIONAL GARDEN ORNAMENTS Who likes traipsing back to the garage all of the time for tools? Not only does the small potting shed in photo 3 make a great garden ornament, and fill some space in a large garden, it can be functional, too. This 4-foot-square structure is perfect for an extra shovel or two, as well as a few other frequently used tools.

You'll notice in the two photos at right that this garden, just like most any garden, has changed and evolved. Several years ago colorful impatiens were planted on both sides of the path every spring. They did a perfectly good job of drawing your view to the path. But for lower maintenance, the two large hostas and clumps of hakonechloa only need to be planted once and can be left alone for many years.

Well, we've made it all the way around the garden. But, there's one more thing to point out — the broad flat lawn in the center. It gives you a place to stand and admire the beds or even play a game of croquet. And the smooth expanse of lawn against the varied textures of the beds really makes a striking contrast.

After touring a great garden like this, I'm always inspired to head home and re-examine mine — especially when I have great new design tips to try out. ◻

— *Jim Childs*

Repeat some of the same plants on both sides of a focal point structure to add balance and draw more attention to the area.

Scatter a few stepping stones among the plants in the border so you have a dry, comfortable place to stand when you're working.

Since the twig arbor doesn't show from far away, but the solid walls of the potting shed do, these two structures don't compete visually.

A smooth lawn gives you a place to relax or play when you're finished gardening.

▶ This symbol indicates the direction the photo was taken in the garden.

(3) Gardens evolve over time. After colorful annuals filled this space for several years, the planting scheme changed to bold hostas that don't need to be replaced each spring.

DESIGN | BACK YARD

THE WEEKEND GARDEN SMARTER GARDENER

Time to Relax

Create a low-care garden getaway.

It's the end of a busy week, and everybody needs a little down time. The best place to spend that time is in a comfortable, private retreat that's quiet and easy to get to. Unlike a large deck or patio with room for cooking and seating for lots of guests, a private getaway, by its very nature, tends to be small and intimate. Contrary to what you may think, creating a garden retreat doesn't have to be a big or expensive undertaking.

FIRST THINGS FIRST Before you do anything, you need to decide where to place your retreat. Depending on how you want to use it, your personal space might be a secret corner to curl up with a good book, a secluded bench for a private conversation or a tiny table for two on a cozy patio. The way you use it will determine where it goes. A personal reading room could easily be tucked into a shady corner far from the phone. But if you'll need to carry food or beverages, a little closer to the house makes more sense.

EASY-GOING GARDEN Placing a private retreat in the garden is a great way to enjoy color and fragrance as you relax, but not if your surroundings need constant attention to look nice. Use the wrong plants and you'll never get to sit down, or, if you do, you'll be nagged by the work that needs to be done. To simplify both your color theme and maintenance chores, choose a few different types of low-maintenance plants and repeat them, like the black-eyed Susans and coleus here. Using ones and twos of lots of plants looks mismatched and increases the chance that some type of garden task needs to be done every day.

Amend the soil with lots of well-rotted manure or other organic matter before you plant. It will provide more nutrition for your plants, making them healthy and strong. That cuts down on fertilizing and you'll see fewer pests and diseases.

And though it's a little more work on the front end, hardscaping cuts down on a lot of work in the long run. A brick patio like this one is much easier to take care of than lawn or a mulched area. For more help to make your getaway as comfortable and functional as possible, check out the tips at right. ☐

— *Deborah Gruca*

Botanical Names

Black-eyed Susan
Rudbeckia spp.
Coleus *Solenostemon* hybrids

Sized right A getaway for one or two doesn't need to be large. Find a corner in your yard for a bench in the shade or a small table and a couple of chairs. When you have seating, allow for 2 ft. of space out from the perimeter of the table to pull the chairs out and walk behind seated visitors. (And, in a small space like this, when you need more seating, you can fit more chairs around a round table than a rectangular or square one.)

Privacy matters Just because you want to get away doesn't mean you have to travel miles to do it. After all, we're talking about a getaway in your own back yard. A change of level — even the single step down to this patio — signals a separation from the rest of the garden.

Another option to create a feeling of protection is a canopy of branches, or even a man-made structure, such as a pergola, overhead. And for a sense of privacy, you need some means of screening your area from its surroundings. A fence offers instant seclusion and there are lots of options. You can see through the pickets in this fence, so you don't feel too cut off from the rest of the world. A warm brown stain that recedes a bit keeps you from feeling hemmed in. Prefer paint? Prep the surface first and use a good-quality coating, so the finish will last as long as possible.

Find furniture When choosing the furniture, consider how you'll be using it. An Adirondack chair or hammock is comfortable and great for relaxing and resting in the shade. But if you'll be eating a meal, sitting at a table is easier and makes more sense. The small round table here is big enough for two to three. Light metal chairs don't require maintenance and can be left outside all summer.

DESIGN | BACK YARD

Bring a blank canvas to life with an ever-changing palette.

Nature's Masterpiece

160 *the* YEAR IN GARDENING   www.GardenGateMagazine.com

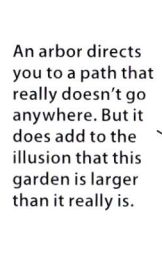

Have you ever thought of your garden as a work of art? Jane LaFlash does. While she loves to spend time outdoors in her Wisconsin garden, it's not always possible. Cold, snowy winter weather and even summer rainstorms mean days spent inside. But Jane has found a way to enjoy the beauty of her garden no matter what's happening with the weather.

Instead of hanging a framed picture on the wall, Jane uses her garden as art. She frames her garden view with a large picture window. And it isn't just a happy accident that this idea works so well. There are some tricks of the trade you can use to make your own garden a work of art.

START AT THE WINDOW A single, large pane of glass means an uninterrupted view. And no curtain implies that you could step into the garden as if you were walking through a doorway. From inside the house, even at a distance from the window, you have a clear view of this garden. If you'd like to try this but are worried about privacy, check the views from your garden window to figure out where you need some taller trees and shrubs. Or maybe a solid fence and lots of plantings will ensure privacy in your back yard.

Notice how some tall plants just outside extend over the edges of the window? That's a good way to blur the line between inside and outside. Want to make an even stronger connection? Set a few plants on or near the windowsill inside the house. That way you're less likely to notice the hard edges of the window frame.

COMPOSE THE SCENE The single birch standing in the lawn is a strong focal point in this picture. Because of its white bark and architectural form, your eye is drawn directly to it. You're much less likely to notice the window frame because you quickly look past it to the tree and garden. And the branches in the top of the frame add a "ceiling," or feeling of enclosure, to the scene.

In the illustration above, you can see that there is a small lawn in the center of the garden. When looking out the window, this bit of turf area allows you an uninterupted view. In other words, it helps add depth and dimension to the picture. You not only see the garden, but like a good painting, you're visually pulled into it. Having a lawn just not your thing? A patio, deck or any kind of open space would work just as well.

AN EVER-CHANGING SCENE This garden view has all the qualities of a fine painting or photograph that you might hang on your wall. But it's a picture that changes with the seasons. The lush look of spring and summer gives way to evergreens for the winter. Plus the structures, like the bench and the arbor, will become much more noticeable when the foliage has turned color and dropped. And did you notice the ornaments tucked in among the perennials? They'll become an important part of the scene when there aren't as many plants to draw your attention.

If you want to learn more design points to make your garden into a work of art, just turn the page.

Botanical Names

Birch *Betula papyrifera*

Illustration callouts:

- An arbor directs you to a path that really doesn't go anywhere. But it does add to the illusion that this garden is larger than it really is.
- The white bark on this birch makes an excellent focal point in any season.
- This bench gives you a spot where you can relax and enjoy a view similar to the one you see when you're indoors.
- 30 ft.
- 50 ft.
- N
- Birch tree
- Lawn
- Panoramic photo
- Patio
- House
- Lead photo taken from picture window

FOCUS ON **DESIGN**

Gardens don't have to be built on a grand scale to be beautiful. In the panoramic shot below you see nearly all of this well-designed garden. But several design techniques help this 30-by-50-foot area look bigger than it really is. Let's take a closer look at how you can use these design ideas in your garden.

WHAT YOU SEE... Even though parts of the wooden privacy fence show in the background, you'll notice that the property lines have been disguised by plantings. You can't see exactly where the edges are, so you're really not sure how large this garden actually is. The plants are dense in some areas and open in others. And they're planted in layers, with a mix of heights, too. That means it's easy to see back into the border, but only in a few spots. Even the lower branches of well-established white pines, with their wispy needles, droop below and soften the horizontal line created by the fence.

FOCUS YOUR ATTENTION While the birch is a strong focal point, this garden has several others, too. In any garden, multiple focal points work if they're on a descending scale. In other words, pick one large one, like the birch; then add a medium-sized one, such

Mix it up A variety of textures and colors makes the area more interesting. That's why in this shade garden you'll find large, bold hostas, as well as lots of other plants with finer foliage, like the white pine, Canadian hemlock and burgundy Japanese maples. While you often hear that you should plant in groupings, that may not be possible in a small garden like this. So, instead, be sure to repeat a few of the plants, such as the Japanese maples, for a unified look.

Angling for interest Let's face it. Most of us have rectangular gardens. But if you can distract the eye from all of those square corners that indicate a boundary, your garden will have the illusion of being bigger. That's why this arbor is placed at an "odd" angle. (It's odd because it doesn't line up with anything around it.) And the path that goes through it meanders back into the distance, behind plantings. Even in a small garden you can create a bit of mystery with careful planning.

as the arbor, in another area; and finally, a small one, like the statue of Shiva in the back. Because they're different sizes and forms, as well as made from different materials, they work together and don't compete for attention with the plants.

GO EASY ON ORNAMENTS There are just a few unobtrusive ornaments nestled among the plants. They have a common theme, Hindu figures, and show well enough to draw your attention, but not so much that you don't see the garden around them first. And later, when the plants go dormant for the winter, they'll come into their own as focal points.

If you like what you've seen, there's still more. Along the bottom of the photo you'll discover four more design tips. While they're pointing out specific elements in this small back yard, each one will help you design your garden, no matter what size it may be.

Whether you're planting on a nice spring day or trapped inside on a cold, snowy one, you can still enjoy the outdoors. Use all of these design tips to turn your garden into an ever-changing piece of art you can enjoy indoors or out.

— *Jim Childs*

Botanical Names

Birch *Betula papyrifera*
Canadian hemlock *Tsuga canadensis*
Hosta *Hosta* hybrids
Japanese maple *Acer palmatum*
White pine *Pinus strobus*

BEFORE

Soften hard lines Take a look at this "before" shot. See all the angles and straight lines? Tree trunks, fences, even the buildings in neighbors' yards kept this back yard from looking like a garden. The lines and angles are all still there, but now layers of plants have blurred or softened them so they blend into the garden better.

Plan for the future No garden is ever really finished. As this garden grows, things will need to change. These Canadian hemlocks will grow to be much too large for this area. But they can be sheared. Or in 20 years or more, as the trees mature, some of the lower limbs could be removed to raise the canopy, and a new garden can go in underneath.

www.GardenGateMagazine.com   *the* YEAR IN GARDENING   163

DESIGN | COLOR PALETTE

Secrets the pros know (but rarely share)

COLOR

Like most people, you probably have a favorite color that you're drawn to. And although that's a good place to start, odds are you won't want to plant your whole garden in one color. So how do you create color schemes? Let me share secrets the pros use when they design gardens. We'll start by seeing what individual colors can do. Then, on the next pages, I'll show you some combos that highlight these colors and I'll help you understand how you can make color work for you.

For this article, just think of true colors, no tints or shades. For example, when you read red, think of a ripe cherry or a fire engine. Yellow is like sunshine on a summer day. Blue reminds me of the sky or the deep ocean. Green? Think of the healthiest oak leaf you've ever seen. Get the picture? Let's take a look.

EXCITING RED This is the color of excitement, strength, danger, passion and desire. Use red where you want to draw attention, maybe at your front door — your eye is immediately pulled to it.

Red is a hot color, just like orange and yellow. Use lots of red in a large garden and the space feels cozier. Imagine a border with a red Japanese maple, a hedge of dark barberries and red shrub roses. Not only does it look warm, but the garden appears smaller because red looks closer to you than it really is. But use this color sparingly in a small space or you may feel crowded. And surprisingly, too much red, especially in a small garden, can seem gloomy.

DEMANDING ORANGE You'd have a difficult time relaxing in a garden planted with all orange. This color is full of enthusiasm, determination and stimulation. A bed filled with Mexican sunflowers and orange cosmos may not be good if you use your garden as a peaceful retreat. But that combo would be great where you like to enter-

Fiesta™ Salsa Red impatiens

'Prinses Irene' tulip

Gerbera daisy

Easy Wave™ Beachcomber petunia

Lady's mantle

Blue Wave hydrangea

tain. And rather than an entire garden of orange, a touch of it here and there will still draw attention and stimulate other color schemes to keep them from being boring.

Other hot colors make good companions for orange. A combo of red sage and orange nasturtiums is energizing. But if you want to calm down those nasturtiums, go with a blue or violet sage.

CHEERFUL YELLOW Joy, happiness and energy come to mind when you look at bright yellow. A border with goldenrod and scarlet mums would cheer up a cool autumn day. But be careful when you combine any of the hot colors like this: Each one is a scene stealer. To avoid chaos, try to use similar amounts of each color. And be sure to use lots of green foliage as a frame. Green is always a good peacemaker between any colors. To keep the goldenrod and mum in harmony and under control, plant them in front of a leafy green hedge or let the foliage from an earlier-flowering perennial weave in among them just a bit.

SERIOUS VIOLET This cool color is somber, great for toning down exuberant orange, yellow or red. However, in doing so, violet often gets lost. Mix red geraniums with violet petunias and at first glance you'll barely notice the petunias. Violet tends to disappear at a distance — probably not a good color for the back of your garden. Enjoy it along a path, near your patio or in a windowbox outside the kitchen window.

AGREEABLE BLUE Blue is the coolest of the cools. Because it has that association with sea and sky that I mentioned earlier, it imparts a feeling of space and distance. Remember how red always seems to move forward and make a garden feel cozy and close? Blue recedes, so it makes a small garden feel a bit larger than it really is. And blue, like the hydrangea in the photo above, is terrific in the evening garden. This color is visible to your eyes later into the twilight than any other color except white.

PEACEFUL GREEN Freshness is often associated with the color green. And since green makes a great companion for most all garden combos, either hot, cool or even a combination of colors, it's the color of harmony and peace. That's good, because it would be hard to create a garden without green. In fact, try to imagine your garden with no green in it. You can't, can you? Is green your favorite color? An all-green color scheme can draw, and hold, your attention as well as a garden full of flowers. Fill a shady garden with clumps of deep-green ferns, yellow-green epimedium and a few hostas with some blue in their foliage for a fresh-looking and peaceful combo.

On the next pages, I'll share plant combinations and design secrets for highlighting these colors.

Botanical Names

Barberry *Berberis thunbergii*
Cosmos *Cosmos sulphureus*
Epimedium *Epimedium* spp.
Geranium *Pelargonium* hybrid
Gerbera daisy *Gerbera* hybrid
Goldenrod *Solidago* spp.
Hosta *Hosta* hybrid
Hydrangea *Hydrangea* spp.
Impatiens *Impatiens* hybrid
Japanese maple *Acer palmatum*
Lady's mantle *Alchemilla mollis*
Mexican sunflower *Tithonia rotundifolia*
Mum *Chrysanthemum* hybrid
Nasturtium *Tropaeolum majus*
Petunia *Petunia* hybrid
Rose *Rosa* hybrid
Sage *Salvia* spp.
Tulip *Tulipa* hybrid

Look my way Red is the ideal color to use near a front door — you can't help but notice it. You don't need a lot of it; even a small bit of red, like this clump of Scarlet Meidiland roses, leads you directly to the entrance. Your eye may slow down just a bit to look at the peachy 'Flutterby' roses and gray lamb's ear. But in the end, the red always wins. Use it to highlight a focal point. Or plant it away from your compost pile. Visitors are less likely to notice the pile of weeds if they have a red distraction.

- **A** Rose *Rosa* Scarlet Meidiland ('Meikrotal'); 3 to 4 ft. tall and 6 ft. wide; blooms in summer; cold-hardy in USDA zones 4 to 9; heat-tolerant in AHS zones 9 to 1
- **B** Rose *Rosa* 'Flutterby'; 4 to 8 ft. tall, 3 to 5 ft. wide; summer blooming; cold-hardy in USDA zones 5 to 10; heat-tolerant in AHS zones 10 to 1
- **C** Lamb's ear *Stachys byzantina*; 8 to 10 in. tall, 12 to 18 in. wide; cold-hardy in USDA zones 4 to 8; heat-tolerant in AHS zones 8 to 1

MAKING COLOR WORK FOR YOU

Whether you're designing a perennial border, landscaping your foundation, or just placing a few containers on your deck, color is important. Sometimes a picture really is worth a thousand words, so I've pulled together four photos to help illustrate how color can work for you. Using information from the previous pages, let me show you examples of color at work. I'm sure they'll help you gain more color confidence! ◻

— *Jim Childs*

Spotlight on yellow Yellow can sometimes look washed out in the bright summer sun. To prevent it from fading into the background, frame yellow with a dark color. Blue, or a somber violet, like this larkspur, is nice. So is lots of green. While hot colors usually make good companions, if the yellow looks washed out it just can't compete. Unfortunately, white and gray also emphasize that washed-out look so you might want to avoid using too much of these colors near yellow.

- **A** Asiatic lily *Lilium* 'Dreamland'; 30 to 48 in. tall, 12 to 18 in. wide; summer blooming; cold-hardy in USDA zones 4 to 8; heat-tolerant in AHS zones 8 to 1
- **B** Larkspur *Consolida ajacis*; 18 to 24 in. tall, 9 to 12 in. wide; summer blooming; annual; heat-tolerant in AHS zones 12 to 1

Fool the eye Blue recedes, meaning it looks further away than it really is. Use it on a small patio or deck like this one and it'll make the area feel bigger. Plus, no matter how big the area, it's the ideal color for a spot where you want to calm down after a busy day. Why? Well, it's not shouting at you to look at it like orange or red would. And blue is such a cool color that just by looking at it you're going to feel a few degrees cooler on those hot, sticky summer evenings. That means you can sit back and relax with lots of blue around.

A **Bacopa** *Sutera* Snowstorm® White; 4 to 8 in. tall, 8 to 10 in. wide; blooms all season long; cold-hardy in USDA zones 9 to 11; heat-tolerant in AHS zones 11 to 1

B **Bigleaf hydrangea** *Hydrangea* Endless Summer® ('Bailmer'); 3 to 4 ft. tall and wide; summer blooming; cold-hardy in USDA zones 4 to 9; heat-tolerant in AHS zones 9 to 1

C **Lily of the Nile** *Agapanthus* Bluestorm™; 15 to 30 in. tall, 18 to 20 in. wide; blooms late spring into summer; cold-hardy in USDA zones 8 to 11; heat-tolerant in AHS zones 11 to 1

Keep it small When you're working with hot colors, like these orange cosmos and marigolds, small dots of them blend into a setting better. Granted, a large hot-colored flower would make a good focal point in this summer combo, but small flowers, separated by some green, won't overpower the scene. Whether you view them from a distance or up close, hot colors are easier to work into a garden if you use small flowers. However, blue and violet can be hard to see, especially from far away. With these cool colors, if you're going to view them from a distance, you may want to go ahead and use larger shapes. Save the smaller cool-colored flowers for a spot where you view them up close.

A **Cosmos** *Cosmos sulphureus* 'Ladybird Dwarf Mix'; 12 to 16 in. tall, 12 in. wide; annual; heat-tolerant in AHS zones 12 to 1

B **Cosmos** *Cosmos bipinnatus* 'Sonata White'; 18 to 24 in. tall, 15 in. wide; annual; heat-tolerant in AHS zones 12 to 1

C **Marigold** *Tagetes tenuifolia* 'Tangerine Gem'; 6 to 9 in. tall, 4 to 6 in. wide; annual; heat-tolerant in AHS zones 12 to 1

D **Zinnia** *Zinnia* 'Dreamland Mix'; 10 to 12 in. tall and wide; annual; heat-tolerant in AHS zones 12 to 1

E **Verbena** *Verbena* 'Heirloom Mango'; 8 to 10 in. tall, 16 to 20 in. wide; annual; heat-tolerant in AHS zones 12 to 1

DESIGN | GREAT COMBOS

4 Fabulous Fall Combos

Keep your garden looking great — even after summer's gone.

Fall doesn't have to be the end of your garden. With a little planning, it can be just the beginning! Make a few changes now and next year you'll have a showcase of autumn color. Choose one area in full sun (that's where most late-flowering plants grow best) and group your late-season performers there. You could scatter plants around the garden but this often just dilutes the colors and textures. Let's take a look at how to get the most bang for your buck in fall.

CONTINUING COLOR Many perennials look wonderful well into fall. And annuals often look even better when the weather cools down a bit, as the exuberant planting in this photo proves. It's not unusual for annuals like these zinnias to grow so large that they spill out onto walkways or over the edges of containers.

TERRIFIC FOLIAGE Of course, it just wouldn't be fall without trees and their changing leaves. But that's not the only foliage you can look forward to. Annuals, perennials and shrubs all give you a great fall foliage show, too, whether it's the showy hues of the Diablo dahlias in the photo or the gently changing colors of an ornamental grass, such as the purple fountain grass.

We'll take a look at more flower and foliage combinations — with a few berries thrown in for extra sparkle — that'll let any garden put on an amazing fall show. Just turn the page for more ideas for *your* fall garden. □

— Sherri Ribbey

1 FLOWER POWER Don't pull your annuals just because summer is ending. With regular watering and feeding, tidy rows of zinnias that were planted in spring can be as large and full as the ones in this photo. Use a liquid fertilizer, such as Miracle Gro®, weekly right up until frost. Some annuals slow their growth in the cooling temperatures, but that just means the flowers will last longer. Because of that, you won't have to worry as much about deadheading, either. After a hard frost has killed the foliage, be sure to remove your annuals and dispose of them. Leaving them in place for the winter gives pests and disease a good hiding place.

A Canna *Canna* 'Louis Cottin'
18 to 24 in. tall and wide; apricot flowers in late summer to fall; cold-hardy in USDA zones 7 to 11; heat-tolerant in AHS zones 12 to 1

B Purple-fountain grass *Pennisetum setaceum* 'Rubrum'
3 to 5 ft. tall, 2 to 4 ft. wide; showy tan plumes late summer to fall; cold-hardy in USDA zones 9 to 11; heat-tolerant in AHS zones 12 to 1

C Dahlia *Dahlia* 'Diablo Mix'
14 to 16 in. tall and wide; dark foliage, flowers in a wide range of colors; cold-hardy in USDA zones 8 to 11; heat-tolerant in AHS zones 12 to 1

D Zinnia *Zinnia angustifolia* 'Crystal White'
12 to 18 in. tall, 9 to 12 in. wide; small, single white flowers from midsummer to frost; annual; heat-tolerant in AHS zones 12 to 1

E Zinnia *Zinnia* 'Profusion Apricot' and 'Profusion White'
12 to 18 in. tall, 9 to 12 in. wide; very free-flowering series with several colors available; annual; heat-tolerant in AHS zones 12 to 1

F Geranium *Pelargonium* 'Maverick Orange'
18 to 24 in. tall, 12 to 18 in. wide; lots of flowers on heat- and drought-tolerant plants; cold-hardy in USDA zones 10 to 11; heat-tolerant in AHS zones 12 to 1

G Cosmos *Cosmos sulphureus* 'Cosmic Red'
18 to 24 in. tall, 12 to 15 in. wide; deadhead orange and red flowers to keep plant blooming until frost; annual; heat-tolerant in AHS zones 12 to 1

H Mealycup sage *Salvia farinacea* 'Evolution'
24 to 36 in. tall, 14 to 16 in. wide; deadhead blue flower spikes to keep plant looking good into fall; cold-hardy in USDA zones 9 to 11; heat-tolerant in AHS zones 12 to 1

MORE **GREAT FALL COMBOS**

2 BERRY GOOD Grow plants with berries and you won't be the only one who enjoys them. Winterberry's fruit holds well into winter so birds can sample these tasty treats when other food is scarce. This shrub is dioecious, though, which means you need a male and female plant for berries to grow. Japanese blood grass has those red tips all summer but the color deepens and intensifies by fall. Bringing the red down into the front of the bed is a good idea as it helps unify the planting. This grass isn't welcome everywhere, as it can be invasive in some states. (See our story on invasive plants on p. 276.) Check with your state's Department of Natural Resources to see if you should grow it in your area. If it's a problem, try 'Nicolas' Japanese forest grass (*Hakonechloa macra*) instead. The habit is more cascading than Japanese blood grass, but it has gorgeous red-orange fall color.

A Winterberry *Ilex verticillata*
5 to 8 ft. tall and wide; best fruit in full sun; cold-hardy in USDA zones 4 to 8; heat-tolerant in AHS zones 8 to 1

B Big leaf hydrangea *Hydrangea macrophylla*
3 to 6 ft. tall and wide; blue, pink or white midsummer flowers fade to tan in fall; cold-hardy in USDA zones 4 to 9; heat-tolerant in AHS zones 9 to 1

C Coleus *Solenostemon* 'Brilliancy'
2 ft. tall and wide; can leave flowers on plant or pinch them off for a tidy look; cold-hardy in USDA zones 10 to 11; heat-tolerant in AHS zones 12 to 1

D Lilyturf *Liriope muscari*
6 to 12 in. tall and wide; mow or shear in early spring to remove tattered foliage; cold-hardy in USDA zones 5 to 10; heat-tolerant in AHS zones 10 to 1

E Bugleweed *Ajuga reptans* 'Purple Brocade'
4 to 6 in. tall and spreading; purple leaf color is best in full sun; cold-hardy in USDA zones 3 to 9; heat-tolerant in AHS zones 9 to 1

F Japanese blood grass *Imperata cylindrica* 'Rubra'
12 to 18 in. tall and wide; red foliage tips more pronounced in cool fall weather; cold-hardy in USDA zones 5 to 9; heat-tolerant in AHS zones 9 to 1

3 FAR-OUT FOLIAGE
Hostas are great in the shade but they can look a little tattered by fall. Why not try this vibrant combo in a part-shade garden? The chartreuse coleus foliage and bright pink impatiens make this combo vibrate with tension and excitement.

Keep the frost-sensitive annuals in this group going even if temperatures take a dip by covering the plants with a lightweight blanket or an old sheet. Don't lay plastic over your plants because it conducts cold, and if it freezes, it will kill any foliage it touches.

A **Bugbane** *Actaea simplex* 'James Compton'
 2 to 3 ft. tall and wide; white flowers in late summer; cold-hardy in USDA zones 4 to 8; heat-tolerant in AHS zones 8 to 1

B **Coleus** *Solenostemon* 'Pineapple'
 12 to 18 in. tall, 10 to 18 in. wide; chartreuse foliage; cold-hardy in USDA zones 10 to 11; heat-tolerant in AHS zones 12 to 1

C **Vinca** *Catharanthus roseus* 'Victory Pure White'
 8 to 12 in. tall, 14 in. wide; white flowers all season until frost; cold-hardy in USDA zones 9 to 11; heat-tolerant in AHS zones 12 to 1

D **Impatiens** *Impatiens* Fanfare™ Orchid
 16 to 20 in. tall, 18 to 24 in. wide; pink flowers from spring to fall; cold-hardy in USDA zones 10 to 11; heat-tolerant in AHS zones 12 to 1

E **Waffle plant** *Hemigraphis alternata*
 6 to 10 in. tall, 12 to 18 in. wide; grown for its colorful foliage, flowers are insignificant; cold-hardy in USDA zones 10 to 11; heat-tolerant in AHS zones 12 to 1

4 PERENNIALS POP!
For colorful flowers well into fall, choose long-blooming or reblooming perennials like the black-eyed Susan and phlox here. Flowers start in midsummer and last for several weeks. Once they fade, deadhead spent blooms and you'll get another round. Wild senna is a native plant that's easy to grow from seed. Look for bumblebees buzzing around the flowers and sulfur butterfly caterpillars munching the leaves.

A **Wild senna** *Senna hebecarpa*
 4 to 6 ft. tall, 2 to 3 ft. wide; yellow flowers in late summer; cold-hardy in USDA zones 4 to 9; heat-tolerant in AHS zones 9 to 1

B **Garden phlox** *Phlox paniculata*
 12 to 48 in. tall, 12 to 36 in. wide; pink, purple or white flowers midsummer to fall; cold-hardy in USDA zones 4 to 9; heat-tolerant in AHS zones 9 to 1

C **Black-eyed Susan** *Rudbeckia fulgida sullivantii* 'Goldsturm'
 2 to 3 ft. tall, 1 to 2 ft. wide; yellow flowers summer to fall; cold-hardy in USDA zones 4 to 9; heat-tolerant in AHS zones 9 to 1

D **Spurge** *Euphorbia dulcis* 'Chameleon'
 12 to 18 in. tall, 18 to 24 in. wide; chartreuse flowers in summer; cold-hardy in USDA zones 5 to 9; heat-tolerant in AHS zones 9 to 1

LOCATION: Lyndale Park Peace Garden, Minneapolis, MN (4)

DESIGN | WILDLIFE

Bring in the butterflies with an easy-care garden!

Warm, Winged Welcome

Purple coneflower

Plant a butterfly garden! Butterflies will like the "buffet" selection of flowers. You'll like the fact that many of the plants are easy-care, long-blooming perennials. Most any yard has a spot where you can tuck in a butterfly bed. This one is about 10 feet long from the corner post to the purple coneflower on the left. And at its widest point, it's just 4 feet deep. Even if you don't have a swimming pool, you can make a similar garden off the edge of your patio or deck, or any place where you can relax and watch these colorful visitors. Find a spot away from lots of activity that might disturb the butterflies as they feast. Then try a few of the pointers and tips you'll find below the photos. They'll help you make visiting butterflies welcome.

Maybe you already have a big garden that will attract butterflies, but you'd like to draw a few of them closer to the deck or patio. That way you'll be able to watch them up close and personal. While butterflies will visit almost any flower looking for food, some are better attractors. Those are the ones to use in a container. Check out our container idea, "Grow a snack-size garden" at left, and then find the planting plan for it in our Web extra. At the end of the season, most of these colorful perennials can be moved into the garden so you can grow them to attract butterflies again next year.

Even if you're only able to use a few of the tips I talk about here, I know you'll enjoy watching lots of butterflies this summer. □

— *Jim Childs*

Illustration: David Kallemyn

Grow a snack-size garden
For a container, you'll want to choose flowers that have lots of nectar, a butterfly's favorite food. That's why we've included aster, lantana, purple coneflower and black-eyed Susan in ours. Add a canna in the center for some height and bold texture. That way your container will look good to you *and* hungry butterflies.

Web extra Plant this **container recipe**

Choose your colors
Vivid shades of red, yellow, orange, pink and purple are colors butterflies look for when they're hungry. Even white flowers are good if they have bright gold centers like these Shasta daisies. And since butterflies' eyesight is not very good, they'll be more likely to find the flowers if you group them in large drifts. Try to choose lots of plants that bloom from midsummer into fall — that's when you'll have the most butterflies looking for food.

Image labels: Shasta daisy, Blazing star, Black-eyed Susan, Campion, Mallow, Garden phlox, Coreopsis

Soak up sunshine

Since butterflies are cold-blooded, they need warmth from sunshine to get moving. Choose a spot for your butterfly garden that gets at least six hours of direct sunlight. And if the garden is near stones or concrete that absorb and hold heat, like this pool edge, your winged visitors can feast later into the evening. A path or patio that is made of stone or brick will work just as well.

Easy eating

Most North American butterflies have a fairly short *proboscis*, or feeding tube. That means flowers with short tubes are best, as are flat-topped or small clustered flowers, like the spikes of the purple blazing star in this photo. And flowers with long, flat petals, such as these Shasta daisies, black-eyed Susans and purple coneflowers, also provide large landing areas with lots of nectar in the center.

Give 'em a break

Imagine being a hungry butterfly on a windy day. Because you're as light as tissue paper, it can be tricky to fly, let alone land on a flower and hang on as you eat. Even in a gentle breeze, a solid fence like this one makes it much easier for butterflies to get around. Don't like the look of a fence? A windbreak of shrubs or tall perennials will do the job just as well.

Botanical Names

Aster *Aster* hybrid
Black-eyed Susan *Rudbeckia* spp.
Blazing star *Liatris* spp.
Campion *Silene* spp.
Canna *Canna* hybrid
Coreopsis *Coreopsis* spp.
Garden phlox *Phlox paniculata*
Lantana *Lantana* hybrid
Mallow *Malva sylvestris*
Purple coneflower *Echinacea purpurea*
Shasta daisy *Leucanthemum* spp.

DESIGN | WILDLIFE

Your winged friends will give this mix-and-match buffet rave reviews.

Butterflies Welcome!

What makes one restaurant more popular than another? I think you can boil it down to three things — location, selection and service. If you're a butterfly looking for a meal, those three things might just make the difference between visiting your garden or moving on to the neighbor's. So, I've put together a buffet for butterflies. Location? Full sun. Service? Help yourself to all you want. Selection? Just take a look at the colorful menu we've put together in the plan below. It's sure to attract a beautiful clientele of monarchs, swallowtails and painted ladies, along with many others.

While butterflies need moisture, they don't drink water from an open source, such as a birdbath. But a mud puddle near the front of this border is what they need. All it takes is a saucer filled with sand and garden soil that's kept wet. The moisture helps butterflies extract minerals they need from the mixture. Toss an old, mushy banana onto the puddle and your guests will get even more nutrients.

Butterflies also need a healthy environment to enjoy their gourmet meal. That's why it's a good idea to limit the use of pesticides. I know — you'd never think of spraying a butterfly! But that hungry caterpillar, munching on the hollyhocks I've included in this plan, later hatches into a colorful painted lady butterfly. Many of the perennials I've included here are noted for having very few other destructive pests so you won't have a need to spray anyway.

As you look over "The main course," you may see flowers that won't grow well in your zone. Or perhaps they don't appeal to you. Don't worry, on the next pages I've included two options, one for each of the plants you see here — another similar shrub or perennial and an easy-to-grow annual. Having choices like this is a good way to customize your garden. Or you can update the menu each year so butterflies have something fresh and new to enjoy.

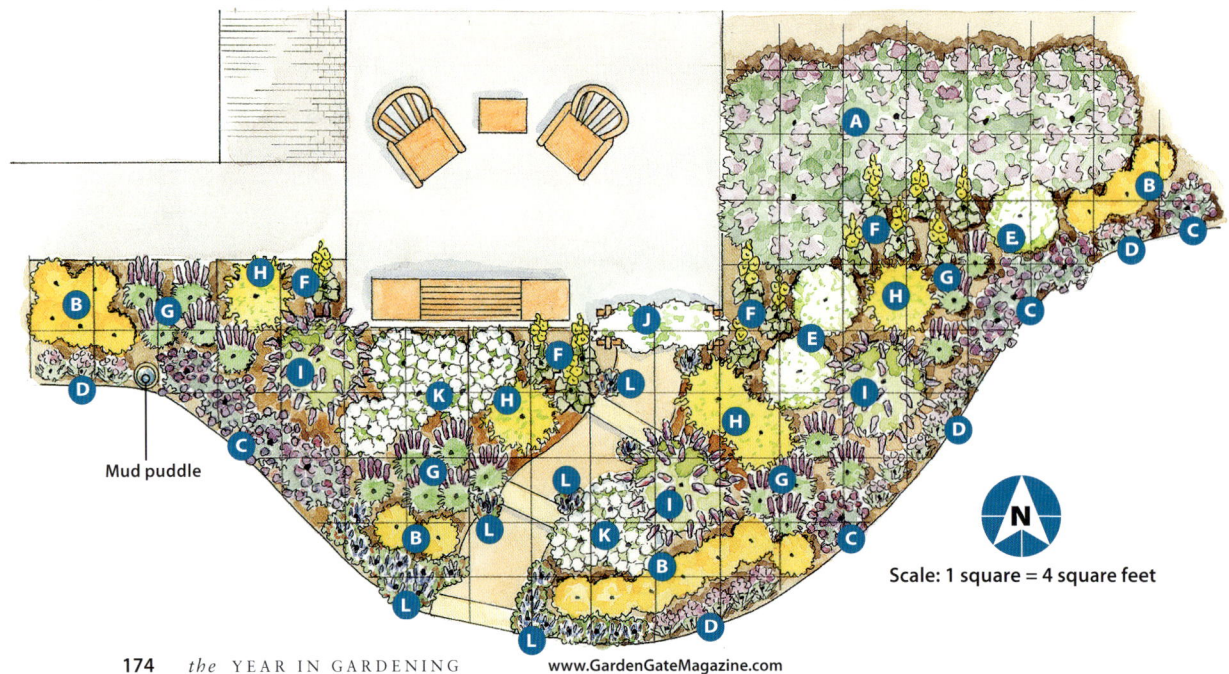

Mud puddle

Scale: 1 square = 4 square feet

THE MAIN COURSE

Code	Plant Name	No. to Plant	Blooms	Cold/Heat Zones	Height/Width	Special Features
A1	**Dwarf Korean lilac** *Syringa meyeri* 'Palibin'	5	Lavender; late spring	3-7/7-1	4-5 ft./ 5-7 ft.	Shrub; flowers have a spicy fragrance; easier to prune to maintain size than most other lilacs
B1	**Threadleaf coreopsis** *Coreopsis verticillata* 'Zagreb'	17	Bright yellow; early to midsummer	3-9/9-1	12-18 in./ 18 in.	Perennial; fine foliage; after first flush of flowers fades, cut plant down to a couple of inches to encourage rebloom
C1	**Verbena** *Verbena* 'Homestead Purple'	9	Purple; midspring to fall	7-10/10-1	6-18 in./ 24-36 in.	Perennial; treat as an annual if it's not hardy in your zone; one of the most popular butterfly plants
D1	**Chives** *Allium schoenoprasum*	16	Lavender; spring	4-8/8-1	12-18 in./ 12-15 in.	Perennial; herb with edible flowers and foliage; deadhead to slow reseeding tendencies
E1	**Boltonia** *Boltonia asteroides*	3	White; fall	4-9/9-1	4-6 ft./ 2-3 ft.	Perennial; covered with billows of small daisies; stiff stems rarely require staking
F1	**Russian hollyhock** *Alcea rugosa*	13	Pale yellow; midsummer	3-9/9-1	5-9 ft./ 1-2 ft.	Perennial; reseeds so cut some of the spikes down before they set seed; painted lady caterpillars eat the foliage
G1	**Spike blazing star** *Liatris spicata* 'Kobold'	19	Deep purple; mid- to late summer	4-9/9-1	18-24 in./ 12-18 in.	Perennial; narrow spires of fuzzy flowers; makes an excellent cut flower for bouquets
H1	**Goldenrod** *Solidago rugosa* 'Fireworks'	5	Golden yellow; late summer	4-9/9-1	2-3 ft./ 2-3 ft.	Perennial; can quickly form large clumps; caterpillars of question mark and comma butterflies feed on the foliage
I1	**Butterfly bush** *Buddleja davidii* 'Nanho Purple'	3	Purple; summer to fall	5-9/9-1	4-6 ft./ 4-6 ft.	Shrub behaves more like a perennial; cut back to within a foot of the ground each spring; slow to leaf out in spring
J1	**Sweet autumn clematis** *Clematis terniflora*	2	White; fall	4-9/9-1	15-20 ft.	Perennial vine; each spring cut back almost to the ground; quickly regrows to cover a sturdy support
K1	**Tall garden phlox** *Phlox paniculata* 'David'	9	White; mid- to late summer	3-9/9-1	2-4 ft./ 2 ft.	Perennial; fragrant flowers; mildew-resistant variety; deadhead to extend bloom later into fall
L1	**Ajuga** *Ajuga reptans* 'Catlin's Giant'	22	Blue; late spring	4-8/8-1	4-10 in./ spreading	Perennial; spreads to form a ground cover; allow it to weave among other perennials

FAVORITE FLOWERS

Somehow, scientists have figured out that butterflies don't have good eyesight. However, if you plant flowers in large blocks of one color, butterflies are more likely to swoop in for a taste. That's why this garden design not only has a variety of nectar flowers, but they're planted in groups so they're easier for butterflies to spot.

As you're designing your "feast," except for the shrubs, you'll notice that the "1s" on the previous spread and "2s" here are all perennials, while the number "3s" are annuals. Go ahead and choose all "1s," all "2s" or all "3s," if you like. Or look over the options and mix and match your favorites to suit your own style and taste. When you swap plants, you may need a few more or a few less than our original plan below shows. If that's the case, I'll let you know with information under the illustration. But no matter which options you choose, this customized full-sun garden is sure to be as popular with butterflies as I hope it will be with you. □

—*Jim Childs*

A2
Summersweet
Clethra alnifolia
3-8 ft. tall/4-6 ft. wide
• 5-9 • 9-1
Shrub with fragrant pale pink to white flowers in late summer

A3
Abelia
Abelia
'Edward Goucher'
4 ft. tall/4 ft. wide
• 6-9 • 9-1
Shrub with pink flowers most of the summer

L2
Sedum
Sedum spurium
'Voodoo'
4-6 in. tall/
10-12 in. wide
• 4-9 • 9-1
Perennial; red flowers in summer; succulent burgundy foliage almost all year round

L3
Heliotrope
Heliotropium arborescens
18 in. tall/18 in. wide
• Annual • 12-1
Annual; fragrant purple flowers in late spring and summer

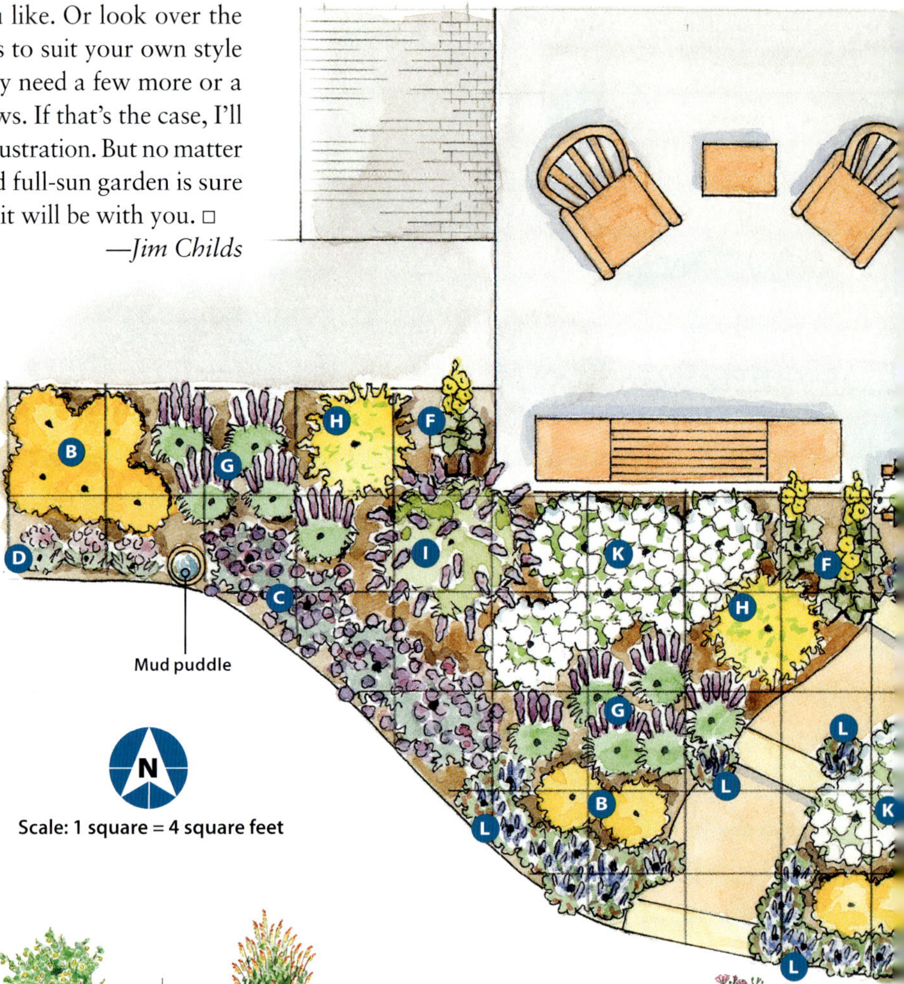

Mud puddle

Scale: 1 square = 4 square feet

K2
Butterfly weed
Asclepias tuberosa
1-3 ft. tall/1-2 ft. wide
• 3-9 • 9-1
Perennial; vivid orange flowers in midsummer; foliage popular food for monarch caterpillars

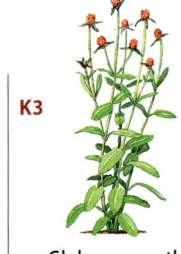

K3
Globe amaranth
Gomphrena
'Strawberry Fields'
18-24 in. tall/
12 in. wide
• Annual • 12-1
Annual; red-orange globe-shaped flowers in summer
(1 plant per sq. ft.)

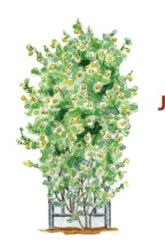

J2
Trumpet honeysuckle
Lonicera sempervirens sulphurea
'John Clayton'
6-12 ft. tall/3-4 ft. wide
• 4-9 • 9-1
Woody vine; tubular yellow flowers in summer

J3
Spanish flag
Ipomoea lobata
6-20 ft. tall/3 ft. wide
• 9-11 • 12-1
Annual vine; sprays of scarlet, yellow and orange flowers in summer; easy to grow from seed

I2
Joe Pye weed
Eupatorium maculatum
'Gateway'
5-7 ft. tall/2-4 ft. wide
• 4-8 • 8-1
Perennial; large clusters of dusty-rose flowers in late summer; rarely needs staking

I3
Cosmos
Cosmos bipinnatus
'Sea Shells'
3-4 ft. tall/12-18 in. wide
• Annual • 12-1
Annual; shades of pink and white flowers in summer
(Thin to 1 plant per sq. ft.)

B2 Sedum
Sedum
'Autumn Joy'
('Herbstfreude')
2 ft. tall/2 ft. wide
- 3-9 • 9-1

Perennial; pink flowers change to copper-red by fall
(1 plant for every 4 sq. ft.)

B3 Pot marigold
Calendula officinalis
12-30 in. tall/
12-18 in. wide
- Annual • 12-1

Annual; shades of gold flowers in summer; direct sow seeds
(Thin to 1 plant per sq. ft.)

C2 Thyme
Thymus vulgaris
6-12 in. tall/
16-18 in. wide
- 5-9 • 9-1

Perennial; tiny pink to purple flowers in early summer; fragrant, edible foliage
(1 plant per sq. ft.)

C3 Petunia
Petunia hybrid Madness™ Plum
12 in. tall/12 in. wide
- Annual • 12-1

Annual; plum-purple flowers bloom all summer long

D2 Black blooming sedge
Carex nigra
12-20 in. tall/
12 in. wide
- 4-8 • 8-1

Perennial; clumps of evergreen grasslike foliage; prefers a spot that has moist soil; caterpillars of several skippers eat sedges

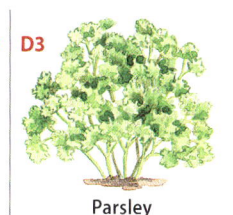

D3 Parsley
Petroselinum crispum
10 in. tall/6-12 in. wide
- 5-9 • 9-1

Can be grown as an annual; mounds of edible green foliage; flowers not showy, but black swallowtail caterpillars love to eat the foliage

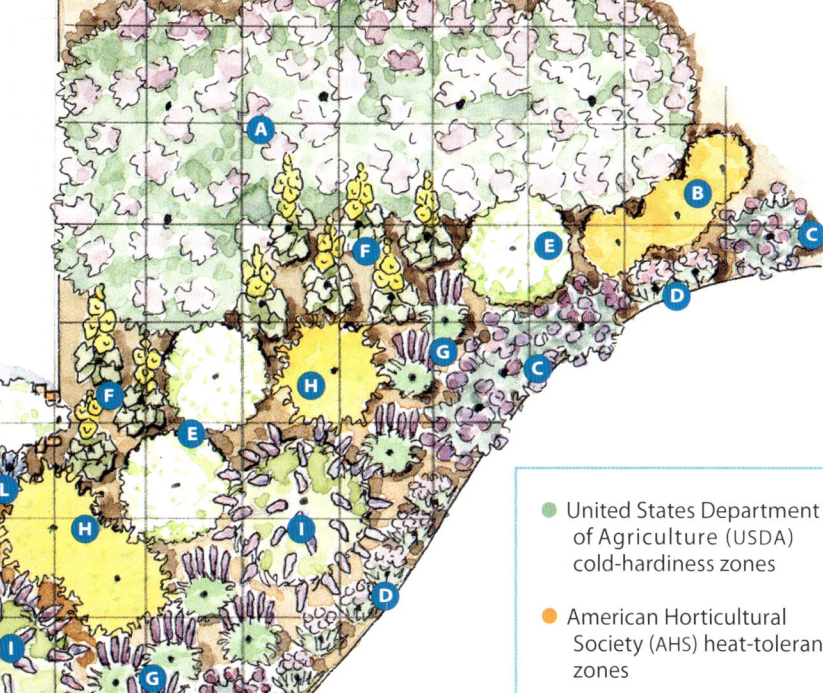

- United States Department of Agriculture (USDA) cold-hardiness zones
- American Horticultural Society (AHS) heat-tolerance zones

E2 New England aster
Aster novae-angliae
'Harrington's Pink'
4-6 ft. tall/2-3 ft. wide
- 3-8 • 8-1

Perennial; loads of small pink daisies in fall; may need staking

E3 Mexican sunflower
Tithonia rotundifolia
2-6 ft. tall/2 ft. wide
- Annual • 12-1

Annual; hot-orange flowers in mid- to late summer; sow seeds directly in the garden

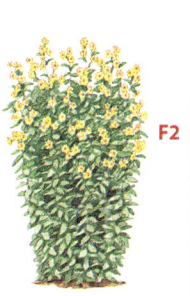

F2 Perennial sunflower
Helianthus
'Lemon Queen'
6-7 ft. tall/3 ft. wide
- 3-8 • 8-1

Perennial; pale yellow daisies in late summer and early fall; painted lady caterpillars feed on the foliage

F3 Annual sunflower
Helianthus annuus
Up to 15 ft. tall/
2 ft. wide
- Annual • 12-1

Annual; shades of yellow and gold flowers in summer; sow seeds directly in the garden; foliage feeds painted lady caterpillars

H2 Bee balm
Monarda
'Cambridge Scarlet'
3 ft. tall/2 ft. wide
- 4-9 • 9-1

Perennial; shaggy scarlet-red flowers in late summer; fragrant foliage

H3 Zinnia
Zinnia elegans
'Benary Giant Mix'
3 ft. tall/1 ft. wide
- Annual • 12-1

Annual; mid- to late-summer blooms
(Thin to 1 plant per sq. ft.)

Turtlehead
Chelone lyonii
2-3 FT. TALL/1-2 FT. WIDE
- 3-9 • 9-1

Perennial; clusters of pink flower spikes in late summer; foliage feeds Baltimore butterfly caterpillars

G3 Mealycup sage
Salvia farinacea
'Victoria'
24 in. tall/10 in. wide
- 8-11 • 12-1

Tender perennial treated as an annual; blue flowers in summer
(2 plants per sq. ft.)

www.GardenGateMagazine.com the YEAR IN GARDENING 177

DESIGN | WILDLIFE

Make your garden bird-friendly

If you have a garden, you probably have birds coming to visit. But how can you make your garden even more attractive to birds so you pull in more kinds and keep them around longer? I talked with Joan McDonald, owner of Gardens by Joan in New York, about tips to make your garden more "bird-friendly." One of her best tips is to plant a bird habitat garden. You'll find plans for one on the next pages. It'll show you that a bird-friendly garden doesn't have to look wild and unkempt and can fit in an average-sized yard. But no matter what size it is, your garden does need to have three basic bird-friendly elements to bring visitors in: Food, water and shelter. And if the birds like the shelter they find, they'll often stick around to raise a family. I'll show you some specific tips Joan shared with me about entertaining birds. Let's start by finding out what they like to eat.

Food For a majority of birds, juicy berries are fast-food favorites. The most popular fruits are small so the bird can quickly gobble them up and move on. Things like holly berries, crabapples and serviceberries are always popular.

KEEP A WELL-STOCKED PANTRY Birds usually need the most food when they're nesting and raising fledglings. And often their preferred foods are prevalent at those times. For example fruits such as serviceberries ripen about the time the first batch of hungry robins is leaving the nest.

Birds that eat mostly seeds and berries will also enjoy a few bugs and worms while they're feeding their young. Let some of the fallen leaves stay under your shrubs and birds will scratch through them looking for a meal.

Because the parents are concerned with protecting the nest, they can't cover as large an area as they normally do in their search for food. That means it's an important time to be sure there's lots of food nearby.

Feeders are a good idea. Always place them in a spot that gets early morning sun — that's when birds do most of their feeding as they appreciate the early warmth.

Water A birdbath is an ideal way to make sure birds get enough water for drinking and bathing. Set a birdbath about 10 feet away from a tall shrub or a small tree. Bathers like a "bird's eye" view of the area to make sure it's safe before they dive into the water. And when they come out, a branch nearby gives them a spot where they can perch and preen before flying away.

SPECIAL AMENITIES ARE NICE Drippers and misters aren't necessities, but if you want to provide deluxe accommodations, check them out. A dripper moves the water ever so gently, but birds are much more likely to spot your birdbath if the water's moving. And on hot days, many birds, especially hummingbirds, love to fly through a cool mist, find a shaded spot to perch, fluff their feathers and relax.

Shelter When it comes time to roost, most birds will choose any protected spot, such as a dense tree or shrub. But when they're ready to build a nest, they may be a bit more particular. It could be the same tree or shrub, a hole in a tree trunk or a ledge tucked up high on a wall. A lot depends on the kind of bird, but anywhere out of the hot sun and soaking rain has potential.

NEW HOME CONSTRUCTION No matter what kind of home birds build, you can help. Drape 6- to 10-inch pieces of cotton string over branches so they can gather it for building material. Or tuck other fibers, such as human or pet hair, in a mesh bag and hang it from a tree. Some birds use mud as cement, so keep a spot in your garden constantly wet so they have a steady supply during nesting season. When you spot birds carrying off the bits of string, or picking up lots of mud and twigs, keep an eye on where

(1) Small berries are ideal for a quick meal. Birds like this robin can swallow them whole and be on their way.

(2) Shallow bird baths, less than 2 in. deep, are best for all birds, even this large male cardinal.

they're headed. It won't be long before you spot where they're building their nursery.

Fledglings need cover as they learn to fly. That's why lots of branches at various heights are a good idea. And if youngsters fall to the ground, low shrubs and dense ground covers will give them protection from predators until they can fly.

If you're trying to attract a specific bird to your garden, you'll want to do some research to find out exactly what they prefer. In "Special requests" at right you'll find tips about five birds and what they look for as they're out scouting for food, shelter and water.

Speaking of keeping your birds happy and well fed, on the next pages Joan has helped create a design for a bird habitat. Let's take a look.

(3) A mother cardinal selected this thorny rose bush as a nesting spot so her babies will be safe from predators.

SPECIAL REQUESTS

OK, so you want to attract some specific birds. A few can be downright particular about where they live and what they eat. Here are five birds that can be found in many parts of North America, with a few clues to help you reel them in. The rest of the decision is up to the bird!

1 CEDAR WAXWING These birds need fruit, and lots of it. Crabapples, holly, hawthorn and mountain ash all have fruit that hangs on much of the winter, at least until the cedar waxwings find it and have a feast.

2 MOURNING DOVE These mournful-sounding birds build loose, fragile nests that sometimes fall from the tree in a storm. To help them build a better foundation, cut a 12 in. diameter circle of ¼-in. mesh hardware cloth. Then cut a pie-shaped wedge into the circle, form the mesh into a shallow cone and fasten the edges together with twist ties. In spring, wedge the cone in the fork of an evergreen. To help deter predators, place it at least 5 ft. from the ground.

3 EASTERN PHOEBE Tuck a small shelf under the eaves on the side of your house and in spring eastern phoebes will build a nest of grass and mud. They won't even mind if it's near a busy patio or entrance — they seem to like the company.

4 GRAY CATBIRD When you want to lure these shadow-colored birds out into the open, give them half an orange or a handful of raisins. Really want to give them a reward for helping rid your garden of insect pests? Pick up some live mealworms at your local pet store and dump them out on a tray.

5 BROWN THRASHER To make your garden attractive to this bird, don't rake areas under shrubs so they can search through fallen leaves for worms and insects. If they like the neighborhood and the food, brown thrashers come back to the same area every year.

PHOTOS: © Jay Gilliam (Eastern phoebe, cedar waxwing, gray catbird, mourning dove, brown thrasher)

bring in the birds

Birds are easy-going guests. But if you want to attract lots of them, growing a bird habitat is the key. Here are some helpful tips, and a garden design, from Joan.

THINK IN LAYERS The best habitat gardens mimic the layers found in nature. There should be tall trees that provide a high perch where birds can safely rest and survey the area for food and water. Next comes a layer of smaller trees and large shrubs, which are also handy for perching as well as providing spots to build nests. Include a few evergreens, like the holly in this garden, for even better protective cover.

Under these two layers are smaller shrubs and large perennials. They're often the main source of food for birds. Finally there's a ground cover of low shrubs or perennials. Birds will find seeds, insects and worms in, as well as under, this layer.

GROW LOCAL Native plants will be acclimated to your region as well as providing familiar food to the birds that live there. And cultivated forms of these plants are fine, too. For example, chokeberry is a native shrub in many areas. But named cultivars like 'Brilliant' are often easier to find. They'll still have tasty fruit the birds will like.

I've "regionalized" the garden plan for you. For example, American holly is great in the northeast and northwest regions, but would suffer in the Midwest. So you'll find regional options for it in the columns below the illustration. And you may have to make some slight adjustments to allow for different plant sizes, too.

Even if you don't have room to plant this entire habitat, just include one or two of the plants to make your garden more popular with visiting birds. □

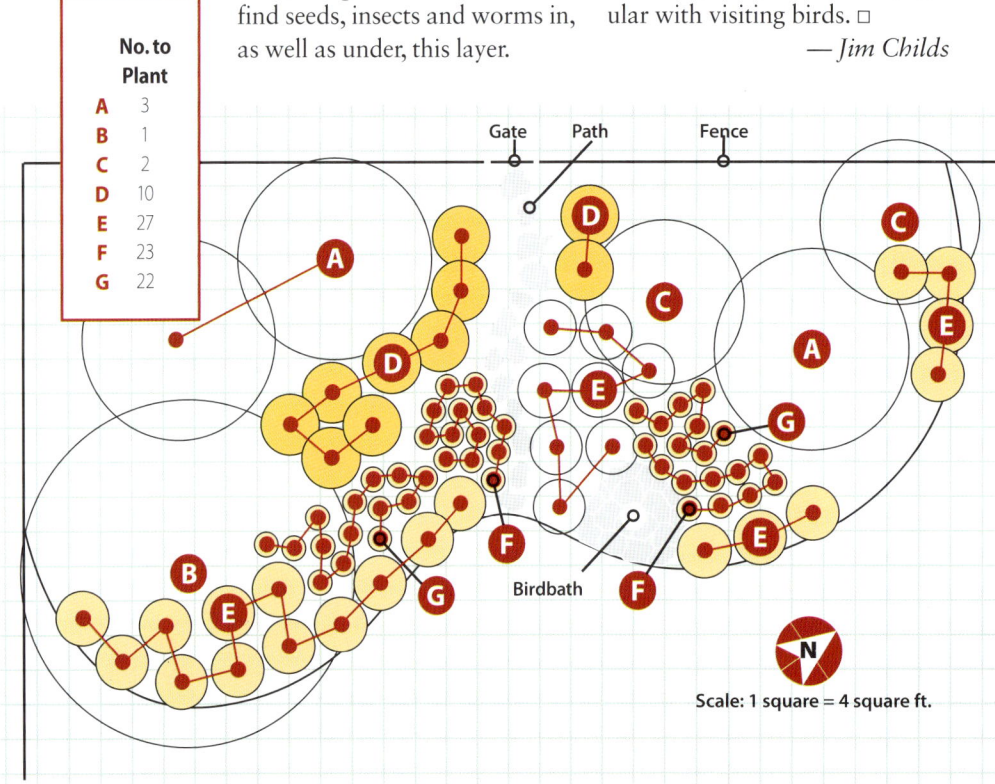

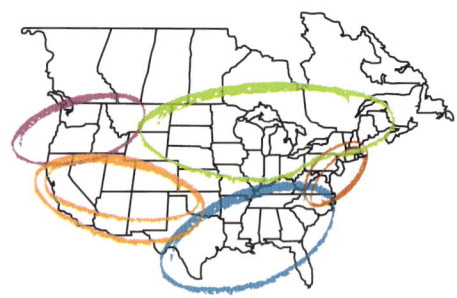

— *Jim Childs*

■ MID-ATLANTIC
■ NORTHWEST
■ MIDWEST & NEW ENGLAND
■ SOUTHWEST
■ SOUTHEAST

Mid-Atlantic

This group of plants is cold-hardy in at least zones 5 to 7.

A American holly *Ilex opaca*
Tree; female plant produces lots of red fruit, spiny evergreen leaves; full sun to part shade; 15 to 30 ft. tall, 10 to 20 ft. wide; cold zones 5 to 9, heat zones 9 to 1

B Flowering dogwood *Cornus florida* Tree; bright red autumn fruit, broad pyramidal form; part shade; 15 to 30 ft. tall and wide; cold zones 5 to 9, heat zones 9 to 1

C Smooth sumac *Rhus glabra*
Shrub; clusters of fuzzy red fruit; full sun to part shade; 10 to 15 ft. tall and wide; cold zones 3 to 9, heat zones 9 to 1

D Chokeberry *Aronia xprunifolia* 'Brilliant' Shrub; glossy red fruit in fall, red fall foliage; full sun; 6 to 8 ft. tall, 3 to 4 ft. wide; cold zones 3 to 8, heat zones 8 to 1

E Black huckleberry *Gaylussacia baccata* Shrub; purple berries in late summer; part shade; 1 to 3 ft. tall, 3 to 4 ft. wide; cold zones 3 to 7, heat zones 7 to 1

F Switch grass *Panicum virgatum* 'Heavy Metal' Perennial; stiff stems hold seed heads well into winter; full sun; 4 to 5 ft. tall, 1 to 2 ft. wide; cold zones 5 to 9, heat zones 9 to 1

G Sweet coneflower *Rudbeckia subtomentosa* Perennial; golden yellow flowers, brown seed cones in late summer; full sun to part shade; 3 to 5 ft. tall, 1 to 2 ft. wide; cold zones 4 to 8, heat zones 8 to 1

No. to Plant	
A	3
B	1
C	2
D	10
E	27
F	23
G	22

Gate Path Fence

Birdbath

Scale: 1 square = 4 square ft.

Understory trees give birds a safe spot to perch before they head to the birdbath.

Dense evergreens give birds protection from bad weather and predators.

Grasses produce seeds many birds find tasty and they provide nesting materials, too.

Northwest
This group of plants is cold-hardy in at least zones 5 to 7.

A American holly *Ilex opaca* Tree; female plant produces lots of red fruit, spiny evergreen leaves; full sun to part shade; 15 to 30 ft. tall, 10 to 20 ft. wide; cold zones 5 to 9, heat zones 9 to 1

B Blackhaw viburnum *Viburnum prunifolium* Large shrub; blue-black berries in fall; full sun to part shade; 12 to 15 ft. tall, 6 to 12 ft. wide; cold zones 3 to 9, heat zones 9 to 1

C Saskatoon serviceberry *Amelanchier alnifolia* Shrub; purple-black fruit in summer; full sun to part shade; 8 to 10 ft. tall and wide; cold zones 3 to 9, heat zones 9 to 1

D Oregon grape holly *Mahonia aquifolium* Shrub; clusters of blue berries in late summer, evergreen; part shade; 3 to 6 ft. tall and wide; cold zones 5 to 9, heat zones 9 to 1

E Lowbush blueberry *Vaccinium angustifolium laevifolium* Shrub; berries in late summer; full sun to part shade; 18 to 24 in. tall and wide; cold zones 2 to 7, heat zones 7 to 1

F Switch grass *Panicum virgatum* 'Heavy Metal' Perennial; stiff stems hold seed heads well into winter; full sun; 4 to 5 ft. tall, 1 to 2 ft. wide; cold zones 5 to 9, heat zones 9 to 1

G Sweet coneflower *Rudbeckia subtomentosa* Perennial; golden yellow flowers, brown seed cones in late summer; full sun to part shade; 3 to 5 ft. tall, 1 to 2 ft. wide; cold zones 4 to 8, heat zones 8 to 1

Midwest & New England
This group of plants is cold-hardy in at least zones 4 to 7.

A Arborvitae *Thuja occidentalis* Evergreen tree; dense foliage for shelter; full sun to part shade; 15 to 40 ft. tall, 10 to 15 ft. wide; cold zones 3 to 7, heat zones 7 to 1

B Flowering crabapple *Malus* hybrids Tree; wide range of fruit sizes late summer into fall; full sun; 8 to 25 ft. tall, 10 to 25 ft. wide; cold zones 3 to 9, heat zones 9 to 1

C Smooth sumac *Rhus glabra* Shrub; clusters of fuzzy red fruit; full sun to part shade; 10 to 15 ft. tall and wide; cold zones 3 to 9, heat zones 9 to 1

D Chokeberry *Aronia xprunifolia* 'Brilliant' Shrub; glossy red fruit in fall, red fall foliage; full sun; 6 to 8 ft. tall, 3 to 4 ft. wide; cold zones 3 to 8, heat zones 8 to 1

E Creeping juniper *Juniperus horizontalis* Shrub; blue fruit, low spreading evergreen; full sun to part shade; 4 to 12 in. tall, 4 to 8 ft. wide; cold zones 3 to 9, heat zones 9 to 1

F Little bluestem *Schizachyrium scoparium* Perennial; late season grass, orange fall color; full sun; 2 to 4 ft. tall, 1 to 2 ft. wide; cold zones 3 to 9, heat zones 9 to 1

G Sweet coneflower *Rudbeckia subtomentosa* Perennial; golden yellow flowers, brown seed cones in late summer; full sun to part shade; 3 to 5 ft. tall, 1 to 2 ft. wide; cold zones 4 to 8, heat zones 8 to 1

Southwest
This group of plants is cold-hardy in at least zones 7 to 9.

A Toyon *Heteromeles arbutifolia* Tree; red fruit in fall, can be grown as a shrub; full sun to part shade; 15 to 25 ft. tall, 10 to 20 ft. wide; cold zones 7 to 11, heat zones 11 to 1

B Mesquite *Prosopis glandulosa* Tree; dry seeds in summer, thorny branches ideal for nesting; full sun; 20 to 30 ft. tall, 15 to 25 ft. wide; cold zones 6 to 10, heat zones 10 to 1

C Sugar bush *Rhus ovata* Shrub; red berries in late summer, evergreen; full sun; 6 to 12 ft. tall and wide; cold zones 7 to 11, heat zones 11 to 1

D Pheasant berry *Leycesteria formosa* Shrub; deep purple berries in fall, prune to the ground each spring; full sun; 6 ft. tall and wide; cold zones 6 to 9, heat zones 9 to 1

E Pinemat manzanita *Arctostaphylos nevadensis* Shrub; pale pink flowers, brown fruit in late summer; full sun to part shade; 12 to 24 in. tall, 4 to 6 ft. wide; cold zones 6 to 10, heat zones 10 to 1

F Mexican feather grass *Stipa tenuissima* Perennial; wispy foliage, late-season seeds; full sun; 2 to 3 ft. tall and wide; cold zones 7 to 10, heat zones 10 to 1

G Prairie coneflower *Ratibida columnifera* Perennial; orange and yellow flowers, brown seed cones in late summer; full sun to part shade; 2 to 3 ft. tall, 1 to 2 ft. wide; cold zones 3 to 10, heat zones 10 to 1

Southeast
This group of plants is cold-hardy in at least zones 7 to 8.

A Wax myrtle *Myrica cerifera* Shrubby tree; waxy gray fruit in late summer, semi-evergreen; full sun to part shade; 20 to 30 ft. tall, 10 to 12 ft. wide; cold zones 7 to 10, heat zones 10 to 1

B Flowering dogwood *Cornus florida* Tree; bright red autumn fruit; broad pyramidal form; part shade; 15 to 30 ft. tall and wide; cold zones 5 to 9, heat zones 9 to 1

C Yaupon holly *Ilex vomitoria* Shrub; scarlet-red fruit in late summer, evergreen foliage; full sun; 10 to 20 ft. tall, 8 to 12 ft. wide; cold zones 7 to 9, heat zones 9 to 1

D Inkberry *Ilex glabra* Shrub; black berries in summer; full sun to part shade; 4 to 8 ft. tall, 3 to 6 ft. wide; cold zones 5 to 9, heat zones 9 to 1

E Wintergreen *Gaultheria procumbens* Evergreen ground cover; scarlet fruits in midsummer; full sun to part shade; 4 to 6 in. tall, spreading; cold zones 3 to 8, heat zones 8 to 1

F Switch grass *Panicum virgatum* 'Heavy Metal' Perennial; stiff stems hold seed heads well into winter; full sun; 4 to 5 ft. tall, 1 to 2 ft. wide; cold zones 5 to 9, heat zones 9 to 1

G Black-eyed Susan *Rudbeckia fulgida sullvantii* 'Goldsturm' Perennial; golden yellow flowers, brown seed cones in late summer; full sun; 2 to 3 ft. tall, 1 to 2 ft. wide; cold zones 4 to 9, heat zones 9 to 1

did you know...

The arches of the circular and scalloped pavers don't match exactly, so you'll need to leave a gap between them.

Mulch mesh
Chick Nihen, Pennsylvania
Wood mulch is great for keeping soil moisture even and weeds down. But Chick was having problems with the local squirrel population rearranging the mulch while they buried their food. More mulch was on the nearby sidewalk than in the garden bed. One day while walking through the local big box store, he spotted a roll of gutter guard and had an idea. This plastic mesh usually runs along roof gutters to keep leaves from clogging the drains. Chick thought it would be perfect for lining his walkway and keeping the mulch in place. After purchasing a 6-inch-by-20-foot-long roll and a box of landscape staples, he took it home and unrolled it. He ran it snugly along the edging, as you can see in the photo below, and anchored it with the staples, as the illustration below shows. Once the daylilies came up in spring, the mesh was invisible and the squirrels looked for another place to bury their loot.

Place landscape staples through the mesh into the mulch as anchors.

The gutter guard isn't noticeable once the foliage grows over it.

Petal paver path
Martha Wells, South Dakota
Martha found a way to jazz up the path through her garden with flowers! She put pre-made pavers from her local hardware store together in an out-of-the-ordinary way.

To create the path, Martha removed the sod and dug down 4 to 5 inches, leaving enough room to put down a 3-inch base of coarse sand plus the thickness of the pavers. Then she laid the round paving stones out where she thought they looked best and added eight scalloped "petal" blocks around each one, as you can see in the illustration above. She filled the whole area in with pea gravel, and her whimsical floral path was ready to go!

Birdbath base redo
Joannie Rocchi, Illinois
When the bowl to your ceramic birdbath breaks, what do you do with the hollow base? It's not always easy to find a replacement bowl that matches, but it seems like a shame to toss it. Joannie had a clever solution. She turned the base upside down and buried the narrow end a few inches in the ground so it wouldn't tip over. Then she filled it with annuals. Since there's an opening at both ends, drainage wasn't a problem. When a second birdbath bowl was damaged, Joannie turned that base upside down, too. To make the combination more attractive and interesting she pushed that base into the soil a little further than the first one.

Homemade hose holder
Erica Anderson, Wisconsin
Erica liked the brass hose hider she saw at the store but she didn't like the price. Later, she found a decorative 24-inch plastic container on sale and got an idea. With a utility knife, she cut a small square hole about 3 inches down from the container's rim. Then she drilled a couple of holes in the bottom, so water doesn't collect. Coiling a 50-foot hose inside the pot, she ran the end through the upper hole and connected it to the faucet.

A brick in the bottom of the lightweight container keeps it from tipping over when she pulls on the hose. Neighbors like her idea so much that homemade hose hiders keep popping up along her block.

product pick

Polymeric sand

Most dry-laid brick patios have sand between the pavers to keep them stable and in place. But over time the sand washes out or wears away. Plus, weed seeds seem to find patios a cozy place to make their home. Polymeric sand can help. There are several major brands available and contractors have used this product for several years. But now homeowners can find it more easily, too! What's so great about it? When this sand is watered in, the polymers enlarge and form a solid joint between the bricks. That keeps them in place, prevents weed seeds from germinating and is impervious to burrowing insects, such as ants. (And you won't track a lot of sand in the house, either.) Prices vary: Expect to pay around $16 for a 25-pound tub, which will give you 8 to 35 square feet of coverage, depending on the width of your joints. Be sure to check the weather and choose a dry day before you start sweeping this sand in. Once it's wet, it sticks to whatever it touches.

Bottom line It's more expensive than plain old sand but worth it.
Source Local hardware or home improvement centers, such as Home Depot and Lowe's

Polymers in the sand form a solid joint.

Bad sand bonding
Bob Stackhouse, Iowa

Q *Part of the polymeric sand I used between my patio pavers last year has washed out. Can I simply add more over the existing sand?*
A Probably not. When you add water to polymeric joint sand, it forms a tough bond between pavers or bricks in patios and walkways. When you sweep it into joints and wet it down, this material hardens and prevents pavers from moving and keeps out weeds and tunneling ants.

The special binders in the sand that got washed out probably didn't set up completely. You could try to sweep in more sand and rewet it, but chances are it won't bond well with the existing sand and you'll end up with the same problem down the road. You're better off removing the existing sand with a pressure washer, letting the pavers and joints dry completely and putting in new sand.

Recycle your old sidewalk
Steff Franklin, Vermont

Q *I'm thinking of using broken concrete to build a raised bed. Will anything leach from the concrete out into the soil?*
A Yes, rain and snow may cause a little lime to leach out, but the amount would be so small that it probably won't affect any plants growing nearby.

The only situation where it might make any impact would be if your soil is already neutral to alkaline and you wanted to grow rhododendrons or other acid-loving plants in the soil.

Actually, using broken concrete for walls is a great way to recycle old materials that might otherwise end up in a landfill. And not only does the material make natural-looking retaining walls, you can often get it free or for just the cost of hauling it.

But in any case, it's always a good idea to do a soil test to find out the pH of your soil before you plant anything. Then you'll know where you stand and if you need to add any amendments to improve it.

did you know... (CONTINUED)

Slip the headboard leg into the piece of pipe so the "gate" will swing open and closed.

Trash to treasure
Sandy Esse, Wisconsin

Another person's trash became Sandy's treasure. She came across a full-sized imitation brass headboard on the curb one day and decided to take it home. Once there, she made it into a rustic-looking gate like the one in the illustration above. To create the "hinge" the gate would swing on, Sandy used a 24-inch piece of galvanized electrical conduit sunk into the ground with about 12 inches above the soil surface. Headboard legs can be different lengths, so measure yours first to see how much conduit you should leave above the ground. Sandy slipped one leg of the headboard into the pipe and it was ready to go!

Creature feature
Molly Vollman, Washington

Molly had a concrete fountain that just didn't work right. Instead of getting rid of it, she made it into a butterfly attraction. All it takes is some sand, a little fresh horse or cow manure and some fruit that's past its prime. Molly filled the large lower bowl of the fountain with sand and mixed in the manure. A couple of tablespoons of manure has all the salts and minerals that butterflies need. Add enough water to keep it damp but not so much that it's soggy. Top the mix off with old fruit and you have a butterfly smorgasbord!

Tool perch
Norma Berry, California

Norma enjoys watching the birds. The only problem was that her garden didn't have any of the mature trees or shrubs that help them feel at home. To entice a few feathered friends to visit, she collected some old long-handled tools. When she sticks the handle end in the ground, hoes, cultivators and rakes provide a high spot so birds can survey the garden before they grab a quick drink from the birdbath.

Turn an old firepit into a water garden
Sheryl Wood, Virginia

When Sheryl moved to a warmer climate, she found she didn't use her metal firepit much. At 30 inches across and 10 inches deep, it was good-sized so she decided to turn it into a water garden. After scrubbing the bowl thoroughly to clean it up, Sheryl spray-painted it a burnished copper color. Then she went shopping at the local garden center and came home with bloody dock (*Rumex sanguineus*), horsetail rush (*Equisetum hyemale*), and pickerel weed (*Pontederia cordata*). She planted them in clay pots and topped the soil off with decorative rock so it wouldn't float away. Then she set the pots in the bottom of the firepit. The terra-cotta blended in with the copper color so well that the pots weren't noticeable. Since there wasn't any moving water, Sheryl added water lettuce and water hyacinth to help keep the water clean. All that was left was to sit back and enjoy the water garden.

Second career for fireplace tools
Kim Croswhite, Washington

Kim felt that she never had enough hose guides. As she watered, it was hard to keep the hose from bending or breaking plant foliage and stems. But when it was time to retire some old fireplace tools, she got an idea. The working end of the brush and the shovel were easy to unscrew and remove from the handle. So Kim took them off and pushed the threaded end of the handle into the soil. They were a little taller than the hose guides you buy, but that turned out to be a good thing because the hose couldn't hop over the top like it sometimes does with others. The decorative finials on top made them nice to look at, and the handles kept her plants safe.

Floating plant roots help keep the water clean.

Place rocks on top of the soil to hold it in place.

product picks

Pure White

Pearl Motif

Mineral Motif

Soji Modern solar lantern

Brighten up the night life in your garden with this new solar lantern. The Soji Modern lantern doesn't need a cord. All it needs is 4 to 6 hours in the sun to soak up some rays. Then when the sun goes down, two LED lights come on for about 6 hours. Like most solar lights, it's not enough to read by, but it adds a soft glow to a summer evening on the patio. Modern lanterns are 9 inches in diameter and come in three patterns. Pearl Motif is white with a white floral pattern, Mineral Motif is white with a gray pattern and Pure White has no pattern.

Bottom line No need for expensive electrical work, just hang them outside.
Source Allsop at www.allsopgarden.com or 800-426-4303 or GardenGateStore.com
Price Retails for about $39.99 each

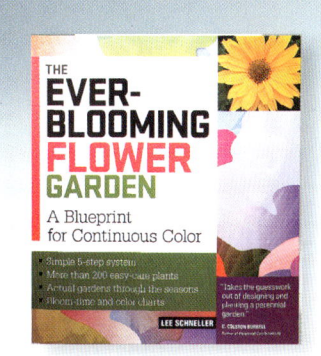

The Ever-Blooming Flower Garden

If you yearn for a garden that blooms from spring to fall, check out this new book by Lee Schneller. Using 220 easy-care plants, the author walks you through her five-step process for designing a garden that's always in bloom. The book includes questionnaires, formulas and checklists, along with a chapter on the plants she recommends. Each profile has a photo and basic care instructions. What's nice about this plant list is that there's something for every zone in North America. So no matter where you live, your garden will always be blooming.

Bottom line Follow the advice in this book for a gorgeous flower garden from spring to fall.
Source Local and online bookstores and GardenGateStore.com
Price $19.95; softcover; 224 pages

Perennial Companions

Getting just the right plants growing together isn't easy. After all, there's a lot to consider even before you put them in the ground. Find plants that look good and grow well together with this new book, "Perennial Companions" by Tom Fischer. Starting with spring and moving to late fall, it's filled with helpful photographs of plant combinations. Each grouping has two to five plants that share the same needs for light, soil and bloom time. Page through this book to get great ideas for filling those empty spots in the garden or starting a whole new bed.

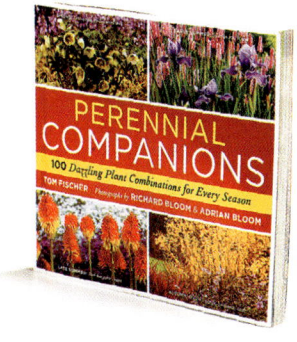

Bottom line It's small in size (only 7x6 in.) but packed with ideas.
Source Local and online bookstores and GardenGateStore.com
Price $14.95; softcover; 216 pages

Here's a stunning solution to a steep back yard. Learn how to do it yourself on page 204.

186 *the* YEAR IN GARDENING   www.GardenGateMagazine.com

design challenge
and drawing board
plans to solve *your* most challenging garden situations

HOW'D YOU DO THAT? is what most folks want to know when they see a gorgeous garden. Let us give you the solutions for six common situations gardeners face. From tips you can apply to your yard to specific planting plans for great-looking beds, it's all here!

Enter Here **188**
An Entry Garden
   for Everyone **190**
Make the Uglies
   Disappear **192**
Hide an Eyesore **194**
Fill in a Big Berm **196**
Easy Tips to Fill
   a Big Garden **198**
Too Much Going On! **200**
Keep it Simple! **202**
Tame a Steep Slope **204**
Beauty on Many Levels **206**
From Simple to Simply
   Stunning **208**
Plant a Little Peace
   and Quiet **210**

DESIGN CHALLENGE | FRONT YARD

garden outside the lines:
enter here!

*See a complete **planting plan** for this entry.*

First impressions are everything — at least when it comes to the garden by your front door. Many homes have a small space that's "trapped" between the house, the sidewalk and the driveway. You don't want to redo the sidewalk, so how do you make a cramped entry garden welcoming?

Diane Buijnarowski of Wallingford, Connecticut, asked that question about her front garden. This two-story house has an awkward space bordered by the house, sidewalk and garage. There's also a long narrow bed that runs along the front of the house. These nearly empty beds needed some help!

BEYOND THE LINES As a rule, foundation beds should extend out two-thirds the height of the house. For example, if your house is 24 feet tall, your garden should be 16 feet deep. But trapped areas are often small and not in proportion with the house. A simple solution is to extend the garden beyond the sidewalk and out into the lawn. Just let the sidewalk pass through. And don't be afraid to include an ornamental tree in an entryway planting — it may seem strange to put a big plant in a small space, but a neatly shaped tree that doesn't get too tall, like the one we've included here, has enough bulk to give the illusion of more garden space. And the tree will cover part of the house, so you're less likely to notice that the house feels too big for the space in front of it.

Repeat some of the plant material from the entryway on the other side of the door and down along the foundation bed, too — it'll make the whole front yard seem more cohesive.

Want to see how these ideas work with different styles of house? Check out some more options starting on p. 190.

CREATE A YEAR-ROUND GARDEN Choosing a plant palette and sticking to it is a good design idea in any size garden. But in this tiny space it's crucial. Too many different types of plants will be confusing. We kept our list to just six plants! But each type of plant serves a distinct purpose. Evergreen shrubs give year-round color and structure, while a small tree adds much-needed height. Then fill in around those two "backbone" plant types with a mix of flowering shrubs, perennials and annuals — that's a combination that'll give you flowers or foliage color year-round.

PAINT WITH PLANTS Take a few color cues from your house to help you make plant color choices. Repeat the trim or accent color with flowers or a container. Here you can see the blue of the shutters and door is repeated in the flowers in the garden. Add splashes of contrasting colors like coral and light green in containers, blooms and ornaments.

ROLL OUT THE RED CARPET For those who get snow in winter, make it easy to keep that path passable by creating a few spots in the garden to pile snow. Heavy snow and de-icing salt can cause serious problems for some plants. See how there's a group of containers near the door? When you put those containers away for the winter, you'll have a spot to pile snow shoveled from the steps.

Combine all (or a few) of these tips for your own entry garden that can't be missed! □

PHOTO: Courtesy of Diane Buijnarowski

Try a tree A small, dense-textured tree will add a formal note to this garden that's right in keeping with the style of the house. But a looser, multi-stemmed ornamental tree would add a more casual feel.

Extra color Containers and obelisks add an extra punch of color and texture in a limited space. You can move them around in different combinations for a new look each year.

Easy-care path Pavers add more interest, texture and color than standard concrete. Speaking of paver colors, dark-colored ones heat up faster in winter sun, making it easier to melt off snow and ice.

Small shrubs In a tight spot like this, you'll want to choose shrubs that don't get too large or sprawling. We chose the arborvitae for this plan, but here are two more options that'll stay neat and tidy without a lot of pruning.

1 Dwarf arborvitae *Thuja occidentalis* 'Hetz Midget' 3 to 4 ft. tall and wide; evergreen foliage is best in a sheltered spot in winter; cold-hardy in USDA zones 3 to 7; heat-tolerant in AHS zones 7 to 1

2 Boxwood *Buxus* spp. 1 to 5 ft. tall and wide; small, glossy semi-evergreen foliage; can be sheared if needed; cold-hardy in USDA zones 5 to 9; heat-tolerant in AHS zones 9 to 1

3 Japanese spirea *Spiraea japonica* 1 to 5 ft. tall and wide; pink or white flowers, green or chartreuse foliage; cold-hardy in USDA zones 4 to 9; heat-tolerant in AHS zones 9 to 1

www.GardenGateMagazine.com   *the* YEAR IN GARDENING

DRAWING BOARD | FRONT YARD

An entry garden for everyone

There are as many styles of front entry gardens as there are homeowners and gardeners. So how you choose to deal with a tiny entryway garden is up to you. To give you some ideas, here are two different houses, each with garden spaces that are trapped by concrete and house walls. Each plan includes a small ornamental tree, evergreen and deciduous shrubs and a mixture of flowering plants. But each plan has its own distinctive style! □
— Stephanie Polsley Bruner and Tigon Woline

House and garden working together

Scale is important when you're designing an entry garden. Too-small plants will make the house look out of proportion and too-big plants will overwhelm both the house and visitors — save larger plants for farther from the door. A good rule of thumb: Near the door, keep the largest plant under 25 ft. tall. The crabapple in this plan has beautiful coral flowers in spring to catch your eye.

This garden doesn't require lots of maintenance, but the hydrangea might need a little attention. 'Dooley' has pale blue flowers in acid soil and lilac to pink flowers in alkaline soil. If your soil is neutral or alkaline and you want blue flowers, work in lots of organic material and elemental sulfur. Feed through the growing season with Miracid® to maintain the soil acidity. Or you could grow the blue hydrangeas in containers sunk in the garden — it's easier to get the soil just right.

Plant list (Number to plant)

A Dwarf arborvitae *Thuja occidentalis* 'Hetz Midget' (8)
3 to 4 ft. tall and wide; low-maintenance background plant; cold-hardy in USDA zones 3 to 7; heat-tolerant in AHS zones 7 to 1

B Clematis *Clematis* 'Blue Light' (2)
6 to 8 ft. tall and spreading; double blue-violet flowers in spring, repeat bloom in fall; cold-hardy in USDA zones 3 to 9; heat-tolerant in AHS zones 9 to 1

C Candytuft *Iberis sempervirens* 'Little Gem' ('Weisser Zwerg') (12)
6 to 12 in. tall, 10 to 25 in. wide; white flowers in spring and early summer, excellent ground cover; cold-hardy in USDA zones 5 to 9; heat-tolerant in AHS zones 9 to 1

D Hydrangea *Hydrangea macrophylla* 'Dooley' (2)
3 to 5 ft. tall and wide; huge blue flower clusters in summer; cold-hardy in USDA zones 6 to 9; heat-tolerant in AHS zones 9 to 1

E Salvia *Salvia* xsylvestris 'Blue Hill' ('Blauhügel') (15)
18 in. tall and wide; profuse blue-purple flowers in summer; cold-hardy in USDA zones 4 to 9; heat-tolerant in AHS zones 9 to 1

F Crabapple *Malus* 'Coralburst' (1)
10 to 12 ft. tall, 12 to 15 ft. wide; coral-pink flowers in spring followed by few fruit; cold-hardy in USDA zones 4 to 8; heat-tolerant in AHS zones 8 to 1

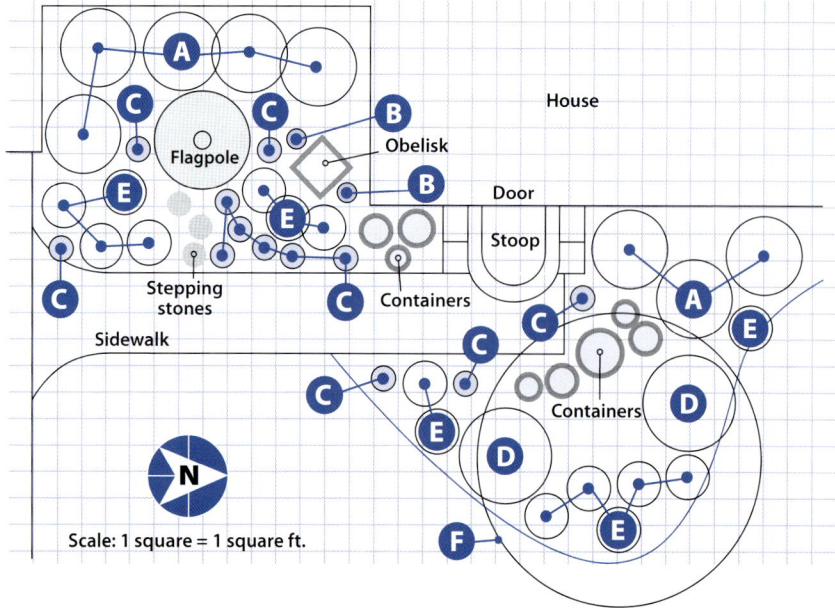

Scale: 1 square = 1 square ft.

Add some pizzazz

Not only does this split-level house have the tight planting space along the front, but it also has an overhang and windows near the ground. Low-growing plants won't block the light. And expanding the planting space beyond the sidewalk gives you room for a big shrub to add a feeling of shelter. Finally, put a stepping-stone path through the bed so your flowers don't get trampled by the mail carrier.

Deadheading is all you need to do for this bright entry. Remove faded flowers from the red-hot poker, blanket flower, canna, and Texas sage. As the summer continues, you may need to trim back the sweet potato vine to keep it from taking over. (Don't worry — it'll bounce right back!) Mix some annuals and tender perennials into a garden — you can change them each year to add a new color or texture.

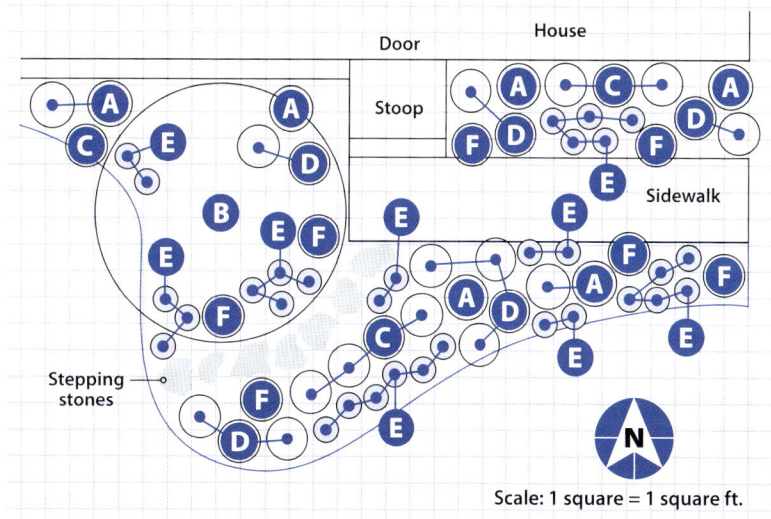

Scale: 1 square = 1 square ft.

Plant list (Number to plant)

A Canna *Canna* Tropicanna™ ('Phasion') (8)
6 ft. tall, 1 to 2 ft. wide; red-, orange- and green-striped foliage and orange flowers; cold-hardy in USDA zones 7 to 11; heat tolerant in AHS zones 11 to 1

B Smokebush *Cotinus coggygria* 'Royal Purple' (1)
15 ft. tall, 10 to 12 ft. wide; burgundy-purple foliage, airy blooms; cold-hardy in USDA zones 5 to 8; heat-tolerant in AHS zones 8 to 1

C Red-hot poker *Kniphofia* 'Flamenco' (8)
30 to 36 in. tall, 18 in. wide; red, orange and yellow flowers in midsummer, semi-evergreen foliage; cold-hardy in USDA zones 5 to 9; heat-tolerant in AHS zones 9 to 1

D Blanket flower *Gaillardia* xgrandiflora 'Kobold' (13)
12 in. tall, 18 in. wide; red-and-yellow flowers from early summer to fall; cold-hardy in USDA zones 3 to 9; heat-tolerant in AHS zones 9 to 1

E Texas sage *Salvia coccinea* 'Spanish Dancer' (31)
24 to 30 in. tall, 12 to 14 in. wide; scarlet flowers attract butterflies and hummingbirds; cold-hardy in USDA zones 9 to 10; heat-tolerant in AHS zones 12 to 1

F Sweet potato vine *Ipomoea batatas* 'Blackie' (7)
4 to 10 in. tall, 18 in. wide and spreading; popular container plant does well in the garden, too; cold-hardy in USDA zones 10 to 11; heat-tolerant in AHS zones 12 to 1

DESIGN CHALLENGE | FRONT YARD

don't look now!
make the uglies disappear

Every yard has one feature that just doesn't look so great. Maybe it's the neighbor's drive, an air conditioner unit, a utility box or a compost pile. Are you doomed to see it every time you drive up to your house? Of course not! But sometimes it does take some careful designing to make the problem fade away.

Kevin and Doris Gomez certainly have one of these not-so-great features in their New York front yard. It's not just one utility box, it's a cluster of four. What do you do about a problem like this? The boxes can't be moved, and they need to be accessible. As is often the case, the right plantings can hide, or at least minimize, this eyesore. However, there are a couple of things to keep in mind for the best coverup.

An obvious solution is to plant something around the box. But your yard will look a little odd if you simply plant a hedge all the way around it — in fact, that will just draw even more attention to the problem. Your goal is to hide as much of the box as possible and to make sure you're obscuring most of those hard, noticeable, "man-made" edges. A mixed planting of evergreen shrubs, grasses and small trees offers softness and texture that'll draw attention away from the box.

And there are other tips you can use to distract your eye from these utility boxes. Clever use of color, plus repeating beds in other parts of the yard, helps distract the focus from the one area you don't want to see. Let's take a look at a few ways to make sure that this electrical box isn't the "focal point" of this yard any more! ◻

Web extra
See a complete *planting plan* for this garden.

PHOTO: Courtesy of Kevin and Doris Gomez

Block and redirect
You don't want to end up with one huge planting that's centered around the eyesore! Create other focal points elsewhere in the yard so you'll notice something else first. Here, clumps of ornamental grasses and bright perennials keep your eye moving around the yard, instead of focused on the utility boxes.

Take a stand Think about where you're most likely to glimpse your problem spot, and how much time you spend at that vantage point. Then factor that into the placement of your cover and focal points. Here, a large shrub screens the boxes from the front door and upper windows, while shorter evergreen shrubs and beds at the outermost corners help screen them from the street.

Do your homework Always check with utility companies (or manufacturers, if you're dealing with an AC unit). You'll need to ask how much clearance these units need, how often they must be accessed and what are acceptable means for covering them. You may be able to paint the outsides, or build a berm or structure around the box. This planting leaves room to stand next to the box for periodic maintenance.

811 Know what's below. Call before you dig.

PICK UP THE PHONE! We've probably all heard the slogan, "Dial before you dig" or something like it. Well, that's good advice — you don't want to hit buried utility lines when you're working in the garden. And it's easier now than it used to be. A couple of years ago, a federal system was set up to simplify all the separate One-Call numbers nationwide. Now, anywhere in the United States, you can call 811, and you'll be connected with your local One-Call number. (Each Canadian province has its own one-call number, listed in the phone book and online.) From there, you can set up a free appointment for someone to come mark where utility lines are buried in your yard.

Even if you've called in the past, call again if you're going to be digging in the same area. Utilities may have changed, or your memory of where the lines run may not be as good as you think.

DRAWING BOARD | FRONT YARD

Hide an eyesore with good design

The only good utility box is one that's not in your front yard! But if that's not an option, you'll have to come up with some ways to conceal it. And actually, that's not as hard as you might think.

START WITH SHRUBS When you're trying to hide an ugly spot in your garden, evergreen shrubs are your best bet. From which direction is your eyesore most noticeable? Cluster the shrubs on the side (or sides) you're most concerned about concealing. Often, you'll need to be able to get close to whatever you're trying to hide, whether it's a compost pile or a utility box. So choose evergreens that are only a bit taller than the eyesore — if you do need to get into the bed for maintenance, you don't want to have to push your way through a jungle to get to the problem spot.

YOUR POINT OF VIEW Most gardeners are primarily concerned about the view from the street. But what about the view you see from the house? Keep in mind that even first-floor windows are probably a little higher than ground level, and of course, second-floor windows are higher still. So plant a large shrub or small tree to block the view of the utility box from above, as well. Then you'll be all set to admire your garden! ◻

— *Stephanie Polsley Bruner*

Sunny screen Low-growing evergreen inkberries cover up the utility box from the street, the side that the gardener most wants to hide. But straight lines or a boxy planting will just draw attention to the problem in the middle. A softly curved planting, on the other hand, distracts your eye. Color provides another distraction. Yellow coreopsis and rosy red daylilies make you look at the sides of the planting, instead of right in the middle. And the upright grass, along with the height of the Peegee hydrangea, keeps your eye moving, as well.

Shady coverup A big shade tree is a wonderful thing. But the combination of a shade tree and utility boxes in the middle of the lawn is a gardening double-whammy. Don't despair: dense, shade-tolerant yews keep the box under wraps in summer and winter, while looser-textured rhododendrons prevent it from looking too stiff. Bright pops of color from astilbe and corydalis make this garden pretty — not just functional — all summer long.

Plant list (Number to plant)

A Coreopsis *Coreopsis verticillata* 'Moonbeam' (12)
18 to 24 in. tall and wide; yellow flowers from early to late summer; cold-hardy in USDA zones 3 to 9; heat-tolerant in AHS zones 9 to 1

B Inkberry *Ilex glabra* 'Shamrock' (5)
3 to 4 ft. tall and wide; slow-growing broad-leafed evergreen; cold-hardy in USDA zones 4 to 9; heat-tolerant in AHS zones 9 to 1

C Catmint *Nepeta racemosa* 'Walker's Low' (2)
18 to 36 in. tall and wide; purple flowers from early to late summer; cold-hardy in USDA zones 3 to 9; heat-tolerant in AHS zones 9 to 1

D Daylily *Hemerocallis* 'Rosy Returns' (10)
15 in. tall, 12 to 18 in. wide; slightly fragrant pink blooms from early to late summer; cold-hardy in USDA zones 3 to 9; heat-tolerant in AHS zones 9 to 1

E Porcupine grass *Miscanthus sinensis* 'Strictus' (1)
5 to 8 ft. tall, 2 to 6 ft. wide; yellow-striped leaf blades, white plumes in late summer to fall; cold-hardy in USDA zones 5 to 9; heat-tolerant in AHS zones 9 to 1

F Peegee hydrangea *Hydrangea paniculata* 'Grandiflora' (1)
10 to 25 ft. tall, 8 to 16 ft. wide; white flowers in mid- to late summer; cold-hardy in USDA zones 3 to 9; heat-tolerant in AHS zones 9 to 1

G Hosta *Hosta sieboldiana elegans* (6)
2 to 3 ft. tall, 3 to 4 ft. wide; textured blue-green leaves, white flowers in midsummer; cold-hardy in USDA zones 4 to 9; heat-tolerant in AHS zones 9 to 1

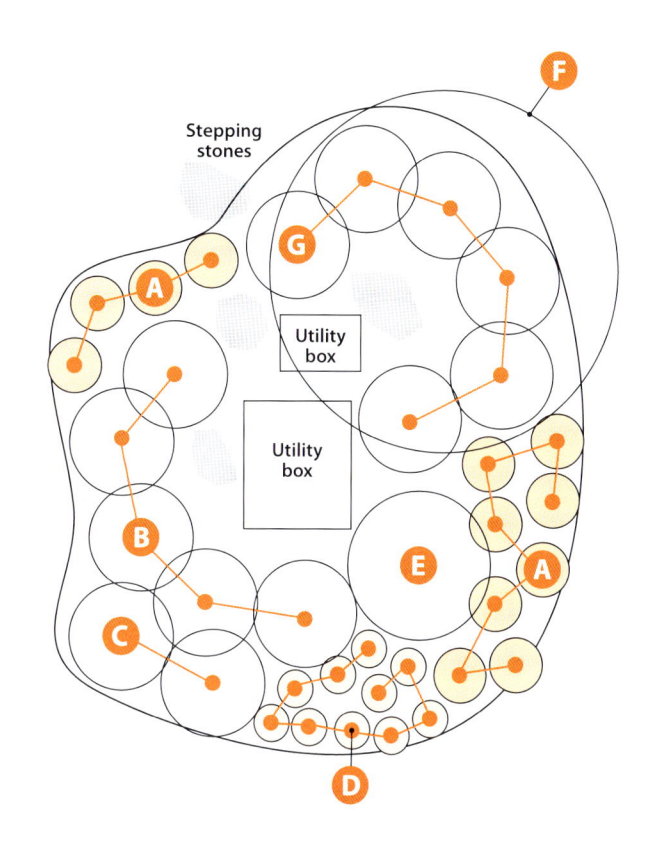

Plant list (Number to plant)

A Spreading yew *Taxus xmedia* 'Densiformis' (4)
3 to 4 ft. tall, 4 to 6 ft. wide; dark-green evergreen foliage; cold-hardy in USDA zones 4 to 7; heat-tolerant in AHS zones 7 to 1

B Astilbe *Astilbe* 'Ostrich Plume' ('Straussenfeder') (12)
2 to 3 ft. tall, 1 to 2 ft. wide; pink flowers in early to midsummer; cold-hardy in USDA zones 4 to 8; heat-tolerant in AHS zones 8 to 1

C Rhododendron *Rhododendron* PJM Group (3)
3 to 6 ft. tall, 3 to 7 ft. wide; magenta flowers in early to midspring; cold-hardy in USDA zones 4 to 8; heat-tolerant in AHS zones 8 to 1

D Hosta *Hosta sieboldiana elegans* (8)
2 to 3 ft. tall, 3 to 4 ft. wide; textured blue green leaves, white flowers in midsummer; cold-hardy in USDA zones 4 to 9; heat-tolerant in AHS zones 9 to 1

E Corydalis *Corydalis lutea* (27)
4 to 18 in. tall, 6 to 12 in. wide; yellow flowers from spring to fall; cold-hardy in USDA zones 5 to 8; heat-tolerant in AHS zones 8 to 1

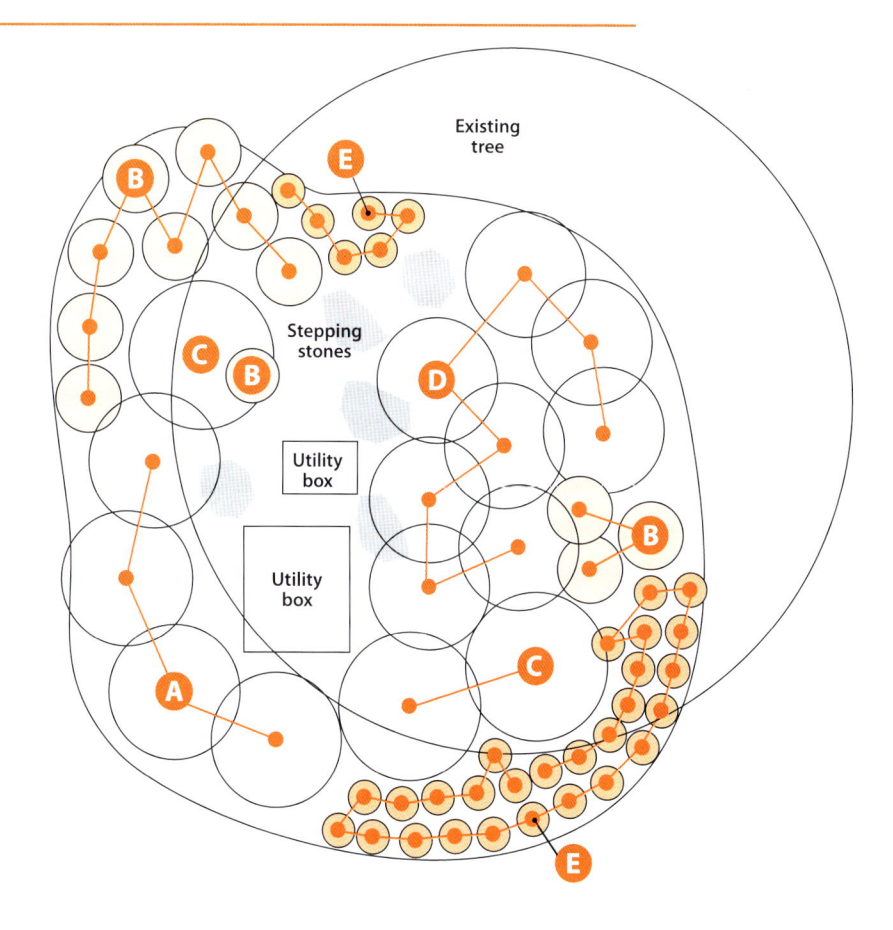

DESIGN CHALLENGE | FRONT YARD

fill in a big berm

If your lot is as flat as a tabletop, you're not alone in wanting something different. Whether they're natural or man-made, hills and berms create focal points and allow you to bring delicate flowers up for closer inspection. But turning a berm into a showstopping garden is a bit tricky, as Debra Richards and her husband have discovered at their Illinois home.

They built a very long berm, about 12 feet wide and 106 feet long, along the road in front of their house. But once they built it, they realized they needed some tips on how to plant it and make it look great.

Out in this country garden, strong winds whip across the yard. The planting needs to withstand strong winds, sandy soil and hot sun. And it needs to be low maintenance because it's so far from the house.

Let's look at a few tips for making the most of any berm. Check out "Berm basics" for more information on how to design the perfect feature for your yard. Then turn the page for a closer look at this beautiful planting plan.

PHOTO: Courtesy Debra Richards

Web extra
See a complete *planting plan* for this berm garden.

Plant placement

As you're planting, keep in mind that a berm acts almost like an easel, getting short plants up closer to eye height. So a plant that's really 3 ft. tall will look like it's 4 or 5 ft. tall if it's planted on a berm. Vary the plants you put right along the top ridge of the berm — it'll give the planting an undulating, natural appearance.

Berm benefit

This berm helps block the wind and creates a colorful ribbon along the road. The extra height can also buffer unwanted views and noises or separate different areas of your garden. Another benefit to any raised planting: It allows you to change the condition of your soil. Build over a soggy spot or create rocky soil for an alpine garden.

196   *the* YEAR IN GARDENING   www.GardenGateMagazine.com

Changing views

The four upright, columnar English oak trees add a punch of drama to this berm. They create a sense of mystery and intrigue as you drive toward the house. You can only see glimpses of the house between the trees, which makes you curious and want to know more. At mature size, these trees are in proportion with the rest of the trees in the surrounding landscape, but their narrow canopies won't shade the plants below.

Stones and steppers

Don't forget about adding stones and steppers. They'll fill up space if your plant budget is tight. Plus, you can step or sit on them to reach into the middle of the bed. Partially bury larger boulders in groups of odd numbers to make them look like they've always been there. Or use smaller rocks around the edge to define the space.

BERM BASICS

Building a berm is a big project. Consider these basics while you're planning, and you're on your way to a stunning garden.

SIZE As with any other large landscape element, make sure your berm is the right size for your needs. A small berm by the front door can add just as much "Wow!" as a bigger one by the street.

GRADE Asymmetrical is the way to go. Natural-looking berms have the highest point closer to one side. The illustration below shows how gradually one side rises out of the ground, while the other side rounds off quickly. And change the height along the berm, especially if it's a long one. It'll be more interesting and more natural this way.

SLOPE Don't make it too steep! The 10-ft.-wide berm in the illustration is only 2 ft. tall at its highest point. This shallow slope allows you to mow the berm safely if you decide to grow grass. Plus, it won't have erosion problems and you'll find it more comfortable to work on.

SUBSTANCE It would be expensive to buy enough topsoil to build an entire berm, and you don't really need to anyway. Instead, use poor-quality soil or sod flipped upside down to build up the shape. Then top it off with a foot or more of good topsoil. Build the berm a little taller than you want the final height, as it will settle a bit. If you compact the sod or poor-quality soil, you'll cut down on the amount of settling.

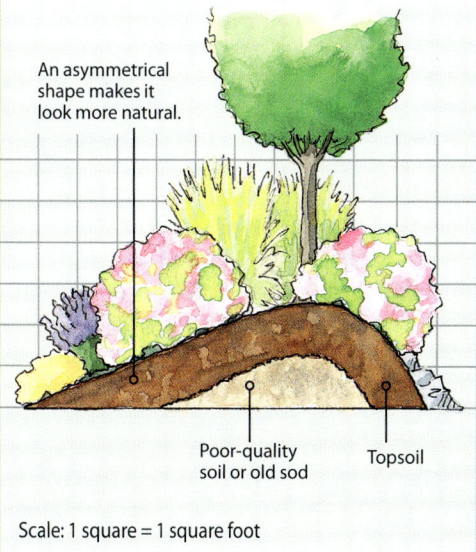

An asymmetrical shape makes it look more natural.

Poor-quality soil or old sod | Topsoil

Scale: 1 square = 1 square foot

DRAWING BOARD | FRONT YARD

easy tips to
fill a big garden

When your garden is away from your house, lugging shovels, hoses and mulch back and forth wears you out. Cut down on the number of trips by planting nearly no-care plants and using some of these tips to help maintain your beds.

DIVIDE TO CONQUER As you saw on p. 196, this berm is really long and, like other big garden projects, the cost of purchasing materials will add up quickly. To help keep the cost more reasonable, develop a planting plan to install the garden over several years. For this plan, start with the oak trees. Then pick an end or section to start planting. The plan below shows the middle section of the berm bed, but you could start at an end instead. Popular, reliable plants, such as the 'Nearly Wild' roses and wild indigo, won't be hard to find at the garden center in the next few years, so only buy what you need for the first section. Many perennials, such as salvia and little bluestem, can be divided in a couple years. Split them up and plant the divisions to fill in the next spot. Add rocks and stones at any time, whether you've planted that area or not.

If the planting is new, it's best to start with an area that's closer to the house and work your way out. You'll be more motivated to keep up with the watering and other chores.

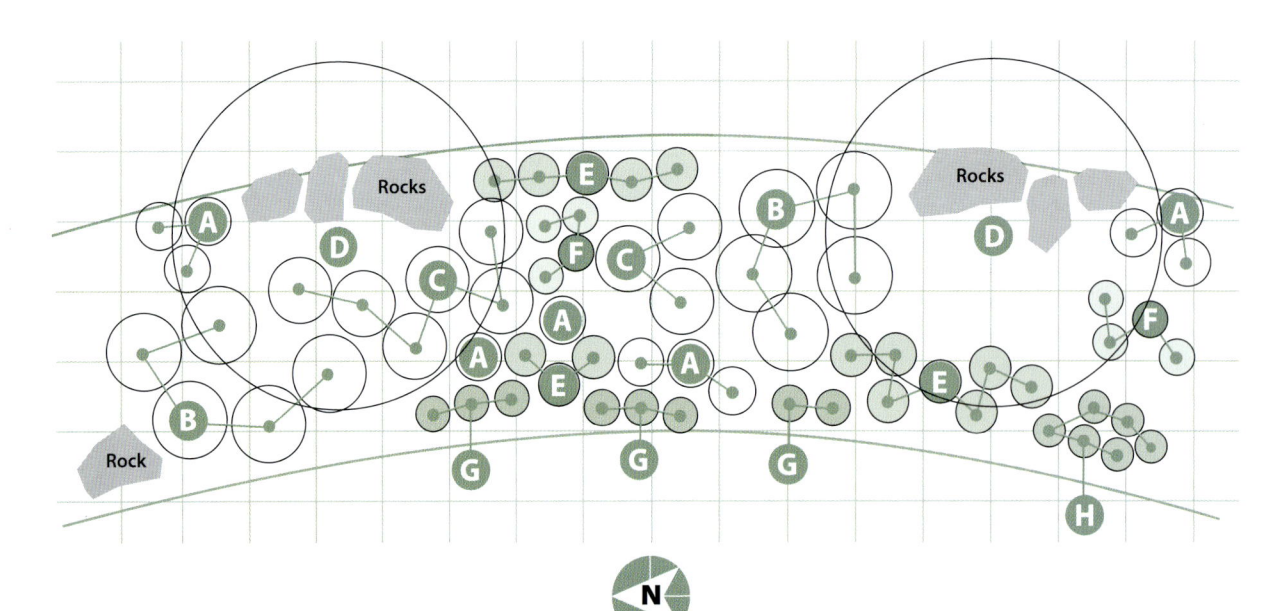

Scale: 1 square = 9 square feet

198 *the* YEAR IN GARDENING www.GardenGateMagazine.com

MULCH IS A MUST Mulch this berm to keep weeds down and the soil moist. To help the mulch stay in place instead of sliding down the sides of the berm, use shredded bark mulch instead of the nugget types. The stringy, shredded texture helps it cling together in a mat. If you find the mulch still slips off, cut pieces of black bird netting and tack them with landscape anchor pins around the plants to keep the mulch in place. Bird netting and landscape pins are available at your local garden center or landscape supplier. (Learn more about holding soil and mulch in place on p. 282.)

ON THE EDGE Another way to cut down on the amount of maintenance this garden needs: Put an edge around it. You can use stone, metal, brick or extruded concrete edging. (If you're not quite ready for a permanent edge, just cut a trench along the bottom of the berm with your spade.) It'll be easy to run a string trimmer along the edging, or if it's flat on top, you can run the mower wheels right along on top of it! An edge will also keep lawn grasses from invading your berm planting.

Berms aren't only for sunny spots. Turn the page for a shady combination.

THE GARDEN'S PALETTE

Code	Plant Name	No. to Plant	Blooms	Type	Cold/Heat Zones	Height/Width	Special Features
A	Black-eyed Susan *Rudbeckia fulgida* 'Goldsturm'	11	Golden yellow; summer to fall	Perennial	4-9/9-1	24-36 in./18-24 in.	Deadhead to encourage blooming and prevent self-seeding; attracts butterflies and hummingbirds
B	Rose *Rosa* 'Nearly Wild'	10	Pink; late spring to fall	Deciduous shrub	4-9/9-1	3 ft./2-4 ft.	Floribunda type rose; single, slightly fragrant flowers attract butterflies; deadhead to encourage reblooming
C	Wild indigo *Baptisia* Midnight Prairieblues™ ('Midnight') **NEW '09**	9	Blue; spring	Perennial	4-8/8-1	4-5 ft./3-4 ft.	Long flower spikes are excellent for cut flowers; second bloom period from low, branches; best if left undisturbed
D	Columnar English oak *Quercus robur* 'Fastigiata'	2	NA	Deciduous tree	5-8/8-1	50 ft./10-18 ft.	Highly drought- and heat-tolerant; holds leaves through winter like other oaks; produces acorns
E	Salvia *Salvia superba* 'Adora Blue' **NEW '09**	14	Blue-purple; early summer	Perennial	4-8/8-1	15-18 in./15-18 in.	Blooms early; flower color last longer; very compact habit; attracts hummingbirds
F	Little bluestem *Schizachyrium scoparium* 'The Blues'	8	Bronze; fall	Ornamental grass	3-9/9-1	24-48 in./18 in.	Blue-gray leaves turn burgundy-red in fall; small seedheads last through winter; cut back to crown in early spring
G	Hummingbird mint *Agastache* 'Cotton Candy' **NEW '09**	8	Pink; summer to fall	Perennial	6-9/9-1	18-24 in./18 in.	Attracts hummingbirds; needs well-drained soil, especially in winter; drought-tolerant
H	Evening primrose *Oenothera fremontii* 'Shimmer'	6	Yellow; late spring	Perennial	4-8/8-1	10 in./15 in.	3-in. lemon-yellow flowers attract butterflies; pinch back in early spring several times to encourage branching

NEW '09 Newly available variety. See p. 60 for 19 more of our favorite new plants this year.

DESIGN CHALLENGE | FRONT YARD

too much going on!

Web extra
See a complete *planting plan* for this entry.

PHOTO: Courtesy of Linda Larson

At first glance, this looks like a pretty garden, doesn't it? But Linda Larson of Iowa wasn't so happy with it up close. Too much fine, wispy texture and too many different kinds of plants made it seem messy and floppy.

What makes a garden look well-planned? Usually the best approach is to pick a core group of five or six plants and stick with it. That way, you're repeating colors and textures, making the garden feel unified. And planting in groups of three to five plants helps, too — you don't end up with lots of little dots of color here and there.

So does that mean she needs to rip everything out and start over? Not at all. It's a lot easier to make a garden look finished quickly if you can keep a few of the existing plants — after all, they're already established. Let's take a look at how to keep some plants while adding in new ones, making this entry feel warm, welcoming and, best of all, well-planned. ◻

Simplify your look Fewer kinds of plants plus a color theme equals a garden with lots of impact. The smokebush in the corner will be the biggest plant in this garden, so pick some other plants, like the coral bells along the front edge, that echo the burgundy leaf color. Plenty of pink flowers, from the veronica, the coneflowers and the sedum (another keeper from the original planting) look great with the burgundy foliage, too. You can find out more about these plants in "Keep it simple" on p. 202.

Challenge Our Designers

Is something about your yard giving you fits? Send a letter describing your landscape problems along with photos of the area. We'll choose a few, come up with ideas to make them work better and share them in future issues. Readers whose challenges are selected for publication will receive a one-year subscription or renewal to *Garden Gate* (not to mention some great garden advice!). Send your design challenge to:

Garden Gate Design Challenge Editor
2200 Grand Ave., Des Moines, Iowa 50312
Or e-mail us at gardengate@gardengatemag.com

A "screen" porch You want a little privacy while you're sitting on the porch, but you don't need huge shrubs to provide a screen. At 4 to 6 ft. tall, the three weigelas that were already in the bed give a sense of separation from the sidewalk and driveway, without completely covering the porch. The existing junipers add a great touch of winter interest. And a smokebush tucked in at the end of the row adds a little extra height to that corner, as well as making a great focal point. Cut the smokebush back hard in early spring, to about a foot tall. That will keep the shrub at a better height for an entryway planting. You won't get as many blooms, but the foliage will be much bigger and showier.

Cut stems back to about 1 ft. in early spring to keep smokebush smaller.

This bed's not big enough for the two of us! It's a great idea to create a bed on the "outside" of the sidewalk, too. But the original planting area wasn't quite big enough. We widened it just slightly, about a foot. That doesn't seem like a big adjustment, but that little bit of extra width allows at least two plants side by side, instead of a single row of plants. Now it'll balance out the big stuff in the main bed better.

Make an entrance This garden should be all about the front door, but there's nothing too striking about this entry in the before photo. Mark the transition from the drive with some vertical elements. On one side, there's the smokebush, and on the other side, tucked into the spreading juniper, there's a metal urn. The urn is a great focal point year-round, and the look can change with the seasons. Plus, it marks the end of the sidewalk, so it's obvious to visitors where they need to walk.

www.GardenGateMagazine.com   *the* YEAR IN GARDENING   201

DRAWING BOARD | FRONT YARD

keep it simple!

Throw a theme party for your garden. When you like plants, it's easy to end up with a few of this, one or two of that. And before you know it, instead of the lovely, colorful effect you'd planned, your garden is a mess.

What do you need to do to pick a garden theme? Not everything in your garden has to match. But a few repeated colors, plant types or common concepts make it a lot easier to put together a planting that looks well-planned, not haphazard. Then, throw in a few contrasts, whether it's a different leaf texture, a bright accent color or even a boulder to stand out against wispy plant material. If you highlight the differences, the contrasts will actually play up your main theme even more.

FOUR-SEASON INTEREST Every garden looks better with year-round appeal, from spring and summer flowers to fall color to winter interest. And that's especially crucial at your front door, because it's a prominent location that you'll view every single day. In the two plans on these pages, you'll see how some medium-sized shrubs offer flowers, leaf color or evergreen winter foliage to give your garden a structure and shape that just can't be beat. □

— Stephanie Polsley Bruner

Echo flower or foliage colors in containers and hanging baskets — they'll feel more like part of the garden that way.

Repeat some plants on both sides of the sidewalk to tie plantings together visually.

Choose shrubs, like this smokebush, that tolerate heavy pruning so they don't overwhelm your porch.

Leave hydrangea heads standing — they'll turn from white to green to tan, and they'll hold well into fall.

Chartreuse hostas and astilbes can stand more sun out of the shelter of the house as long as they're given extra water.

Pink and red perfection

Just like your outfit, you want your garden to look coordinated and pulled together. Choose a bold foliage plant, like the smokebush here, and use it for the inspiration for the rest of the garden. Burgundy coral bells pick up the smokebush's leaf color. Then pink-flowered weigela and pink spikes of veronica, along with dusty-pink coneflowers and sedum, keep a great accent color coming all season. This garden thrives in full to part sun. In full sun, give the coral bells a little extra water to keep the leaves from scorching.

Scale: 1 square = 1 square ft.

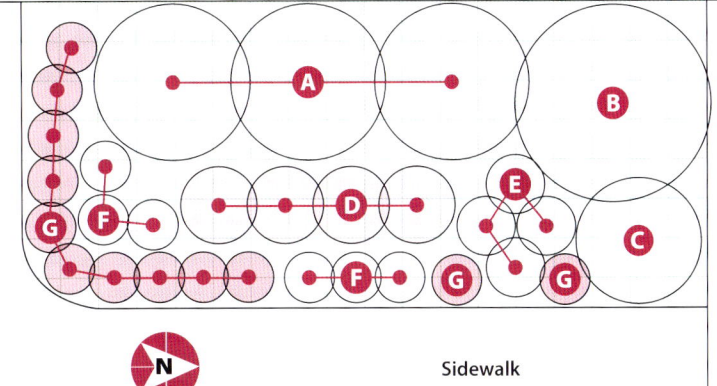

Code	Plant Name	No. to Plant	Blooms	Type	Cold/Heat Zones	Height/Width
A	Weigela *Weigela florida* 'Pink Princess'	3	Pink; late spring to early summer	Shrub	4-8/8-1	4-6 ft./4-6 ft.
B	Smokebush *Cotinus coggygria* 'Velvet Cloak'	1	Pink-gray; spring	Shrub	5-8/8-1	6-15 ft./6-15 ft.
C	Juniper *Juniperus sabina* Calgary Carpet® ('Monna')	1	NA	Evergreen shrub	3-8/8-1	9-12 in./36-72 in.
D	Sedum *Sedum* 'Autumn Joy' ('Herbstfreude')	4	Pink; late summer to fall	Perennial	3-9/9-1	24 in./24-36 in.
E	Purple coneflower *Echinacea purpurea* 'Kim's Knee High'	4	Pink; mid- to late summer	Perennial	3-9/9-1	18-24 in./18-24 in.
F	Veronica *Veronica spicata* 'Red Fox' ('Rotfuchs')	6	Pink; mid- to late summer	Perennial	3-8/8-1	12-24 in./15-24 in.
G	Coral bells *Heuchera* 'Amethyst Myst'	12	Pink; midsummer	Perennial	4-9/9-1	12-16 in./15-18 in.

Dark but not dreary!

Nothing is more relaxing on a hot summer day than walking up to a cool, shady house. If shade is what you have, try lighting it up with some white flowers, like the 'Annabelle' hydrangeas and goat's beard here. And a bit of chartreuse foliage and flowers, from the hosta and the lady's mantle, also lightens up that shade. Don't forget a little pop of excitement — a group of bright-red astilbes is a midsummer exclamation point. (Keep them well-watered so the foliage holds up even after blooming.) Last but not least, a sweetshrub adds some springtime fragrance.

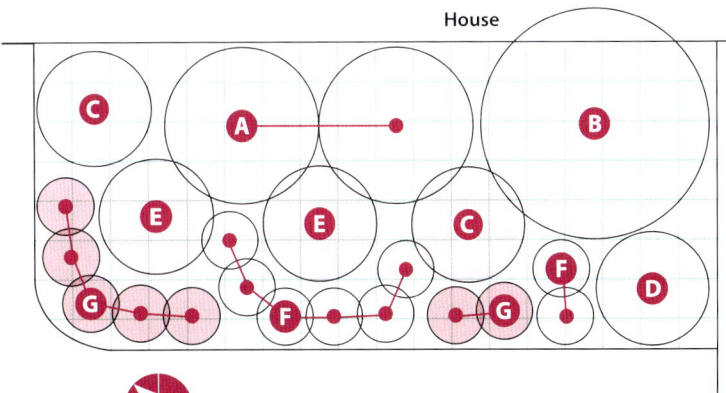

Scale: 1 square = 1 square ft.

Code	Plant Name	No. to Plant	Blooms	Type	Cold/Heat Zones	Height/Width
A	Hydrangea *Hydrangea arborescens* 'Annabelle'	2	White; early to midsummer	Shrub	3-9/9-1	3-5 ft./4-6 ft.
B	Sweetshrub *Calycanthus floridus*	1	Red-brown; late spring to early summer	Shrub	4-9/9-1	5-10 ft./5-10 ft.
C	Goat's beard *Aruncus dioicus*	2	White; spring	Perennial	3-7/7-1	4-6 ft./2-4 ft.
D	Russian cypress *Microbiota decussata*	1	NA	Evergreen shrub	3-8/8-1	1-2 ft./3-6 ft.
E	Hosta *Hosta* 'August Moon'	2	White; midsummer	Perennial	3-9/9-1	18-24 in./36-42 in.
F	Astilbe *Astilbe* 'Red Sentinel'	8	Red; early to midsummer	Perennial	4-9/9-1	24-30 in./18-24 in.
G	Lady's mantle *Alchemilla mollis*	7	Chartreuse; late spring to early summer	Perennial	4-8/8-1	10-18 in./18-30 in.

DESIGN CHALLENGE | BACK YARD

tame a steep slope

When it's cold and bleak in winter, it's nice to daydream about sitting out on the deck and enjoying the warm summer weather. If you don't have the yard of your dreams yet, this is the perfect time to plan it.

Betsy and Michael Alessi of Pennsylvania have a great big second-story deck and screened-in-porch, but it's hard for them to enjoy it. The neighbors can see onto the deck, and the hot summer sun limits the time they want to spend out there. They'd really like to plant around it but have no idea what to do with the steep slope along the side.

So we started this plan with two multi-stem birch trees. Planted near the corners, they enclose the area and provide shade. And a series of short terraces across the slope will prevent erosion problems — plus, it creates three new levels for planting!

Let's take a look at a few ideas for dealing with slopes and creating privacy around an elevated deck. Then turn the page for a closer look at the garden.

PHOTO: Courtesy of Betsy and Michael Alessi

Web extra
See a complete *planting plan* for this back yard.

Tie it all together

Bringing all the elements of a great landscape together is a daunting task. Make it easier by selecting only a few plants and using them over and over. Here, sweeps of cranesbill are repeated along the edge of the bed. Another technique to unify a garden is to have a continuous path through the middle of it. The path in this garden connects the deck, the terraces, the garden and the grassy back yard.

Exposed!

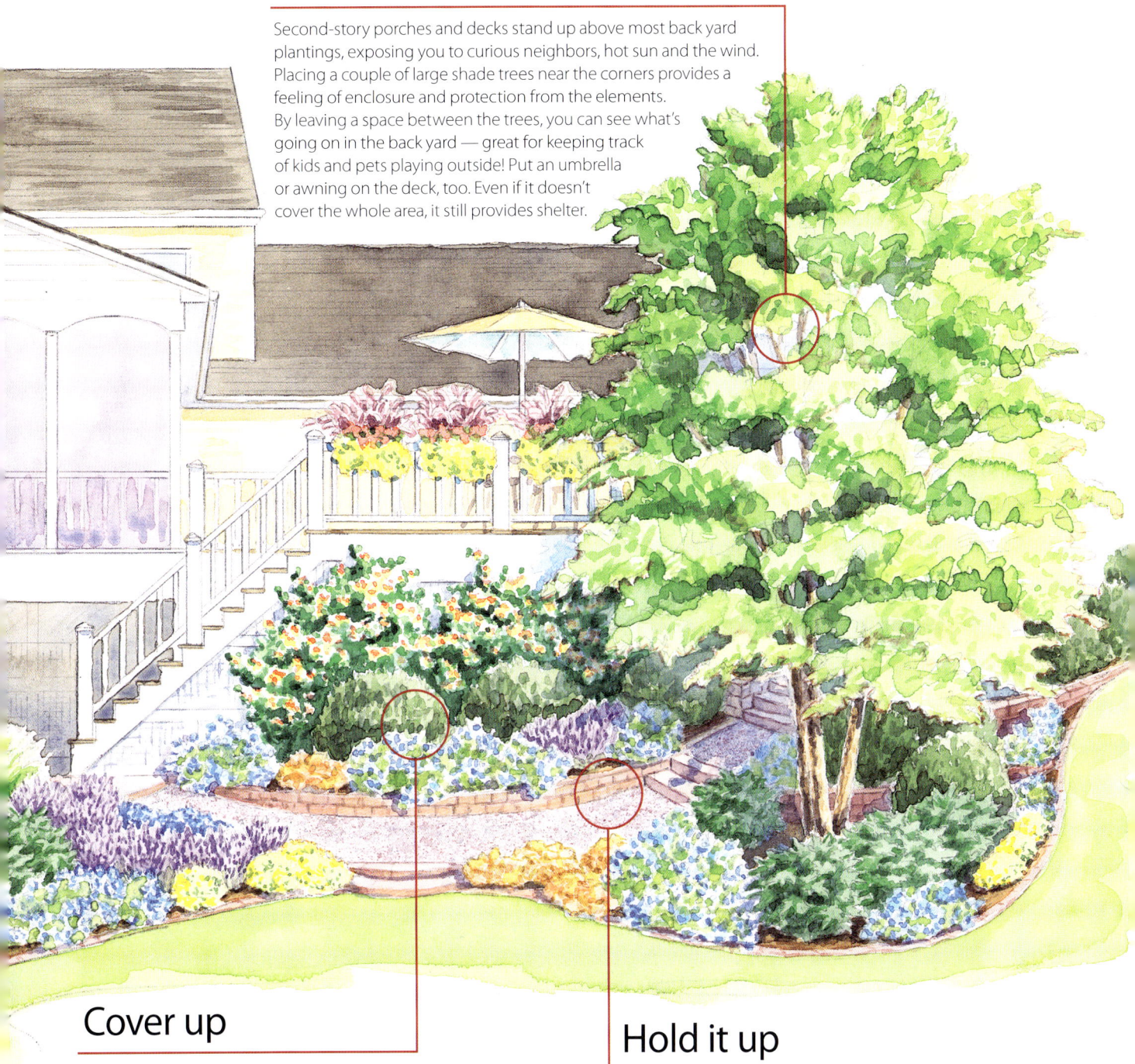

Second-story porches and decks stand up above most back yard plantings, exposing you to curious neighbors, hot sun and the wind. Placing a couple of large shade trees near the corners provides a feeling of enclosure and protection from the elements. By leaving a space between the trees, you can see what's going on in the back yard — great for keeping track of kids and pets playing outside! Put an umbrella or awning on the deck, too. Even if it doesn't cover the whole area, it still provides shelter.

Cover up

Elevated decks have tall supports and large spaces under them that usually aren't very attractive, especially if that space is used for storage. A common solution is to install lattice screening around it so it looks nice. To help the deck blend into the landscape more, train vines, such as honeysuckle or clematis, up the lattice. Trailing annuals, such as calibrachoa or sweet potato vine, in planter boxes can hide parts of the railing and bring the garden up. They also provide a bit more screening and privacy.

Hold it up

This slope is pretty steep and could present an erosion problem if you just dug up the sod and started planting. Installing retaining walls or terraces breaks the slope into manageable spaces. They will stop any erosion problems and create level planting areas where the soil can be amended more easily. Whenever you're planning major work on a slope, it's best to consult a landscape architect or engineer before you get started to make sure you don't create new drainage problems.

DRAWING BOARD | BACK YARD

beauty on many levels

Even the most beautiful deck doesn't look finished without an equally beautiful garden around it. Here, a planting on four terraced levels adds privacy and season-long color — and it looks great from any angle. Cool purples and soft yellows keep a potentially harsh, hot site looking cooler and more inviting. Plus, this garden is easy to care for!

SEASONAL COLOR Glossy green 'Carissa' holly forms a backdrop for creamy yellow and white peonies in spring, bright purple-blue cranesbill all summer and golden-tan maiden grass in fall. Add even more spring and fall color by tucking in clusters of bulbs along the walkway where they can be enjoyed up close. And the cranesbill will cover the ripening bulb foliage as it grows.

LOOKING UP The view from the back yard toward the terraces is an enticing garden scene with a path that draws you in to experience the garden. Fragrant lavender and cheerful tickseed dot the edge of the walkway, begging you to stop and enjoy the flowers. The view from the deck toward the back yard is just as pleasing. Because the bed swings out away from the house, you can see a good portion of it from the lofty perch. A narrower planting bed couldn't be enjoyed from the deck. Plus, the tall back wall of the house needs to be balanced by a wide planting.

LOW-CARE BEAUTY You wouldn't want to have to keep climbing up and down the steps to maintain this garden, so it has to be low care. The perennials don't need much through the growing season. Deadhead the peonies after they're done blooming, but leave the foliage, as it'll make a great filler for the rest of the season. The other flowering perennials will take care of themselves. Prune the holly once each year in early spring before new growth starts to keep the shape you want.

Terracing is a great solution for managing a slope in full sun or shade.

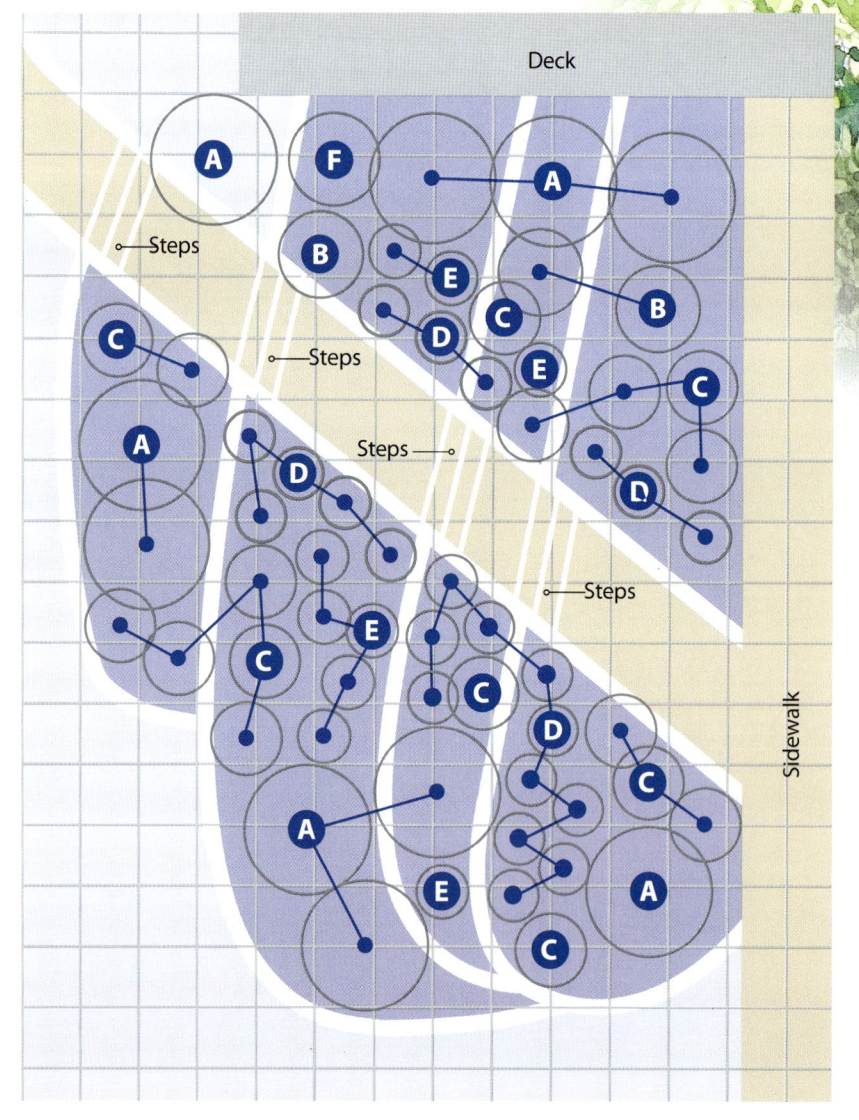

Scale: 1 square = 4 square feet

206   *the* YEAR IN GARDENING   www.GardenGateMagazine.com

THE GARDEN'S PALETTE

Code	Plant Name	No. to Plant	Blooms	Type	Cold/Heat Zones	Height/Width	Special Features
A	Holly *Ilex cornuta* 'Carissa'	10	White; spring	Evergreen shrub	6-9/9-1	3-4 ft./3-4 ft.	Glossy green leaves have single spine at tip; great background for flowering plants; shear annually in early spring to maintain shape
B	Peony *Paeonia lactiflora* 'Primevère'	3	White with yellow; midspring	Perennial	4-8/8-1	34 in./32 in.	Anemonelike blooms; cut buds before they're fully open to bring inside; deadhead faded flowers
C	Cranesbill *Geranium* 'Johnson's Blue'	17	Blue-violet; spring to fall	Perennial	4-8/8-1	18 in./30 in.	Fast-growing, mat-forming ground cover; cut back when it gets leggy in summer
D	Tickseed *Coreopsis verticillata* 'Zagreb'	22	Yellow; summer	Perennial	3-9/9-1	15 in./18 in.	Blooms from late spring into late summer; deadhead promptly with shears to encourage rebloom in fall
E	English lavender *Lavandula angustifolia* 'Hidcote'	9	Lavender; summer	Perennial	5-8/12-1	18 in./18 in.	Excellent fresh cut or dried flowers; drought-tolerant; attracts butterflies; fragrant
F	Maiden grass *Miscanthus sinensis* 'Morning Light'	1	Red-bronze; late summer	Perennial	5-9/9-1	5 ft./3 ft.	Narrow green leaves with white margin; drought-tolerant; seedheads provide winter interest

DESIGN CHALLENGE | BACK YARD

Soften the edges Tuck a few taller shrubs and perennials around the garden shed to help disguise it.

from simple to **simply stunning**

Here's a yard most of us can relate to. It's not terrible — there are trees and a nice privacy fence and plenty of green grass. But it's pretty boring, isn't it? Matt and Lynn Walker of Austin, Texas, really want a garden. And they'd like some outdoor living space with a little privacy from the surrounding two-story houses. They already have the basics; they just don't know where to start dressing it up.

TAKE A SEAT Bigger isn't always better, but this 10x10-foot patio is a bit cramped. An easy solution: Add on with 2x2-foot concrete pavers. (If you have more money in your budget, you could use stone or brick.) We extended the pavers to create a path through the garden to the garden shed. For a casual look, leave a few open spaces for planting. Check out "Paving with pizzazz" at right, for some tips on making that work.

DON'T FIGHT THE SHED Garden sheds are kind of like clothes hampers. They're not especially attractive, but everyone needs one. This garden shed *could* actually look quite a bit nicer. Soft paint colors will help it blend into the surroundings better than its original stark white. Simple plantings around the base of the shed cover some of the walls and make it feel anchored in the beds, like a part of the garden. And we put in a hard-surfaced path to the shed, so it's easier to get to garden equipment that's stored there.

PROTECT YOUR PRIVACY When your garden is surrounded by taller houses, it's hard not to feel exposed. But you can't build a 20-foot fence (this isn't Fort Knox!), and this yard isn't big enough to plant lots of trees to block every view.

So instead, "target" your privacy — plant trees or create structures to shelter the areas of the yard you use the most. In this case, an existing shade tree screens this patio from one side, while an additional small ornamental tree will screen

Build some privacy A pergola creates overhead privacy from surrounding two-story homes. Need even more shade or privacy? Add vines to the pergola.

Blend it in To tie the pergola and house together visually, paint or stain the pergola to match or complement the house trim.

Dress it up Choosing a couple of colors, like the blue and yellow here, makes a garden look well-planned.

Paving with pizzazz Planting within pavers brings your garden right up to your seating area. Choose plants that can take the reflected heat from the hard surface. The low-growing thyme, yellow euphorbia and tufted blue fescue in the photo are good candidates. So is the lavender cotton in the plan on p. 210. Leave the planting spaces near the edge of patios or paths, out of the way of your most-used traffic patterns. That way, you won't step on or trip over plants as you move through the garden.

the other side. (You can see a detailed planting plan for this patio area, plus an alternative, on p. 210. If you'd like a plan for the whole back yard, check out our Web extra.) And best of all, a pergola along the back of the house screens most of the patio from above. Not only does it create a nice, shady place to sit, but it keeps your main seating area out of neighbors' view. That way, it doesn't matter so much if some other areas of your yard are more easily seen. No room for a pergola? A well-placed patio umbrella can offer the same sense of shelter to allow you to enjoy your garden in peace! ▢

Botanical Names

Blue fescue
Festuca glauca
Euphorbia
Euphorbia spp.
Thyme
Thymus serpyllum

Web extra
See a complete *planting plan* for this getaway.

www.GardenGateMagazine.com *the* YEAR IN GARDENING 209

DRAWING BOARD | BACK YARD

plant a little peace and quiet

You already have a privacy fence, but your back yard still doesn't feel private… what do you do? Plants to the rescue! Here, a simple planting, using only six different plants, creates a sheltered, welcoming, easy-care oasis. A mix of trees, shrubs and perennials will keep it looking great year-round. And it doesn't need a lot of heavy-duty maintenance, either, so you'll have time to sit down and enjoy it.

What if you don't have the privacy fence? We have another solution that provides a quick screen and an unusual, elegant garden feature. Here, vines do the work of providing both privacy and height when grown on a structure of posts and chain. And colorful perennials at ground level hold the focus inside the garden. Keep reading for easy privacy solutions! □
— *Stephanie Polsley Bruner*

Tougher than tough These plants are pretty…and they're also pretty tough! They'll take hot, dry conditions without missing a beat. And they'll look good most of the summer with very little maintenance, too. In fact, all you need to do is some deadheading on the daylily, and shear the lavender cotton back after the first flush of blooms to neaten the plants a bit. A little gravel mulch around these plants will help keep weeds down. (Believe it or not, even rock mulch will help conserve some moisture.) And the crisp combination of yellow, white and blue looks sunny and fresh no matter how dusty and dry the summer may get.

No fence? No problem! Here, a climbing rose drapes itself across swags of lightweight chain supported between posts. You can still see around and through it, but it gives this back yard a sense of enclosure. And it doesn't cast as much shade as a tree would, so if you prefer a sunny getaway, this is a good bet. (Besides, it'll grow a lot faster than a tree will!) Live in a zone where climbing roses aren't that reliable? Try a sweet autumn clematis, American bittersweet or trumpet vine instead. They'll fill in a structure like this quickly, too.

tip Just like bark mulch, apply 2 or 3 in. of rock mulch around plants — it'll help keep weeds down and hold moisture in the soil.

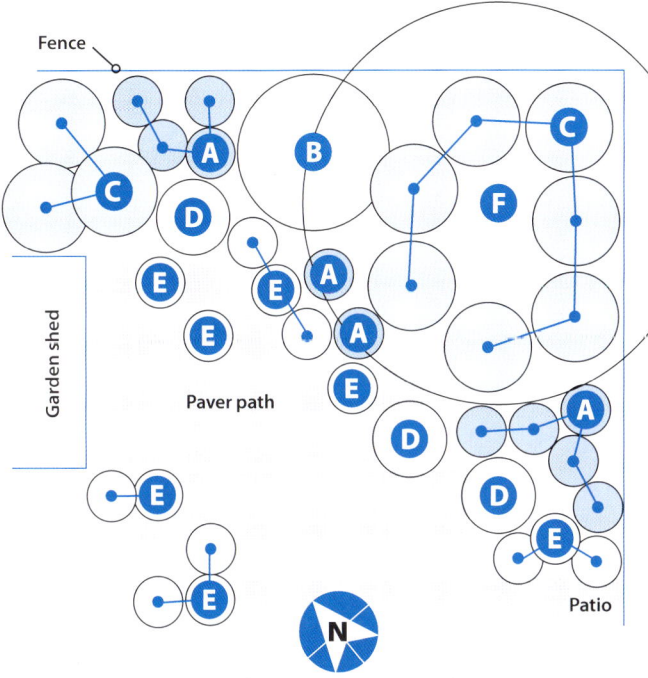

Plant list (Number to plant)

A Daylily *Hemerocallis* 'Hyperion' (11)
24 to 40 in. tall, 24 to 36 in. wide; fragrant yellow flowers in midsummer; cold-hardy in USDA zones 3 to 10; heat-tolerant in AHS zones 10 to 1

B Oakleaf hydrangea *Hydrangea quercifolia* (1)
4 to 8 ft. tall and wide; white flowers in early summer fade to pink; cold-hardy in USDA zones 5 to 9; heat-tolerant in AHS zones 9 to 1

C Southern shield fern *Thelypteris kunthii* (10)
3 to 4 ft. tall and wide; more drought-tolerant than most ferns; cold-hardy in USDA zones 6 to 9; heat-tolerant in AHS zones 9 to 1

D Salvia *Salvia guaranitica* 'Black and Blue' (3)
2 to 5 ft. tall and wide; blue flowers in mid- to late summer; cold-hardy in USDA zones 7 to 9; heat-tolerant in AHS zones 9 to 1

E Lavender cotton *Santolina chamaecyparissus* (14)
12 to 18 in. tall, 24 to 36 in. wide; yellow flowers in early to midsummer; cold-hardy in USDA zones 5 to 9; heat-tolerant in AHS zones 9 to 1

F Texas redbud *Cercis canadensis texensis* (1)
15 to 25 ft. tall and wide; lavender pink flowers in spring; cold-hardy in USDA zones 6 to 10; heat-tolerant in AHS zones 10 to 1

Scale: 1 square = 1 square ft.

---

tip Use 10-ft.-long, 4x4-in. posts to support the chains. When the posts are set in the ground, they'll be about 8 ft. tall.

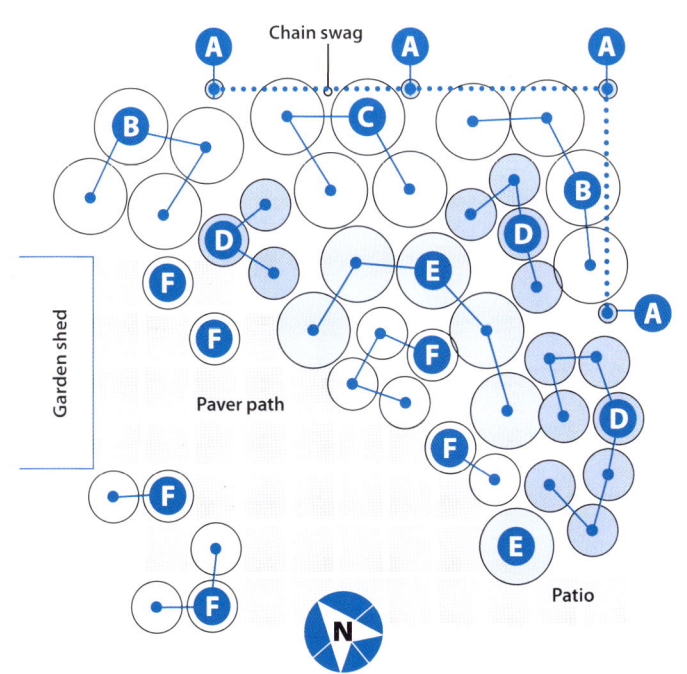

Plant list (Number to plant)

A Climbing rose *Rosa* 'Mermaid' (4)
15 to 30 ft. tall; creamy yellow blooms from summer to fall; cold-hardy in USDA zones 8 to 9; heat-tolerant in AHS zones 9 to 1

B Rosemary *Rosmarinus officinalis* 'Tuscan Blue' (8)
5 ft. tall, 2 to 4 ft. wide; blue summer flowers, fragrant foliage; cold-hardy in USDA zones 8 to 10; heat-tolerant in AHS zones 10 to 1

C Salvia *Salvia guaranitica* 'Black and Blue' (4)
2 to 5 ft. tall and wide; blue flowers in mid- to late summer; cold-hardy in USDA zones 7 to 9; heat-tolerant in AHS zones 9 to 1

D Daylily *Hemerocallis* 'Sherwood Gladiator' (14)
48 in. tall, 18 to 24 in. wide; fragrant yellow flowers in rebloom from summer to fall; cold-hardy in USDA zones 3 to 9; heat-tolerant in AHS zones 9 to 1

E Rose *Rose* 'Country Dancer' (6)
3 to 4 ft. tall and wide; pink flowers in summer followed by red hips; cold-hardy in USDA zones 5 to 9; heat-tolerant in AHS zones 9 to 1

F Lavender cotton *Santolina chamaecyparissus* (13)
12 to 18 in. tall, 24 to 36 in. wide; yellow flowers in early to midsummer; cold-hardy in USDA zones 5 to 9; heat-tolerant in AHS zones 9 to 1

Scale: 1 square = 1 square ft.

Botanical Names

Sweet autumn clematis
  Clematis terniflora
American bittersweet
  Celastrus scandens
Trumpet vine
  Campsis radicans

This container was inspired by a larger space. Learn the whole story on page 236.

all about containers

grow your *best containers* ever!

THERE'S NO SECRET RECIPE for fabulous container gardens. We're happy to share the ingredients for showy containers in every season. And we'll show you the steps to designing great-looking containers of your own. Our readers have put together some pretty spiffy containers, too! See them and learn how-to tips for making container gardening easier, as well. It's all here!

Container 1-2-3	**214**
Instant Spring!	**218**
Basket of Flowers	**220**
Sunny Sizzler	**221**
Getting the Hang of it	**222**
Grasses = Great Containers	**228**
Readers' Best Containers	**230**
Create a Super Bowl	**234**
Warm Sunshine	**235**
Cool Idea	**236**
3 Ways to Shape Up a Container	**238**
Container Cleanup	**240**
Overwintering Plants	**241**
Did You Know	**244**

CONTAINERS | DESIGN BASICS

Create a great container around a great plant!

Container 1-2-3

Looking for excitement? Go to your favorite garden center! It seems that nearly every time I go, I find a plant that's begging me to take it home. What to do with them once I unload them is the tricky part. Sure, you could shove any plant in the ground, but how do you really show off the qualities that made you fall in love with it? On a recent trip, I discovered three plants I loved — a lantana trained as a standard, a variegated Jacob's ladder and a pretty pink geranium. I thought they would all make great container plants. Let me take you from my initial sketches to my final favorite planting for each.

READ THE TAG Healthy plants are beautiful plants. Before you think about how a plant looks, consider how it grows. The most important thing is to check the growing conditions it likes — such as light and moisture — and pick companions that like similar ones. For example, if you put a moisture-loving canna with a dry-soil-loving succulent, one of them will suffer. But also consider the area where your container will be. Do the plants in it need to tolerate heat reflected from pavement or wind, for instance?

FOR STARTERS Whatever your starter plant, you want the end result to be a pleasing design. This means you'll want to begin with a focal point. The orange flowers in the container at left are the first things you notice. A focal point may be a bright color or a bold leaf — anything that grabs your attention first. Then, it's often nice to soften the edge of the pot with a trailing plant of some sort. And finally, you'll want to fill in the design with other plants. In the design at left, a taller grassy plant adds height and shape to balance the planting with the container. But if your focal point were a large plant, you might need to fill in the space between that and the trailers with some medium-sized plants.

TRY ON PLANTS If you're able to do it, it's easiest to walk around the garden center with your new plant in your hand. Hold it up to possible companions to see how the colors, textures and shapes go together. For a sophisticated look, keep the colors similar. For a more casual look, use lots of different colors, but be sure that at least a few of them are "echoed" by companions. This creates a more pulled-together look. Try to vary the textures and shapes of foliage and flowers, too. If your plants all look too much alike, the effect will be humdrum.

I used these tips for my three plants. On the next pages I'll show you a few of the combinations I came up with and the ones that rose to the top. ☐

— *Deborah Gruca*

A focal point grabs your attention with bright color or bold texture.

Add more plants to balance out the overall design and create contrast.

Trailing plants soften the edge of the pot.

Color and contrast make this combination pop!

think it through

I've always liked the look of plants trained as standards, but have avoided using them in containers. Their "lollipop" shape makes them challenging to use in a design.

But this 'Confetti' lantana inspired me. So I brought it home and made a few sketches to experiment with different plant combinations. I wanted plants that would echo the colors of the lantana flowers and leaves, but at the same time offer some contrast to keep the planting interesting.

IDEA #1 The lantana's bright flowers needed companions of the same intense hues. I tried crazily ruffled 'Peter's Wonder' coleus and salmon twinspur to make the pot buzz with energy. The coleus would provide great color all summer and would definitely get tall enough to fill in the space around the tall stem of the lantana. And all of the colors would give the pot a casual feel that I liked. But I didn't think these plants really went with the clean, sophisticated look of the white pot I wanted to use.

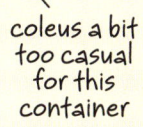

tons of color!

coleus a bit too casual for this container

IDEA #2 I next tried a combination with a more sedate feel with black mondo grass and 'Illumination' vinca vine. Alternating these two plants around the pot would let their foliage weave together in an interesting way. And having low plants like these at the base of the lantana would create a "living mulch" that would let the lantana shine.

Still, it seemed that the lantana really needed to have more colorful companions than the ones in this reserved planting. Take a look at my final picks at left.

great texture contrast!

What I planted I like the way this combination looks balanced. The large leaves of the Swedish ivy contrast with the other smaller foliage in this grouping, while the light green and silver color of its foliage echo the off-white container. Also, the colors of the purple cape daisies and the tiny apricot twinspur tie to similar tinges in the lantana flowers above. This container's classy and fun at the same time!

Code	Plant Name	No. to Plant
A	**Lantana** *Lantana camara* 'Confetti'	1
B	**Twinspur** *Diascia* Diamonte™ Apricot	6
C	**Cape daisy** *Osteospermum* Sunny™ Mary	3
D	**Swedish ivy** *Plectranthus oertendahlii* 'Emerald Lace'	2
E	**Evolvulus** *Evolvulus* Hawaiian Blue Eyes	1

Container is 18 in. square.

2 MORE GREAT CONTAINERS

think it through

Good-looking foliage is a great feature for a plant, particularly if it's growing in a container. The variegated leaves of this 'Brise d'Anjou' Jacob's ladder practically jumped up and grabbed me, even from across the garden center.

IDEA #1 So naturally, I picked it up and started to choose other shade-loving plant neighbors for my terra-cotta bowl. A variegated carex and a Japanese painted fern could have been good companions for the Jacob's ladder because all three will thrive in a shady spot. The painted fern brought in other subtle tones to the combination and the grasslike carex would give it some spiky accents. But all of that fine texture looked just a bit too busy.

no deadheading needed!

IDEA #2 Next, I tried a beautiful, leafy deep-red coleus to back my Jacob's ladder — wow, talk about snap! Color contrast strikes again! All this planting needed now was another low plant — maybe a trailer, like 'Blackie' sweet potato vine, to add some deep-colored drama. It'd be perfect, but these plants would have quickly overtaken the Jacob's ladder and would get too large for this size container. Check out what I planted in the end.

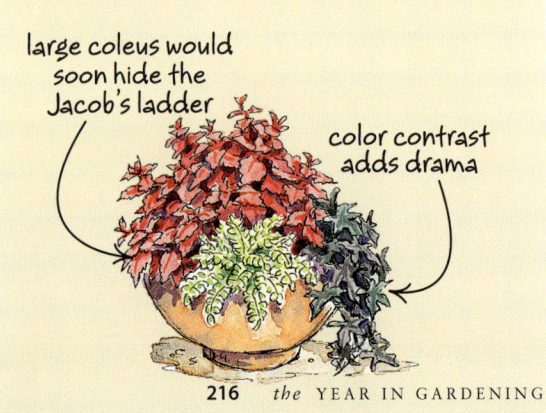

large coleus would soon hide the Jacob's ladder

color contrast adds drama

Two pale-colored rocks add contrast and anchor the planting.

Deadnettle and bugleweed will fill in the bowl after the Jacob's ladder dies back.

What I planted I chose plants with bold, solid colors to back up and enhance the Jacob's ladder pattern. I love variegated plants, but use too many in one place and you'll actually diminish their effect. Instead, chartreuse deadnettle picks up one of the colors of the Jacob's ladder leaves, while the coral bells and bugleweed sport a deep burgundy that really complements them.

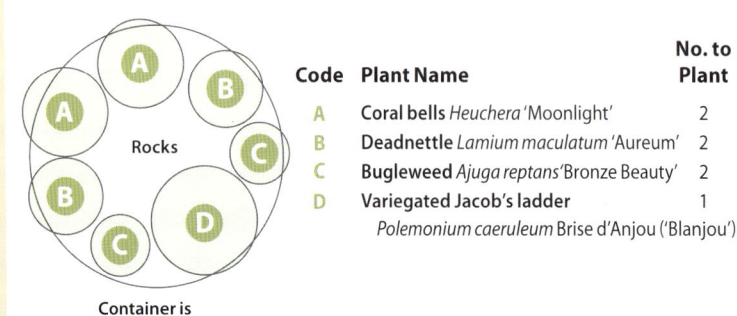

Code	Plant Name	No. to Plant
A	Coral bells *Heuchera* 'Moonlight'	2
B	Deadnettle *Lamium maculatum* 'Aureum'	2
C	Bugleweed *Ajuga reptans* 'Bronze Beauty'	2
D	Variegated Jacob's ladder *Polemonium caeruleum* Brise d'Anjou ('Blanjou')	1

Container is 15 in. in diameter

think it through

Ahh, annual geraniums! You just can't beat these dependable container workhorses. With a little fertilizer and a bit of deadheading, they'll bloom happily and beautifully all summer long. I pick up at least a few of them every year.

IDEA #1 For a bright, flowery combination, I tried pairing geraniums with yellow calibrachoas and pink verbenas. These full-sun annuals thrive on the same conditions as the geraniums and bloom like mad. And the tiny trumpet-shaped calibrachoa flowers and the masses of verbena blooms would enhance those of the geranium. But the deadheading *can* be a bit much.

loads of flowers all season

IDEA #2 I also tried the geranium with a purple fountain grass and some bacopa — the classic "focal point, spiller, filler" formula. The fountain grass would add height and also a bit of hypnotic movement when it's tousled by wind. Bacopa would break up and soften the sides of the ceramic pot and provide an ongoing shower of petite white flowers and trailing, fine-textured green foliage. Nice? Yes. But I thought I could do even better than this with a couple more exciting plant partners.

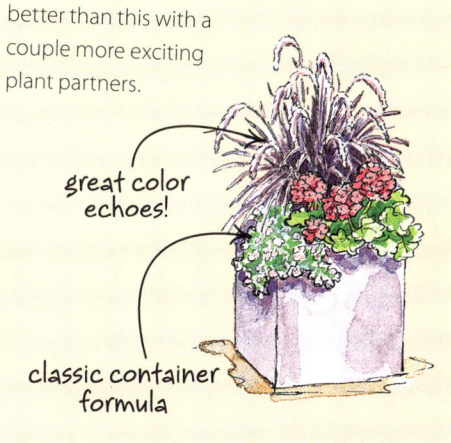

great color echoes!

classic container formula

Limit your color palette for a sophisticated look.

What I planted Now here's a pot with real pizzazz! The deep pink of the geranium is reflected in tinges of pink in the straplike leaves of the New Zealand flax, as well as the undersides of the coral bells foliage. Even if the ever-blooming geraniums should take a flowering break, the two foliage plants, as well as the glazed pot, guarantee continuous color.

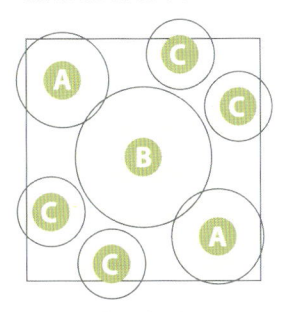

Code	Plant Name	No. to Plant
A	Coral bells *Heuchera* 'Marmalade'	2
B	New Zealand flax *Phormium* 'Rainbow Sunrise'	1
C	Geranium *Pelargonium* Americana Violet	4

Container is 15 in. square.

CONTAINERS | RECIPES

Combine a few pots of grocery store plants for an early boost.

Instant Spring!

If you're like me, the holidays are barely over before you start dreaming about spring. Those few months before the weather starts to warm seem unbearably long. Well, here's an idea to help you beat that spring fever and enjoy a preview of fresh spring flowers and color with just a little imagination and a trip to the grocery store.

Florists, the floral departments of many supermarkets and even home improvement stores stock live plants year-round these days. But their color really packs a punch when the view outdoors is dreary. In addition to house plants, in late winter you'll see pre-chilled spring bulbs, such as hyacinths, daffodils and tulips, ready to bloom. Blooming gift plants, like cyclamen and primrose, are also easy to find now. You can buy them already combined in pretty containers, but I think it's more fun to buy individual ones and put together different combinations. It's easy — create your own! □

— *Deborah Gruca*

Add a furry accent with cut stems of pussy willow.

Kitchen basket

First, look around your house for a fun, unique container. You can use almost anything that'll hold plants, as long as it has drainage. I pre-soaked and wrung out sheet moss to line a wire basket, added a plastic bag (with a couple of drainage holes poked in the bottom) and filled it with some potting mix. Next, I popped the plants out of their plastic pots and tucked them into the mix. Or, if you prefer, just set them, pots and all, into your container and top with more moss to hide the pot edges. (Either way works fine, since this isn't a very long-term arrangement.)

A few cut stems of pussy willow add flair to the combination. Use a saucer — either in the bottom of the basket or underneath — to keep any water droplets from damaging the table. In a cool room, expect your combination to last several weeks.

Code	Plant Name	No. to Plant
A	**Variegated English boxwood**	
	Buxus sempervirens 'Variegata'	2
B	**Cyclamen**	
	Cyclamen persicum (2 colors)	3

Mail-order sources

Blooming Bulb
www.bloomingbulb.com
800-648-2852. *Online catalog only*

Plow & Hearth
www.plowhearth.com
800-494-7544. *Catalog free*

Tulip World
www.tulipworld.com
866-688-9547. *Catalog free*

Spring greeting Do you garden where the winters are cold but not frigid? Put together a pot of blooming plants and set it in a sheltered spot outdoors. This front stoop is perfect for a beautiful spring surprise.

Don't worry about lugging out bags of potting mix. Just set small pots (each with one or more plants) into an empty container, top with a little mulch and stand back! In cool weather you probably won't need to water them very often. I purchased all the plants here at the grocery store, but you can also order containers of pre-chilled, ready-to-bloom tulip, hyacinth, daffodil and other bulbs from mail-order sources. I've included some of my favorites above.

All of these plants stand up well in temps as low as the mid-40s F., and will keep looking fresh for at least a couple of weeks. If you're expecting it to drop below that, pull the pot into the garage until it gets warmer. And choose an area protected from harsh winds to keep your container colorful for as long as possible.

Code	Plant Name	No. to Plant
A	**Primrose** *Primula polyanthus* 'Pacific Giants'	8
B	**Hyacinth** *Hyacinthus orientalis* 'Delft Blue'	2
C	**Tulip** *Tulip* 'Gabriella'	1
D	**Daffodil** *Narcissus* 'Tete a Tete'	3

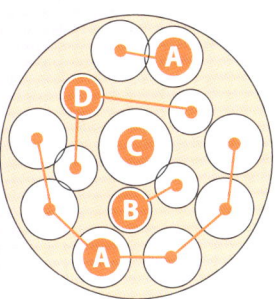

www.GardenGateMagazine.com

CONTAINERS | RECIPES

basket of flowers

Hot-colored geraniums and pinks in this basket grab your attention instantly. The deep-pink and lavender-pink are closely related to the purple colors of the calibrachoas and annual baby's breath. And if those were the only colors in the container, the effect would be very sophisticated. But adding a splash of yellow calibrachoas (the color opposite purple on the color wheel) gives the whole combination a friendlier, more light-hearted look that we like. Meanwhile, the fresh, deep green of the foliage provides a rich background color for all those bright flowers.

BUILD A BASKET While it's a joy to design with color, it's even more fun to put this planting together. Start with a sturdy wire basket, like this recycled creamery tote. Soak some sphagnum moss in water, gently wring it out and use it to line the inside. Top with a sheet of plastic (with several holes punched in it) to retain moisture longer. Next, fill the basket about two thirds full with a soil-less potting mix. I like to mix in a little slow-release plant food, or you can buy the potting mix with the fertilizer already in it. Then start planting. As with all containers, forget about the suggested spacing for plants. The plan at right shows you how tightly these plants are packed. That's the best way to get a full, flowery look fast.

If you want to keep these plants looking and blooming their best all summer, give them weekly food and even moisture. To neaten up the calibrachoas and keep them compact, snip a few inches off the longer stems once a week. While you're at it, deadhead the faded pinks and geraniums to encourage more blooms and to keep the planting looking fresh and gorgeous. □

Tips for care
- Full sun
- Even soil moisture
- Apply ¼-strength water-soluble 15-30-15 fertilizer once a week

Code	Plant Name	No. to Plant
A	Dianthus *Dianthus* Bouquet™ Rose Magic	2
B	Calibrachoa *Calibrachoa* Superbells® Yellow Chiffon	2
C	Calibrachoa *Calibrachoa* Callie® Purple	2
D	Geranium *Pelargonium* Fantasia™ Strawberry Sizzle	2
E	Bacopa *Sutera cordata* 'Snowflake'	1
F	Annual baby's breath *Gypsophila elegans* 'Rosea'	1

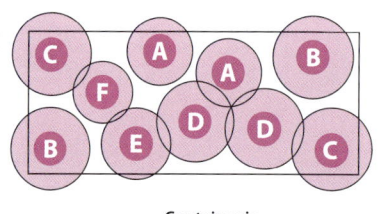

Container is 24 in. long x 10 in. wide.

sunny sizzler

Want an easy tip for creating great plant combinations? Use lots of bright color. There are only five different plants in this pot, but look at the impact they make! And while there are multiple colors (most of them are similar in intensity, so they create a great effect), a bit of color repetition helps keep the planting looking pulled together. The mealycup sage, cockscomb and evolvulus (with its morning-only blooms) nod to a blue-purple theme while the yellow of the black-eyed Susan echoes similar hues in the lantana blooms.

In addition to color, these flowers also differ in size and shape. Tiny evolvulus flowers set off the much larger black-eyed Susans, while the other three vastly different-looking blooms add sizzle and spark. Delicious, citrus-colored globes of lantana play off those fascinating fuzzy magenta "claws" of cockscomb. Nearby butterflies will find all of these plants irresistible.

GROWING KNOW-HOW These colorful companions have a lot in common, too. They all like sun and heat. In fact, the lantana and black-eyed Susan don't really hit their stride until midsummer. But even though most of these plants are drought-tolerant when growing in the garden, they need regular water in a pot like this. So check the soil every day and water when the top inch is dry.

While the black-eyed Susan is small, pinch back the growing tip once to encourage branching. You'll get lots of blooms on a fuller plant. Deadheading will give you nonstop color. In particular, watch the lantana. If it starts to form berries, remove them to keep the plant blooming. With a little effort, you can enjoy the flowery finery right up to frost *and* satisfy your craving for color!

Container is 14 in. in diameter.

Code	Plant Name	No. to Plant
A	Black-eyed Susan *Rudbeckia hirta* 'TigerEye Gold' **NEW '09**	1
B	Lantana *Lantana camara* Luscious™ Citrus Blend™ **NEW '09**	3
C	Mealycup sage *Salvia farinacea* 'Evolution'	2
D	Evolvulus *Evolvulus glomeratus* 'Hawaiian Blue Eyes'	1
E	Cockscomb *Celosia* 'Dark Caracas'	3

NEW '09 Newly available variety. See p. 60 for 19 more of our favorite new plants this year.

Tips for care

- Full sun
- Even soil moisture
- Apply ¼- to ½-strength water-soluble 15-30-15 fertilizer weekly

CONTAINERS | DESIGN

Getting the Hang of It

Grow gorgeous hanging baskets in any situation.

Who doesn't love the look of hanging baskets on a porch or trellis? But have you had the sad experience of planting one with high hopes, only to spend the summer watching it wilt between waterings, or refuse to bloom because it's under the eaves of your porch?

Hanging baskets are tougher to grow than most containers. Often, the spot you'd choose for a hanging basket, close to a house or garage, has periods of intense sun and periods of heavy shade, and that can be challenging for plants.

Let's take a look at four great places for hanging baskets. I'll also share some tips to help you get the most out of your baskets, no matter where you put them. Plus, I'll introduce you to good planting techniques, as well as some gadgets that make hanging basket care easier. Speaking of planting, there are more great plant choices than ever when it comes to hanging baskets. "New plants for hanging baskets," below, will introduce you to three varieties that we've tried the last couple of summers that have really knocked our socks off.

Let's get started exploring how to make the most of your hanging baskets.

BY HOOK OR BY CROOK A basket or two out in the garden adds color to a dull spot. It's easy to fit a shepherd's hook in where there's not really room for a container to sit on the ground, like the skinny strip between a privacy fence and a sidewalk. Hanging baskets can add some vertical interest, too. I especially like to use them to bridge the gap between large shrubs or trees and a lower, ground-hugging planting. Or try hanging baskets in a shady spot where spring-flowering shrubs have finished — you'll perk that area right back up.

How many baskets do you need? Well, of course, that depends on how much space you have to fill. But repeating baskets, just as you repeat plants in a border, makes a strong statement. See how the orange begonias and the burgundy coleus in photo 1 echo some of the colors from the surrounding garden? This makes it fit in nicely.

One last thing to keep in mind about hanging a basket on a hook: Unless it's in a very sheltered spot out of the wind, you'll probably need to water it more often than you would one that's up next to the house. On p. 227, I'll give you some helpful planting tips to keep any hanging basket from drying out too quickly. Turn the page to see a couple more classic hanging basket scenarios, and how to make them work.

NEW PLANTS for hanging baskets

These plants performed well for us — and they'll do the same for you! Technically, they're all tender perennials, but you can grow them as annuals in your baskets.

1 Mandalay™ Mandarin begonia
Begonia hybrid Trailing stems with bright-orange flowers all summer; 10 to 12 in. tall, 18 to 30 in. wide; USDA zones 10 to 11; AHS zones 12 to 1 **NEW '09**

2 Supertunia® Vista Silverberry petunia
Petunia hybrid Silver-white with pink eye; turns more pink in cooler weather; 16 to 20 in. tall, 18 to 24 in. wide; USDA zones 10 to 11; AHS zones 12 to 1 **NEW '09**

3 Aztec® Red verbena *Verbena* hybrid More mildew-resistant than most verbenas; 8 to 10 in. tall, 12 to 18 in. wide; USDA zones 10 to 11; AHS zones 12 to 1 **NEW '08**

NEW '09 Newly available variety. See p. 60 for 19 more of our favorite new plants this year.

(1) Move your baskets as the seasons change. These part-shade baskets were under trees for the summer so the foliage didn't scorch. But in fall's less intense sun, they were moved out to be the stars of the garden.

PLANT THIS BASKET
A **Begonia** *Begonia* Bonfire®
B **Coleus** *Solenostemon* 'Trailing Burgundy'
C **Foxtail fern** *Asparagus meyeri*

SITUATIONS AND **SOLUTIONS**

One of the biggest problems with hanging baskets on a structure is that odd light and shade patterns make it hard to give plants the conditions they need to bloom, or even to thrive. But don't give up on them — nothing dresses up a porch or pergola like hanging baskets.

PERGOLA PERFECTION First, let's look at pergolas. These are actually fairly easy situations for hanging baskets. You can hang them just about anywhere under a pergola. Just be careful that they're not hanging right where you walk the most, or you'll have to keep ducking. And make sure they aren't right over your outdoor furniture — you don't want dirty water to dribble out of the basket and onto your favorite chair.

Most pergolas provide enough shade to protect the plants a bit. But they still let in plenty of light for sun-lovers, like the vinca, petunias and calibrachoa in photo 2. That's an important consideration — let's face it, most flowering plants need some sun to look their best. (I'll show you some colorful baskets that grow great in shade, too.)

Consider your viewing angle when you're planting up hanging baskets. If you're going to see them primarily from a distance of 10 feet or more (the far end of the pergola, or as you walk up to the house), don't worry about covering up the basket. But if you'll be seeing them up close, include more and longer trailing plants so you aren't stuck with a view of the basket itself.

PLANT THIS BASKET
- **A Calibrachoa** *Calibrachoa* MiniFamous™ Dark Blue Evolution®
- **B Alternanthera** *Alternanthera dentata* 'Purple Knight'
- **C Petunia** *Petunia* Cascadias™ Great Spark
- **D Vinca** *Catharanthus roseus* Cora™ Lavender

(2) Trailing plants cascading over the edge hide the basket. When you're viewing these at close range, you want to see plenty of plants, not just the bottom of the basket.

(3) Turn baskets around every couple of days to keep them blooming evenly on all sides. These shade-loving fuchsias won't need to be turned as often as plants that like a little more sun.

PRACTICAL PORCH POINTERS Now let's tackle some tougher situations. A shady porch dressed up with a row of hanging baskets is a classic garden look. But here's where tricky light and shade patterns really come into play. Take a look at photo 3 above. This porch lets in more light than most porches. It faces east, so these baskets get full sunlight for a few hours early in the day, and are in complete shade by midmorning. These fuchsias are a good choice — they're obviously happy with those conditions.

If your porch wraps around two sides of your house, baskets will get different amounts of light depending on which side they're on. You'll need to move them from one side of the porch to the other every few days to keep them blooming equally. Or choose different plants for each side of the house. That can look great if you choose some similar colors and plant shapes so the baskets all look coordinated.

In photo 4, you see one of the toughest spots of all for hanging baskets. This house faces west, although the garage to the right blocks a lot of sun. So these baskets are in full shade until mid- to late afternoon, and then they're in hot sun, particularly the one on the left. Again, you'll need to switch these baskets to keep them blooming about the same amount. That's especially important when there are only two of them, because it's going to be really noticeable if one is much more developed than the other.

Turn the page for one last scenario, helpful gadgets and tips for a perfect basket planting.

PLANT THIS BASKET
A **Begonia** *Begonia* Mandalay™ Mandarin **NEW '09**
B **Coleus** *Solenostemon* 'Pete's Wonder'

(4) Add a length of chain to drop your baskets down an extra 6 to 12 in. It gets them farther from the porch overhang, allowing the plants to enjoy more light. And it makes them easier for you to reach, too, when it's time to water or fertilize.

SITUATIONS AND SOLUTIONS (continued)

KEEPING IT CLOSE You don't need a porch or a pergola to enjoy having hanging baskets around the house. A simple bracket keeps this shade-loving container right at eye level.

You'll notice an interesting thing about the basket in photo 5. Unlike the others in this story, this one doesn't have any trailing plants. Why is that? One drawback to hanging a basket on a bracket is that if the wind picks up, it can bang the basket against the house, which is hard on trailing plants. So keep that in mind, or choose a bracket that holds the basket farther out from the wall. Ideally, the bracket should hold the side of the basket at least 6 inches from the wall, although you'll have to make some adjustments depending on the size of your basket and how much room you have. No matter where you hang baskets, it's a good idea to lift them down and set them on the ground if it's going to storm. In a high wind, they can blow right off their hooks. (For a couple of handy hanging gadgets, see "Great gadgets for hanging baskets," below.)

Now that you know how to cope with some of the situations that can lead to hanging baskets looking just so-so, you're on your way to plantings that look beautiful! □

— Stephanie Polsley Bruner

PLANT THIS BASKET
- **A** Sedge *Carex buchananii* 'Red Rooster'
- **B** Coleus *Solenostemon* 'Chocolate Mint'
- **C** Oxalis *Oxalis vulcanicola* 'Molten Lava'

(5) Think about the background when you're choosing plants. These browns and burgundies, plus the bright notes of chartreuse, look great against the dark-toned brick wall of the house.

GREAT GADGETS
for hanging baskets

These simple products can make caring for your baskets easier.

SWIVEL LINK With one of these swivels, you won't have to lift the basket down to turn it. Just give it a half turn every couple of days to keep the basket blooming on all sides.

PULLEY No more lifting a watering can or reaching with a hose! With the pulley in place, just bump the bottom of the basket to lower it for watering, then lift it back up into place.

You'll find similar products at garden centers. Or purchase them from Charley's Greenhouse and Garden, www.charleysgreenhouse.com, 800-322-4707; or from the *Garden Gate* Store, www.GardenGateStore.com.

PLANTING SUCCESS

Planting a hanging basket isn't so different from planting a regular container. But because hanging baskets are often shallower than standing pots, and are placed in different locations, they have slightly different needs.

LINE UP First, you need a frame and a liner. Frames range from coated wire to wrought iron. Just keep in mind the finished weight of the basket, as well as the structure or bracket that's going to hold it.

Two popular lining options are coconut-fiber liners or long-fiber sphagnum moss. Coconut-fiber liners are preshaped and come in different sizes. I like them because they're quick and easy, and I can reuse them for several years. Sphagnum moss gives a softer, more rustic look. You can buy it loose in bags, or as preformed liners. If you use loose moss, you'll have to dampen it and pack it into place. (Check out our Web extra for tips on how to do this.) Preformed liners just need to be moistened to plump up (they're available from the *Garden Gate* Store, www.GardenGateStore.com).

Hanging baskets dry out quickly. Punch holes in a piece of plastic, like the white garbage can liner in the photo. Use it to line the basket before you add potting mix. The plastic will prevent the basket's liner from leaching water from the potting mix. You could also tuck a plastic hanging basket inside a moss-lined one, and use mulch to hide the edge of the plastic pot.

TIME TO PLANT Once your plastic liner is in place, fill the basket. Add potting mix, with a layer of water-absorbing crystals and slow-release fertilizer. You can also stir the crystals through the potting mix, if you prefer. Sometimes I like to mix a few scoops of compost into the lightweight potting mix. That helps it absorb and hold moisture better, and it adds nutrients to the soil, too. It does make baskets a little heavier, so if weight is a concern, just stick to the moisture crystals.

Even with these precautions, you'll still need to water your baskets often, especially during hot weather. Don't fill the baskets to the top with soil — leave an inch or two of space to allow water to soak in, instead of running off the surface.

Finally, finish off your hanging basket with a layer of mulch, to help retain more moisture and prevent precious water from splashing out and all over you. Your container will stay moist and look tidy.

Web extra Learn how to **line a basket** with moss.

Labels: Mulch · Soilless potting mix · Slow-release fertilizer and water crystals · Plastic liner with holes · Sphagnum moss

Moisture matters

These "crystals" are really super-absorbent polymers. One teaspoon of water crystals can expand to almost a quart's worth when water is added, and they can last 10 years. Be sure to keep them a few inches below the potting mix's surface — if they're too close to the top, they can expand right out of the container.

CONTAINERS | DESIGN

grasses = great containers

Five favorite grasses

Blue oat grass *Helictotrichon sempervirens* 24 to 36 in. tall, 24 to 30 in. wide; silver-blue foliage goes well with soft pastel colors

Fiber optic grass *Isolepis cernua* 6 to 12 in. tall, 8 to 12 in. wide; delicate-looking grass cascades down the side of a pot

Lemon grass *Cymbopogon citratus* 4 to 6 ft. tall, 2 to 3 ft. wide; bright-green foliage on a large, easy-to-grow grass; good as a focal point; smells good

Napier grass *Pennisetum purpureum* 'Princess' 2 to 4 ft. tall, 18 to 24 in. wide; large grass with burgundy foliage and stiff, sturdy stems; makes a good specimen

Orange New Zealand sedge *Carex testacea* 18 to 24 in. tall, 18 to 24 in. wide; wispy foliage tints orange in fall and trails 12 in. down the side of a pot

You know how striking ornamental grasses can be in your perennial garden. But have you thought about adding a few to your containers? They can be just as striking there. Rita Randolph, co-owner of Randolph's Greenhouses in Jackson, Tennessee, is known for her container designs incorporating grasses. She shared a few tips that are sure to perk up your containers, plus her "Five favorite grasses" at left. Let's take a look at how she puts these and other grasses to work.

KEEP IT IN BALANCE Your choice is only limited by the size of your container. You want the finished design to look balanced. That usually means the ultimate height of the tallest plant, whether it's a grass or something else, should be a bit taller than the height of the container. If the top of the plant is airy and open, like the maiden grass in photo 1, you can go even taller. But for a dense, solid-looking choice, shorter is better.

CHOOSE GOOD NEIGHBORS In the small combo in photo 2, a simple "lawn" of toe tickler grass massed together creates a lush carpet under a small figurine. The delicate texture of the grass makes you want to get up close and even run your fingers over the surface. Here it's used all by itself. But grasses make terrific companions to lots of plants. Like any neighbors, some get along together better than others. If you have a lovely upright form, like the maiden grass in photo 1, don't overcrowd your combo. You want the arching foliage to fan out over the other plants, not be constricted.

PLANT THIS CONTAINER
- A **Maiden grass** *Miscanthus sinensis* 'Little Kitten'
- B **Croton** *Codiaeum variegatum pictum*
- C **Lantana** *Lantana camara* 'Kolibri'
- D **Ornamental pepper** *Capsicum annuum* 'Black Pearl'

(1) Wispy maiden grass and orange crotons look like a sunrise on a foggy day. Leave the tropical crotons in individual pots and you can swap them out with other foliage or flowering plants for a fresh, seasonal look.

PLANT THIS CONTAINER
A Toe tickler grass *Eleocharis acicularis*
B Maidenhair fern *Adiantum* spp.

(2) Toe tickler grass, sometimes called "needle spikerush," likes it moist, even wet. Plant it in a container that won't dry out quickly, or set the pot in a saucer and always keep it filled with water.

Rita thinks it's this fine texture that makes grasses so useful in container designs. Take a look at photo 3. Notice how the wispy blades of the blue fescue break up the "chunky" foliage forms around it? The grass weaving into the coarser foliage creates a dramatic, and very interesting, texture contrast. In this case, the low mounding fescue is used to spill over and soften the hard edge of the container, too.

SEASONAL IMPACT Check out photos 1 and 3 again. House plants, such as croton, mother-in-law's-tongue and inch plant, combine beautifully with grasses. Plant everything in the same container if you like, or leave the house plants in their individual pots. Later you can pull them out quickly and move these tender plants indoors before frost. Since the grasses look good well into fall, pop a hardy plant, such as a mum or aster, into the hole left behind for a fresh, seasonal change.

GROWING CONCERNS As you would with any container combo, be sure to match the growing requirements of the plants. And while you may think of grasses as only full-sun plants, don't fret if you have shade. Many of the fescues and sedges actually prefer part shade.

Any general-purpose potting mix is fine for grasses. For the best results, when you plant, add a scoop or two of compost and a slow-release fertilizer with an analysis of 5-3-3 or something similar. Most grasses are grown for their foliage, so they respond well to the nitrogen in fertilizer, which encourages foliage growth.

These are just a few of the grasses that adapt beautifully to confined living. If you have your own favorite, give one a try in a container. ◻

— *Jim Childs*

PLANT THIS CONTAINER
A Blue fescue *Festuca glauca*
B Moses-in-a-boat *Tradescantia spathacea*
C Coral bells *Heuchera* 'Pewter Veil'
D Mother-in-law's-tongue *Sansevieria trifasciata laurentii*
E Oxalis *Oxalis triangularis* 'Mijke'
F Japanese painted fern *Athyrium* 'Ghost'
G Inch plant *Tradescantia zebrina*

(3) Shades of silvery gray, with touches of rich burgundy, make this container striking. But it's also the dramatic texture contrasts of all these foliage plants that encourage you to examine the combo more closely.

CONTAINERS | RECIPES

2009 container challenge
Readers' Best Containers

What's so great about container gardening? The answers are as varied as the gardeners. For one thing, you can change plants every year, growing classic geraniums one season and tropical hibiscus the next. If your garden soil is poor, containers allow you to grow plants that might struggle in the ground. You can even garden where there isn't *any* soil, such as on decks or patios. Is there a bare spot in the garden? No problem, move a container to hide the gap. But I think the biggest reason container gardening is so popular is the variety it provides. Variety is also what's great about our Container Challenge. We get to see all the creative ways our readers have combined plants, and then share them with everyone! Let's take a look at the latest and greatest reader-designed containers. ☐

— *Sherri Ribbey*

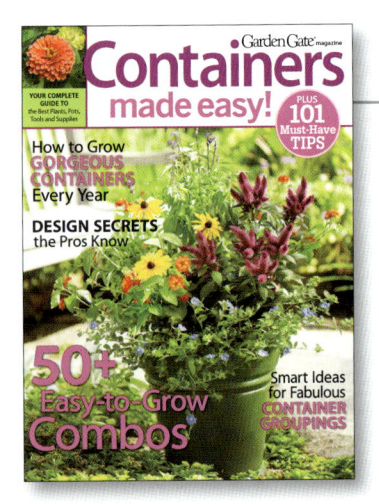

Garden Goods Hard work deserves a reward. Thanks to the generosity of the companies listed here, we're sending these gardeners some great stuff. Editor's Choice, Jennifer VanWagner, will receive a Campania container, Organic Mechanics™ potting mix, Quench™ water crystals and a box of Simply Beautiful® plants from Ball Horticulture. Our top pick for each category gets *Pots in the Garden* by Ray Rogers, along with a soil knife and sheath. We'll also send all these gardeners our latest special interest book, *Containers Made Easy!* You can get your copy online at www.GardenGateStore.com.

230   *the* YEAR IN GARDENING   www.GardenGateMagazine.com

Editor's choice
Jennifer VanWagner, Michigan

Here's a deck planting that really makes a great first impression. Tough and reliable annuals, such as geranium, licorice plant, lantana and calibrachoa, mean this exuberant planting doesn't need any fuss.

A self-watering container helps keep it looking good, too. Once the reservoir is full, plants have easy access to water for several days, which cuts down on garden chores. Jennifer did find that during a long dry spell last summer, she still needed to water daily. But the reservoir kept the water from evaporating too quickly, and the plants still looked fantastic.

The container on the railing is 9 in. wide and 39 in. long and is watered through a fill tube like the one in the illustration above. You can get your own from a local garden center or from Gardener's Supply at www.gardeners.com or 888-833-1412.

Pour water into the fill tube to water plants. The floating level tells you how much you've added.

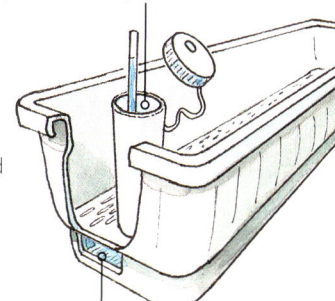

Water reservoir

Code	Plant Name	No. to Plant
A	**Lantana** *Lantana camara* Patriot™ Classic™ Cherry	3
B	**Licorice plant** *Helichrysum petiolare* 'Licorice Splash'	2
C	**Calibrachoa** *Calibrachoa* Superbells® Tequila Sunrise	2
D	**Geranium** *Pelargonium* Americana® Bright Red	2
E	**Bacopa** *Sutera cordata* Scopia™ Gulliver White	2

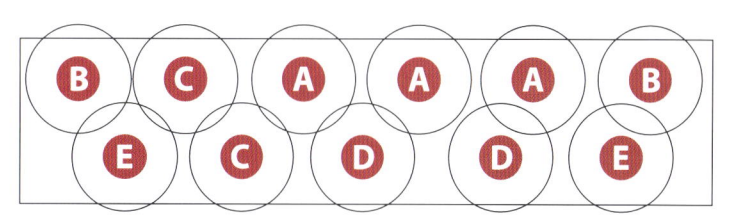

Best sun container Susan Hoblit, Illinois

Put sun and shade plants together in one container? No problem. This combination of sun-loving and shade-tolerant plants worked perfectly because it was grown in four to five hours of morning sun, or part sun. The morning light was gentle but still strong enough that the New Zealand flax and alternanthera kept their nice burgundy foliage color. But it wasn't enough to scorch the coleus leaves or fade the impatiens flower color.

Susan recommends regular watering even for big, 18-in. containers like this one, especially in hot weather. That's what makes the plants look so good all season long. How do you know when to water? Insert your finger into the potting mix up to the first knuckle. If the soil is dry, it's time to give your container a good soaking.

Code	Plant Name	No. to Plant
A	**New Zealand flax** *Phormium* 'Rainbow Warrior'	1
B	**Alternanthera** *Alternanthera* Red Threads	1
C	**Impatiens** *Impatiens walleriana* Super Elfin XP™ Punch	2
D	**Coleus** *Solenostemon* 'Black Dragon'	2

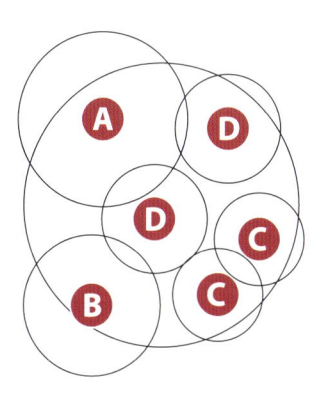

www.GardenGateMagazine.com

the YEAR IN GARDENING   231

MORE CONTAINERS!

Best shade container *Deborah Trickett, Massachusetts*

Shade gardeners have a limited number of flowers to choose from, so they've learned to get creative with foliage. This elegant container is colorful without a single flower. Broad caladium leaves provide a nice contrast to the fluffy asparagus fern, while the smaller burgundy bugleweed leaves add depth. Deborah bought her caladium already growing in a gallon-sized container, but if you buy a bag of tubers, three or four should be enough. Take a close look at the bugleweed and you'll notice the color varies from leaf to leaf. That's common for this plant and is caused by the amount of light it receives. The more light, the darker the leaf. Speaking of light, this 16-in. urn was grown in shade, so it didn't dry out as quickly as one in full sun would. But since most of these plants appreciate moist conditions, Deborah used water crystals in the potting mix to ensure success.

Code	Plant Name	No. to Plant
A	**Asparagus fern** *Asparagus densiflorus* Sprengeri Group	1
B	**Caladium** *Caladium* 'Florida Cardinal'	3
C	**Bugleweed** *Ajuga reptans* 'Bronze Beauty'	4
D	**Deadnettle** *Lamium maculatum* 'White Nancy'	2

Best whimsical container *Lawrie Morello, New Jersey*

Brightly colored containers can be a real challenge to design with, whether they're a familiar shape or something fun like this big teacup that's about 12 in. across. The key to using strong colors like these is to match one or two of them with your plants, like Lawrie did. Here, the orange begonia and yellow Dahlberg daisy go well with their corresponding stripes, while purple calibrachoa and white verbena provide a nice contrast and keep it interesting.

Begonias like this one are often sold as gift plants, so you're more likely to find it in the florist's shop rather than the garden center. Instead of tossing your begonia in the fall, try overwintering it inside. Once the plant stops blooming, cut it back to a few inches above the soil. Place it in a cool, dry area and keep the soil dry. When you see new growth, move it to a sunnier spot and start watering and fertilizing again.

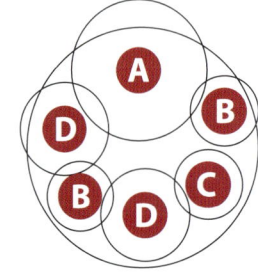

Code	Plant Name	No. to Plant
A	**Begonia** *Begonia* Rieger group	1
B	**Dahlberg daisy** *Thymophylla tenuiloba*	2
C	**Calibrachoa** *Calibrachoa* Superbells® Blue	1
D	**Verbena** *Verbena* Babylon® White	2

BONUS CONTAINERS!

With so many great entries, we couldn't narrow it down to only four. Here are five runners-up. You'll find the plant lists and plans in our Web extra.

A Color for part shade
Patty Sutherland, Minnesota
Talk about easy-care — this container is full of plants that look great with hardly any help from you. Consistent moisture is the one thing you can do to keep it looking good.

B Cozy teakettle
Karen Dozier, Iowa Don't throw that old teakettle out: Drill a few holes in the bottom and fill it with flowers like Karen did! Since it's so small, keep it in part shade and water daily.

C Bulb bonanza
Macel Posey, Oregon To chill the bulbs in this container, Macel left it outside in a protected spot all winter. In spring she got to enjoy the sunny daffodils, tulips, hyacinths and pansies. She let the bulb foliage turn brown before pulling them out and planting them in the garden for another spring of blooms.

D Shady sophistication
Sylvia Murdoch, Ohio Sylvia found that an eastern exposure works best for this plan. Morning light gives black mondo grass foliage its best color, and there's still enough sun to encourage the salvia to bloom. Pinch the polka dot plant back occasionally to keep it tidy.

E Perfectly purple
Jennifer VanWagner, Michigan
You can't tell from the photo, but this container is really the lid of an old grill. Jennifer left the vent in the top open for drainage. To keep these sun-loving plants compact and in scale with the container, pinch stems back if they get too tall.

Web extra See complete *planting plans* for these containers.

CONTAINERS | RECIPES

create a super bowl

Imagine coming up the front walk of a house and being greeted by the sunny personality of this beautiful bowl. You can't help but feel warm all over!

Waves of cheery yellow flowers engulf the red, pink and salmon geraniums in the center of this combination. (Take off the faded geranium flowers to keep the plants looking tidy and blooming well.)

As the petunia grows, feel free to clip back the more exuberant stems to keep it growing full and lush. A steady feeding schedule will keep it and the other annuals floriferous all summer.

Now, as the weather gets hotter, the yellow cape daisies will start to flag. (I usually cut them back to 3 or 4 inches.) But by that time the geraniums and the white bacopa will have grown enough to fill the resulting gap.

A good rule of thumb is to keep plants no more than one and a half times the height of your container. That's especially true for a low bowl like this. Plants much taller than that will look out of scale and make the planting look top-heavy. I like the way these plants "hug" the pot — just what you'd expect from one with such a warm personality!

Tips for care

- Full sun
- Even soil moisture
- Apply ¼-strength balanced water-soluble fertilizer monthly

Code	Plant Name	No. to Plant
A	**Petunia** *Petunia* Surfinia® Patio Yellow	1
B	**Bacopa** *Sutera* Abunda™ Giant White	1
C	**Cape daisy** *Osteospermum* 'Lemon Symphony'	1
D	**Geranium** *Pelargonium* Maestro™ Pink Parfait	1
E	**Geranium** *Pelargonium* 'Starlette Salmon'	1
F	**Geranium** *Pelargonium* Maestro™ Bright Red	1

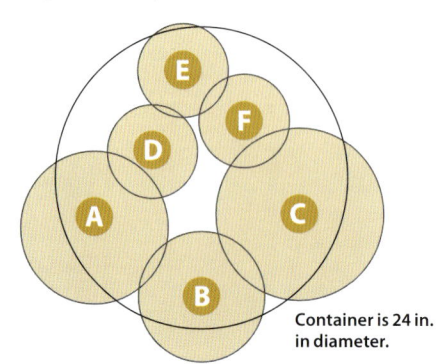

Container is 24 in. in diameter.

234   the YEAR IN GARDENING   www.GardenGateMagazine.com

warm sunshine

One of the great things about container gardening is that you can create a planting almost any time of year. In fall, for example, many garden centers get in lots of fresh plants that look fantastic in cooler weather.

This container planting uses traditional fall colors of orange and gold, but, except for the kale, pretty unconventional fall plants. These gorgeous yellow and orange 'Julie' begonias echo the color of this big terra-cotta bowl, while adding a fresh bright look. In the background, large ornamental kales provide a more traditional touch of fall, along with interesting color and texture contrasts.

And who says you can't use indoor plants in fall containers? Croton and begonias are typically considered house plants, but here they bring autumnal shades and fascinating textures. Keep them in their individual pots when you place them in the larger container. Then you can just pop them back out and take them indoors before frost hits.

For a big pot like this, try mounding the soil in the center before planting to give the middle plants a bit more height. And a few unobtrusive green bamboo stakes will keep the begonias standing nice and straight. The combination will look good for just a few weeks, so don't bother to feed the plants.

Don't forget about the container itself. A raised oak leaf and acorn pattern reinforces the fall theme in this combo. The design will gain even more character as the pot ages and takes on a deeper tinge or maybe even a bit of moss. And the plants in this design won't trail over the edge of the pot and obscure the distinctive design. □

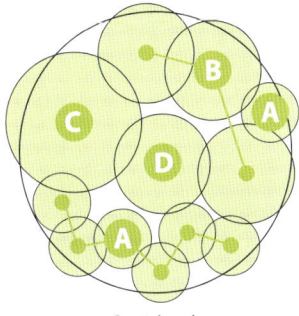

Tips for care

- Full to part sun
- Even soil moisture
- Short-term fall container doesn't need fertilizer

Container is 19 inches in diameter.

Code	Plant Name	No. to Plant
A	**Begonia** *Begonia xhiemalis* 'Julie'	7
B	**Ornamental kale** *Brassica oleracea* 'Peacock Red'	3
C	**Croton** *Codiaeum variegatum pictum*	1
D	**Foxtail fern** *Asparagus densiflorus* 'Myersii'	1

CONTAINERS | RECIPE

cool idea

SOOTHING ESCAPE Think a color palette of cool greens and purples sounds too dark for shade? It doesn't have to be! Punches of white brighten this soothing palette and make it just the thing for a garden planted in the shade of several large trees.

There's a lot to love about this large island bed. It's overflowing with variegated hostas, tall spikes of daffodil foliage and delicate white corydalis. A patch of lavender mazus spills over into the grassy path. The effect is a garden full of color and texture contrast. Who could resist?

Not us! We recreated the same filled-to-the-brim look by choosing the fullest plants we could find. That meant choosing two house plants: dieffenbachia, to stand in for the hostas, and Rieger begonias, to echo the corydalis' white blooms. Spike plant is a near-perfect (but smaller) copy of the daffodil foliage, and deep purple wishbone flower spills out of the pot, just like the mazus spills from the bed. The result? Similar color, fullness and texture, in less space!

Give this container part to full shade, and keep it consistently moist, but not too wet. A high-quality potting soil will provide excellent drainage, and a layer of mulch along the soil's surface will retain moisture.

This planting looks great all summer long, but once the begonias are done blooming, it's time to move on. Bring the dieffenbachia inside to brighten a living room or spare bedroom, and toss the rest of the plants.

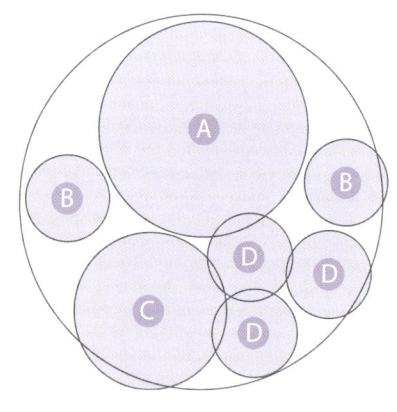

[the inspiration]

Container is 16 in. in diameter

Code	Plant Name	No. to Plant
A	**Dieffenbachia** *Dieffenbachia* hybrid	1
B	**Spike plant** *Cordyline* hybrid	2
C	**Rieger begonia** *Begonia xhiemalis*	1
D	**Wishbone flower** *Torenia* Catalina® Midnight Blue	3

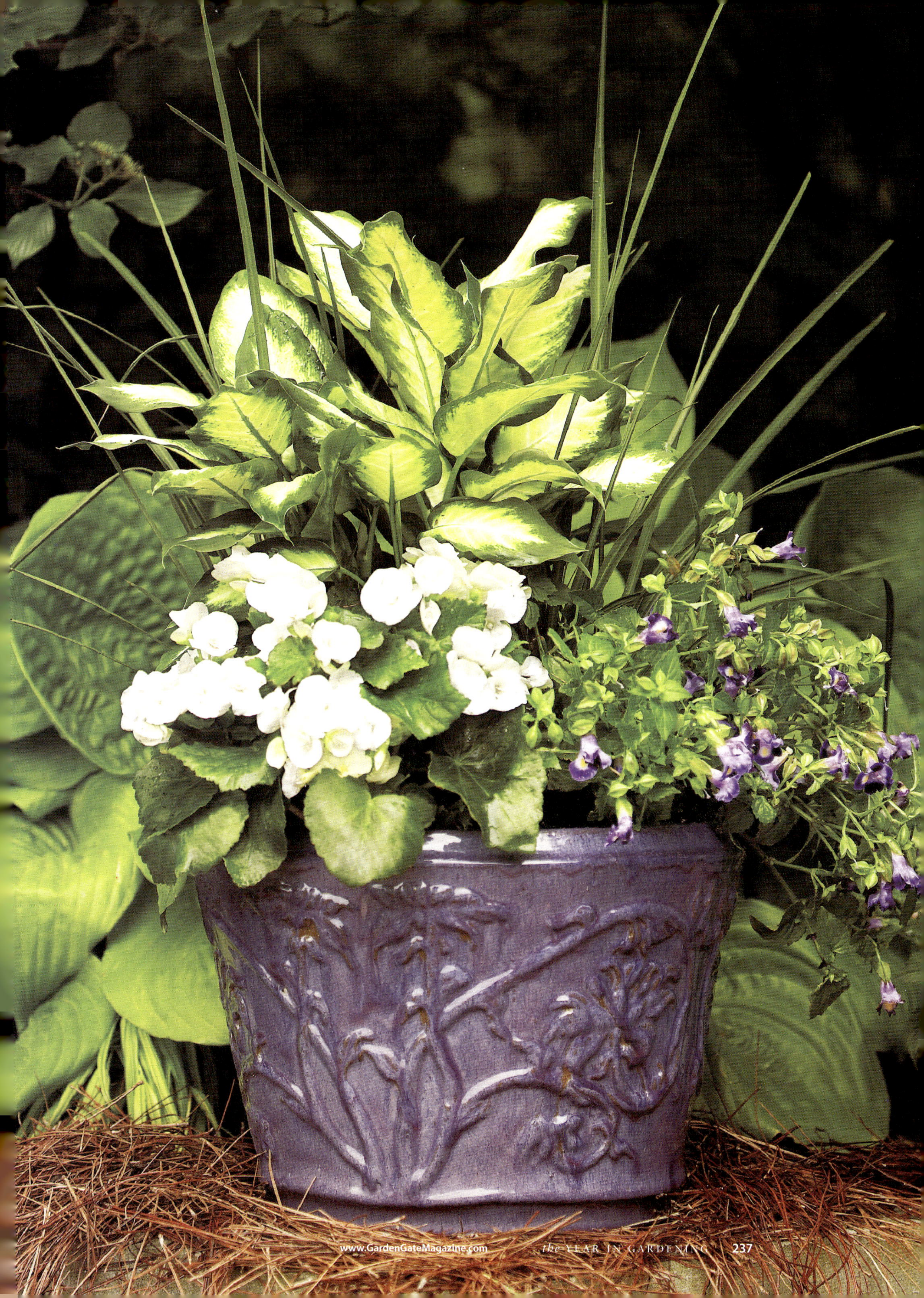

CONTAINERS | BASICS

3 ways to shape up a container

Many container plants are vigorous and low-maintenance. They don't complain when you squish their roots or put them in tight quarters. In fact, with a little food and water, they'll repay you by growing furiously! Why not give them a little makeover in return?

The techniques here aren't vital to plants' survival, but they leave foliage and flowers looking, and growing, much better than they would without the attention. Each of these procedures is simple, and takes just minutes.

I'll show you how to do three techniques and tell you which plants benefit most from them. Then I'll share a recipe at right that uses some of these techniques. □

—*Deborah Gruca*

1 PINCHING BACK Some common container plants, like the coleus below, are fantastic growers. But the flipside is that they can get a bit leggy and start taking over the entire container. Cutting or pinching back is easy, and works really well on foliage plants that are growing out of bounds.

Snap off overgrown stems about a third or half the way back, just above a healthy set of leaves. Not only does this give the plant a neat and tidy "after" appearance, but it also encourages a less leggy, more bushy habit — perfect for containers!

Another situation where pinching or cutting back comes in handy is when you want to revive annuals that bloom in spring and fall, but hibernate in summer.

PLANTS TO PINCH
- **Browallia** *Browallia speciosa*
- **Coleus** *Solenostemon* hybrids
- **Dichondra** *Dichondra* spp.
- **Joseph's coat** *Alternanthera* hybrids
- **Licorice plant** *Helichrysum petiolare*
- **Persian shield** *Strobilanthes dyeriana*
- **Sweet potato vine** *Ipomoea batatas*

2 DEADHEADING Deadheading is one of the essential techniques you need to know. It has a number of benefits — it keeps plants looking good, encourages them to keep blooming and prevents reseeders from taking over your garden. For annuals like the geraniums in the photo below, all you need is your fingers. Snap off the spent bloom at the bulge in the base of the stem, so you don't see the empty stem. For marigolds, just remove the flowers and seedheads. But for plants with tough stems, like dianthus, use a pair of scissors to shear off the faded flowers. However, there are some plants that are termed "self-cleaning" — they drop their spent blooms on their own, so you don't have to deadhead them at all! Meet some of those in the second list below.

PLANTS TO DEADHEAD
- **Marigold** *Tagetes* spp.
- **Dianthus** *Dianthus* hybrids
- **Zonal geranium** *Pelargonium* hybrids

SELF-CLEANING PLANTS
- **Angelonia** *Angelonia angustifolia*
- **Dragon Wing™ begonia** *Begonia* hybrids
- **Marguerite daisy** *Argyranthemum* hybrids
- **Moss rose** *Portulaca grandiflora*

3 UNDERCUTTING The trailing petunias in the built-in planter below have formed a lush, thick mat of color, which looks great. But unfortunately, our petunias are feeling a little stressed. See how tangled the stems are? When plants form a carpet of flowers, they also form a thick web of stems that block water and sunlight from reaching the lower branches. This eventually slows the growth of the plant or even kills it. To prevent this, you need to undercut.

Lift the carpet of flowers so you can see the stems underneath. Then use pruners to snip stems as I'm doing in the photo below. It doesn't matter which ones you cut; the goal is to thin the mat and stimulate new growth. As you snip, pull cut stems out of your way until the remaining ones look loosely interwoven, and you can see through the mat a bit. Check the top side from time to time so you don't create a hole.

PLANTS TO UNDERCUT
- **Bacopa** *Sutera* hybrids
- **Calibrachoa** *Calibrachoa* hybrids
- **Lobelia** *Lobelia erinus*
- **Petunia** *Petunia* hybrids
- **Swedish ivy** *Plectranthus forsteri*
- **Twinspur** *Diascia* hybrids

ORANGE ACCENT

Do you love bright color? Here's a way to work color into your containers without going overboard: Use it in small doses! In this pot, the hot-colored dahlias and orange anagallis establish the orange color theme. The other plants pick up on that theme, but in an understated way. See how that succulent echeveria has pink hints along its edge? In another container, that subtle accent might be missed. But surrounded by such warm tones, it really stands out!

This container needs full sun, and plenty of moisture. The only exception is the echeveria. Succulents like dry, sharply drained soil. To keep it happy here, plant all of the other plants, then dig out a hole for it. Add a handful of gravel or turkey grit to the bottom of the hole, then plant the succulent at an angle (to cover the edge of the container and encourage water to drain away from the plant's crown). Finally, add a light mulch of gravel or grit around the plant. Keep the dahlia going by deadheading spent blooms, but don't worry about the anagallis — it's self-cleaning. Do pinch its stems back though, along with those of the Joseph's coat, to keep both plants neat and compact. (You'll find great tips on pinching in "3 ways to shape up a container" at left.) ☐

Tips for care
- Full sun
- Even soil moisture, except near the echeveria
- Apply ¼-strength water-soluble 15-30-15 fertilizer once a week

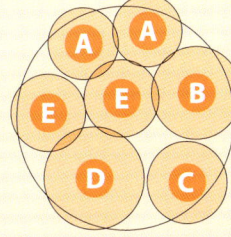

Container is 14 in. in diameter.

Code	Plant Name	No. to Plant
A	**Dahlia** *Dahlia* 'Mystic Desire'	2
B	**Wood spurge** *Euphorbia* 'Efanthia'	1
C	**Anagallis** *Anagallis* 'Wildcat Orange'	1
D	**Echeveria** *Echeveria* 'Afterglow'	1
E	**Joseph's coat** *Alternanthera* 'Red Threads'	2

the YEAR IN GARDENING

CONTAINERS | BASICS

container cleanup
in 3 easy steps

You've invested a lot of time and money in your containers to make your garden look great all season. When the weather cools in fall, it's time to take care of that investment. Exposed to freezing winter elements, glazed and terra-cotta containers often crack or flake apart. But with a little time and effort, you can prevent that and get many years of use from them. Here's how.

1 CLEAN OUT After you've removed the plants from your container, it's important to empty your pot. In most cases, the mix and other materials don't harm anything. But if the plants in your pot had disease problems during the season, these materials can harbor the disease until next year. So, just to be safe, it's good to clean them up.

I use the stiff-bristled brush you see in photo 1 to scrub off as much potting mix, moss and mineral deposits as possible. (The mineral deposits are white material that builds up on the pot from water or fertilizer.) Then I wet down the entire container with water to loosen anything remaining and scrub it again. If there's still some mineral build-up left on the pot, daub on a solution of 1 cup vinegar in 1 quart water and brush it down again. Rinse it with plain water.

2 STERILIZE Once your pot is clean, it's time to sterilize it with a 1:10 bleach and water solution. Spray down the inside, as I'm doing in photo 2, to kill any diseases in the pot.

Next, set them up off the floor in a warm, dry spot, like on a garage workbench, for a few days until they are totally dry.

3 STORE THEM Garden containers are best stored indoors, where they're protected from rain and snow. Stash them in your garage, potting shed, basement — anywhere dry and out of the way. You don't want to accidentally knock a pot over and crack it. Ideally, you should store your pots unstacked to prevent breaking them. But if you're short on space, you can stack them — upside down if they're outdoors (so they won't collect rain or snow), upside down or right side up if they're inside. See how I've propped my pots up on a pair of 2×4s in photo 3? This keeps them off the ground and improves air circulation (which helps them stay dry). Place long strips of cardboard between the pots to separate them and prevent them from sticking together. That way, in the spring, they'll be easy to lift apart.

Of course, you don't have to put away *all* your containers for winter. Check out "Mini masterpiece" at right for a simple two-plant container that will look great even when the snow flies! ☐

— *Deborah Gruca*

1 Remove soil from containers with a stiff-bristled brush.

2 Use a spray bottle to direct the bleach solution where you want it so you don't accidentally bleach your clothing.

3 As fall approaches, keep the cardboard boxes from new shoes or electronics, so you have enough on hand to protect all your stacked pots.

Mini masterpiece

Snow adds the finishing touch to the red-and-green combo in this small wood-and-bark container. Tuck in fresh or frozen cranberries as a colorful mulch that may even entice a few birds to take a closer look. And add several cut stems of red-twig dogwood for a little vertical accent.

Code	Plant Name
A	**Atlantic white cedar** *Chamaecyparis thyoides* 'Top Point' (1)
B	**Holly** *Ilex* 'Rock Garden' (2)
C	**Red-twig dogwood** *Cornus sericea* (Cut stems)

Container is 7 in. in diameter

It's best to transfer plants from pot to ground before the weather gets very cold. But moving perennials on hot or humid days is hard on them, too. Choose a day with temperatures in the 60s or low 70s, and be sure to give the new transplant plenty of water as it settles in.

overwintering plants

No matter how hard you try to fight it, winter will arrive. But that doesn't mean you have to lose all of your favorite plants! Here's how to save them.

Containers used to be the domain of annuals alone. But lately, gardeners have been adding more perennials and tubers to the mix. The result is plantings with great texture and bold colors. But even the hardiest plants won't survive most winters in containers (there's not enough soil to keep them warm). You could just toss them with the annuals at the end of the year, but with a little extra effort, your favorite tubers and perennials can live to bloom again.

PERENNIALS Perennials, like hostas, coneflower and bugleweed (shown above) look fantastic in containers. But when the end of the year comes, it's a shame to just toss them. Instead, after the summer's over, plant them in your garden so they'll keep growing, year after year. In zone 6 or cooler, you'll want to pull the perennial from its container and transplant it in early fall, before there's any chance of frost. This ensures that the ground will be soft enough to dig into, and it'll give your perennial plenty of time to get settled in its new home before the soil freezes.

Dig the perennial out of the pot. If you end up breaking or slicing a few roots, that's not a big deal. Then, dig a hole in your garden, and plant the perennial at the same depth as it was in the pot. Give your plant a deep drink of water. Finally, add a 3-in. layer of mulch over the roots to protect them from cold. Next year, simply treat the transplanted perennial like any other plant.

continued

CONTAINERS | BASICS

TUBERS YOU CAN STORE
Calla lily *Zantedeschia* spp.
Caladium *Caladium* hybrid
Canna *Canna* spp.
Elephant ear *Colocasia esculenta*
Giant elephant ear *Zanthosoma* hybrid
Upright elephant ear *Alocasia* hybrid

Elephant ear

Elephant ear tubers

Banana

1   **2**

Tropical tubers, like elephant ear, can be very fragile, and lifting the plant by its foliage can damage it. Instead, dig your hands under the tubers and lift up from below.

Set aside a corner of your garage or basement for over-wintering. If you have a carpeted floor, lay down a tarp to catch any spilled soil.

If you live in an area where the ground freezing isn't an issue, the perennials can stay in their pots until you're ready to dismantle them (in the fall or in a few years). Plant and treat the perennials as usual. While you can technically dig up the plants again in the spring and put them back in containers, it's not the best idea. Perennials do best, long-term, in a garden.

TENDER TUBERS Elephant ears (shown in photo 1), cannas and caladiums all make stunning and dramatic container plants. But, they may not be winter-hardy in your area. If that's the case, and you want to save them, there's a simple solution: winter dry-storage. This storage technique works for all tubers, bulbs and rhizomes, but we show it using elephant ear tubers.

You can leave tender tubers in their pots until a light frost (between 30 and 32 degrees Fahrenheit) arrives and damages the foliage. However, be sure to get them indoors before a hard freeze (28 degrees or colder) comes through, or cold will damage the tuber.

Use a small spade or soil knife to cut a circle into the soil around the plant's base. Make sure it's as wide as the foliage above the plant to avoid cutting the tubers. Lift the clump from the pot, making sure you don't damage any of the little shoots you see coming off the tuber in photo 1.

Snip back the foliage 2 or 3 in. above the tuber, and crumble off any large clumps of soil. Then set the tuber in a warm, dry spot, like the shade of a tree or a basement workbench, to dry for a few days. This will help you brush the rest of the soil off the tuber without causing any damage. Make sure the tubers are completely dry. If they're stored with any moisture, they could rot.

When the tubers are dry, then you can store them. Wrap each one loosely with newspaper, as you can see in photo 2, and store them in a cardboard box or a basket. If you prefer, you could also fill a plastic tub with sawdust or peat moss, and bury the tubers in there. Keep them in a cool, dark room — 45 to 50 degrees is about right. Any warmer, and they may begin to sprout new foliage.

Throughout the winter, it's a good idea to unwrap a few tubers to check for soft spots (signs of rot). Just give the tubers a squeeze. If you do find a soft spot, don't panic. You might be able to save the tuber. Cut out the soft spot with a sharp knife, and sprinkle the wound with dusting sulfur, a fungicide available at many garden centers, to stop the spread of rot. Let the tuber dry out for a few days, then wrap it in fresh paper and put it back in the basket. It shouldn't have any more problems. And as long as the tuber still has a portion of the roots and last year's growing tip, it'll grow just fine next summer.

BOLD TROPICALS Tropical perennials are hard to resist, and why should you? Their exotic foliage and flowers add new dimensions to container gardens. And many tropicals, like bananas, flowering maples and gingers, can easily be overwintered if they aren't hardy in your zone.

Bananas are unique in their storage preferences. Pull these giants from their containers before frost, and shake off as much soil as you can. Cut off all the leaves except for the top one, and move the plant to a cool garage or basement — 50 degrees is optimal. Spritz the roots with water, then wrap them loosely in a plastic bag, as you can see in photo 2. Some air should circulate, or they'll rot. Pull back the bag to check on the roots throughout the winter, and give them another spritz of water if they're dry. Then rewrap. When temperatures warm, replant the banana in a pot, and set it outside.

For most tropical plants, like flowering maples and gingers, the best option is to keep them in their pot. Before night temperatures drop to the 40s, remove any container companions from the pot, and pull the tropical indoors. While tropicals can stand cooler temps, they'll go into shock if they're moved from a cold yard to a warm house. (If it's too big to fit in the house, prune it back by a few inches or even a few feet and it'll still return next year.) Put the container in a room that gets filtered light (a north-facing window is great) or in a basement with bright lights, and keep the soil just barely moist. A few weeks before you're ready to put it back outside, move the pot to a room with bright light, like one with a south-facing window, and return to a normal watering schedule. Then, once night temps are consistently above 40, set it back out for another gorgeous year!

ANNUALS Last but not least are annuals and tender perennials, like pansies, petunias and impatiens. You can try to overwinter these flowering beauties, but for the amount of effort that you put in, you probably won't get much in return. When winter hits and your annuals and tender perennials start to fade, pull them from their pots and add them to the compost pile. They'll break down over the winter and throughout the next year, and create a rich compost with lots of nutrients for a new batch of annuals!

wrapping a tree or shrub

There's one category we haven't covered yet: trees and shrubs in containers. In zones 6 or colder, your best bet is still to get the tree out of the container, and put both in a garage or basement. Keep the tree planted in a plastic nursery pot, rather than planting it in the container itself, for easy removal. Then turn to page 240 for more information on how to clean out your pots for the winter. But in zones 6 or warmer, you can leave your tree outside, in its container. Here's how to keep it warm and toasty.

Give your trees a warm winter coat. It helps keep the plants' roots at an even temperature. First, wrap the container in a few layers of insulation. Bubble wrap, in the photo at right, is handy — the pockets of air help insulate — but burlap or an old quilt will work, too.

Next, drape the branches with burlap. This fabric will buffer wind and protect bark against uneven warming.

Secure the burlap with twine. You can see at right how to wrap it in a spiral, going from the top to bottom. The twine shouldn't squeeze the branches too tightly — just enough to hold the burlap in place. When that's done, your potted tree is ready to face Old Man Winter.

Stop fertilizing your container at this point. You won't resume fertilizing until spring, when you unwrap your tree for good. Also, cut back on the watering. During winter, you want to keep the soil just barely moist, not wet. Two or three times during the winter, pull back the burlap and give your tree a drink. Water as usual, until you see the liquid coming out the bottom of the pot. Rewrap, and it should be fine until spring!

did you know...

Take containers to new heights
Sharon Whitney, Washington

Whiskey barrels are popular garden containers. Take a look at the illustration below to see how Sharon found a way to add some extra height and interest to hers. She fills a 28-inch-wide whiskey barrel to within a few inches of the top with potting mix. Then she sets a 12- to 14-inch-diameter container in the center of the whiskey barrel. To anchor the smaller container, she works it down into the loose mix. Next, she places tall plants, such as purple fountain grass (*Pennisetum rubrum*), in the top container. Then she takes a step back from the container to see how it looks. If the small container seems too tall, she pushes it down. Or she adds extra soil underneath if it's not high enough.

Once the height is right, Sharon fills the upper container with medium-sized upright annuals and a trailer to soften the edge. In the lower level she adds more flowers and another trailer, such as Wave™ petunias, to complete the planting. Every year this container has a different look!

Bring spring inside
Ginnie Judd, Illinois

Can't wait for spring? Do what Ginnie does and get a head start. During a warm spell in late winter, Ginnie steps outside with her trowel and a container she'd like to fill. She gently removes the mulch on her lily of the valley, looking for the new growth, called "pips." These small points stick ¼ to ½ inch above the soil.

Ginnie digs them up, soil and all, and places them in her container at the same level they were in the ground. (She's had success with digging up plants as early as January.) Then she brings her new house plant inside and sets it in a sunny, south-facing window. She keeps the soil moist but not soaked. It takes a week or two to start growing, and flowers open a week or so after that.

Show off seashells
Paula Smith, Georgia

When Paula goes on vacation, she walks along the beach and collects seashells. Back at home, she enjoys container gardening. She's found a way to combine the two so her beautiful containers are a reminder of favorite vacation spots.

Paula takes the shells from her forays to the beach and uses them as mulch around the plants in her containers. Before applying the seashell mulch, Paula rinses the shells off in tap water to get rid of sand and salt and to keep them from smelling bad. The mix of small- to medium-sized shells is attractive to look at and also helps keep the soil moist. And it's a great way to show off her collection instead of storing it away in a box.

The hole story
Linda Lindgren, Montana

Linda fills a lot of her old nursery pots with new divisions for the garden club plant sale. Instead of using coffee filters or rocks to cover the holes in the bottom of the pots, Linda uses leaves! She's found that hollyhock and mullein work best. Since the new plant will be transplanted quickly, there's no worry about the leaf decomposing, leaving the hole uncovered.

Push the smaller container down into the potting mix so it won't tip over.

Add trailing plants above and below for a unified container.

Easy pot feet
Diane Johnson, Minnesota

Designer pot feet look great but they can get expensive if you have a lot of containers. Diane makes her own and saves that extra money for more plants. How? With soap molds from the craft store. You'll also need mortar mix, vegetable oil or spray, water, a container and a stir-stick for mixing. If you want a specific color, get some concrete dye, too.

To make a set of pot feet like the ones in the photo above, add water slowly to the mortar mix until it's the consistency of a thick cake batter. Now's the time to stir in the dye if you want colorful pot feet. Spray the mold lightly with vegetable spray and pour in the mix. Then tap it gently to get rid of air bubbles. Let the mold dry for 24 hours. If the mortar is dry to the touch, go ahead and pop the feet out. Let them cure another day or two to harden. After that, your new pot feet are ready to hold up containers.

To prevent sticking, spray the mold with vegetable oil before pouring the mortar mix in.

Let the mortar mix cure for at least a day before removing the pot feet from the mold.

product pick

Monrovia Organic Potting Soil

Monrovia® Nurseries has been selling plants to garden centers for years. Now it's also offering its custom Organics Potting Soil in bags. When we cut open a bag of this mix the first thing we noticed was the rich, earthy smell. One handful and you could tell it was full of materials to help plants grow. Monrovia Organics mix includes peat moss, composted bark, perlite and compost. It also has something you can't see — mycorrhizae, a fungus that helps roots grow. The coarse texture is a breeze for roots to grow in, and our containers looked great!

Bottom line Good soil means healthy plants.
Source Independent garden centers
Price $12.99 for a 1.5-cubic-foot bag

did you know... (CONTINUED)

in the news

Feel-good flowers
If you've had to spend a few days in the hospital, you know how welcome flower bouquets or potted plants from family and friends can be. Now researchers at the Department of Horticulture, Recreation and Forestry at Kansas State University have found that this caring gift can actually help patients get better. They compared patients recovering from abdominal surgery who had plants in their room to those who didn't. Patients with plants used significantly less pain medication and had less pain, anxiety and fatigue, as well. In addition, they showed more positive physical responses, such as lower blood pressure and heart rate and felt more satisfied with their rooms. So the next time someone you know has surgery, be sure to send them some flowers or a plant to speed up their recovery.

Sack of potatoes
Rick Biel, Wisconsin

Most old water softener salt bags end up in the garbage. But when Rick noticed the small perforations on the front of a salt bag he'd emptied, he got an idea. Those holes would help water drain, so why not grow something in it? First, he enlarged the opening and rinsed out the bag with the hose. Then Rick filled the bag about two-thirds full with a mixture of peat moss, compost and potting soil. That done, he added two potatoes that had been sprouting.

Once the potatoes were planted, Rick picked up the bag and hung it on his picket fence as the illustration above shows. The handle slid over the picket and came to rest on the stringer, the board that runs horizontally to support the pickets. In a couple of months he had a nice harvest of potatoes. Next year he's going to try cucumbers!

Filled with potting mix, the bag weighed about 15 lbs.

Terra-cotta tragedy
Ron Steffen, Washington

Q I broke a big terra-cotta pot. I tried to patch it with silicone caulk, but it won't stay patched. Is there anything else I can do?

A With a few tools and some patience, you can "sew" a pot together with wire, forming a more durable patch than caulk alone.

You'll need wire, a drill and a masonry bit (available at hardware stores). Make sure the wire is smaller than the diameter of the drill bit.

With the broken piece in place, make pairs of pencil dots about ½ inch in on both sides of the break. Take the broken piece out, and use the masonry bit to drill holes at each pencil dot.

Cover the broken edges with Liquid Nails® or other adhesive, and slip the piece into place. When the adhesive is set, cut lengths of wire, poke them through the paired holes, and twist the ends together on the inside of the container, forming a "stitch."

For a little extra support, cut a piece of wire long enough to go around the outside of the pot just under the lip. Twist the ends together and tighten with pliers (not too tight!), then snip the ends short.

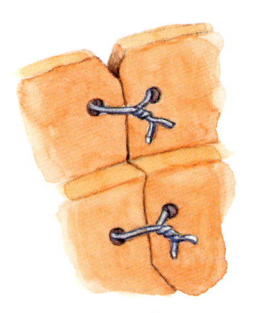

You may need to snip the ends of the wire once it's twisted.

Even when the patch is in place, don't pick the pot up by the edges, and store it where it won't freeze.

Leaky pot gets the seal
Jennifer Strickley, California

Q What can I do to keep water from seeping out of my concrete pot so quickly?

A Of course you'll lose water through the drainage hole and any cracks in the container, so make sure all cracks are filled. Repair them with either latex caulk or a concrete repair kit available from your local hardware store. If your container doesn't have cracks (or you've repaired them), water is probably seeping through the sides. Some concrete mixes are dense and don't leak, but many are porous, and water seeps right through. To prevent plants from drying out — and your water bill from increasing — seal the container.

There are many products available from your local hardware store. One we have had success with is GBS Penetrating Sealer. Paint one saturating coat on the inside surface and let it dry. You can buy the sealer in different finishes and colors.

product picks

FabricPots

Don't keep your house plant in the boring plastic pot it came in. Jazz it up with a FabricPot™! It really is made of fabric, and yes, you can put the plant, soil and all, in this container. The inside is coated with a high-tech material similar to waterproof sportswear so water stays in but the fabric still breathes. Excess water escapes through drainage holes into the saucer below. If you want to change pots, the FabricPot collapses down for easy storage. There are two styles: Narrow-mouthed Frusto comes in three colors: Citron (yellow), Pinot Noir (shown) and Turquoise; tall Silo comes in two colors: Pinot Noir and Citron.

Bottom line Stylish and functional, it's a great way to add a little sparkle to indoor plants.
Source Hova Design at 888-456-3040 or www.hovadesign.com
Price Silo $30; Frusto $40; both are 7½ inches tall and 8½ inches at the base

Frusto-style pot in Pinot Noir

Better Than Rocks

Whether you're trying to lighten up a heavy container or want to save on potting mix, this new product is a great solution. Better Than Rocks® is made of 100 percent recycled plastic and looks like a furnace filter. The strands of plastic are tight enough to hold soil in but they still let water flow out of the hole in the bottom of the container. You can buy it precut in 10-inch squares or as a roll that you cut to size yourself with scissors. At 1½ inches thick, one layer of Better Than Rocks is usually enough for small containers. In larger containers, you may need several layers. Though this product is a little pricey up front, you can reuse it for years. You don't have to rinse the pieces off with water in the fall but if you're worried about disease problems, you might want to.

Bottom line Lightweight and reusable, Better Than Rocks is worth the extra investment.
Source Kinsman & Co. at 800-733-4146 or www.kinsmangarden.com or www.GardenGateStore.com
Price $13.95 for two 10-inch squares or $52.95 for a 16-inch-by-96-inch roll it came in. Jazz it up with a FabricPot™!

The dense fibers hold in the soil but allow water through.

We manage to grow a good-looking garden, despite regular visits from deer. We'll let you know what works (and what doesn't) on page 274.

gardening basics

how to *grow* the garden you've always wanted

PESTS. WEEDS. DISEASES. HARD WORK. If you garden, you can't avoid these and other challenges. But they don't have to take all the fun out of gardening. We'll share tools and techniques that make the dirty work easier on you. Plus we'll pass along great tips for perfect planting, a new way to fertilize, how to divide your lilies, our favorite reader tips over the last 15 years and more!

Off to a Great Start	**250**
Fertilizer: Get the Facts	**254**
Feed Your Plants What They Love	**256**
No Pests, No Chemicals	**258**
The Secrets to Dividing in Summer	**260**
Lots of Lovely Lilies	**262**
Garden Smarter: 7 Easy-Does-It Tips	**264**
Point, Click, Plant!	**266**
Get Your Garden in Shape Now	**268**
15 Years of Readers' Best Tips	**270**
Deer Diary	**274**
Attack of the Invasives	**276**
Garden Coverups	**280**
No-Mow Slope	**282**
Sharpen Your Edges	**284**
Digging Tools That Work	**286**
Bulb Tools That Really Work	**288**
Think Small, Save Time	**290**
Did You Know…	**292**
Beneficials You Should Know	**304**
Pests to Watch	**305**
6 Weeds to Know	**306**
Know Your Zones	**308**

BASICS | SMART GARDENING

Off to a Great Start
in 4 Simple Steps

Shopping for perennials is fun — planting them is work. Don't let your labor go to waste — plant them right!

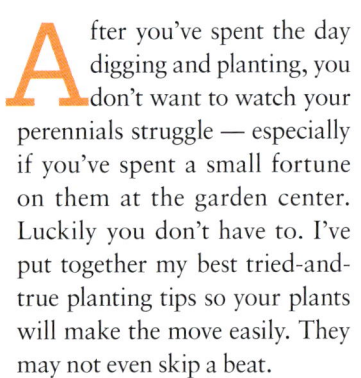

After you've spent the day digging and planting, you don't want to watch your perennials struggle — especially if you've spent a small fortune on them at the garden center. Luckily you don't have to. I've put together my best tried-and-true planting tips so your plants will make the move easily. They may not even skip a beat.

To start, of course, you'll want to get your soil in great shape with compost and other amendments. In a large planting bed, tilling in advance not only makes the soil easier to dig, it'll save you time and energy. If you're just putting in a plant or two, shoveling compost into each hole and working it in is fine, too.

To prevent stressing your new plants, the best time to get them in the ground is when it's cool and cloudy, a day or two after a light rain. The next best time is when you have time to do it! So, make sure the plants and the garden are ready when you are.

1 ADVANCE PLANNING Set the potted perennials in place the night before you're going to plant. It's much easier to adjust the design now than after everything is planted. That's exactly what I've done in photo 1. I'm also watering the plants. After all, you don't want to plant wilted, dry perennials; it'll be much too stressful for them. The garden soil gets a light sprinkling, too. Why the soil? The moisture is good for all of the beneficial bacteria that may have been disturbed as you worked the soil. You don't need to water until it's muddy, just moisten the surface a bit.

Now turn off the water and relax until tomorrow. Then it's time to get down and dirty!

2 DIG THE HOLE Most perennials will survive in a planting hole that's less than perfect. But our objective is to get your plants off to the best possible start *and* make sure they'll thrive in your garden for many years.

In photo 2 I'm digging a wide, shallow hole — I like to call it an "extravagant" hole. That's a good name because it's much larger than the gallon-size perennial I'm going to plant into it. A wide hole, at least twice as wide as the pot, will allow the roots to push out into the loosened soil quickly to gather moisture and nutrients. The faster they can do that, the faster they will adapt to their new home and grow.

Water the day before you plant.

Dig a wide, shallow hole.

Don't bother digging a deep hole. Almost all perennials will have a majority of their roots near the surface of the soil, so they don't really go down very far. Plus, a shallow hole with gently sloping sides is usually easier to dig.

Loosening lots of soil in the bottom of the hole could cause the plant to sink too deep after it's watered. Later, especially over winter, water will collect in the low spot and rot the crown. As a rule of thumb, don't dig the hole any deeper than the depth of the pot the plant came in. The illustrations at right show you the "hows" and "whys" of hole size and shape.

If you've prepared the soil in your new bed with lots of compost, you won't need to add more to the hole. The roots may never push out into the surrounding soil if you make the soil in the hole too rich. But if you're planting in an established bed, you'll want to amend the soil with extra compost as you dig. In either situation, don't add granular fertilizer now — it can burn the tender new roots. Wait at least until the following spring before you use a granulated fertilizer on your new plants. I'll talk a bit more about fertilizer later.

Now, don't get too ambitious and dig all of the holes at one time. With tender roots, moisture is critical, and an open hole dries out quickly. That means you had better keep planting before the soil in this hole dries out. On the next pages I'll show you the best way to get the plant out of the pot and into the ground.

Good depth to avoid crown rot.

Plenty of room for roots to spread out.

DO dig a hole that is wide and shallow.

Raising the plant up with loose soil may cause the plant to sink later.

Nowhere for the roots to grow.

DON'T dig a deep, narrow planting hole.

www.GardenGateMagazine.com   the YEAR IN GARDENING   251

READY TO PLANT!

Tip the pot and ease the root ball out.

Loosen circling roots.

3

Knock potting mix from the crown.

You have the perfect hole ready to receive the new plant. It's time to take the perennial out of its container and get it into its new home. Let's start planting!

Really rootbound? Make one slice, about a third of the way up, into the solid mass of roots. Then make shallow cuts on two sides to keep the upper roots from continuing to spiral. Gently pull the two halves apart. When you set the plant into the hole, keep these sections spread apart.

3 OUT OF THE POT Sometimes just getting the plant out of the container can be tough. If roots are poking through the drainage holes, cut them off so the root ball will slide out easier. Then put your fingers over the crown as I'm doing in photo 3 and tip the pot. The soil will hold together and you're less likely to drop the plant or break stems this way. If the plant won't slide out, squeeze the sides of the pot a bit and the roots should come out easier. Still won't budge? Hold the plant upside down and tap the lip of the pot on a hard surface.

In the top right photo, see how the roots are circling around the bottom of the root ball? Pull them loose or they may continue to circle in the hole instead of spreading out into the surrounding soil.

Don't worry if a few roots tear, the plant will recover.

In the lower right photo there aren't many roots in the upper portion of the root ball. Use your fingers to knock the top couple of inches of potting mix away. Now you can see the crown better so it's easier to plant at the correct depth. And since the potting mix is lighter than your garden soil, it could wick moisture up and dry out the roots if it's left exposed. Make sure the mix is completely covered with garden soil and you will avoid this problem.

You may come across a plant that's been growing in its pot so long that the roots have grown into a solid mass. If that's the case, you'll need to take more drastic measures. Find out what they are in "Really rootbound?" at left.

4 INTO THE HOLE Put the root ball in the hole and spread the roots out in the bottom. Lay something straight, such as the yardstick in photo 4, across the top of the hole. It'll help you check the depth so you don't set the crown too deeply. Keep in mind that if in doubt, it's best to plant the crown a bit too high rather than too deep.

Now push a couple of inches of soil back into the hole as I'm doing in the next photo, and adjust the depth if you need to. Gently firm the soil around the root ball to hold it in place.

See in the final photo how I'm pouring water around the roots, not directly on the crown? The plant is less likely to sink this way. You can use an organic liquid fertilizer now, such as fish emulsion, to help get the roots moving faster. Let the water drain away and check the depth again. Finish backfilling the hole, making sure to cover all of the potting mix. Don't bother tamping this upper layer of soil. Now you're ready to move on to the next perennial.

After you have all your new plants in place, soak the area with a sprinkler. Run it as needed to keep the bed moist for the first week or two. After that, slowly decrease the watering so the roots will push out into the surrounding soil. A mulch of shredded bark will help conserve water and reduce weeds that would compete for moisture and nutrients.

In the coming weeks, keep an eye on things. Wilted plants, especially when you spot them early in the morning or late in the evening, need a drink. But wilting during the heat of the day is often normal, so be careful you don't overwater and drown your new garden.

Once the plants are growing, it's OK to use a 10-10-10 fertilizer, or one with a higher middle number. Apply it at half the recommended rate on the label, at least until next spring when you can begin a full-strength feeding. And continue to monitor watering. Even after it's fully established, which is usually an entire growing season, the average perennial garden needs an inch of water per week. It could be from rain or a hose — the plants won't object to either.

Success is judged by healthy, lush perennials. While some will flower the first summer, you'll get the full show the following year and, because you took the time to plant properly, for many more years to come. □

— *Jim Childs*

Set the crown level with the surrounding garden.

Backfill with a couple inches of soil.

Soak the soil before backfilling the rest of the hole.

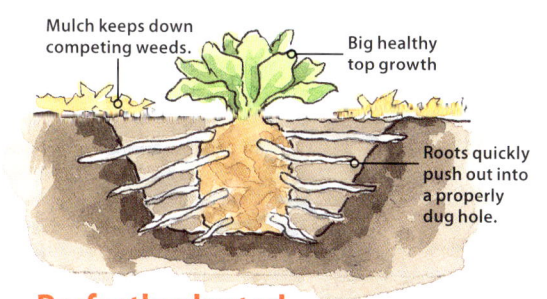

Perfectly planted This perennial has been growing for a while. Notice how the roots have pushed into the surrounding soil? All of the potting mix is under the soil and the crown is at the proper depth. Spread a layer of mulch several inches away from the crown so the roots are kept moist, but water won't collect and cause crown rot.

- Mulch keeps down competing weeds.
- Big healthy top growth
- Roots quickly push out into a properly dug hole.

BASICS | SMART GARDENING

Fertilizer: Get the Facts

Ever wonder if you're feeding your garden right? We can help.

All of you who have questions about fertilizer, raise your hands. I thought so! Fertilizer can be so confusing. And I don't mean all the jargon about NPK and what fertilizer is made from, either. Just trying to figure out when and how much to apply always leaves me wondering if I really should try this without taking a class first. And then there's the question about organic vs. inorganic! What's a gardener to do? I've pulled together some information that will show you it's not as frightening as you might think. Let's take a look at it together.

Should I fertilize everything?

The quick answer is no. If you've worked lots of organic matter into your soil before planting, then added more every year or two, it may not need extra fertilizers. Some plants actually prefer lean, infertile soil. For example, feeding a tall sedum can make the stems weak and floppy so the plant falls open in the center. And applying the wrong fertilizer won't help your plants much, either. If you give lawn fertilizer to a lilac, for instance, you'll get lush foliage but few flowers.

How can I tell if I'm buying the right stuff?

Just as you do when you buy food for your family, start by reading the label. There are three main ingredients in every fertilizer:
- N=nitrogen, feeds foliage
- P=phosphorus, produces flowers and fruit
- K=potassium, keeps plants healthy and strong

You'll find them listed in that order on every package. It's the combinations of these ingredients that determine the best fertilizer for your plants. If you're not sure what a particular plant needs, try feeding it at a quarter to half the recommended rate and see what happens. A water-soluble fertilizer works well for this because it gives a quick result. If the plant improves, feed a bit more the next time. Or switch to a granulated fertilizer with a similar analysis for long-term feeding. Take a look at the table below to see what fertilizer analysis different types of plants need. (The actual numbers will vary from brand to brand, but the proportions will be similar.)

Which fertilizer do you need?

	N	P	K
Annual and perennial flowers	15	30	15
Deciduous trees and shrubs	15	10	9
Evergreens	12	6	12
Most vegetables	24	8	16
Lawns	30	2	3
Roses	9	18	9
Tomatoes	8	18	21

There are two basic options for fertilizer: Liquid and granulated.

What's the best way to apply fertilizer?

There are two basic options — liquid or granulated. Here are some pros and cons for each:

Liquid or water-soluble fertilizer

What's good about it?
- Easy to mix and pour over or around the plant
- Great for fast-growing plants, like annuals and vegetables, because it's absorbed quickly through roots and foliage and it rarely "burns" leaves

What are the drawbacks?
- Flushes though the soil quickly, so needs to be replaced often

Granulated fertilizer

What's good about it?
- Easy to broadcast on the soil
- Some kinds release quickly if your plants need a fast fix; others are slow release (may be called timed-release on the package) for gentle, long-term feeding
- All release more slowly than water soluble, so they don't need to be applied as often, making them the easy feeding choice for trees, shrubs, lawns and perennials

What are the drawbacks?
- Can "burn" leaves and stems if applied too heavily
- Need moisture to work, so must be applied right before rain or watering
- Can damage roots if it's left in the soil dry

Can I use too much?

"If a little is good, more is better" definitely does *not* apply to fertilizer. Read the label, then apply a bit less than that, even just half the amount. It's easy to add more fertilizer later, but hard to pick up any excess once it's been applied. An overfed plant usually isn't productive. And the roots and leaves could be burned, or even killed, by too much fertilizer.

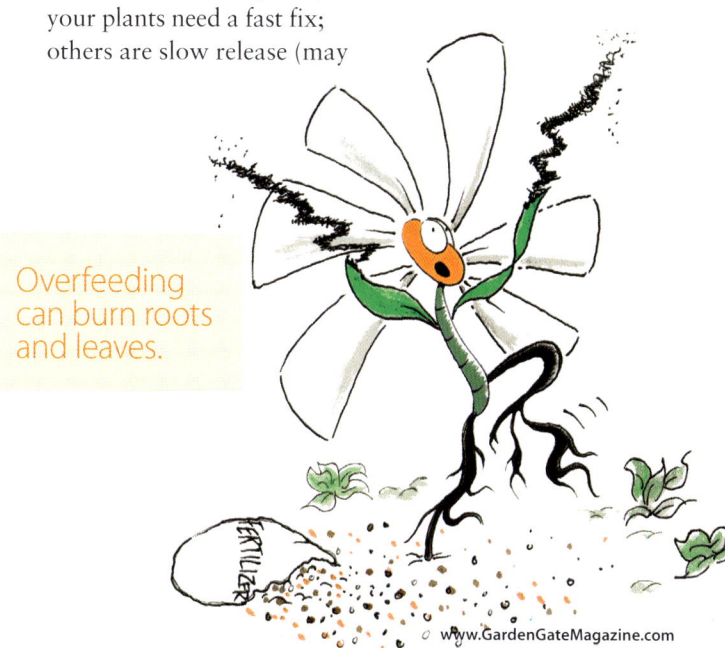

Overfeeding can burn roots and leaves.

When should I fertilize?

There's no best time for feeding all plants. On annuals you can apply water-soluble fertilizers all season, starting in spring and repeating about every two weeks. Use granulated fertilizers more sparingly, usually once or twice a growing season on trees and shrubs. But stop feeding by mid-August so the plant slows down for winter.

When plant growth resumes in spring, it's a good time to apply slow-release fertilizers to take care of the whole season. But with regular granulated fertilizer, do a light feeding. Then just before the plant blooms, do a regular feeding to put more energy into flower and fruit production. □

— *Jim Childs*

There's no best time for feeding.

WHAT'S (IN) ORGANIC?

Does the label mention plant- or animal-based ingredients, like manure or seaweed? It's probably organic. Sound more like a chemistry class? That's probably a synthetic or inorganic fertilizer. Here are the differences to help you decide which is best for your garden.

ORGANIC
- Slow feeding
- Rarely burns
- Won't kill beneficial bacteria in the soil

INORGANIC
- Quick feeding
- Often less expensive
- Can burn and damage plants as well as beneficial soil organisms

BASICS | SMART GARDENING

feed your plants
what they love!

Chemical fertilizers are just like fast food — they satisfy a plant for now. But why not put your garden on a healthy diet? Your plants will grow bigger and faster and stay healthier.

Jeff Lowenfels, author of *Teaming with Microbes, A Gardener's Guide to the Soil Food Web*, tells me that if you take care of the beneficial microbes in your soil, you can improve its structure and nutrient retention. Plus, these microscopic critters help protect plants against diseases and make them more resistant to insect damage, too.

What if you discovered you could improve an entire garden's beneficial microbes with just a few scoops of compost? It's true, when you make actively aerated compost tea. This tea is packed with these microbes, and it's almost free! Here's how to make, and use, this amazing stuff. There's a little more to it than just soaking compost in a bucket of water, but not much.

WHAT FLAVOR IS BEST? If your compost is made mostly from green materials — lawn grass, fresh weeds, vegetable parings — it contains beneficial bacteria. If you make it from dried leaves and debris from cleaning the garden in spring — mostly brown stuff — then your compost will have more fungus in it. Why does this matter? Fast-growing veggies and annuals do best with bacteria. Perennials, trees and shrubs prefer more of the beneficial fungus microbes in their soil.

THE BREWING PROCESS You can soak compost in water and make tea, but it won't have as many microbes in it as actively aerated tea. The brewing process pulls lots more healthy microbes from the compost. Find out what you need and how to make it in "4 easy steps make the perfect brew" below.

Brew on a warm day, with water that's about 72 degrees Fahrenheit. Set the brewer in a shady spot — strong sunlight can kill microbes. Before you fill the bucket with water, put the air equipment together and place it in the bucket as you see in the illustration below.

4 easy steps make the perfect brew

1 SET UP Hook up an aquarium pump with two air valves to two air stones. This one's rated for an 80-gal. tank, which gives you lots of bubbles. Place the stones in a 5-gal. plastic bucket and duct tape the tubing to the bottom so they don't float.

2 ADD WATER Fill your bucket with water. If it's chlorinated, let the pump run for several hours before adding compost to get rid of the chlorine, which could kill the microbes.

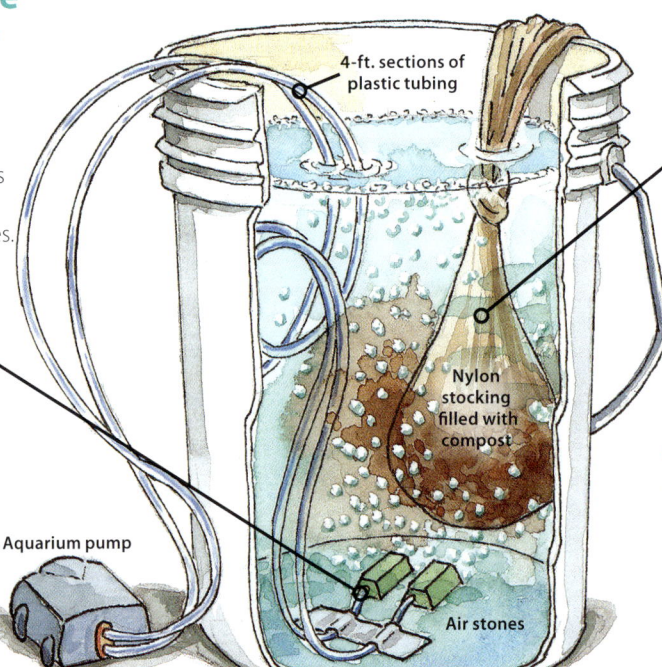

3 DROP IN THE COMPOST Put 4 to 5 cups of well-rotted compost in an old stocking or cloth bag and sink it in the water. The nylon stocking will keep the debris out of the tea so it won't clog up your sprayer later on.

4 START BREWING Run the pump for 24 to 36 hours. When the tea turns coffee brown, it's ready to use — the sooner, the better.

Unlike tea that's made from compost simply soaked in water, actively aerated compost tea is brewed and will have a pleasant, earthy smell.

Add the water and put the compost in a brewing bag — an old stocking works great — and place it in the water. Turn on the pump. All of the small bubbles tease the microbes out of the compost. Let the pump run for 24 to 36 hours until the tea turns the coffee brown color in the glass above.

HOW DO YOU APPLY IT? The easiest application method is to pour the freshly brewed tea onto the soil. Notice I said fresh — compost tea doesn't store well. If you must hold it longer than five hours, keep it refrigerated. Even so, the microbes will run out of food and start to eat each other. If it starts to smell bad, you need to make a fresh batch.

Unlike most chemical fertilizers, you can drench your plants with full-strength compost tea without any damage. In fact, you really can't overdo it. But if you want to dilute it and spray it on, just a cup or two of tea to a gallon of chlorine-free water will treat a large garden.

WHEN TO APPLY IT Late fall, before the ground turns cold, is a good time to pour compost tea on the soil. Hungry microbes will begin to break down the leaf litter and will get right to work again in spring. Spray foliage just as your plants start to leaf out in spring, too. It'll help prevent plant diseases and insect damage.

If you're pouring tea as a soil drench, any time of day is fine — the microbes quickly sink into the soil. But if you're applying tea to foliage, ultraviolet rays will kill microbes. So before 10 a.m. or after 3 p.m., when the sun isn't quite as strong, is the ideal time to spray it on.

YOU'RE ALMOST DONE As soon as you finish, make sure to flush the equipment with clean water. If the slime begins to dry, you may need to use baking soda for a little extra muscle. Don't let the slime harden because it'll clog the hoses and air stones.

With regular doses of actively aerated compost tea, your soil will thrive, and so will your plants!

— *Jim Childs*

It's as simple as water, air and compost

These three things are all it takes to give your soil and plants a healthy boost with beneficial microbes.

WATER
If you use rainwater you've harvested, you can start brewing your tea right away. But if your water is chlorinated, run the bubbler for several hours to get rid of the chlorine before adding the compost.

AIR
The bubbles created by the pump help pull the microbes that are already at work in the compost into the water. But once the bubbles stop, the microbes start to disappear, so use your tea as soon as possible after it's brewed.

COMPOST
Microbes are already active in well-rotted compost. The tea allows you to collect them in a concentrated form. Spraying annuals or vegetables? Use compost made with mostly green material, or add a couple tablespoons of unsulphured molasses to the compost before you brew it. Feeding perennials and shrubs? Use compost made with mostly brown stuff or add a tablespoon or two of liquid kelp or a hydrolyzed fish fertilizer to your brew.

BASICS | SMART GARDENING

Keep your garden safe!

No Pests, No Chemicals

Aphids

Scale

Everyone wants a good-looking garden. But when pests like the scale, aphids and caterpillar in the photos at right get out of hand, what can you do and still be considerate of the environment? Choose "green" pesticides!

What makes a pesticide "green"? First, in most cases, it's organic, which means it's made from natural ingredients. Second, it's easier on the environment than its non-green counterparts. Because it breaks down quickly after it's applied, it won't hang around in the soil or water for a long time. And many green pesticides tend to target specific pests, as in the case of Bt.

But not all "organic" products are totally safe. For example, if someone suggests you use nicotine-based pesticides, think twice. While nicotine does come from a plant, it can harm people, animals and even some plants.

Be sure to read the label directions for any pesticide. And follow all safety precautions. For help deciphering those labels, check out "Read the label" on the next page.

You'll find that there are a lot of choices out there, including products that combine these pesticides. So to help you figure out what fits your situation best I've put together this chart of some of the greenest pesticides available. Whatever you choose, you'll have a beautiful garden that's safe for you, your kids, pets and all the wildlife that live nearby. ◻

— *Sherri Ribbey*

	Pests it kills	How does it work?
Bt	A specific strain of B_t attacks each pest: • Caterpillars (B_t kurstaki) • Beetle larvae (B_t tenebrionis) • Fly larvae (B_t israelensis) • Gnat larvae (B_t israelensis) • Mosquito larvae (B_t israelensis)	• Destroys the insect's digestive system when it's eaten. • Used most often for lawns, vegetables, water gardens and ornamentals. **Buy as spray, dust or mosquito dunks for water gardens**
Horticultural Oil	• Aphids • Insect eggs • Mites • Scale	• Suffocates the insect. • Used most often on trees and shrubs. • Apply lightweight summer oil in the growing season to treat problems and heavy dormant oil in winter before insects do damage. **Buy as spray, pre-mixed or concentrate**
Horticultural Soap	• Aphids • Boxelder bug nymphs • Japanese beetles • Mealybugs	• Washes away the insect's protective outer coating so it dehydrates. • Used most often for smaller plants and house plants. **Buy as spray**
Neem	Broad spectrum (kills all insects); most often used for: • Aphids • Mites • Whiteflies • Beetles • Scale	• When eaten by pests, it interferes with hormones, preventing eating and growth. • Used for ornamentals and vegetables. **Buy as spray**
Pyrethrum	Broad spectrum (kills all insects); most often used for: • Aphids • Beetles • Caterpillars • Wasps • Whiteflies	• When it's eaten or absorbed by insects, it affects the transmission of impulses to and from the brain. It also works as a repellent. • Used most often on ornamentals, fruit trees and vegetables. **Buy as spray or dust**
Spinosad	• Caterpillars • Flies • Leafminers • Thrips	• When it's eaten or absorbed, it disrupts the insects' nervous system. • Used most often for lawns, fruit trees, ornamentals and vegetables. **Buy as spray**

Caterpillar

Read the label

Look for these *signal* words to know how toxic a pesticide is. All the products in our chart are labeled "Caution" in the ready-to-use form, but concentrates may have a higher rating.

CAUTION Relatively non-toxic to mildly toxic. This product may cause a mild reaction if eaten, absorbed by the skin or inhaled. If you get it in your eye or on your skin, it may cause a slight irritation.

WARNING Moderately toxic. Look for a stronger reaction if this product gets on your skin, is inhaled or gets in your eyes.

DANGER Highly toxic or poisonous. A product like this could cause irreversible damage if mishandled.

For more information about signal words and pesticide safety, check out the National Pesticide Information Center at www.npic.orst.edu.

What's in it?

The soil-born fungus *Bacillus thuringiensis*

Highly refined petroleum oils combined with an emulsifying agent
Did you know? Vegetable oils used in home remedies don't work as well. Because they're not as refined, they don't mix well with water. Manufactured oils are more refined and easier to apply.

Specially formulated soap with fatty acids — some are natural, others are synthetic

Oil from the seeds of the neem tree (*Azadirachta indica*)

The seeds of Dalmation chrysanthemum (*Chrysanthemum cinerariaefolium*)
Did you know? You may also see products called "pyrethroids." They're synthetic forms of pyrethrum that are more toxic and hold up in sunlight better than their natural counterparts.

The soil-born fungus *Saccharopolyspora spinosa*

Green facts

- B_t isn't recognized by receptors in the digestive system of people or animals. If you accidentally ingest it, it's not harmful.
- Each strain of B_t is effective on a specific type of pest.

- Horticultural oil has little effect on beneficial insects. Since they are larger and faster than the pest insects, they can usually get away before being coated in too much oil.
- It's also effective against powdery mildew.

- Chemically similar to liquid hand soap, so it's pretty mild.
- Beneficial insects are not as susceptible because they often have an exoskeleton, or protective outer shell.

- Neem also smothers fungus spores, making it a good fungicide. It's especially effective against powdery mildew and leaf spot.

- People have an enzyme in the body that detoxifies pyrethrum, if ingested, before it can do any serious damage.
- It works quickly, so it's also used in many wasp sprays.

- Most beneficials aren't harmed by this pesticide. There's one exception, bees. Apply it early in the morning or late at night so it dries before the bees become active.

Look out!

- B_t for pest caterpillars kills butterfly caterpillars, too.
- Breaks down in sunlight, so you may need to reapply every three to five days.

- Follow label directions carefully. Too much oil applied in too much heat or cold can burn plant foliage. Japanese maples, evergreens, redbuds and smoke trees are especially sensitive.
- Needs to coat the insect thoroughly to work.

- Check the label — an incorrect mixture or too many applications can burn plant foliage.
- Needs to coat the insect thoroughly to work
- Won't affect caterpillars or beetle larvae.

- Some studies show people can have an allergic reaction to neem.
- Toxic to fish and aquatic life.

- Breaks down quickly in sunlight, so needs to be applied about every week.
- Some insects have developed resistance.
- Highly toxic to fish, tadpoles and beneficial insects.
- It can cause a rash or an allergic or asthmatic reaction in some cases, so wear safety equipment.

- Don't use around ponds or water sources. Spinosad degrades more slowly in water and is toxic to fish and mollusks.

BASICS | SMART GARDENING

Need to divide a perennial in summer's heat? No sweat.

The Secrets to Dividing in Summer

Do you know the signs of a plant that needs dividing? If you're noticing fewer flowers, a dead center or a plant that is shrinking, it may be time to divide. And while spring and fall are traditionally the best time to divide, there are plenty of reasons you may *need* to divide a plant in the summer. Whether you're moving or just haven't had the time until now, many plants take summer division just fine as long as you follow the tips I'm about to share. There are even some plants, such as bearded iris and Oriental poppies, that are better off being split this time of year.

SUPER SUMMER Summer's heat and lack of rainfall are hard on plants, so water the plant *and* its future home the day before you dig.

The next day get out the spade. But before you dig, cut the foliage back by half: This way a smaller root system won't have to support lots of foliage in the heat later. Shear plants whose leaves go all the way to the base, such as daylilies. But if a plant's leaves are mostly at the ends of the stems, you'll need to trim individual leaves. Coral bells is one example.

Dig up your plant, slicing 4 to 6 inches out from the edge of the crown. Then you can divide. The red lines in "The root of the matter," below, show you where to split the different root types. Get your new plant in the hole quickly so the roots don't dry out.

Once the plant is in place, fill the hole halfway with soil and water well. That way the water soaks in and doesn't evaporate or roll off the soil's surface. I've found that adding an organic liquid fertilizer, such as Neptune's Harvest, to the water helps get plants off to a good start. Fill the hole the rest of the way with soil, water it again and put down a layer of mulch.

Full-sun plants will benefit from a shade shelter for a week or two. Insert a few bamboo stakes in the soil on the west side of the plant to protect it from the hottest sun of the day. Clothespin some landscape fabric or an old sheet to the stakes to make a screen.

Finally, check your plant each day, and if it looks wilted in the morning or late evening, give it a drink. You may need to water daily for a few days after planting.

Look over the list at right and you'll find a lot of plants that take summer division in stride. Don't see yours on the list? Our Web extra lets you know which plants don't like division anytime.

Now you know what and how to divide this summer... no sweat! □

— *Sherri Ribbey*

THE ROOT OF THE MATTER

RHIZOMES Bearded irises have rhizomes for storing food. Make sure each new plant has at least one fan (three to four leaves) and a good cluster of roots. Toss the rest on the compost pile.

— = Where to divide

Throw away rhizomes without a fan of at least three leaves.

CLUMP Dividing plants with fibrous or spreading roots like this daylily is easy. Just pull them apart or cut through them with a sharp spade. For bigger plants faster, divide the original plant in half or thirds.

If roots are too tangled, tease them apart with a garden fork.

WOODY CROWNS Some plants, such as the coral bells below, have a woody crown. Cut pieces off to replant. Don't worry about getting roots with each transplant. They'll sprout from the stem.

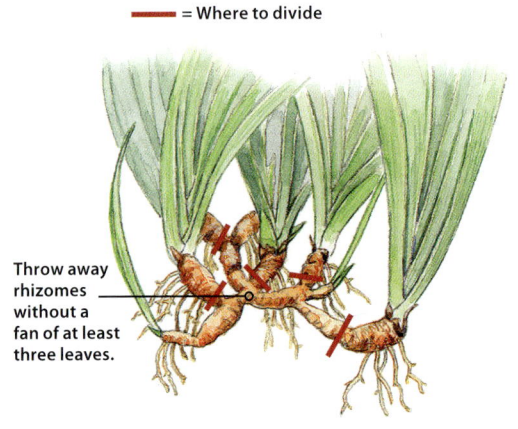

Leave one set of leaves attached to the main root and replant.

The hot list: 27 plants you can divide in summer

Web extra: Take a look at our *list of plants* that *don't* like dividing at all.

Plant Name	Cold/Heat Zones	Height/Width	Root Type	Comments
Bellflower, clustered *Campanula glomerata*	3-9/9-1	15 in./18 in.	Clump	Divide after the first flush of blooms is finished; second, smaller rebloom will be sacrificed
Bellflower, spotted *Campanula punctata*	4-9/9-1	26 in./spreading	Clump	Spreads quickly; divide frequently to keep it in bounds; provide new divisions with shade
Bergenia *Bergenia cordifolia*	3-9/9-1	8-24 in./12-24 in.	Clump	Look for fewer flowers or a crowded-looking plant; usually needs division every 4 to 5 years; cut leaves back by half
Bleeding heart, fernleaf *Dicentra eximia*	3-9/9-1	12-18 in. tall and wide	Clump	Foliage may go dormant after dividing, but don't worry, the plant will come back next spring
Bleeding heart, old-fashioned *Dicentra spectabilis*	3-9/9-1	12-24 in./12-30 in.	Clump	Divide as foliage goes dormant in the heat or mark plant location; roots are brittle, handle carefully
Bugleweed *Ajuga reptans*	3-9/9-1	4-6 in./10-24 in.	Clump	Plants root as they spread; no need to dig whole plant; cut off rooted outer pieces and replant
Catmint *Nepeta xfaassenii*	3-9/9-1	12-24 in./18-36 in.	Clump	Doesn't need division often; cut back whole plant by half so roots have less foliage to support
Columbine *Aquilegia* hybrids	3-8/8-1	5-36 in./6-18 in.	Woody crown	Seedlings don't always look like parent plant so divide hybrids every few years to keep this short-lived perennial around
Coral bells *Heuchera* hybrids	3-9/9-1	6-18 in./10-24 in.	Woody crown	Don't worry about getting roots with each piece, they'll sprout from the stem; cut individual leaves back by half to conserve moisture
Coreopsis *Coreopsis grandiflora*	3-9/9-1	18-24 in./18-24 in.	Clump	Division every 3 to 4 years helps this short-lived perennial stay around longer; cut plant back by half
Corydalis *Corydalis lutea*	5-8/8-1	4-18 in./6-12 in.	Rhizome	Don't keep new plant too wet after you divide or it will rot
Daylily *Hemerocallis* hybrids	3-9/9-1	12-36 in./9-24 in.	Clump	Divide every 5 to 7 years to keep clumps healthy; rebloomers are best lifted in spring before they flower
Dianthus *Dianthus* spp.	3-9/9-1	3-24 in./8-24 in.	Clump	Mat-forming types root as they grow; cut a rooted piece from the edge and replant
European wild ginger *Asarum europaeum*	5-7/7-1	4-8 in./9-12 in.	Rhizome	Easy to dig and split; likes moist to wet soils, so keep new plants well-watered
Foxtail lily *Eremurus stenophyllus stenophyllus*	6-9/9-1	24-36 in./9-12 in.	Woody crown	Roots are brittle so only divide mature plants in midsummer; wait for the leaves to die down for the season
Garden phlox *Phlox paniculata*	4-9/9-1	1-4 ft./1-3 ft.	Clump	Divide every 3 years or when flowering diminishes; discard the woody center and plant the edge pieces
Hardy geranium *Geranium* spp.	4-9/9-1	2-4 ft. tall and wide	Woody crown	A ring of foliage around a dead center tells you it's time to divide; usually every 3 to 4 years is sufficient
Iris *Iris* hybrids	3-9/9-1	8-40 in./18 in.	Rhizome	Needs division every 3 to 4 years in midsummer to remain vigorous; cut leaves back so there's 4 to 5 in. left above the rhizome
Lamb's ear *Stachys byzantina*	4-8/8-1	6-18 in./spreading	Clump	This hardy plant roots along the stem; cut a piece off the edge and replant; cut leaves back by half; don't overwater
Lily-of-the-valley *Convallaria majalis*	3-8/8-1	10 in./12-18 in.	Rhizome	Rhizomes pull apart easily; make sure each new division has a leaf and a cluster of roots
Lungwort *Pulmonaria* hybrids	3-8/8-1	6-12 in./15-40 in.	Clump	Big leaves wilt easily; cut each leaf back by half and keep summer plants well-watered
Maltese cross *Lychnis chalcedonica*	3-9/9-1	36-48 in./18-24 in.	Clump	Divide after flowering in midsummer; cut plant back by half; may lose the second bloom
Oriental poppy *Papaver orientale*	2-9/9-1	18-36 in./18 in.	Woody crown	Divide in midsummer; foliage goes dormant quickly after flowering so mark the plant's location; keep new transplants watered
Peony *Paeonia* spp	3-8/8-1	2-4 ft. tall and wide	Clump	New plants will take a few years to flower; set new plants at the same depth or they won't bloom; keep watered
Snowdrop anemone *Anemone sylvestris*	3-9/9-1	12-18 in./6-12 in.	Rhizome	Can spread quickly in well-drained soil but more slowly in clay; cut rhizomes so each plant has one bud
Speedwell *Veronica* hybrids	4-8/8-1	6-48 in./15-18 in.	Clump	Easy to slice into pieces; make sure to get plenty of roots with each new section
Yarrow *Achillea* spp.	3-10/10-1	24-36 in./15-18 in.	Clump	Divide every 2 to 3 years; cut foliage back by half so roots don't have as much foliage to support

the YEAR IN GARDENING

BASICS | SMART GARDENING

lots of **lovely lilies**

Beautiful, fragrant flowers, glossy green leaves…these are the things you love about lilies. But have you ever stopped to think about what's happening underground? You should! If you want more of these lovely plants, you can dig and split a big clump, for a garden full of lilies.

These 'Scheherazade' Orienpet lilies, like the one in the photo above, were stunning last summer. But I needed to move the clump to another area. When I dug them up in the fall, I found, to my delight, the enormous cluster of bulbs you see below, just ready to divide and scatter around the garden.

Let's take a look at how to dig and handle these beauties. After all, who could say no to more lilies? □
— *Marcia Leeper*

See the red blush on these bulbs? Often, the color of the lily bulbs echoes the color of the flowers.

1

A garden fork loosens and lifts bulbs easily. But it won't slice into the clump and do as much damage as a spade would if you misjudge where to dig.

Dig 'em up

Of course, the first step is to get the lily bulbs out of the ground! Midfall is the best time to dig them. These bulbs were about 10 in. below the soil's surface. I like to use a garden fork to lift the clump out of the soil because it won't slice into the bulbs the way a spade will if you get too close. Push the fork straight down into the soil, about 10 in. away from the stalk. Then loosen the soil all the way around the clump before you gently pry the whole thing up with the fork. Shake the loose soil off the clump so you can see what you're doing.

Now take a closer look at the bulbs above. See those fibrous roots on top of the bulbs? They feed the bulb and help keep the lily upright. But don't worry if you break or damage them, because they die along with the stem and regrow every year.

Pull 'em apart

Now that the clump is out and most of the soil has been removed, it's time to separate the individual bulbs. This is the fun part, as you ask yourself, "How many bulbs can I find in the large clump?" I like to use my fingers (or sometimes an unusual tool, a chop stick!) to work my way into the roots and soil. Tease the roots out with your hands and use the sticks to open up the space between bulbs. This is a little time-consuming, but you don't want to bruise or break the bulbs. When you've teased out most of the soil, it's time to do a little pulling. See how I'm gently rocking the stems back and forth in the photo? Work each bulb and its roots out of the clump and see how many more lilies you will have to plant in your garden. I got 12 blooming-sized new bulbs out of this cluster.

These fibrous roots regrow every year, so you can gently pull them off the stem if they're in your way.

This flattened ridge at the base of the bulb is its basal plate. Each individual scale can grow as long as there's a little bit of the basal plate attached to it.

3

2

Only the larger bulbs will have stems, as the smallest ones may not have produced any foliage yet.

Plant 'em again

So what's that golf ball doing in the photo? Well, all the bulbs larger than the ball should bloom next season. But go ahead and plant the smaller ones, even the single scales that break off larger bulbs, like the ones in the foreground. They won't bloom for a couple of years, but eventually they will flower. It's best to replant them immediately after you dig them up. But if it's going to be a few days, store them somewhere cool, moist and dark.

When you replant, set the large bulbs at the same depth they were already growing, from 6 to 10 in. deep, measuring from the top of the bulb, and set them 6 to 12 in. apart. Choose a spot with good drainage for the happiest lilies. Plant smaller bulbs and single scales 2 to 3 in. deep. Believe it or not, as they grow, their own roots will pull them down to their preferred depth. Water the lilies in and give them a little mulch for added protection, but don't fertilize them yet. In spring, you can treat them to a handful of a balanced 10-10-10 fertilizer, just about the time the new leaves are starting to unfurl.

Plant these single scales, and you'll have blooming plants in a few years.

BASICS | SMART GARDENING

garden smarter:
7 easy-does-it tips

Botanical Names

Pachysandra *Pachysandra terminalis*
Vinca *Vinca minor*

Rush! Rush! Rush! The world seems to go faster every day! Who has time to garden at a leisurely pace? And if you're trying to save money and garden as "green" as possible, it can all start to seem a bit difficult. To get a handle on this, I spoke with Kris Medic, author of *The New American Backyard* and principal with Groundsmith Consulting, a firm dedicated to helping grounds managers evaluate and care for their properties. She shared helpful, smart tips to make gardening more enjoyable, as well as easier on you, your wallet and the environment.

1 SHADE THE AC Central air conditioner units sitting in the hot sun use more energy than they would in the shade. You could move the unit to the north side of your house, but that's not always possible. The trees in the illustration at left shade the AC unit during the summer, especially during the hottest part of the day. This could save you up to 10 percent on your cooling costs. Just make sure you don't block the movement of air from the unit by planting too close. Check to see where the warm air exits your AC so you don't trap it around the unit and end up making it run more.

THE PAYOFF How's your monthly energy bill? Conservation is the way to go, and with the money you save, you can buy more plants!

2 MAKE A PLAN Every gardener spends the winter dreaming about what to plant where in next year's garden. Many counties' Geographic Information Systems (GIS) will provide a layout and measurements of your property to get you started. To find the Web site for your area, use a search engine and type in the name of your county and state, followed by the words "assessor" or "surveyor." When you find it, follow the prompts from there to locate a printable image of your lot. Each county is different, and not all of them have this service at this time. But it's worth a try to find out more.

THE PAYOFF You get to start playing around with your design right away instead of spending your time taking tedious measurements.

3 WHEN PRUNING'S A PROBLEM Do you have shrubs that need to be pruned more than once a year so you can see out your windows? Why waste time pruning? It's time to choose a shrub that stays smaller. The list below, "Five under five," is a good place to start. None of these shrubs will grow more than 5 feet tall, and they're all ideal for a foundation planting.

THE PAYOFF Choose the right plant the first time and you won't have to do any drastic pruning. And most plants look more natural if you aren't always hacking away at them. On top of that, you won't have to figure out how to get rid of all of those unwanted trimmings.

Five under five

Abelia *Abelia* 'Edward Goucher' 4 to 5 ft. tall and 4 to 6 ft. wide; cold-hardy in USDA zones 6 to 9; heat-tolerant in AHS zones 9 to 1

Boxwood *Buxus* 'Green Velvet' 2 to 4 ft. tall and wide; cold-hardy in USDA zones 5 to 8; heat-tolerant in AHS zones 8 to 1

Dwarf fothergilla *Fothergilla gardenii* 2 to 3 ft. tall and 3 ft. wide; cold-hardy in USDA zones 5 to 8; heat-tolerant in AHS zones 8 to 1

Japanese spirea *Spiraea japonica* 'Goldflame' 3 to 4 ft. tall and wide; cold-hardy in USDA zones 4 to 9; heat-tolerant in AHS zones 9 to 1

Slender deutzia *Deutzia gracilis* 2 to 5 ft. tall and wide; cold-hardy in USDA zones 5 to 8; heat-tolerant in AHS zones 8 to 1

Don't let limbs hang directly over the AC or they direct warm air back down to the unit, keeping it warmer.

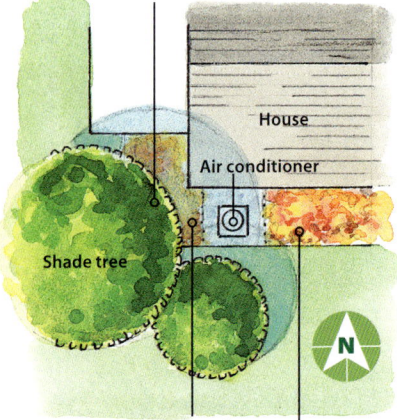

Make sure the air conditioner is shaded during the hottest season.

For the best efficiency, keep plants at least 2 to 3 ft. away from the sides of the AC where fresh air is drawn into the unit.

(1) Pretty potting A bright coat of paint, a clean plastic tub and a few colorful linens mean your potting bench can do double duty on your patio instead of hiding behind the garage.

4 DOUBLE-DUTY DECORATING
Need more patio space? We all do. Why not make some of your garden "furniture" do double duty? Instead of hiding your potting bench, give it a fresh coat of colorful paint every year or two and you can just hose it off to use as a sideboard or buffet table. And as you can see in photo 1, swap out the soil bin with a clean plastic tub to hold ice for drinks. Want to dress it up even more? Keep a washable tablecloth handy and toss it over the potting bench.

THE PAYOFF Most of us try to crowd too much onto our patios anyway. And this way you get to work at your potting bench on your pretty patio instead of behind that dirty garage!

5 REDUCE MOWING TIME
If you feel you spend your entire Saturday afternoon mowing, ground covers are the solution. Plants that spread, such as vinca and pachysandra, planted under trees or on hard to mow slopes, can greatly reduce your mowing time. Not only are they good looking, but you'll spend less time trimming grass around tree trunks, too. Want even less labor? Enlarge your hardscaping areas, such as patios and paths. Sure, this may be more expensive up front, but it can save you time and energy in the long run.

THE PAYOFF With fuel prices staying high, mowing any size lawn with gas-powered equipment is not going to get any cheaper.

6 SPEAKING OF LAWNS
Do you really need to keep spreading herbicides over the entire lawn? Not if you have your weeds pretty well under control. However, seeds will always find ways to invade your lawn. Weed seeds are less likely to sprout in shade, so mow your grass at least 2½ to 3 inches high during the summer. And for those weeds that do grow, keep a bottle of premixed selective herbicide or a sharp hoe handy as you mow. You can quickly spot treat any weeds you see before they become established, set more seeds and spread.

THE PAYOFF A beautiful lawn can be yours, even without overusing herbicides.

7 SHARPEN YOUR EDGES
When you do a garden task can be as important as *how* you do it. For example, see all that fresh soil being exposed while the edge is being cut in around the bed in photo 2? That means you're bringing weed seeds to the surface that are just waiting for a chance to sprout. Annual weeds, such as crabgrass and lamb's quarters, sprout fast in moist spring weather. But edge in summer and fewer seeds will sprout. Even if they do grow later in the season, they won't have as much time to set a crop of seeds and spread in the hot, dry soil you uncover.

THE PAYOFF A crisp edge makes your garden look good. And you probably have more time to edge in summer than you do in spring anyway. □

— *Jim Childs*

(2) Time to edge Knowing the best time of year to cut a fresh edge around your flower beds will help prevent a weed takeover. Use a garden hose to get the best curves and a sharp spade for a clean and crisp cut.

BASICS | SMART GARDENING

Point, Click, Plant!
The best mail-order Web sites

Gardeners like plants. Problem is, if there aren't a lot of garden centers or nurseries close by, it can be hard to find unusual, new or rare plants to grow. But if you have access to the Internet, you can easily find and buy virtually any plant you want. Online shopping is simple and quick, and there are thousands of plant Web sites — but how do you find the best places to shop? Well, based on my own experience, plus that of lots of people who do extensive online ordering, here's a list of what I think are some of the best. I'll touch on these companies' strengths and weaknesses, including my favorite features on their Web sites. Next, I'll give you the price range for their most common size of perennials and the cost of shipping three of those plants. (See the "Pricing key" at left for help deciphering my shipping ratings.) And speaking of shipping, I'll share a few tips on how to save on these costs at right in "Shopping for shipping."

The three companies that specialize in bulbs are grouped together at the end of the story. Prices and shipping listed for these are for 10 similar-sized common daffodil bulbs, just for comparison.

Check out these Web sites easily — go to our Web extra for links to these, plus 20 more you may want to visit. □

— *Deborah Gruca*

PRICING KEY
Use this guide to compare shipping costs for three perennials to most locations in the United States.

Shipping
$ $6 to $14
$$ $15 to $23
$$$ $24 to $30

Web extra
Check out the *links* for these, plus 20 more companies.

Most of Bluestone Perennials' plants are sold in their jumbo 3-packs.

Perennials

ANNIE'S ANNUALS & PERENNIALS
www.anniesannuals.com
Looking for the rare and unusual? If you want plants none of your neighbors have, start here. This business, based in California, has tons of annuals and perennials, some of them hard to find anywhere else. It's a great place for cottage garden or California native plants. And talk about inspiring — be sure to check out the slide shows! "Totally Useful Plant Lists" offers interesting categories like "True Blue," "Fragrant," "Good for Cutting" and "South African."

4-in. square pots
$4.95 - $12.95
Shipping $$$
Also sells annuals, bulbs, shrubs, trees and vegetables.

BLUESTONE PERENNIALS
www.bluestoneperennials.com
A fantastic selection of plants awaits you at this Ohio company's Web site. And because the plants are small and reasonably priced, you can afford to buy enough for an impressive planting or a hedge. I really like the "Custom Plant Search" feature on Bluestone's site that allows you to narrow your search to the exact qualities you want. Clear photos let you see what the plant looks like, with detailed descriptions about conditions it likes and how to care for it. And if you return the packing peanuts, you even get free shipping on your next order.

Priced by jumbo 3-pack (each pot is 2¼x 3-in.)
$10.95 - $16.95
Shipping $
Also sells annuals, bulbs and shrubs.

FORESTFARM
www.forestfarm.com
Forestfarm isn't kidding about having one of the largest plant selections in the country. This Oregon company offers thousands of plants, many of them unusual, and many cold-hardy to USDA zones 3 and colder. Their smaller plant sizes will save you money, and the common name index helps you learn botanical names. Plus, a list of potentially aggressive plants will steer you clear of garden thugs.

2-in. x 4- to 5- in.-deep tubes
$5.95 - $15.95
Shipping $$
Also sells trees and shrubs.

GARDEN CROSSINGS
www.gardencrossings.com
Garden Crossings, in Michigan, has a great selection of large, good-quality plants, along with lots of care information. They carry container and garden plant combinations and recipes, and their "Garden Accents" section offers tools, ornaments and accessories. Not sure how to spell a plant name? Type in the first few letters and the plant search fills in the rest to help you find the correct name.

5½-in. square pots $9.95 - $19.95
Shipping $$$
Also sells annuals, shrubs and edibles.

266   *the* YEAR IN GARDENING   www.GardenGateMagazine.com

HIGH COUNTRY GARDENS
www.highcountrygardens.com

This site, based in New Mexico, is the place to go for xeric plants — they have hundreds. You can buy preplanned gardens for different looks and situations and container combinations, with pots, if you want. How-to videos help you get started planting. Pick the week you want your order to ship, and plants arrive in time for weekend planting.

5 x 5-in.-deep pots $5.49 - $9.99
Shipping $

Also sells turf grasses, bulbs, seeds, shrubs and conifers.

KLEHM'S SONG SPARROW
www.songsparrow.com

Passionate about peonies? How about daylilies, hostas or clematis? Klehm's has page after page of hard-to-find plants in these groups, plus lots of others. Plant collectors will want to check out the "Sparrow's Nest Fresh Picks," a selection of the best plants and trees to grow, hand-picked by owner Roy Klehm. Large, healthy plants from this Wisconsin nursery are carefully sleeved and well-packed.

2-qt. pots $12.95 - $29.95
Shipping $$$

Also sells shrubs, trees and conifers.

LAZY S'S FARM & NURSERY
www.lazyssfarm.com

Lazy S's sells more than 2,000 varieties of perennials, shrubs and trees, but unlike other mail-order businesses, they grow most of the plants themselves, right there in Virginia. You'll find three dozen types of sedums and geraniums and nearly 100 hostas, just to mention a few. The Web site is a bit clumsy to use, with descriptions and photos on different pages, but plants are staked and well-packed to arrive in good shape.

1-qt. pots $7.99 - $17.99
Shipping $$$

Also sells trees and shrubs.

Bulbs

BRENT AND BECKY'S BULBS
www.brentandbeckysbulbs.com

I love to order from Brent and Becky's because I'm sure of getting large, healthy bulbs from this Virginia-based company. Every plant description on the Web site is accompanied by suggestions of good companions with similar bloom times. Videos let you see many of the plants they sell growing in garden settings. The Web site is a little clunky but the selection is excellent.

10 'Carlton' daffodil bulbs $12.10
Shipping $

Also sells seeds, perennials and cut flowers.

EASY TO GROW BULBS
www.easytogrowbulbs.com

You'll find tons of planting and growing information and videos on a wide variety of bulbs and perennials here. Every plant has a great description, a large photo and information on the size of plant or container you're ordering. Be sure to check out the "Weird and Wonderful" tab, where this California company promotes wacky and very unusual bulbs they offer in small numbers.

10 'Carlton' daffodil bulbs $9.95
Shipping $

Also sells perennials.

OLD HOUSE GARDENS
www.oldhousegardens.com

Hooked on heirloom flower bulbs? Old House specializes in them, especially the rare ones. The site is simple and easy to use and, because it's a small company, the staff is warm and personable. Click on the "Learn More" tab to read dozens of articles about bulbs and Old House Gardens. Prices are moderately high, but reasonable, considering that many of the bulbs are hard to find anywhere else.

10 'Carlton' daffodil bulbs 15.75
Shipping $

SHOPPING FOR SHIPPING

Buying plants online isn't perfect. One of the drawbacks is paying for shipping and handling. While some companies charge more for shipping than others, take into account the quality and prices of the plants, too. It may be worth spending a little more on shipping for bigger plants. Here are a few tips for saving on shipping.

1 BUDDY UP Some sites require a minimum order or charge a flat rate for shipping. If you want just a few plants, combine your order with your friends' and split the shipping. This also works for places that offer free shipping on orders over a certain amount.

2 CHECK THE NUMBERS Because of the way some companies pack plants, you'll sometimes pay the same shipping for four plants that you would for two or three. Before you buy, play with the numbers of plants to see if you can save money this way (or get more for your dollar).

3 LOOK FOR DEALS For places that base shipping on the amount of your order, look on the Web site for specials and coupons on plants.

4 GO LOCAL Want just seeds? Ask if theirs are carried in local retail stores and go there instead. If the store doesn't have the exact seeds you want, they'll often order them and not charge you shipping.

Check bulbs over right away to ensure they are large and firm. Torn or missing tunics don't affect the bulbs' quality.

BASICS | SMART GARDENING

THE WEEKEND GARDENER · Garden Smarter

Have 10 minutes, half an hour or a day?
Get Your Garden In Shape Now!

As the season dwindles down, garden tasks often seem to increase. But your work doesn't have to be overwhelming. Whether you have 10 minutes, a half hour or a day to garden, there's more than one way to get the results you want. Prioritize and make a plan of action based on how much time you want to spend.

Here are a few things you can still tackle late this fall. For each I've given you three maintenance options — good, better and best. If you only have a few minutes, go with the good option. More time? Go with the better or best to make sure your garden is in shape and ready for spring.

— Jim Childs

Better: Remove leaves and dead grass with a leaf rake that has flexible teeth.

Lawn — now is the time to make sure you'll have a gorgeous one next year.

GOOD Mow the lawn to chop and mulch dry leaves after they fall from the trees. Just let the fine particles disintegrate into the lawn.

BETTER After chopping leaves, rake the area to remove large particles. Then spread a fall lawn fertilizer. And if there's a weed problem, apply a herbicide now.

BEST Rent a power dethatcher to take out the layer of spongy dead material that builds up near the surface of the lawn and can smother the grass. Once you've finished, overseed and then fertilize. Don't apply a weed control if you're spreading seed — it'll prevent seeds from sprouting.

Garden tools — taking care of them now will save time next spring.

GOOD Haul your tools indoors to prevent rust on metal parts. And if you live where temperatures drop below freezing, disconnect the hose from the spigot. Drain hoses, sprinklers and nozzles so they won't freeze and break.

BETTER Remove caked-on dirt with a wire brush and soapy water and dry the tools thoroughly. Wipe down pruning tools with sanitizing wipes to kill bacteria on the blades and let them dry.

BEST Use a file to remove nicks and dings from shovels and hoes. Then lightly sand down wooden handles and rub them with boiled linseed oil. Wipe the steel blades with vegetable oil to protect them from rust.

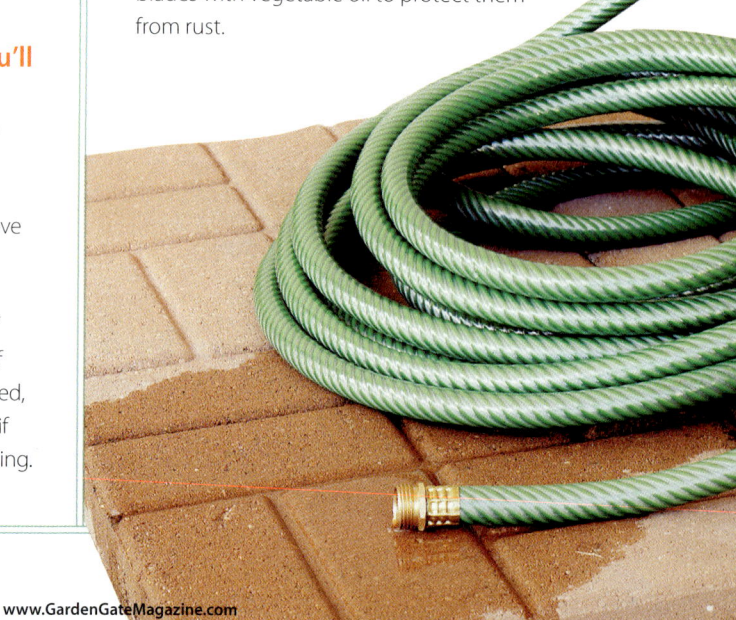

Best: Bind shrubs with twine so you can make smaller chicken wire hoops and save money.

Trees & shrubs — protect your investment.

GOOD Before the ground freezes, make sure the soil around your trees, evergreens and large shrubs is moist. If it's dry, lay a hose a foot or so from the base of the plant and let it run at a trickle for several hours.

BETTER After you water, protect tree trunks from frost cracks with tree wrap you can pick up at any garden center. Put it on young trees with smooth bark after a hard freeze. Then remove it as the tree starts to leaf out, so bugs don't have a chance to move in.

BEST Even if you wrap the trunks, critters can quickly ruin a healthy tree or shrub. Rabbits, deer, voles and mice, among others, get hungry just like you do. And they often have expensive tastes — your most prized trees and shrubs. There are lots of repellents on the market, and many work well. But the best protection method is to surround the plant with a fence of chicken wire or hardware cloth.

Critters — safeguard your newly planted spring-flowering bulbs.

GOOD If you're still planting, go with critter-resistant bulbs, such as daffodils, alliums, hyacinths and fritillarias. Squirrels won't dig them up, and even deer pass over these flowers when they're looking for a meal.

BETTER Pin sections of chicken wire over your beds of tulips so critters can't dig them up.

BEST Pick up some ¼-in. hardware cloth and make protective cages. Form a cylinder and add a bottom. Set it into the ground, plant your bulbs in it and lay a piece of mesh on top so mice and voles can't get to the bulbs.

GET PERENNIAL BEDS READY FOR SPRING

☐ **REPAIR AND REPLACE TAGS** Sure, you think you'll remember the name of that new perennial next spring. But a tag is a big help. Now is the time to check old tags to make sure you can still read them, or put out new tags.

☐ **ONE LAST WEEDING** Get ahead of next year's weeds now. Perennial weeds will be popping up at the same time as your flowers, and you don't want to give them a head start. Annual weeds are still spreading their seeds, so pull them out carefully. Don't add these weeds to your compost — it may not be hot enough to kill the seeds. If you can't send them away in the trash, bury them in a trench, at least 3 ft. deep, and the seeds won't sprout.

☐ **CUT OR LEAVE STANDING?** Research shows that perennials are more likely to survive winter if you don't cut them off until spring cleanup time. The exceptions are plants that harbor pests, such as peonies with botrytis or iris with borers. Cut the foliage down, and if possible, burn it. Can't burn in your municipality? Bury the material in the trench with the weeds.

☐ **TUCK 'EM IN FOR THE WINTER** If you live where the ground freezes, a thick blanket of mulch over your perennials is good as an insurance policy. Your objective is not to keep the soil warmer, but to keep it at an even temperature. Wide temperature fluctuations between cold and warm damage roots and often cause winter kill. Once the plants are completely dormant and the ground is beginning to freeze, 4 to 6 in. of straw or crisp oak leaves (don't chop them up first or they pack down too tightly) will do the trick. Leave this winter mulch in place until the weather warms up in spring. You'll know it's about time to remove it when the forsythia starts to bloom.

Push tags deep so you don't pull them out when you rake.

Cut away peony foliage after it yellows to prevent the spread of diseases.

Spread 4 to 6 in. of leaves after the ground begins to freeze.

BASICS | SMART GARDENING

reader tips

GARDEN GATE · 20 Great Tips · 15 YEARS

Every time we ask, you tell us that you love reader tips. And there have been some good ones over the last 15 years. We thought you might enjoy seeing 20 of our favorite tips.

Getting creative with recycling is always a popular topic so you'll find 10 of these tips to start. And everyone's always looking for and sharing their favorite ways to save time and money or make gardening easier. So I've divided these 20 ideas into "recycling tips" and "gardening easier." I hope all these tips inspire you to send in one of your own! ❑

— *Sherri Ribbey*

recycling tips

1 Seed-starting rolls Peat pots are a great way to start seeds, but they can be costly. Helen Trautman from Idaho uses cardboard paper towel tubes to start her seedlings. She cuts the tubes in half using scissors, then cuts them in half again, for four "pots." After that, she lines the cylinders up in a cake pan without holes in the bottom and adds seed-starting mix. She found that the thin cardboard gets soft after watering but if the tubes are packed in tightly they hold each other up. When the seedlings are ready to set in her garden, Helen pulls down the side of the roll so the cardboard is buried underground. Like peat pots, if the edges stick up above the surface, they'll wick moisture away from the roots.
From issue 31, February 2000

2 Give cuttings a lift Make sure your coleus cuttings (and other easy-to-root plants) get a good start with a vase like Donna Saverino's of Michigan. To make the vase, cut off the top of a 12-ounce plastic water bottle where it narrows for the neck. Then cut V-shaped notches for the stems to catch on. It keeps the stems off the bottom so they easily absorb the water. It also holds the leaves out of the water so they don't rot.
From issue 77, October 2007

3 A gardener's clean haul When it's time to retire your old plastic shower curtain, don't toss it. Recycle it like Jackie Maas of Minnesota did. She uses the curtain as a drop cloth inside her vehicle when hauling compost and mulch. And when cleaning up the garden, she lays a shower curtain on the ground to collect debris. When the pile is large enough, she simply grabs one corner of the curtain and drags it over to the compost pile.
From issue 23, October 1998

4 Floppy foliage Deloris Kline of West Virginia likes growing bulbs but the flopping leaves of her fading daffodils and naked ladies get in the way of planting. So she took a three-tier tomato cage and, using wire cutters, cut the cage just above the bottom circle. That left her with two short cages — a one-tier and a two-tier one. Then she cut each circle once, so she could open the cages and wrap them around the bulb leaves. The cages held the foliage up and were easy to take out along with the dried foliage.
From issue 68, April 2006

5 Creative staking Looking for something different to keep your plants from leaning? Rose Wingert of Ohio found just the thing at an antique store: A fireplace screen. She placed it in her garden, bending back the "wings" on each side to keep it upright. For added stability, she placed wooden stakes at each corner where the panels meet. Plants in front grow up and cover the stakes. Now Rose's false sunflowers stay upright.
From issue 75, June 2007

6 Confine that twine Konnie Smith of Oregon was fed up with losing balls of twine, so she came up with an easy dispenser. She hung a metal funnel in her shed by nailing one edge to the wall. Then she dropped the ball of twine into it. She can pull out as much twine as she needs through the small end of the funnel without any tangling, and the ball is always in one place.
From issue 55, February 2004

270 *the* YEAR IN GARDENING   www.GardenGateMagazine.com

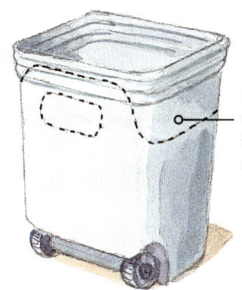

Use a utility knife to follow the line and cut away the excess plastic.

7 New life for an old can

Rita Bush-Anderson of Illinois turned an old wheeled garbage can into a "garden can" for hauling garden debris. To remodel the can, Rita drew a line that followed the lip edge at the back of the can. Then she dropped the line down about 8 inches along the side and front, as you can see above. For a handle, she drew a rectangle centered on the back. Rita used a utility knife to cut it out, following the lines she'd drawn.
From issue 82, August 2008

8 Vacation watering

Rosa Hernandez of Texas liked to take weekend trips but didn't like losing her containers because they dried out. So she got the idea to use her kids' plastic wading pool. For each container, Rosa lays two bricks in a "V" on the bottom of the pool. She sets a container on top of them with the drainage hole exposed in the notch of the "V." Then she fills the pool. The wicking action of the soil draws water into the pot. This is a perfect watering solution for a few days, but left longer than that, the roots may rot. When Rosa gets home, she pulls the pool side down to drain the water and lets the pots dry. That way, they aren't too heavy to lift.
From issue 42, December 2001

9 Safe pruning

Maryland's Albert Pippi was tired of getting poked by rose thorns when he cut blooms for his vase. Now he protects his hands by holding the top of the stem with a spring-type clothespin. Grasp the rose stem with the clothespin and snip to the desired length.
From issue 3, May 1995

10 Blooming bed guards

If you don't have a built-in irrigation system, chances are you need something to protect your garden from the dragging hose. R.M. Gallagher of Washington has a unique solution that serves double duty. First, he found the spots in the curve of his garden bed where the hose was most likely to jump the border and flatten plants. Then he found a couple of 1-foot sections of clay drainage tile (check with a local tiling company or home improvement store), and sank them upright into the ground about 5 inches deep. R.M. filled the tiles with soil to keep them from tipping when the hose hit and planted petunias in each little hose guard/planter. The tiles hold moisture well, but it still doesn't hurt to keep an eye on the "planters" because they dry out more quickly than the rest of the garden bed. *From issue 24, December 1998*

PHOTO: Brent Isenberger

gardening easier

11 Vegetable pruning
Lots of vegetables keep on producing until cold weather stops them. But some fruit will never have enough time to ripen. Emily Davis of Iowa prunes to keep her pumpkin plants from wasting energy on those pumpkins that will just die on the vine anyway. Three to four weeks before the first average frost, Emily gets to work. Starting at the ends of the vines, she works her way back to a point where the flowers are beginning to form fruits. She cuts the vine just above that leaf or fruit. This way the fruit already on the plant grows bigger and ripens faster. By the way, this technique also works on squash, melons, cucumbers and tomatoes.
From issue 34, August 2000

12 Snowscaping
Sometimes winter seems to last forever. David Johnson helps satisfy his urge to garden during winter by using snow to plan new garden beds. In New York, David usually gets quite a bit of snow every year, so he shuffles through the fluffy white stuff to make a clear line in the shape of the bed or path he's thinking of adding. This works best with a light snow because it's easier to see the contrast between the snow and the footprints. When there's a heavy snow, he piles it into mounds to approximate the size and shape of mature plants. This gives him an even better idea of how big he needs to make his beds.
From issue 54, December 2003

13 Seed-sharing photos
When friends ask Janet Maulick of Pennsylvania for seeds from her garden, she gets out her digital camera and takes a photo. Then she prints out the picture and glues it to an envelope. On the back of the envelope, she makes notes on the size and care of the requested plant, along with any tips she's found helpful. After the seeds ripen, Janet puts them in the envelope and seals it up. Next spring, when her friends look through their seeds, they'll know exactly what they're planting and how big it will get.
From issue 83, October 2008

14 Get a handle on measuring To help determine planting depths and plant spacing, garden trowels often come with measurements right on the metal. Rolando Galvan of Texas took this idea a step further. He marked off the handle of his shovel in increments of 6 inches so he has a measuring tool handy every time he digs — without having to take along the measuring tape.
From issue 21, June 1998

15 Stake and tomatoes
Isn't it great when one tool does the work of two? That's what Judy Stahley of South Dakota developed in her tomato staking and watering system. First, she cut a 5-foot length of 2-inch PVC pipe and made a mark 1 foot in from one end. After pushing the marked end of the pipe into the ground as far as she could, she set a length of 2x4 on top of it and hammered the 2x4 — pounding directly on the pipe might break it. She hammered until the mark was level with the ground, leaving 4 feet of the pipe sticking out. Judy planted tomatoes a few inches from the stakes. As the plants grew, she tied them to the pipes with strips of nylon stockings. The PVC is sturdy enough to hold the plants upright. But these stakes have an added bonus: Filling the PVC pipe gets water or a fertilizer solution down to the roots. Depending on how quickly the water drains, she may fill it several times. On the last refill, she puts a PVC cap on the pipe, to keep water from evaporating and critters out.
From issue 63, June 2005

16 Shoot for better pruning Prune the easy way like Josephine Borut of New York does — use a digital camera! After the leaves are gone, she photographs trees or shrubs that need pruning, taking care to get shots from several angles. It's easier to see which branches need to be removed when there's no foliage. Different vantage points give her a good idea of the overall shape of the plant. Once the photos are printed, Josephine uses a marker to indicate on the photo any branches that need to be removed. At the appropriate time for pruning each plant, Josephine goes to work with her photo and her pruning tools.
From issue 78, December 2007

17 A clean cut Ornamental grasses add interest to a garden through winter, but in spring they need to be cut back to make way for new growth. That's a lot of work added to the list of spring cleanup chores. But Sonia Sugarman of New York has found a simple and tidy way to do this. She wraps a length of duct tape (or two, depending on how tall the grass is) around the clump of grass before cutting. Make sure to overlap the ends of the tape since the adhesive doesn't actually stick to the grass. With the tape wrapped around the middle, Sonia had an instant bundle that's easy to carry to the compost pile or stick in a yard waste bag. And since the tape doesn't stick to the grass, it's easy to cut it off. Make things even easier on yourself and do what Valerie Reihl of Maryland does. Use electric hedge trimmers to cut the grass down near the base.
From issues 50 & 74, April 2003 & 2007

18 Clip and save What is it about gloves? It seems that one always disappears, leaving its mate behind. Karen Cochran Hasler from Indiana "clipped" this problem with a binder clip from the office supply store. While she works in the garden, Karen fastens the clip to the hem of her shirt or the back of one glove so it's always handy. When she's done working, she takes her gloves off and clips them together by the cuffs. Then she hangs them up so they're ready for her next trip to the garden.
From issue 35, October 2000

19 Easy out You don't want a back injury to ruin your gardening fun. Here's a tip from Louis Maureen of Colorado to make it easier to empty those heavy bags of topsoil, compost or mulch. After transporting a bag in a wheelbarrow to the right spot, most of us cut open one end, then lift and dump out the contents. But Louis lays the bag flat on the ground and cuts a slit across the middle from side to side. Then he rolls the bag over, gripping both ends, and lifts. All the contents pour through the slit, and he doesn't have to lift such a heavy bag. It's a simple change in technique, but it can spare your back for other garden tasks.
From issue 62, April 2005

20 Keep deer away We get a lot of questions about how to keep deer out of gardens. Here's a recipe from Sandy White of California to help keep those four-legged eating machines from munching on your plants: She blends three raw eggs and a quart of water in a blender, pours it into an old milk jug and lets it sit for 24 to 48 hours. After that, it's ready to spray on her plants. Eggs contain sulfur compounds which wildlife experts speculate smells like a deer's own "alarm scent." You will need to mix up a new batch and spray it on again after a heavy rain.
From issue 53, October 2003

Web extra Learn 12 more *tips* to get rid of or attract wildlife to your garden.

We pay $25 for garden tips*!
- Money-saving ideas
- Cool structures
- Pest-proofing techniques

→ Submit a tip – Upload images ←

www.GardenGateMagazine.com

Or, mail to *Garden Gate* Tips, 2200 Grand Ave., Des Moines, IA 50312. Please include your name, address and daytime phone number in case we have any questions.

*tip must be published

sharing is easier than ever!

BASICS | PROBLEM SOLVER

deer diary...
what *really* keeps deer out of your garden!

Deer have their place, but that place is *not* enjoying a buffet in the *Garden Gate* test garden! After all, when I plant hostas, I want them to look like the ones at left, not the nibbled stubs in the inset. Over the years, I've tried different products and techniques for keeping them away from my plants. Some of those things worked, some didn't — but I never really took good notes, so every year, I'd have to start all over again.

Last summer, I decided to get organized. I kept track of my deer-scaring strategies from May to September, when I see the most problems. There wasn't a foolproof solution that worked all summer — I had to keep switching techniques and products as the deer got used to certain repellents.

But in the end, I figured out a system that kept our garden fairly safe. Let's take a look at some of my ideas. You might find them helpful in your own fight against deer.

(1) Like humans, deer have different preferences. But hostas are always a favorite deer snack.

Off to an easy start

I've used Shake Away®, a granular, predator-urine scent repellent before. So I decided to start the summer deer program with that. I knew it worked, but I wasn't sure how long. It's easy to apply, since you just shake the crystals onto the ground. And it doesn't take much — one shake at each entry to the test garden usually heads deer off. (Deer don't always use the gate. Look for tracks and droppings to figure out how they're getting in.) I like this product because there's no odor when you apply it, and the granules don't damage foliage.

HOW DID IT WORK? It worked well until it rained! One night of rain, and still no deer damage. But after two rainy days, the deer were up to their old mischief again. So I had to reapply it after every heavy rain.

Finally, after two weeks of continued use, the deer weren't scared anymore. Free hosta buffet!

Try some spray repellents

There are lots of spray repellents out there, so after the Shake Away lost its effectiveness, I decided to try a few. The first one was Deer Stopper®, which is supposed to be safe for organic growers. It's both a smell and a taste repellent — a double whammy for the deer. (Rosemary oil, mint oil and egg give this product its punch.) The label claims it won't wash off after a heavy rain. When you're applying spray repellents, you usually need to get a light misting on any plant you think the deer might nibble.

I sprayed in the evening, just in case the scent was annoying to humans, too. There was a definite odor, but when it dried I didn't smell it anymore. After I applied it, there were no deer problems for three nights. But the fourth night, it rained, and on the fifth night, the deer were browsing again. But if I reapplied it after every rain, it was effective. I did notice that the deer were still eating the hostas at the back of the garden. Some plants that the deer really love may need extra protection. (Try "layering" products in these areas — I used both the spray repellent and the Shake Away, and that seemed to do the trick.)

I also tried a product called Liquid Fence®. Liquid Fence is a spray that uses garlic and egg compounds to make plants smell and taste bad to deer. Believe me, I wouldn't eat anything that smelled like Liquid Fence! It has quite an odor, so I had to spray in the evening, after garden guests were gone. (The smell dissipates, for humans, in about an hour.) I also noticed some spotting on flowers, like the impatiens blooms you see above. I found that spraying the sides of containers or the ground near plants worked almost as well as spraying the plants directly, and that way the flowers aren't damaged.

HOW DID IT WORK? I learned a lot about applying spray repellents! First, watch the direction of the wind as you're spraying — you don't want to get a face full of spray. Early morning or evening is usually best, as the wind generally isn't as strong then. I always wore a mask over my nose and mouth, as well as eye protection, just to be on the safe side. And I wore gloves and washed my hands after applying any of these products: One bad-tasting peanut-butter sandwich taught me that! A last bit of knowledge: Even products that claim to be rainproof need to be reapplied after a rain.

Over the summer, I tried a couple more brands of spray repellent, including Bobbex™ and Deer Off®. All of these repellents are easy to find in any garden center, and the application is just about the same for all of them. They all worked fairly well, but it seemed like the deer got used to each one after a few days. So each time I sprayed, I used a different one, just to keep the deer from getting accustomed to any of them.

Hearing voices

A final tip I learned from another gardener: A radio playing in the garden all night keeps deer at bay. I set an inexpensive radio on a brick and turned a small plastic trash can upside down over it to keep moisture off. (You could also set it inside a garage or garden shed.) Just to check the effectiveness, I didn't do any spraying for a day or two.

HOW DID IT WORK? Believe it or not, this does help! I had to let the neighbors know that the radio would be on, and you do have to turn it up fairly loud. There was a little deer browsing right around the edges of the garden, but they didn't come too close to the radio. It might be my imagination, but sports stations and talk radio seemed to be the scariest for deer! But like all deer-repelling techniques, eventually they got used to the noise, so I had to rotate this along with my other products.

So that's the tale of my summer of scaring the deer. The most important thing I learned is that you can't let up — keep rotating products, because a couple of days' lapse can allow the deer to do a lot of damage. But our test garden made it through the season mostly intact. So this year, I'll start the rotation again, and hope for the same good results! □

— *Marcia Leeper*

(2) Spray repellents can mark some flowers, but it's not too noticeable from a distance.

Share your tips on our *deer forum*.

BASICS | PROBLEM SOLVER

Attack of the Invasives!

Stop them before they take over your neighborhood!

Botanical Names

Obedient plant
Physostegia virginiana

W ho would have thought that plants could cause so many big problems? No matter what you call them — exotic, non-native, alien or noxious — invasive plants have become a menace in all areas of North America. While sources vary, it's estimated that these plants are invading an area the size of Yellowstone National Park every year. Imagine more than 2 million acres of native trees, shrubs and wildflowers being forced out of their homes by a gang of thugs. Even the animals that rely on the native plants for food could face extinction if they don't find any of these interlopers tasty.

INVASION TACTICS Some of these invasives infiltrate native areas by wide-spreading root systems. Others produce seeds that travel any way they can. Seeds can even hitch a ride on the bumper of your car, crossing borders with ease. And all of these seeds are opportunists. Many sprout in the shade of mature trees or dry cracks in a sidewalk. Several of these aliens spread by both seeds *and* roots.

When an invasive moves away from its native home, it leaves behind foraging animals, insects and diseases that would ordinarily keep its spread in check.

KNOW YOUR ENEMY Now, you may be wondering if you should worry about some of the fast-spreading plants in your garden. While some perennials, such as obedient plant, may be aggressive, even annoying pests, they haven't scooted under the fence, looking for wide open spaces to colonize. Perennials like this don't pose much of a threat to native plants, so they're not really invasive.

Then there is purple loosestrife. Introduced from Asia and Europe, it used to be sold as an ornamental. However, its seeds escaped from cultivation and it's now growing rampantly in the wetlands of at least 36 states. Its stems and roots are so tough and dense that fish even find it hard to swim through the tangle. Every year approximately $45 million is spent by taxpayers and private companies to fight this pest. So not only is it is not only harming nature, it's hurting your wallet!

You'll also find large shade trees, such as Norway maple and white poplar, on the invasives list. And shrubs that have been sold at garden centers for many years, such as burning bush and Japanese barberry, are among the biggest problems. They're in lots of regions because they've been so widely planted.

PLAN YOUR ATTACK How do you know which plants you need to be wary of? In the list at right and on the next pages, I'm going to point out some of the worst offenders. But this is by no means a complete list, so check out our Web extra for a link with information specific to your state. You may have some of these plants in your garden or spot them at your local garden center. Unless a plant is invasive in your region, it may be OK to plant it. Just be aware of its potential problems, and if you have an option, try to choose a friendlier plant.

With each plant, I've included information on where it's hardy, how big it'll grow and where it's become a problem. This list shows perennials. Turn the page for trees, shrubs and vines.

Believe it or not!
One purple loosestrife can produce 3 million seeds each year. They spread by wind, water, animals and humans.

ILLUSTRATIONS: Jeff Bash

Invasive perennials

● Northwest ▲ Northeast
● Southwest ■ Southeast

Web extra: Want to know if a plant's a problem in your state or county? Check out our *links*.

Plant Name	Cold/Heat Zones	Regions	Height/Width	How it Spreads
American water lotus *Nelumbo lutea*	4-11/11-1	■ ● ▲	3-6 ft./spreading	Aquatic perennial; spreads by roots and seeds; clogs waterways and forces out native aquatic plants
Bamboo, golden *Phyllostachys aurea*	6-11/11-1	■ ◆ ●	6-30 ft./spreading	Spreads by underground rhizome; hard to kill or remove the wide-spreading aggressive roots
Bishop's weed *Aegopodium podagraria* 'Variegata'	4-9/9-1	■ ◆ ▲	6-12 in./spreading	Escapes by underground rhizomes; frequently planted as a ground cover in shady areas
Butterfly bush *Buddleja davidii*	5-9/9-1	■ ◆ ● ▲	3-10 ft./3-10 ft.	Shrub spreads by seeds and layering; forms colonies in ditches and prairie areas
Cactus, jointed prickly pear *Opuntia aurantiaca*	4-9/9-1	■ ◆ ● ▲	6-12 in./spreading	Cactus with very sharp thorns; sections break off to sprout a new plant; travels by attaching to animal fur
Chinese lantern *Physalis alkekengi*	3-9/9-1	▲	18-30 in./36 in.	Grown mainly for its ornamental orange seed pods; seeds spread rampantly and sprout easily
Chinese silver grass *Miscanthus sinensis*	4-9/9-1	■ ◆ ● ▲	3-12 ft./2-6 ft.	Spreads by seeds; forms colonies of large plants; most of the cultivated varieties will reseed
Chives, garlic *Allium tuberosum*	3-9/9-1	■ ◆ ▲	10-20 in./10-24 in.	Spreads by seed and bulbs; invades native areas, as well as lawns and perennial gardens; pungent odor when stepped on
Cogongrass *Imperata cylindrica*	5-9/9-1	■ ◆	12-18 in./12-18 in.	Spreads by roots and seeds; related to 'Rubra' Japanese blood grass, which is also invasive
Crownvetch *Securigera varia*	4-9/9-1	■ ◆ ● ▲	8-36 in./spreading	Widely planted for erosion control along highways; escaped by spreading roots and prolific seeding
Cup plant *Silphium perfoliatum*	3-9/9-1	■ ▲	4-8 ft./1-3 ft.	Spreads by seeds and roots; grows mainly in wet areas; most seeds travel by water; large leaves shade out other plants
Daisy, ox-eye *Leucanthemum vulgare*	3-8/8-1	■ ◆ ● ▲	1-3 ft./1-2 ft.	Looks similar to Shasta daisy, but smaller and much more aggressive; spreads by seeds and surface rhizomes
Fountain grass *Pennisetum alopecuroides*	5-9/9-1	■ ◆ ●	2-5 ft./2-5 ft.	Reseeds into sunny areas, displacing native grass species, as well as flowering plants; some cultivars are also invasive
Iris, yellow flag *Iris pseudacorus*	5-9/9-1	■ ◆ ● ▲	3-5 ft./2-3 ft.	Needs wet soil at the edge of ponds or streams; multiplies quickly to form dense colonies
Japanese knotweed *Fallopia japonica*	3-9/9-1	■ ◆ ▲	4-6 ft./6-8 ft.	Spreads by underground roots; hard to control; sometimes called American bamboo
Jerusalem artichoke *Helianthus tuberosus*	3-9/9-1	■ ◆ ● ▲	8-10 ft./3 ft.	Once planted for its edible rhizome; fast-spreading by underground tubers; hard to remove once established
Loosestrife, purple *Lythrum salicaria*	4-9/9-1	■ ◆ ● ▲	2-5 ft./2-4 ft.	Spreads mainly by seed; once extensively grown as an ornamental in the perennial border
Reed, common *Phragmites australis*	4-10/10-1	■ ▲	15 ft./spreading	Spreads by seed and deep underground rhizomes; roots can spread 10 ft. in one season; found in wet areas
Scouringrush *Equisetum hyemale*	3-11/11-1	■ ◆ ● ▲	2-4 ft./1-6 ft.	Usually found in damp or wet areas but can adapt to dry conditions; no leaves give it an unusual look; often best to remove it by digging
Spiderwort *Tradescantia virginiana*	4-9/9-1	■ ▲	18-24 in./18 in.	Seeds sprout easily to spread this native perennial; cultivars can reseed, but not as aggressively as the species
Star of Bethlehem *Ornithogalum umbellatum*	6-10/10-1	■ ◆ ● ▲	4-12 in./6-12 in.	Bulbs multiply to form large colonies; bulbs can be hard to kill or even separate from other plants; also reseeds
Water hyacinth *Eichhornia crassipes*	9-11/12-1	■ ◆ ● ▲	6-12 in./18 in.	Floating aquatic clogs ponds and streams; even where it is not hardy it can float downstream to areas where it can survive
Water lettuce *Pistia stratiotes*	9-11/12-1	■ ◆ ● ▲	4-6 in./6-10 in.	Floating aquatic; even where it is not hardy it can float downstream to bodies of water where it can survive and clog lakes and streams

INVASIVE MANEUVERS

Web extra
Find lots more *tips* on how to get rid of invasive plants.

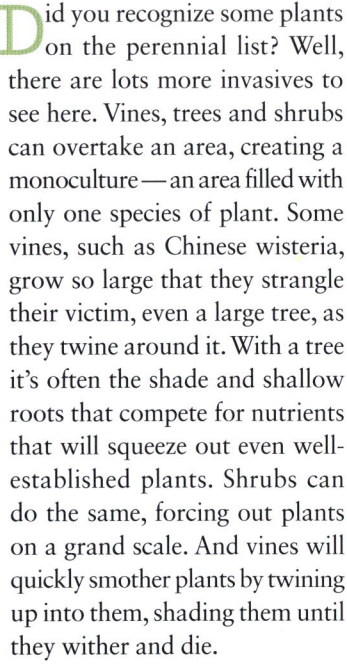

Did you recognize some plants on the perennial list? Well, there are lots more invasives to see here. Vines, trees and shrubs can overtake an area, creating a monoculture — an area filled with only one species of plant. Some vines, such as Chinese wisteria, grow so large that they strangle their victim, even a large tree, as they twine around it. With a tree it's often the shade and shallow roots that compete for nutrients that will squeeze out even well-established plants. Shrubs can do the same, forcing out plants on a grand scale. And vines will quickly smother plants by twining up into them, shading them until they wither and die.

MARKED FOR ELIMINATION
All of the invasives that spread by seed can be pulled while they are small. But if they multiply by sending out aggressive roots, you may want to use a systemic herbicide, such as Roundup®. Why? If you leave even a tiny piece of root in the soil, odds are it'll regrow. You could end up spreading the pest. Even if you can only mow down an area, keep the plant as short as you can to prevent it from setting seeds.

Older trees, shrubs and vines will need to be cut down. And even then, their stumps could resprout. Apply a brush killer you paint or dribble onto the cut surface to kill the roots. And check out our Web extra to learn more about getting invasive plants under control.

Noxious shade Norway maples cast very dense shade and have such a wide net of shallow roots that few plants (other than their own seedlings) can grow under them.

Scientists are helping win the battle in large and wild areas using natural controls. For example, insects that feed on purple loosestrife have been imported from Europe to help eradicate this pest. But natural controls can pose their own set of problems — we don't want to solve one problem, only to release another.

So, this battle will be ongoing. Once invasive plants make themselves at home, you're going to have trouble evicting each and every one. Sure it's going to take some time and energy, but getting rid of these pests will help protect our wildlife and native plants. □

— *Jim Childs*

A bouncing baby ivy English ivy shades out and chokes everything it covers. But did you know it won't flower and set seed until it matures, which only happens when it's able to grow vertically?

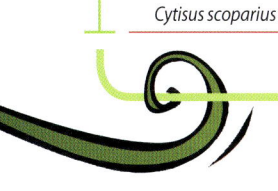

Invasive vines, trees and shrubs

◆ Northwest ▲ Northeast
● Southwest ■ Southeast

VINES

Plant Name	Cold/Heat Zones	Regions	Height/Width	How it Spreads
Akebia, fiveleaf *Akebia quinata*	4-8/8-1	■ ▲	20-40 ft./climbing	Semi-evergreen twining vine; spreads mainly by seeds; stem pieces can also root and spread
Bittersweet, Oriental *Celastrus orbiculatus*	4-8/8-1	■ ▲	40-60 ft./climbing	Twining vine; spreads mainly by seeds; its relative, American bittersweet (*C. scandens*) is not invasive
Euonymus, climbing *Euonymus fortunei*	4-9/9-1	■ ▲	2-40 ft./climbing	Evergreen; climbs tree trunks and other surfaces with rootlets along its stems
Honeysuckle, Japanese *Lonicera japonica*	4-10/10-1	■ ● ▲	30 ft./climbing	Evergreen to semi-evergreen twining vine; spreads by seeds; stem pieces can also take root
Ivy, English *Hedera helix*	4-9/9-1	■ ◆ ● ▲	1-80 ft./3-40 ft.	Planted extensively as a ground cover; so dense it shades out anything it encounters, including trees
Porcelainberry *Ampelopsis brevipedunculata*	4-8/8-1	■ ▲	15 ft./climbing	Twining vine reseeds easily in both sunny and shaded areas; easy to dig or pull out; variegated form is also invasive
Wisteria, Chinese *Wisteria sinensis*	5-9/9-1	■ ▲	30 ft./climbing	Twining vine; can strangle a large tree; spreads by seed and roots where stems touch the ground

TREES AND SHRUBS

Plant Name	Cold/Heat Zones	Regions	Height/Width	How it Spreads
Alder, European/black *Alnus glutinosa*	3-7/7-1	▲	40-80 ft./20-40 ft.	Fast-growing shade tree; seeds sprout easily in wet areas along streams and ponds
Barberry, Japanese *Berberis thunbergii*	4-8/8-1	◆ ■ ▲	3-6 ft./4-8 ft.	Dense shrub with thorns; spreads mainly by seeds; can form an impenetrable thicket; most cultivars are also invasive
Blackberry, Himalayan *Rubus armeniacus*	4-9/9-1	■ ◆ ● ▲	10 ft./40 ft.	Spreads by arching stems, roots and seeds; forms dense, thorny thickets that force out native species
Buckthorn, common *Rhamnus cathartica*	2-9/9-1	■ ◆ ● ▲	12-20 ft./12-20 ft.	Sharp spurs on branches; birds ingest seeds and spread them; easy to pull young sprouts
Burning bush *Euonymus alatus*	4-9/9-1	■ ▲	8-20 ft./10 ft.	Large shrub; red fall color makes it popular, but seedlings can grow into dense thickets; cultivars can also be invasive
Empress/Princess tree *Paulownia tomentosa*	5-8/8-1	■ ▲	30-50 ft./30 ft.	Fast-growing tree; spreads by seed; large leaves cast dense shade
European highbush cranberry *Viburnum opulus*	3-8/8-1	◆ ▲	8-15 ft./10-15 ft.	Large shrub; spreads by seeds carried away by birds; American highbush cranberry (*V. o. americanum*) is not invasive
Honeysuckle, Tatarian *Lonicera tatarica*	3-9/9-1	■ ◆ ● ▲	8-12 ft./6-12 ft.	Large shrub often used in windbreaks; birds spread seeds that force out other shrubs
Locust, black *Robinia pseudoacacia*	3-9/9-1	■ ◆ ● ▲	30-80 ft./20-25 ft.	Fast-growing suckering tree; treat cut stump with a brush killer to prevent resprouting; spreads by seed and suckers
Maple, Norway *Acer platanoides*	3-7/7-1	◆ ▲	40-60 ft./30-50 ft.	Large dense tree; spreads by seeds; most plants can't cope with the dense shade or the aggressive roots
Pear, Bradford *Pyrus calleryana* 'Bradford'	5-9/9-1	■ ▲	30-50 ft./20-25 ft.	Once planted as a street tree; flowers hybridize with other species of pear and reseed
Poplar, white *Populus alba*	3-9/9-1	■ ◆ ● ▲	50-75 ft./50-60 ft.	Fast-growing tree; aggressively spreads by seed; once planted as a windbreak
Privet, common or European *Ligustrum vulgare*	4-7/7-1	■ ◆ ● ▲	10-15 ft./8-15 ft.	Often used as a sheared hedge; birds eat black fruit and spread the seeds; easy-to-pull young sprouts
Russian olive *Elaeagnus angustifolia*	2-8/8-1	◆ ● ▲	12-35 ft./12-20 ft.	Large shrub or small tree; fruit is popular with birds, which help spread this plant; sharp spurs on branches
Saltcedar *Tamarix ramosissima*	3-8/8-1	■ ◆ ●	10-15 ft./6-15 ft.	Once planted for its airy pink flowers; usually found in moist soil; spreads aggressively by seeds and roots
Scotch broom *Cytisus scoparius*	6-8/8-1	■ ◆ ▲	4-6 ft./4-6 ft.	Twiggy shrub with slender arching branches; yellow flowers in late spring

BASICS | PROBLEM SOLVER

make the most of your fading beauties!
garden coverups

Of course, it would be nice if plants could bloom all season. But unfortunately, some of the prettiest flowers arrive in a blaze of glory… and then wimp out. You're left with a big bare spot or maybe some ratty foliage in the garden for the rest of the summer. Are you doomed to live with it, or can you improve things? Of course you can! Creative planting, careful pruning and some imaginative work with containers can help your garden look beautiful from spring to fall. Let me show you three of my favorite, tried-and-true techniques for keeping a garden looking great all summer long.

— Marcia Leeper

The earlier-blooming lily gets a chance to show off before the coverup plant steps in for the rest of the summer.

Look for a planting companion with similar leaves: See how much these two look alike?

Snip the stems of the spent early-season plant back to the height of the late-season coverup.

When you plant the late-season coverup, tip the plant a little away from the early-season bloomer to give it plenty of room.

Blending in Many perennials bloom in early or midsummer. If you're lucky, the foliage that's left after they finish blooming is attractive. But sadly, sometimes it just doesn't look all that great.

Let's consider trumpet lilies. Their big, bright flowers are gorgeous. But when they're done blooming and you've deadheaded them, those stumpy stalks look terrible, and you can't cut them back because the plants need the leaves to manufacture food for the rest of the season. So plant something in front of them. But choose carefully: I've found that the key to a successful pairing is to choose a coverup plant to go in front that has a similar habit and foliage to the spent plant. Mexican bush sage, with upright stalks and slender leaves, would never be mistaken for a lily, but the leaf shape and texture are similar enough that the lilies seem to disappear behind it. In this case, because Mexican bush sage is a fast-growing annual, I like to tip it a little bit away from the lilies to give them some breathing room. But if you're pairing two perennials, watch the spacing. You want them to be close enough for the coverup to work, so it's OK if they billow into each other. But you don't want one crowding the other out of the garden!

Hide this…	with this!
Bee balm Monarda spp.	**Black-eyed Susan** Rudbeckia spp.
Yarrow Achillea spp.	**Dusty miller** Senecio cineraria
'Husker Red' penstemon Penstemon digitalis	**'Eva Cullum' phlox** Phlox paniculata
Trumpet lily Lilium hybrids	**Mexican bush sage** Salvia leucantha

Plants on a pedestal

Quite a few early blooming perennials, like old-fashioned bleeding heart, go dormant in summer. A well-established bleeding heart can be a couple of feet wide, so, as you can imagine, that leaves a big hole in the garden. You can't plant a bunch of annuals in the space because that'll disturb the bleeding heart's roots.

So do you have to wait for surrounding perennials to cover the space? Nope! Containers to the rescue! A showy container, full of summery blooms, is the perfect way to cover this space. But it's not as easy as just plopping the container into the empty space. Take it a step farther and set the container up on a couple of bricks. That'll keep moisture and air accessible to the crown of the plant underneath, and if it's a perennial that puts out a little new growth in late summer, the bricks will hold the container up and out of the way.

Perennials that do a disappearing act

- **Old-fashioned bleeding heart** *Dicentra spectabilis*
- **Bloodroot** *Sanguinaria canadensis*
- **Oriental poppy** *Papaver orientale*
- **Primrose** *Primula* spp.
- **Trillium** *Trillium* spp.

After it's finished its early show, let the perennial plant go dormant at its own pace — don't cut the foliage back until it's completely yellow.

Tip bricks on their sides and place on either side of the crown to give plants underneath plenty of air circulation.

Cut back dormant plant

Even on large, established plants, the crown is usually small enough to be covered by one container, once the stems are cut back.

Cut cool-weather bloomers back to a couple of inches (or a tuft of foliage) to get them through the summer.

Spring — In spring, this Cape daisy looks great in the container.

Summer — By summer, the Cape daisy has been cut back, but the red dwarf salvia takes over during the heat.

Fall — As fall's cooler weather approaches, the Cape daisy will resume growth, weaving through the salvia.

Early summer slow-down

Is there some way to make a container look great from spring through fall without totally replanting? Absolutely!

Try a summer fill-in. Cut those cool-weather annuals, such as Cape daisy, back to a few inches high. Then tuck in some hot-weather bloomers, like the red dwarf salvia in the illustration. Leave a few inches of breathing room, and check on your plants occasionally during the summer. You may need to pinch or prune back the summer bloomer to make sure it doesn't totally take over the container and shade out the cool-weather plants. Besides the salvia here, annual geraniums and marigolds are good choices — they'll fill in the container, but they won't sprawl and take up more than their fair share of space.

Come fall, your cool-weather annuals will grow and take their place in the container again. You can either leave the cover-up plants in place or remove them to give the cool-weather beauty more room to bloom.

Spring beauties you can save

- **Calendula** *Calendula officinalis*
- **Cape daisy** *Osteospermum* hybrids
- **Dahlberg daisy** *Thymophylla tenuiloba*
- **Pansy** *Viola* hybrids
- **Snapdragon** *Antirrhinum* hybrids

BASICS | PROBLEM SOLVER

create an easy-care no-mow slope

Botanical Names

Bugleweed *Ajuga reptans*
Sedum *Sedum* spp.
Vinca *Vinca minor*

Mowing is one of those jobs like weeding. I don't really enjoy it, but I have to do it. Now, I know that some gardeners actually do like to mow. But everyone agrees — mowing a steep bank like the one here isn't fun, and sometimes it can even be dangerous. Why bother? A ground cover can solve your problems, turning that garden eyesore in the inset photo into an asset, like the gorgeous planting of vinca in the big photo below.

So why don't more people use this easy solution? The problem is, a steep bank is a tough place to get plants started, even ground covers. Soil washes away easily, exposing plant roots and making it difficult for them to get established. But I've planted quite a few areas like this, and I've come up with some tips that make it easier. Just keep two main goals in mind: You need to give the plants a chance to get their roots established. And you need to keep the soil on the bank from washing away until the ground cover has taken over. Let's take a look at how you get a great ground cover going on a slope. □

— *Marcia Leeper*

This shady slope is pretty rough. Grass doesn't grow well in shade, so bare soil is exposed. And it's steep enough to make mowing both difficult and dangerous. A shade-loving ground cover, like the one below, would be a great solution for this spot.

Pin the plants

This is a shady bank, so I'm using perennial vinca, a tough, vining ground cover. Like most ground covers, it'll take off quickly, but it does need just a bit of encouragement. First, remove the competing weeds and tufts of grass, but don't till up the soil or loosen it too much. (I'll tell you more about keeping the soil in place in a minute.) The biggest difficulty with planting on a slope is that young plants can be dislodged by watering or rain, and you'll end up with bare spots. I've found that securing the plants with a metal landscape pin (available at any garden center) keeps them in place while they get going. (Forked twigs or homemade pins made from clothes hangers work, too.) See how I'm just pushing that U-shaped pin into the soil right over the crown of the plant? In a month or so, you can pull the pins out, although they won't really hurt anything if you miss a few. As the plants send out new shoots, pin those to the ground, too — they'll root where they make contact with the soil.

Rocks to the rescue The pins are great, but what if you're using a ground cover with fleshy stems, like sedum or the bugleweed you see here, instead of a wiry, vining plant? I tried pinning bugleweed in place, too, but the stems tended to break where they were pinned. Instead, a rock or a brick, wedged into the ground right below the plant, keeps the soil and the plant in place while the roots get established. If you like the look, you can leave the stones. Or just pick them up in a month or two and fill in the depression with a little extra soil.

Push the pin down gently but firmly right over the crown of the plants.

Save the soil

How steep is your slope? Pinning the plants in place is one part of a successful planting, but keeping the soil where it belongs is just as crucial.

If the slope is gentle enough, you can mulch around the plants and the mulch will hold the soil down. But on a steep bank like the one at left, you'll need to use burlap, which you can purchase at most garden centers. (How do you know if it's steep enough to need this? A good rule of thumb is if it's hard to keep your footing walking sideways along the bank, it's steep!) Burlap's loose weave allows the ground cover to root through it, and eventually the threads rot away. (Don't use weed barrier — it won't allow the plants to root.) Put the burlap down before you plant, then cut X-shaped planting holes in it as I'm doing here. Pin the burlap every couple of feet to hold it against the slope. The plants will hide the burlap before you know it, and you won't have to mow that bank again!

BASICS | PROBLEM SOLVER

These 4 great-looking edgings won't drain your energy (or your bank account)!

Sharpen Your Edges

THE WEEKEND Garden Smarter GARDENER

You can really enhance the look of a bed or border with garden edging. But edging doesn't just make the bed *look* nice: It also keeps the lawn and rambling plants from invading each other's spaces. A crisp edge is easier to mow or trim along and keeps mulch where it belongs.

Here, we'll take a look at four kinds of edging that don't cost an arm and a leg or take much trouble to maintain.

First mark where your edging will go: Lay out a garden hose so you can make adjustments before you dig. Push a mower along the line to check that the curves are easy to maneuver. Then mark the line with flour or paint and you're ready to start edging. If you're concerned about keeping mulch in place, the tops of brick, stone and metal edging should be at least an inch above the surrounding soil.

1 TRENCH IT IN This is by far the easiest, least expensive option for edging a bed. All you need is a sharp spade or half-moon trenching tool and some time to get the effect in the photo. Cut straight down 3 to 4 inches and remove the sod and the soil as in the illustration at left. Top the bed and trench with a few inches of mulch. This edge will get a little overgrown by the end of the season, so you'll need to touch it up now and then. But it's also easy to expand the size of your garden as your plants or your ambitions grow. **Cost: $**

2 MARK IT WITH METAL Depending on your garden style, you can pound metal edging down so it barely shows, or leave enough exposed to highlight the bed edges as you see in the photo. Either way, you have a crisp edge that rarely needs any touch-up. This type of edging comes in 8- or 16-foot lengths of steel or aluminum. Aluminum is lighter and won't rust like steel but may heave with frost. Secure the edging with flat stakes to help it keep its shape. **Cost: $$$**

3 SET IT IN STONE (OR BRICK) For a more permanent look than a trenched edge, you can't beat brick and stone. They can be installed different ways for different effects. Dig a narrow trench and line the bottom with a couple inches of ⅜-inch gravel or sand to create a stable base. Level and tamp the sand and set the bricks or stone in end to end. You'll need more of them if you set them with the long sides together, but it creates a much wider border that's easier to mow along. Random-sized pieces of stone in the lower photo evoke a casual, informal look, while large pieces of cut stone could double as a path along your bed. Set the brick or stone solidly by tapping it with a rubber mallet to ensure that it's level. (You may need to add or remove sand later, as settling occurs.) Sweep sand into the spaces between to fill the gap. Either stone or brick is a good fit for gardens with plants that spill out of the bed because they provide a buffer between bed and grass, meaning grass isn't as likely to be smothered. Keep the top about an inch above the soil. **Cost: $$**

4 SHOW A LITTLE WHIMSY For an informal or cottage-style garden, try lining your bed with bottles, shells or any other found objects. Or craft the willow hoops you see here, reminiscent of old English wattle fences. Use our design or create your own. (Check out our Web extra to see a video of how to create this look.) This rustic edging would be time-consuming for a large bed, and not as long-lasting as metal, brick or stone. But it's a great way to call special attention to a favorite bed. **Cost: $**

If you've been wanting edging, I hope this guide helped you make a decision that your back and bank account can agree upon! □

— *Deborah Gruca*

HOW MUCH WILL IT COST?
$ = Free
$$ = Up to $5 per linear foot
$$$ = $5 to $10 per linear foot

Fill a trenched edge with mulch to keep weeds from sprouting or grass from spreading into the bed.

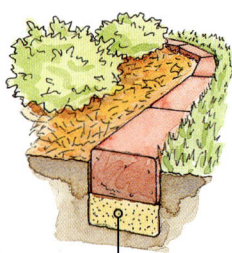

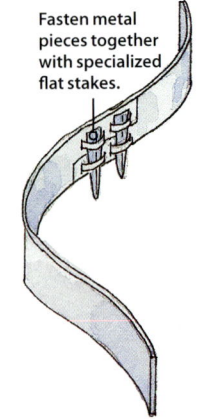

Fasten metal pieces together with specialized flat stakes.

Create a sturdy base for bricks or stones with a couple inches of sand or gravel.

1. Trenched
2. Steel
3. Brick
4. Willow Stone

Web extra
Watch our *video* to see how to make this willow edging.

www.GardenGateMagazine.com

BASICS | TOOLS

digging tools
that work

Gardeners spend a lot of time digging, whether it's moving soil, planting or dividing. The right tool makes all the difference. If you're digging planting holes with a square sand shovel, you're going to end up with blisters, an aching back and not much to show for your hard work. But pick up a pointed perennial shovel, and that hard job suddenly gets a lot easier.

Let's take a look at some common tasks and I'll show you my favorite spades, shovels and garden forks for these jobs, plus alternatives. You'll see some overlap — there's more than one way to dig a hole! Then I'll share tips on picking the tool that's the right fit for you.

As you read, you'll notice that I'm talking about shovels and spades. Some folks think they're the same. But actually, there are some differences. Spades have sharp, small, flat blades, and they're good for tight spaces, breaking new ground or loosening soil. You'll find them handy for edging and dividing, too. Shovels' curved blades help you scoop soil out of a hole easily, so they're great for planting. You'll notice that spades have straight handles, so they're better for working and loosening soil than lifting it. Shovels, however, have a curve to the handle that makes it easier to lift loads. Depending on the garden center or catalog where you're looking for tools, you may find them called all sorts of things. (Check out A.M. Leonard, www.amleo.com, 800-543-8955, for a great selection of digging tools.) But just keep in mind the shape you need for the job, and you'll be all set to dig! □

— *Marcia Leeper*

Small perennial shovel

Dig that hole!

What's your first mental image of gardening? If you're like most gardeners, probably the first thing you think of is planting. And to do that, you need to dig holes.

MY FAVORITE I couldn't garden without the perennial shovel you see at left. It's small enough — the blade is 6 in. wide and 9 in. high — to dig between plants without damaging anything, and it's light enough for me to work a long time without getting tired.

WHAT TO LOOK FOR Do you do a lot of digging in tight spaces or transplanting in between existing plants? A small shovel like mine is easy to maneuver. But if you dig a lot of big holes in fairly soft soil, a big shovel, with a blade that's 8 or 9 in. wide and 11 or 12 in. high, will help you dig faster.

ANOTHER TOOL TO TRY Digging a trench for drainage or planting a row? I like this rabbiting or transplant spade. The blade, 5½ in. wide and 10½ in. long, is longer than the one on my perennial shovel, so it works well if you need a deep, narrow hole.

Rabbiting spade: The long, narrow blade is handy for digging trenches or working in a tight space.

Scoop that pile!

You've just ordered some lovely compost or soil for your garden…and now you have to move the pile.

MY FAVORITE When I have soil, compost, sand or fine mulch delivered, I like the square-tipped sand shovel at left because I can move a lot of material quickly, but it's not too heavy to lift. Upturned edges hold the material, and the flat blade edge makes it easy to scrape the last traces off a sidewalk or out of a truck.

WHAT TO LOOK FOR The bigger the "business end" of the tool, the faster you'll be able to move stuff, as long as you can lift it. A short D-ring or strap handle helps balance the weight. (Check out "Get a handle on it," below, to learn more about handles.)

ANOTHER TOOL TO TRY This large, pointed-tip shovel is a bigger version of the little perennial shovel I showed you at left. If you're scooping mulch or compost out of a pile, instead of off a flat surface, you may find the pointed blade digs into the pile more easily than a flat blade does.

Square-tipped sand shovel

Pointed-tip shovel: It's great for moving a lot of material quickly, but don't wreck the point on the blade by scraping it along a driveway or sidewalk.

Stick a fork in it!

A lot of gardeners aren't sure how or why to use garden forks. But they're great for loosening soil, dividing plants and moving mulch.

MY FAVORITE My little border fork, at right, lifts plants without cutting the roots, and I also use it for harvesting root crops. The small, narrow head makes it easy to use in tight spaces. I like to have two garden forks around when I'm splitting perennials — use them back-to-back to pry apart tough root balls.

WHAT TO LOOK FOR The sturdy, square tines you can see poking out from under the root ball in the photo will withstand a lot of prying and digging.

ANOTHER TOOL TO TRY If I have a big pile of mulch to load or spread, I like a wide scoop fork. The broader head means you can move more mulch with one scoop. And the tines on this are sharp and slightly curved instead of big and square, so they dig into a pile of mulch with ease.

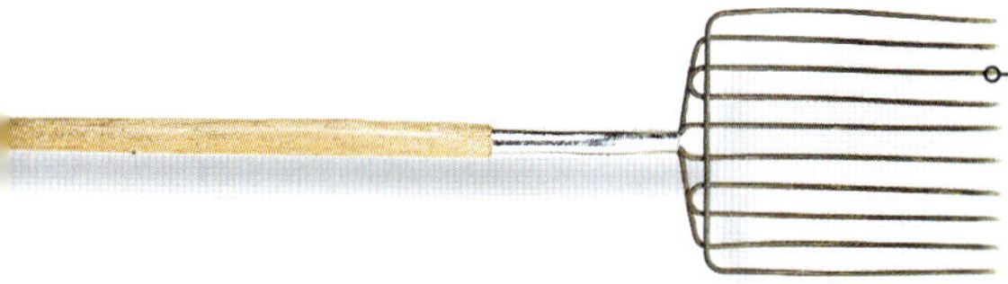

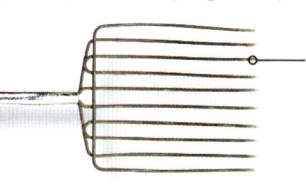

Wide scoop fork: These sharp, thin tines aren't meant for digging heavy soil — stick to moving mulch or compost with this scoop fork.

Garden or border fork

GET A HANDLE ON IT

What about the handle? After all, that's the end you have to hold! Here are a few things to consider as you're purchasing your new digging tool:

WHAT SHAPE IS IT? Long, straight handles (A) give you a little extra leverage when you're digging. And if you're tall, the length may make these handles easier to use. D-ring or strap handles (B) give you a place to grip the end of the tool so it doesn't twist or tip when you're moving a full load. These handles are short, too, so they're easy to maneuver in a tight space or if you're not very tall.

WHAT'S IT MADE FROM? Wooden handles, often made of ash, are heavy and long-lasting. Many gardeners like the extra weight of wood, because it makes the tool feel well-balanced. Of course, it's a good idea to store your tools inside regardless of material, but wooden handles deteriorate quickly if left outside. Metal or fiberglass handles are strong, lightweight and fairly weatherproof, but without the extra "heft" of wood. When you're buying a digging tool, pick up several and hold them like you're going to use them to see what feels best to you.

BASICS | TOOLS

THE WEEKEND Garden Smarter GARDENER

Make it easier on yourself this fall!

Bulb Tools That Really Work

Botanical Names

Daffodil
Narcissus spp.
Crocus
Crocus hybrids
Grape hyacinth
Muscari armeniacum
Snowdrops
Galanthus nivalis

Not many flowers rival the welcome splash of color that spring bulbs can give you. But if you've ever planted them in fall, you can appreciate the effort that goes into planting…it's not always easy! However, it doesn't have to nearly kill you every year. After years of trial and error, I've found that the right tool really can make the difference. No one tool is the answer. It depends on what kind of bulbs you're planting, how many you have to plant and what shape your soil is in.

Let me show you how you can save some time and prevent aches and pains this fall.

These tools are what you'll use when you can't (or don't want to) dig a trench, arrange the bulbs and cover them back up. Maybe you just have a few bulbs to plant. Maybe you don't have room to dig a trench. Maybe you're planting in your lawn. Whatever your plans are this fall, I hope these tips can make your work easier. ☐

— *Kristin Beane Sullivan*

When you have a lot to do
Simply tighten this attachment into your drill and you can dig a lot of holes without much effort.

You can use an auger in lawns and even tough garden soil (but stay away from tree roots and hard-packed clay). Just make sure you're using a 12-in. or shorter length auger (this one is 7 in.). The longer ones are more likely to bend when the going gets tough. However, the long-shafted augers *are* more comfortable to work with (you don't have to bend as much) and they're fine if you're working in prepared soil. I use an electric ½-in. drill with my auger because running an extension cord is no big deal in my small yard. A powerful battery-operated drill also works, but you may have to recharge or switch battery packs frequently. See how the auger is kicking dirt out of this hole? Run it both as you push down and pull up to get the cleanest hole. (And wear eye protection.) Need a bigger hole for giant daffodil bulbs? Drill two holes side by side.

MAKE IT EASIER ON YOURSELF When you're planting bulbs 6 in. or so apart, here's a tip: Enlist a friend. Why? If you drill more than one hole at a time, holes this close together tend to cave in on one another. So use a drill-and-drop planting technique: One person drills, the other drops the bulb into each hole and refills it. This means you won't have to drill a hole, put down the drill, drop a bulb in, refill the hole, drill another hole, etc.

For a few bulbs A traditional bulb planter can be handy because it digs the right size hole and gives you planting depth at a glance. The long-handled version makes it easy on your back and knees. Just step on it to plunge the digging end into the soil. Do wear sturdy shoes if you'll be digging lots of holes so you don't bruise the bottom of your foot. It works best in prepared soil and pretty well in turf because you're able to put your body weight into the digging. But steer clear of using it in heavy clay. Even if you did manage to muscle this tool through heavy clay, it would smooth and compress the sides of the hole, making future root growth more difficult.

If you're buying a bulb planter, look for one that's welded together rather than attached with bolts or rivets. Those connections get wobbly after a bit of use. The tool at left, The Bulb Hound®, has a lever that opens the hinge at the bottom to drop the soil back out. Check out how it works in the inset photos.

THE SHORT-HANDLED ALTERNATIVE I like the planter at right better than the traditional short-handled version because of its quick-release lever. Even so, using it can still be tiring, so I only get it out if I'm planting a few bulbs in well-prepared soil. It's also handy for planting small annuals in spring.

Mail-order sources

A.M. Leonard
www.amleo.com
bulb augers, soil knife, dibble

The Garden Gate Store
www.GardenGateStore.com
bulb auger, soil knife

Amazon
www.amazon.com
bulb planters, augers

This Oxo bulb planter has a quick-release lever that drops the soil out of the planter.

The solution for small bulbs For minor bulbs like grape hyacinth, crocus and snowdrops, a soil knife is really simple to use: Slice it into the soil to the depth you want, rock it back to open a hole, drop in the bulb, slide the blade out and close the hole up again. It works well in lawns if you want to start a patch of naturalized crocuses, and it's easy in prepared soil. The soil knife is narrow enough that I don't make a bigger hole than I need. If you have a narrow trowel in your shed, try it, too. A similar alternative for prepared soils or in containers is a dibble (in the inset), which you usually use for planting seedlings. Open a hole, drop in a bulb, fill the hole. That's all there is to it!

WHAT TO LOOK FOR I really dislike a cheap tool that bends backward when I push it into the soil. Cast or forged tools that aren't welded or riveted to the handle are the least likely to bend or fall apart with use.

Like this soil knife? Get your own plus our *Garden Gate* leather sheath at www.GardenGateStore.com.

BASICS | TOOLS

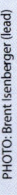

think small, **save time!**

It's often the little things that make your day go well — that just-right cup of coffee, that parking space showing up when you need it. Why not round up a few little things that will make an afternoon in the garden perfect? Whether it's having a hose washer at hand when your watering wand springs a leak or saving yourself the pain of a sunburn, this collection of small items makes gardening more pleasant. Best of all, a lot of them are things you probably have around the house anyway. And several of them have more than one use, maybe even a use you hadn't considered.

Here's my little garden tool kit — I try to have it out in the garden with me, or at least right inside the door so it's easy to find when I need it. This wire-mesh basket is a handy carrier because it's easy to rinse off if it gets a little grimy, and it doesn't hold water. But you could also use a small toolbox or even a plain old bucket. The key is just to keep all these items in one place. That way, you won't waste time looking for them when you're right in the middle of a garden project. Let's take a look at what I carry around!

— Marcia Leeper

Time savers
Keep these often-needed little helpers right at your fingertips.

MAGNIFYING GLASS Once in a while, you notice a plant with drooping or discolored foliage. You can see most insects with the naked eye, but for small ones like spider mites, it's easier to make a quick diagnosis with a magnifying glass. The quicker you identify the problem, the sooner you can save your plant's health.

MEASURING SPOON A lot of fertilizers and garden remedies don't come with measuring scoops. It's tempting to use a kitchen spoon when you're in a hurry, but you don't want to run the risk of contaminating food later. I keep an old plastic measuring spoon with my garden gear so I don't waste products or accidentally overdose my plants with fertilizer.

POCKET PRUNERS If I'm planning to do a lot of heavy-duty pruning, I take my full-size pruners. But during other garden tasks, I like to take care of little cleanup jobs right away. Small pruners like these are perfect for deadheading perennials, and they'll snip a small branch, too. Plus, they fit easily into my basket or even a pocket.

WASHERS I used to keep hose washers in my little basket, but they kept falling out and getting lost. Now I slip two hose washers onto my garden-shed key ring so I can fix a leaky connection right away.

Quick fixes
Repair a leak or control loose stems without having to hunt for supplies.

PLANT TIES Plain old garden twine is handy for many tasks. You never know when you might need to tie up a plant or bundle up some cut stems. I used to carry a whole roll of twine, but it often unspooled and got all tangled up. So now I keep a handful of shorter lengths coiled up together in my garden tote.

DUCT TAPE It's true — you really can fix just about anything with duct tape. It's a great quick fix for a hose puncture (or a tear in the seat of your gardening pants!). I also like to use it for fall or spring cleanup. Wrap it around grasses and other stems to keep them from blowing all over the place when you cut them down. You can learn more about this technique on p. 7 of "Reader Tips."

PUTTY KNIFE This inexpensive tool is a garden wonder. Use it to weed between cracks in pavement, brick or stone, or to grab tiny weeds close to the base of plants. Mud on your tools or shoes? Scrape it off with the putty knife. It's even good for planting small annuals!

SMALL PLIERS You might think of pliers as a home-repair tool, but they're pretty useful outside, too. I keep a pair of small, inexpensive pliers in my garden carryall to pull small saplings and tough-stemmed weeds. Besides, they come in handy for cutting wire or tightening a bolt on a wheelbarrow or gate.

Take care of the skin you're in
While you're caring for your garden, don't forget to take care of yourself.

INSECT REPELLENT I never notice mosquitoes until I'm in the middle of a project, then I hate to trek back to the house for repellent. But in these days of West Nile virus, it's foolish not to take precautions, so I carry insect repellent wipes or a small bottle of spray with me.

ADHESIVE BANDAGES If you get a nick in your skin, cover it quickly to keep dirt out until you have time to clean and disinfect the area. Or if your garden clog or a tool handle is starting to rub your skin, slap a bandage on right away to prevent a blister from forming.

SUNSCREEN Protect your skin with a sunscreen of SPF 30 or higher. You could carry a big bottle, but I like this small-size container with its loop to attach to my belt. That way, I remember to add more sunscreen now and then.

PLASTIC BAGS Those long, thin bags that cover newspapers when they're delivered are perfect quick "gloves" if you need to pull some poison ivy. Place a bag over your hand and arm, pull the weed, then roll the bag down and throw the whole thing away.

Great gift idea
Your friends probably already have wheelbarrows and spades, but a basket of these handy items would make their gardening easier, too. You can collect them all for about $25 (depending on the pruners), and you'll find nearly all of these items at your local hardware store!

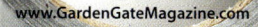

did you know...

Squirrel deterrent
Rowena Low, British Columbia
Are squirrels making you crazy by digging up your plants? Try this tip from Rowena. When she prunes thorny canes from her roses, she doesn't put them in the compost pile. Instead, she lays them carefully around newly planted perennials or bulbs. Then she anchors the canes with landscape pins to keep them in place. You could also cut a wire hanger into 4-inch pieces and bend them into U-shapes to make your own pins. Rowena says the thornier the rose, the better it keeps the squirrels away!

Buried barrier
Cheryl Wissler, Idaho
Cheryl found just how disruptive the tunneling from moles and voles can be in a garden. Rather than try to get rid of them, Cheryl asked her husband, Ed, to build her a raised bed. So he built a 4-by-8-foot frame from 2x6 cedar boards. Using fence staples, Ed attached ½-inch hardware cloth to the bottom of the frame to keep these pests from tunneling up into the bed. The openings in the wire hardware cloth are too small for the moles and voles to get through. Since Cheryl is growing vegetables, the bed is deep enough for their shallow roots.

Hummingbird feeder shake-up
Rose O'Mahony, North Carolina
It's not easy cleaning hummingbird feeders, especially if mold gets a foothold. Rose knows how important it is to keep feeders clean, so she came up with a technique to make quick work of cleaning.

After dumping any remaining nectar, she sprays a couple squirts of a bleach cleaning solution from the store into the feeder to kill the mold. Then she adds a tablespoon of uncooked rice (not the instant kind), replaces the cover and shakes the feeder. The rice works as an abrasive to dislodge the mold. Once the feeder is clean, she throws the contents out and rinses it thoroughly with water. If you're concerned that your cleaning solution is too strong for this, use the recipe recommended by the Hummingbird Society (www.hummingbirdsociety.org) of 1 tablespoon of unscented bleach to 1 quart of water. A clean feeder will keep your hummers happy and healthy.

product pick

Nectar Gem

These airtight pouches of hummingbird nectar prevent spoiling and keep the ants and wasps out. You can toss the pouch when it's empty or wash it in a 1:4 vinegar and water solution to reuse it.

Bottom line Easy to use, easy to keep clean and brings in the hummingbirds.
Source Nectar Gem™ at www.nectargem.com or 800-393-0333
Price $12.99 for two 16-oz. feeders and nectar mix for two replacement pouches

The pressure-sensitive valve is easy for hummingbirds to use but leaves ants and wasps looking elsewhere for food.

in the news

Weeds from birdseed?
Researchers at Oregon State University tested 10 brands of wild bird seed mix commonly sold in retail stores. Along with the feed, they found seed from more than 50 species of weeds! In addition, a short-term study looked at what happens when that same bird seed drops to the soil. The results? Between three and 17 species sprouted and grew from those 10 brands. So does this mean you need to stop feeding the birds? Not at all. Here's what you can do to feed your feathered friends without letting weeds take hold:
- Put out seeds that won't sprout, such as sunflower hearts or peanuts.
- Use feed other than seed, such as peanut butter, raisins, mealworms or plain suet cakes.
- Keep an eye out for sprouting weeds under your feeder and pull them right away.

Save our pollinators
Habitat loss, pesticide use and disease have taken a big toll on the creatures that pollinate our flowers and edible crops. As gardeners, we can be a big help by making our yards pollinator friendly. If you'd like to pitch in but aren't sure where to start, visit www.pollinator.org and download a free "Pollinator Friendly Planting Guide." It's as easy as typing in your zip code. Each guide tells you how to create a yard that butterflies, birds, bats and insects will visit. In addition, there are plant lists so you'll know what to look for when you go shopping.

Have we lost our ladybugs?
There are more than 400 ladybug species native to North America, but did you know that some are now considered rare? The Lost Ladybug Project is trying to find out just how many native species are left. You can help: Visit www.lostladybug.org for tips on identifying and photographing these familiar insects. Then take a look around your garden to see what you can find. Once you've found and photographed a few ladybugs, submit the photos to the Web site. Scientists hope to get a better idea of just how many of the native species are left, which exotic ladybugs are taking over and how this might affect our gardens.

Lantana lunchroom
Lantanas and butterflies just seem to go together. But a study at Auburn University has found some lantana varieties are more popular with these winged wonders than others. Of the 10 varieties tested, 'New Gold' and 'Radiation' got more visits from native butterflies than the other varieties. 'White Doves', 'Firewagon', 'Confetti' and *Lantana montevidensis* were the next most popular plants.

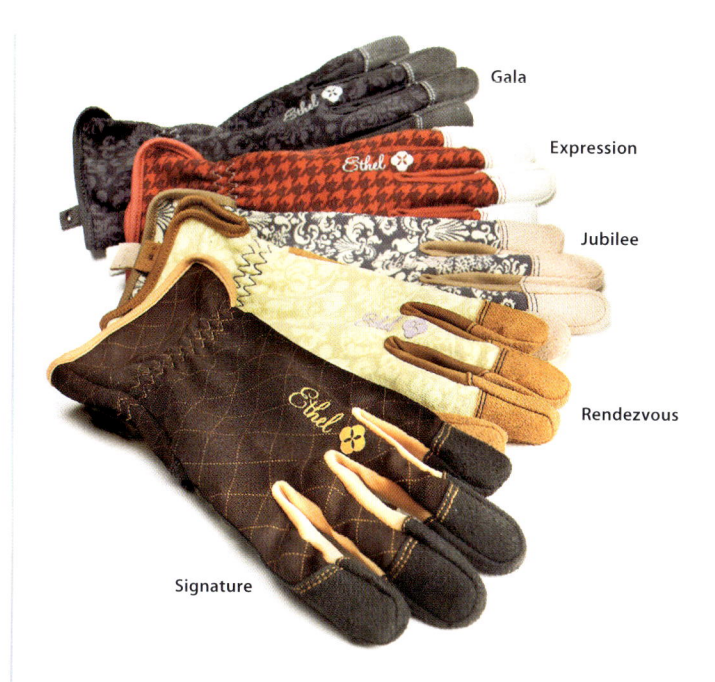

product pick

Ethel gloves

Throw out that old pair of garden gloves and treat yourself to a pair (or two!) of these new Ethel® gloves. They're made of synthetic material that's durable and stretches with your hands. When ours got dirty, we just threw them in the washing machine and they came out almost like new. Reinforced fingertips prevent the ever-present hole that appears on the fingers of everyone's favorite gloves, and the extended cuff keeps dirt from sneaking in. Ethel gloves come in women's sizes small, medium and large. There are five different colors and patterns in all.

Bottom line These are hard-working gloves that are stylish, too.
Source Ethel Gloves at www.ethel-gloves.com or 877-384-4587
Price $18

did you know... (CONTINUED)

Up and over!
Dot Montigillion, West Virginia

Have you ever tried growing overly enthusiastic pole beans or cucumbers on a teepee or fence? Dot had, and wasn't satisfied. The vine would twine over itself, making it hard to find the produce.

Now she grows her veggies on an arbor made of cattle panels like the one in the illustration below. This heavy-duty steel fencing is available at farm supply stores or online at Tractor Supply (www.tractorsupply.com). Cattle panel fencing comes in various sizes and the height of the arch can vary depending on the length of the panels. Dot's roll of fencing was 4 feet wide by 16 feet long.

To create an arch, she had a friend hold one side of the fence while she pulled the rest out and over. This formed an arbor 6½ feet tall with a 5-foot opening. To keep it sturdy, anchor each corner to a steel post driven into the soil with wire or zip ties.

Growing vegetables up instead of out like this has a lot of benefits, besides saving space. Vines are healthier because they get better air circulation and more sunshine, which means there's more produce. Harvesting is easier, too. Just reach up and pick your beans!

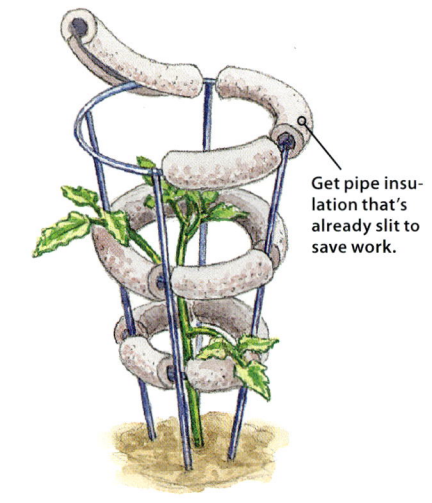

Beans are easier to pick as they hang through the holes in the fencing.

Place steel posts at the corners to help keep the arch sturdy.

Get pipe insulation that's already slit to save work.

A cushier tomato cage
Roxie Reinking, Idaho

Long tomato vines get heavy once the tomatoes start growing. And there's nothing worse than having your hard work (and taste buds) frustrated when vines break because they hang over thin wire tomato cages. Roxie found a solution to keep the plants healthy and the fruit crop coming.

She fits a length of pipe insulation from the hardware store over the top hoop of the cage. Notice how the plant is still young in the illustration? That makes it easier to put the insulation on. If the lower vines grow extra long, go ahead and cover the lower rings, too. With the insulation in place, the vines have a soft resting place, and Roxie has plenty of tomatoes to eat all summer.

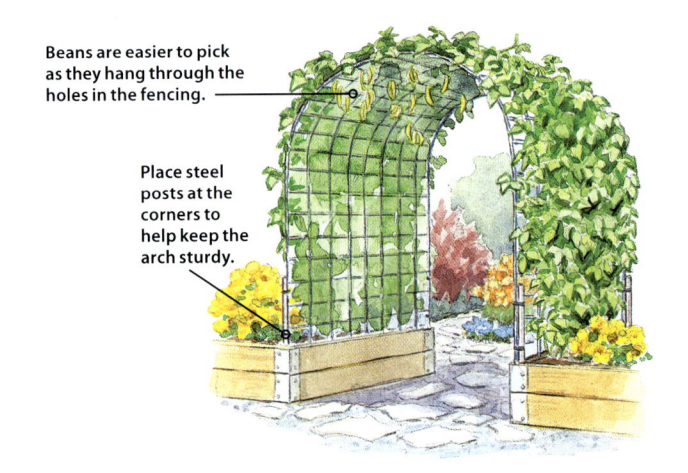

---

product pick

The Truth About Organic Gardening

Confused by all the claims made about organic gardening products? Cut through the hype with this book by Jeff Gillman, professor of horticulture at the University of Minnesota. It's filled with information about organic and synthetic methods of fertilizing, dealing with garden pests, weeds and disease. And it explains the ways these products or materials affect our environment. Each chapter gives some of the basic science behind the products, along with their benefits and drawbacks. What's really helpful is the bottom line statement that sums up what you've just read.

Bottom line You'll get the whole picture on organic gardening with this book.
Source Local and online bookstores and GardenGateStore.com
Price $12.95, 208 pages, softcover

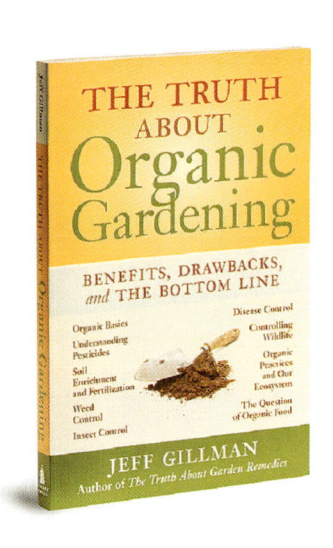

Raspberry patch pointers
Bonnie Wilcoxson, Idaho

Q Can I grow red, gold, black and purple raspberries in the same patch?

A Yes, you can plant different colored raspberries together. They won't cross pollinate, so it won't affect the flowers or fruit. Be sure to start with disease-free plants from a reputable source.

You might want to keep red and gold plants separate from black and purple ones to make maintaining them easier. Red and gold raspberries have upright, suckering habits while the black and purple types have arching canes that come from a single point. Planted together, they could grow into a big mass that would complicate pruning and picking for you.

Plant any combination of the four colors of raspberries and you'll have fresh fruit for most of the summer.

How many veggies?
Lisa Ridley, Georgia

Q I'm planting my first vegetable garden. How many plants do I need to feed my family?

A That all depends on how many people are in your family and how much you like vegetables! The chart at right shows the number of individual plants you'll need to grow vegetables for fresh eating. It also shows how many plants can be grown per foot of row so you can figure out how much space you'll need. For crops such as beans and peas, plant multiple times one to two weeks apart during the growing season. That way, you'll get just the right amount for fresh eating for a longer period of time.

If you really like a vegetable or want to have plenty to share, plant more than is suggested. And if you want to preserve some, do one big planting so you can freeze or can all the produce at one time.

in the news

How many seeds do you need?
Find out exactly how many seeds you need to order this spring at Johnny's Selected Seeds. Visit www.johnnyseeds.com/CustomerService/InteractiveTools/SeedCalculator.aspx and try out the seed calculator. Several drop-down boxes let you choose your form of measure (English or metric), the plant you're interested in and whether you want to direct-sow seed or transplant young plants. Then enter the row length and the calculator will tell you how many seeds or plants you need so you know exactly how many to order!

Fear the freeze no more
Scientists at Miami University and the University of Alabama have developed a spray called "Freeze-Pruf," which improves a plant's cold tolerance by 2.2 to 9.4 degrees F., depending on the species. This solution works kind of like antifreeze by lowering the level at which a plant's tissue is damaged by cold. In addition, Freeze-Pruf prevents ice crystals from forming in a way that damages plant cells. It's been used successfully on palms, house plants, bananas, citrus plants and a variety of flowers. The ingredients are already used in food production so it's safe for vegetables, too. Spray Freeze-Pruf once in the fall, right before a freeze, to extend your tomato season. Or improve your temperature zone by about 200 miles for your favorite banana. If there's been a lot of snow and rain, you may need to reapply it in a couple of months. Developers expect to have Freeze-Pruf available for purchase within the year.

Save trees, get fewer catalogs
When seed catalogs start to fill up your mailbox, don't you wish you could do some thinning? Now you can. Visit Catalog Choice at www.catalogchoice.org and choose to stop receiving the catalogs you get duplicates of or just don't want. Use your customer number from the mailing label for the best success. If the catalog you're looking for isn't there, you can suggest that it be added. The service is free, and Catalog Choice won't sell, rent or share your information with anyone else.

Crop	Per Person	Family of 4
Asparagus (1 plant/ft. of row)	5-10 plants	25 plants
Bush beans (2 plants/ft. of row)	10-12 plants	45 plants
Cucumbers (1 plant/2 ft. of row)	1 vine or 2 bushes	4 vines or 6 bushes
Peas (6 plants/ft. of row)	15-20 plants	70 plants
Peppers (1 plant/ft. of row)	3-5 plants	12-18 plants
Tomatoes (1 plant/2 ft. of row)	2-4 plants	8-12 plants

did you know... (CONTINUED)

Use two nails to mount the rake head. That way you can hang heavier objects without the rake tipping.

Recycle a rake
Darla Weaver, Ohio
While cleaning the clutter out of her garden shed, Darla found an old garden rake that didn't have a handle and wasn't much good for its original purpose anymore. But by attaching it to the wall of the shed, Darla had an instant set of hooks at no cost!

She hung the rake at an easy-to-reach height. See the two nails in the illustration? There's one at each end so something heavy won't throw the rake off balance. You could also attach it to the wall with 1¼-inch fence staples. The steel rake tines face out, forming small hooks that can hold trowels, pruning shears and other small tools. Darla even stores her gardening gloves there by laying them on top of the tines.

Get organized!
Patricia Stevens, Washington
Patricia found rummaging through boxes and drawers in search of plant tags frustrating. One day while cleaning her son's room, she discovered the solution. Those plastic storage pages for sports cards were perfect for holding plant tags. Most tags fit just fine but you may need to cut off the pointed end that goes into the soil to make them fit. The clear plastic makes it easy to see both sides of the tag with a turn of the page. And because each page has holes punched along the edge, it fits in a three-ring binder. Now Patricia's plant tags are right at her fingertips whenever she needs them.

Slip-on shoes
Katherine Raye, Washington
Changing shoes every time you take a break from gardening and come in the house can be a pain. Katherine found a simple, inexpensive way to modify her favorite old sneakers — elastic! After removing the shoe laces, she put the shoes on and pulled an 18-inch piece of ¼-inch elastic through the top two sets of eyelets and tied a tight bow. (The length of the elastic may vary, depending on the size and type of shoe.) With elastic in the eyelets instead of shoestrings, it's easy for Katherine to get her feet in and out with no trouble. Now when she needs to come in for a quick drink of water or to cool down, she can slip her shoes off and back on easily.

product pick

Garden boots

Midsummer Black pattern

How would you like to have footwear as colorful as your garden? You can with these new garden boots from Sloggers. Wide openings make it easy to tuck in your pant legs and there are firm insoles to support your feet. These waterproof boots come in women's sizes 6 to 10 and there are four patterns and two solid colors to suit anyone's taste.

Bottom line These boots keep your feet dry and comfortable and they're just plain fun.
Source Local garden centers or Sloggers at www.sloggerstore.com or call 877-750-4437
Price $39.99

product picks

Powergear bypass pruners

It's not unusual to find you have sore hands and wrists, maybe even a blister or two, after a long session of pruning shrubs or deadheading perennials. Save your hands with the new Powergear® pruners from Fiskars®. With ergonomic handles, these pruners are almost effortless to use. What's unique about the Powergear is that the bottom handle rotates smoothly on a ratchet as you squeeze the handles together, which helps prevent fatigue. Powergear bypass pruners come in two sizes, too, so you can pick the ones that work best for your hand size. In fact, they're so comfortable that the Arthritis Foundation has awarded Powergear bypass pruners its Ease-of-Use Commendation. Powergear pruners come with a lifetime warranty.

Bottom line These are comfortable, easy-to-use pruners and are reasonably priced, too!
Source Local hardware stores or Fiskars at www.fiskars.com
Price $29.99

Garden Gear Organizer

How many times have you gone digging through a bag or cupboard searching for your twine, only to find it at the back of a drawer? You'll find your stuff a lot faster if it's stashed in this new Garden Gear Organizer. Made of heavy-duty cotton canvas, it's 44 inches long and 23 inches wide so it holds plenty of what you need to work in the garden. Stash seed packets, hardware or other small items in the clear vinyl pockets so you can see what's there right away. The deeper bottom pockets work well for bulkier items like your kneeling pad. Dirty gloves or tools leave a mark? Use a damp cloth to wipe it away. Up top are three sturdy steel rivets to hang your organizer from hooks on the wall. You can also use the over-the-door holder, like the one in the photo, that comes with it. No matter what you're storing there's a clip, loop or pocket to hold it.

Bottom line This will help you get organized so you can spend more time in the garden instead of looking for your supplies.
Source Gardener's Supply Co. at www.gardeners.com or 888-833-1412
Price $49.95

did you know... (CONTINUED)

Cover the lawn with a layer of cardboard and several inches of compost where you want your new bed.

An easy way to make a bed
Cheryl Hansen, Tennessee

Q *I'd like to start a flower bed in my lawn next spring. Is there an easy way to kill the grass?*

A You could hand dig, use a rototiller or rent a sod cutter to remove the sod where you want your new bed. But those involve a lot of work. There are a couple of ways to create a bed without having to remove the sod first. The easiest way is to mow the area and kill the grass by applying a herbicide like Roundup®. Be sure to spray only on calm days to prevent killing any surrounding plants or lawn. In about a week the grass will turn brown and you can dig holes and plant in the bed. You can till in the dead grass or remove it and add it to the compost pile, if you prefer, but you don't have to.

A chemical-free way to do it is to simply smother the grass and let it compost right in the bed. Cover the area with cardboard or five or six layers of newspaper. On top, pile several inches of organic material like compost, grass clippings, shredded leaves, kitchen parings, chipped prunings or rotted manure. Keep all the material moist so it'll break down. Do this in fall and by spring you'll have a nice loam that you can plant in. After planting, top your bed with a couple inches of mulch, such as wood chips or shredded leaves, to help hold in moisture.

Nutshells on the compost pile
Jon Baker, Colorado

Q *Is it OK to put nutshells in the compost pile?*

A Most nutshells make great additions to the compost pile. However, don't add walnut husks and shells, as they contain juglone, a chemical that can prevent some plants from growing properly.

Before adding nutshells, crush them into small pieces so they'll break down faster. Put them in an old pillow case and break them with a hammer (this will probably destroy the pillow case). Since they're a high-carbon ingredient, mix the crushed shells with a high-nitrogen ingredient, like manure or fresh grass clippings, before adding them to the pile. The fresh manure and grass clippings will help the nutshells break down into compost faster.

New-plant screen
Frank Bondzinski, Illinois

Once new transplants are in the ground, a little shelter from the sun and wind can help get them off to a strong start. Frank gives new hostas, ferns and other plants a helping hand with old political yard signs. After an election, these signs end up in the trash, so they're easy to come by. Frank collects a few to keep on hand for the following spring.

Creating a plant shelter is easy. Just push the metal legs into the ground so the bottom of the sign touches the soil. For taller plants, "stack" signs by taping two together with duct tape. If the stacked signs are too floppy, use a couple of bamboo stakes to keep them upright.

No more lost bulbs
Evelyn Henry, New York

Like a lot of us, Evelyn would sometimes accidentally dig up her old bulbs when she was planting new ones in the fall. She found that clear plastic utensils help her avoid this. When the bulb foliage has ripened, Evelyn pulls out the brown leaves and replaces them with a plastic fork, knife or spoon. Because the utensils are clear, they don't show in the garden during the growing season.

product picks

Easy Bloom

Looking for an easy way to find out which plants will grow best in your garden? Or maybe you're wondering why some plants aren't doing well. Give Easy Bloom a try. This little sensor monitors light, temperature, water and humidity. Leave it in the garden for a few hours or next to a plant on your desk at work, then hook up the sensor to the USB port on your computer. It connects you to the Easy Bloom Web site, where you can access a plant database of more than 5,000 entries and see which plants will work for you.

This gizmo is easy to use and comes with a detailed instruction manual. Or, if you prefer, get on the Web site and walk through the process that way. In addition, once you've registered (don't worry, it's free), you have access to all those plant profiles online. The information is somewhat limited, though, and won't work for more specialized plants, such as cactus. But it is a helpful tool for beginning gardeners or anyone who has moved and has a new garden to set up.

Bottom line It's easy to use and a good way to get specific plant recommendations for your garden.
Source Burpee at www.burpee.com or 800-333-5808
Price $59.99

Write + Erase Plant Tags

You won't forget which hosta you've planted or which zinnia variety you have this year with these new labels. Made of rubber, they're UV treated so they won't deteriorate in the sun. And as long as you use gel-ink pens, you can erase the name with soap and water at the end of the growing season and use it again next year with a different plant. (If some of the writing remains, use a little rubbing alcohol to get rid of it.) Each tag has a decorative image on one side. There are two sets: The Botanical series has colorful flower silhouettes, while the Herb series has silhouettes of common herbs in shades of green.

Bottom line A pretty and durable way to identify your favorite plants.
Source Allsop at 866-425-5767 or www.allsopgarden.com or www.GardenGateStore.com
Price $15.99 to $19.99 for a set of 6

did you know... (CONTINUED)

If the lid doesn't have ventilation holes like these, poke a few. Good air circulation helps prevent disease.

Carry-out seed starter
Tamara Westphal, New York
Tamara doesn't spend a lot of money on fancy seed-starting setups — she just cleans and reuses the plastic containers that rotisserie chickens come in.

Place moistened seed-starting mix in the bottom tray. (You may want to poke a few holes in the bottom for drainage.) Plant the seeds according to directions, sprinkle water over the top and snap on the lid. Tamara finds she doesn't need to water much because condensation on the lid trickles down into the soil. Her recycled seed pan fits in the windowsill, but you could also place it under a grow light.

Once the seedlings have a second set of leaves, move them up to larger pots. If the weather is warm enough, you can plant them outside.

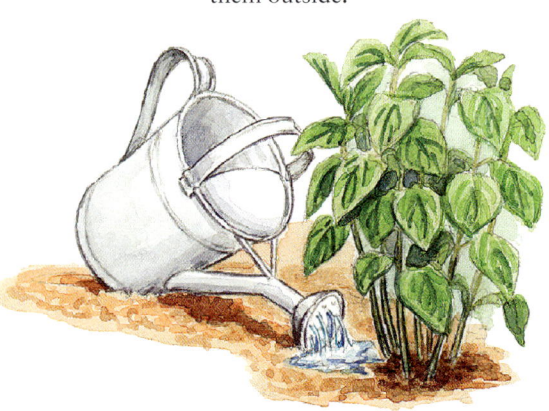

Water as you weed
Sarah Hamilton, Iowa
There's a lot to do to keep a garden looking good, and it can be hard to stay on top of both the weeding and the watering. But Sarah gets both jobs done quickly with a simple trick. She fills her watering can and tips the can so the rose at the end of the spout sits on the soil next to a plant. You can see the angle in the illustration above. As the water gently pours through the holes, she has time to pull a few weeds in the vicinity. When the water stops flowing, she pours the rest out, fills the can and moves on to the next thirsty plant.

Make your own watering can
Michelle McNeel, Illinois
Big watering cans can be expensive. But Michelle has found that an empty laundry detergent container works just as well for watering and doesn't cost her a thing. Plus, reusing it means it doesn't end up in the local landfill.

To start, she rinses the jug thoroughly to get all the soap out. Then she uses an ice pick to make 10 to 12 holes in the lid. You could use a nail or an electric drill, too. The holes give her the option of "sprinkling" the water lightly on the plants instead of pouring it. Once the jug is filled with water and the lid is screwed back on, it's easy to carry around, and she doesn't worry about water slopping out of the opening on top, either.

Cap that soaker hose
Mary Nall, Missouri
Soaker hoses are a great way to water. Mary likes to keep the end that connects to the supply hose capped between uses so mulch and soil don't sneak in, clogging the tiny soaker holes. She discovered that the white vinyl caps you put on furniture legs work really well. Check the size of your hose before buying caps as sizes vary. One other benefit: See how easy that white cap is to spot in the mulch?

Check the size of your garden hose before buying this vinyl furniture leg cap as sizes vary.

Perennial fertilizer schedule
Carolyn Foust, Iowa

Q Is it true you shouldn't fertilize perennials after July 4?

A Actually, lots of perennials put on most of their growth after July 4, so you can continue your regular fertilizing schedule through the summer.

In zones with frigid winter temperatures, stop feeding perennials water-soluble fertilizers that promote new foliage growth (Miracle-Gro® 24-8-16, for example) around Labor Day. Continuing to feed plants after that won't let them slow down growth in preparation for winter dormancy.

Instead, in fall when weather cools, give perennials a dose of fertilizer high in phosphorus (the middle number), such as 5-10-5. This promotes strong roots to help your plants survive winter and get an early start on next year's growth. If you don't get it done in fall, you can also apply this in early spring, as the daffodils start to bloom. You'll encourage good root development and healthy plants to start the new season.

Strong, upright seedlings grow when the light is kept very close.

Great way to start
Staci Parent, Nebraska

Q I started seeds inside, but now I'm worried because the plants are spindly and leaning. What's wrong?

A If the seedlings you start don't get enough bright light, the young plants will stretch and become very leggy. Light is very important to seedlings. You can start seeds in a south-facing window, but they'll do better if you set up an artificial light source for them.

They don't need fancy grow lights — basic shop lights with one warm-white and one cool-white fluorescent bulb work just as well. Use chains to hang the light over the flat so you can move it up as the seedlings grow. Always keep the light no more than 3 inches above the tops of the plants. See the difference in the illustration above? If you notice the seedlings starting to lean to one side, rotate the tray 180 degrees so they'll straighten up again.

Keeping the light too high will make seedlings "stretch."

product pick

Sprout House and Relocation Station

Your seeds won't miss a beat when you grow them in the Sprout House (at left) and move them up to the Relocation Station (below right). The pots are made of biodegradable coconut coir, which is easy for roots to grow in and through. Since there's no need to dig the plants out of plastic cell packs, the roots aren't disturbed, so there's less chance of transplant shock. Our pansy seedlings here didn't miss a beat when we moved them up to the bigger pots of the Relocation Station.

Each kit comes with Wonder Soil®, a compressed potting mix with added worm castings. Just pour water onto the pellets in each pot and the mix expands to fill it perfectly.

Bottom line Roots grow through these biodegradable pots with ease and keep seedlings growing strong.
Source Gardener's Edge at 888-556-5676 or www.gardencrsedge.com or Garden Gate Store at www.GardenGateStore.com
Price $29.98 for both

This small water reservoir holds the overflow so you don't have to water quite as often.

These larger Relocation Station pots go directly in the garden when plants are ready.

did you know... (CONTINUED)

Trunk flare

Spread the roots over a cone of soil to keep the tree from sinking.

Annual or perennial?
Pam Bradberry, Arkansas

Q Could you please explain the exact difference between an annual and a perennial?
A Annuals complete their life cycle in just one year. Starting as seeds in spring, they grow, flower, produce seed, then die in fall or winter. Popular annual flowers include zinnias, marigolds, petunias and impatiens. You'll need to plant new seeds or seedlings each year.

Perennials, such as daylilies, hostas, peonies and coneflowers, grow for two or more years. They sprout, grow, flower and produce seed just like the annuals, but they'll come up again next spring. Typically perennials have shorter periods of bloom than annuals, but you don't have to replant them every year.

Fascinating fasciation
Chris Thompson, Michigan

Q One of my lilies has a huge flower head and the stem is flattened and crowded with leaves. What's going on?
A It's called "fasciation" and often looks like several stems have fused together into one flattened stem with lots more leaves.

Experts aren't sure what causes fasciation. Some think it's caused by a virus; others think bacteria are responsible. Either way, it doesn't spread to other plants — you can leave the stems or remove them. This growth is unpredictable and likely won't return next year. Some fasciated plants are propagated by stem cuttings to keep the unusual growth. That's how you get crested saguaro cactus and fantail willow.

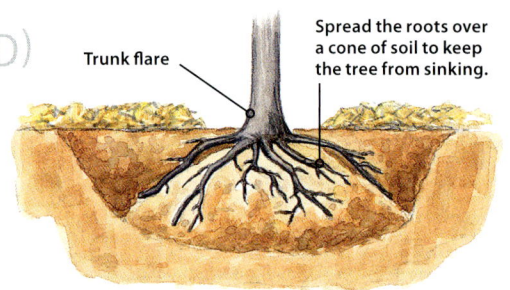

Find the flare
Carlie May, Iowa

Q When planting bare-root trees, how do you know where the "trunk flare" is?
A The "trunk flare" is the union between the trunk and the roots where the trunk widens slightly. When properly planted, a tree's shape should have the gradual transition from trunk to ground that you see in the illustration above. If it looks like a telephone pole sticking straight out of the ground, it's been planted too deeply and the trunk flare is underground.

Your planting hole should be just deep enough so the trunk flare sits slightly above the ground. It should be wide enough to fit all of the roots without trimming or cramping. When in doubt, it's better to plant the tree too shallow than too deep (where there is less oxygen and water available to the roots). Build a cone of soil in the bottom of the hole, as shown in the illustration, to provide a firm foundation so it doesn't sink or lean as the soil settles. Spread the roots out and fill the hole halfway with soil. Then water it to remove any air pockets. Finish backfilling, gently tamp and water again. Top it off with 2 inches of bark mulch. Make sure your tree gets an inch of water each week. In windy spots, stake bare-root trees for the first year to keep them standing tall.

What's the difference?
Gene Hamlish, Iowa

Q I'd like some bulbs that'll grow in my lawn in early spring. What's the difference between bulbs that naturalize and those that perennialize?
A A planted bulb that grows and blooms for at least three years in a row is considered a good perennializer. The same bulb regrows and may increase in size, but doesn't really spread. A bulb that will not only return but also multiplies and spreads is considered a good naturalizer. These work well growing in a lawn. You'll find four good early to midspring-blooming naturalizers at right. Some grow better in some regions than others — we'll let you know which are best where. When growing naturalizers in the lawn, try to let the bulb foliage turn yellow before you mow the grass in spring.

'Ice Follies' daffodil is a good naturalizer.

Checkered lily (*Fritillaria meleagris*) 6 to 12 in. tall, 6 in. wide; checkered, bell-shaped purple or white flowers; tolerates wet soil; cold-hardy in USDA zones 3 to 8; heat-tolerant in AHS zones 8 to 1

Daffodils (*Narcissus* hybrid) 4 to 24 in. tall; 4 to 12 in. wide; white, cream, yellow, or orange flowers; different cultivars thrive in nearly every region; cold-hardy in USDA zones 3 to 9; heat-tolerant in AHS zones 9 to 1

Snowdrops (*Galanthus nivalis*) 4 to 9 in. tall; 2 to 3 in. wide; lightly fragrant white flowers; plant grows in many areas but flowers last longest in temperatures below about 60 degrees; cold-hardy in USDA zones 3 to 9; heat-tolerant in AHS zones 9 to 1

Spring snowflake (*Leucojum vernum*) 6 to 12 in. tall, 12 to 18 in. wide; white or green flowers; very cold-hardy but also adapts to hot spring temps in Southern gardens; cold-hardy in USDA zones 3 to 9; heat-tolerant in AHS zones 9 to 1

Use your largest bit and drill several holes a few inches deep into the stump.

So long, suckers!
Don Martin, Washington

Q How can I get rid of all of the suckers sprouting from the stump of a willow tree I cut down?

A The suckers are coming up from the tree's stump and the roots. One solution is to remove the stump by digging out the surrounding soil and cutting off the roots. Hire a tree company to grind out the old stump.

If you don't want to go to that much work or expense, there are other solutions. For a stump less than 8 inches in diameter, cut it down as close to the ground as possible with a handsaw or chainsaw. Then mow off any suckers with a lawn mower. If you're persistent, this will eventually kill the stump.

You can also kill a larger stump (either freshly cut or an older one) by helping it to break down faster. Drill several holes in it like the stump at left and wet it down to encourage the wood to rot. Place a high-nitrogen fertilizer in the holes and on the surface of the stump. (It's a good way to get rid of leftover lawn fertilizer.) Keep the material wet or use a 4-inch layer of bark mulch to hold in moisture and speed up the process even more. Check the stump from time to time, and apply more nitrogen or compost. Stump removal chemicals from the garden center can speed up decomposition.

The chemical route is to prune the suckers off and paint the freshly cut surfaces of the suckers and the edge of the bark with brush killer. Use one containing triclopyr, such as Roundup® Poison Ivy Plus Tough Brush Killer. In the illustration below, you can see how a small brush gives you the most precision so you don't put chemicals anywhere that you don't need them. It may take several applications and one to six weeks to kill the stump.

Paint brush killer on the freshly cut suckers and at the edge of the stump, where the tree will take up the chemicals.

Use two tension rods to hang the curtain between the ribs of the roof panel.

Need to move your plant? No problem, you can move the curtain, too.

Greenhouse shades
Patricia Peters, Ohio

Greenhouses are great for keeping plants warm in winter, but sometimes the bright summer sun is too hot. Ready-made products to shade your greenhouse are expensive, so Patricia came up with her own version made of woven landscape fabric, not plastic (it's difficult to sew and holds too much moisture). She cut a piece of fabric the same size as the 24-inch wall panel and sewed a 2-inch hem in one end. Then she ran a tension rod through it and hung the curtain between the ribs on one of the panels, like in the illustration above. As the sun moves across the horizon during the year, it's simple to move the curtain. Or if a plant needs to be moved, the curtain goes, too. Patricia made a similar curtain for the roof panels using the same fabric but with a casing at both ends for two tension rods. Now Patricia can keep her greenhouse plants happy no matter how bright the sun is.

Quick cuts
June Grimm, Michigan

Fall garden cleanup is easier with the shortcut June uses. Instead of pulling the annuals that she grew in her perennial bed, she waits until a hard frost kills the plants and cuts the stems off at the soil line with a soil knife. (You can use pruners for this, too.) That way, the roots are left to decompose, adding organic material to the soil. And she's not disturbing the roots of nearby perennials, either. June finds this works best with soft-stemmed annuals like begonias, coleus and impatiens. Annuals with woody stems, such as marigolds and cosmos, are harder to cut and the roots don't rot as quickly.

beneficials you should know

Little brown bat
Myotis lucifugus

IDENTIFICATION Long feared as dark-winged predators of the night, little brown bats are actually great to have flitting around your garden.

These airborne mammals eat thousands of flying insect pests each night, including mosquitoes, flies, moths and beetles. One bat can devour more than 600 mosquitoes in an hour — that's 10 bugs a minute! In the summertime, bats will eat almost half their weight in insects every night. A little brown bat weighs only ¼ to ⅓ ounce and is 3 to 4 in. long, with a wingspan of 6 to 8 in. Its large ears help the little brown bat echolocate, or hear a high-pitched frequency that helps it to "see" insects in the dark.

LIFE CYCLE This bat is found everywhere in the United States and in parts of southern Canada and northern Mexico.

Little brown bats have one offspring, or pup, a year. The pup hangs onto its mother for the first few days after birth, even when she's flying! In three weeks, it is ready to fly on its own and begin hunting insects. Unlike other small mammals that live only a year or two, the little brown bat can live up to 32 years.

To attract bats to your garden, plant flowers like nicotiana, four o'clocks, petunias and moonflower, which are food sources for night-pollinating insects. Once the bats show up, they're sure to make a dent in the local mosquito population, too. Avoiding insecticides whenever possible and providing a water source will also encourage bats to make your yard their hunting ground.

Bats migrate to caves, cellars, tunnels, attics or old buildings to hibernate as temperatures and insect populations drop in late autumn. Although they're great to have in the yard, you don't want them spending the winter in your house. Make sure you seal all openings that are larger than ½ in.—bats can get into some pretty tiny spaces. ☐

Minute pirate bug
Orius tristicolor

IDENTIFICATION It may be tiny, but this ¼-in.-long bug has a big appetite — for other bugs, that is. The minute pirate bug is most common in the western United States and Canada. It has an oval shaped body with black and white wings like the one in the illustration.

Both the adult and nymph form of the minute pirate bug will eat just about any small insect. Thrips, mites and aphids are some of its favorites. That makes this feisty little bug a big asset in the garden. When prey is scarce, the minute pirate bug feeds on pollen and plant sap.

If you pick up a minute pirate bug, watch out! It will bite. Reactions range from nothing other than the initial discomfort to a small bump similar to a mosquito bite, without the itch. Think you've seen this bug in the Midwest? It's probably the insidious flower bug (*O. insidiosus*), a close cousin.

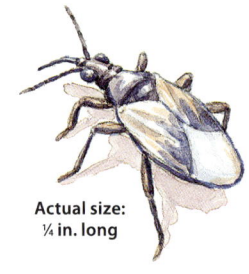

Actual size: ¼ in. long

LIFE CYCLE In spring, minute pirate bugs lay eggs in plant stems or leaf tissues. Eggs hatch in three to five days, and the nymphs immediately start looking for small insects on which to feed. It takes about 20 days and five stages for a minute pirate bug to reach adulthood. Then it lives about a month and dies. Several generations of this bug can occur over the course of a growing season.

You probably already have minute pirate bugs or insidious flower bugs in your garden. But to keep them around and perhaps attract a few more, avoid spraying insecticides. Also, grow flat-topped flowers like daisies and yarrow, whose pollen is easy to get at. That way, these little garden helpers will have something to keep them going once they've whittled down the pest population in your garden. ☐

Bull snake
Pituophis catenifer sayi

Actual size: 3 to 6 ft. long

IDENTIFICATION Snakes may give you the creeps, but the bull snake is one of the good guys. You'll find it and its close relative, the gopher snake, all over the United States, Canada and parts of northern Mexico. Neither snake is poisonous — they constrict their prey. Hunting by day, the bull snake looks for mice, rabbits, rats and just about any rodent it can catch. So you can see why it might be good for a gardener to have this reptile around.

The bull snake is tan to brown, fading to white around the neck with large dark spots all over the top part of its body. When startled, it hisses loudly and vibrates its tail and is sometimes mistaken for a rattlesnake. But rattlesnakes have wide heads, narrow necks and chunky bodies that end in blunt, rattle-filled tails. The bull snake, in this photo, is long and slender with a pointed tail. If a bull snake feels threatened, it can inflict a painful, but not dangerous, bite.

LIFE CYCLE In early spring, the hibernating bull snake wakes and emerges from its den to warm up in the sun, shed its skin and mate. Females lay three to 24 large eggs in sandy soil, beneath rocks or logs. Eggs hatch in two to three months. Baby snakes are 12 to 18 in. long and are grayer in color than adults. These young snakes are ready to start hunting small mice and other rodents right away.

Like all reptiles, the bull snake can't maintain its own body temperature, so it will seek sun or shade depending on how hot or cold it is. Most hunting is done in the early morning and evening hours. As fall turns into winter, it'll seek shelter in an underground burrow, where it can hibernate through the cold weather. ☐

PHOTO: Bull snake courtesy of the U.S. Fish and Wildlife Service

pests to watch

Squash vine borer
Melittia cucurbitae

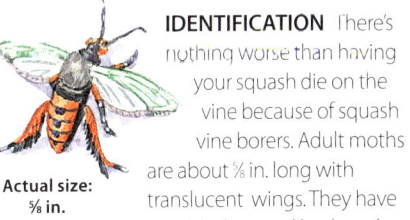

Actual size: ⅝ in.

IDENTIFICATION There's nothing worse than having your squash die on the vine because of squash vine borers. Adult moths are about ⅝ in. long with translucent wings. They have an orange and black striped body with fringed hind legs. Females emerge in spring to lay pinhead-sized eggs on the lower 3 to 4 ft. of squash vines.

Once the eggs hatch, the larvae bore into the stem and start eating. They grow up to an inch long with a white body and brown head. Larvae live and eat in the vine for four to six weeks, then move from the plant into the soil, where they spend the winter in a cocoon.

DAMAGE Squash, zucchini, pumpkins and gourds are all susceptible to attack by these pests. Their favorite variety is Hubbard squash. Butternut squash, cucumbers and melons are less palatable but are sometimes affected. If the vines in your garden suddenly wilt, take a look at the base of the plant. Look for small holes in the vine, along with an accumulation of sawdustlike material. That's frass, the debris larvae produce as they eat their way through the vine. As they eat, the larvae cut off water and nutrients, which kills the plant.

CONTROL Because squash vine borer larvae are inside the vine, it's difficult to get rid of them. But if you keep at it, you can minimize damage.

In late spring, spray the vines weekly with an insecticidal soap to smother the eggs. Or spray the vine with B$_t$ before the eggs hatch. This natural insecticide is safe to use on vegetables but needs to be eaten by the pest to be effective. (Find out more about this and other green pesticides on p. 258.) In fall, destroy the vines as soon as possible after harvest to get rid of any remaining larvae. If you can till the soil to expose any cocoons to cold and predators, that will help, too. ☐

Actual size: 1 in.

Bacterial leaf scorch

IDENTIFICATION You wouldn't be surprised to find a few brown leaves on a tree near the end of summer. But take a close look: Do the leaves have an irregular pattern of browning with a pale yellow or red band between the brown and healthy green leaf tissue? If so, it could be bacterial leaf scorch. This disease, caused by the bacterium *Xylella fastidiosa*, clogs the plant's water-conducting tissues. It's spread by spittlebugs, leafhoppers and treehoppers as they feed and is mostly confined to the Eastern and Southern United States. Sycamore, mulberry, maple, dogwood, American elm and several species of oak trees are affected.

DAMAGE Symptoms start showing up in early summer and get worse by autumn. Each tree species is affected a little differently, but generally you'll notice premature browning, or scorching, of leaves first. As browning spreads toward the middle of the leaf, the edges curl in and the leaf may drop off the tree. Each year more leaves turn brown. Then twigs and whole branches start to die and growth is stunted. Once weakened by this, the tree becomes vulnerable to other infections or infestations. It can take as long as five to 10 years for the whole tree to die.

CONTROL There's no cure for bacterial leaf scorch. It can usually be diagnosed by symptoms alone but for a definitive diagnosis, check with your local extension agency. If you need time to select and plant a new tree, you can keep the old tree going by hiring an arborist to administer trunk injections to suppress the symptoms. Or delay the development of the disease by removing infected limbs and avoiding drought stress. Mulching around the tree and watering during dry spells will help keep moisture even. Whatever treatment you choose, the tree will eventually need to be removed. ☐

Bacterial leaf scorch starts at the outer edges of the leaf and moves inward.

Emerald ash borer
Agrilus planipennis Fairmaire

IDENTIFICATION If you have an ash tree (*Fraxinus* spp.), keep an eye out for emerald ash borer. Native to Asia, this pest is a serious problem in Michigan, Indiana, Ohio and Ontario. Several surrounding states, on the map below, have infestations to a lesser degree.

Emerald ash borers (EAB) are slender with metallic green wing covers. But you don't have to see the insects to know that they're there. Adults chew small, ⅛-in.-diameter D-shaped exit holes in the tree in spring. Soon after they emerge, females start laying eggs in the crevices of ash tree bark. Larvae burrow back into the tree bark to overwinter, pupating into adulthood in early spring.

DAMAGE Adult emerald ash borers feed on leaves and don't do a lot of damage. It's the larvae, which feed under the bark of the tree, that cause problems. They disrupt the flow of water and nutrients, which eventually girdles and kills the tree. The tree can die within two years of initial symptoms. White, green and black ash trees are equally tasty to EABs. Dieback usually starts in the top third of the canopy and works downward.

CONTROL New treatment methods provide hope that this pest can be beaten. The new pesticide Tree-äge™ did very well in 2007, its first year of use. It's applied every other year by trunk injection and can only be purchased and applied by certified arborists or landscapers. In Canada, a similar treatment, TreeAzin™, is working, too. Predatory wasps native to China have been released in Indiana, where results are still pending.

You can help prevent movement of EAB by not transporting firewood or logs from quarantined states to others. For more information check out www.emeraldashborer.info. If you suspect your tree has an infestation, contact your local extension agency to report it. ☐

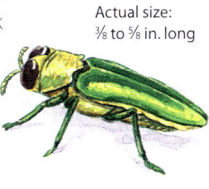

Actual size: ⅜ to ⅝ in. long

EAB larvae burrow into bark, leaving behind a maze of winding tunnels as they feed.

www.GardenGateMagazine.com

6 weeds to know

Curly dock
Rumex crispus

IDENTIFICATION With its attractive green flowers on 5-ft.-tall stalks, and its stems and leaf margins that turn red-brown in fall, curly dock is rather pretty — for a weed. Even many waterfowl and songbirds like the tasty seeds. But you probably don't want this common perennial weed in your garden.

Also known as sour dock or yellow dock, it's common across much of North America. A basal rosette of long, wavy leaves comes up in fall. Early the next summer, a flower stalk emerges from the rosette with green blooms that turn red-brown as they age. Curly dock spreads by seed and root pieces.

FAVORITE CONDITIONS Found in meadows, lawns and landscapes, curly dock prefers moist, undisturbed areas like around culverts or low-lying areas that have occasional standing water. But you can find it in your garden beds and lawn, too.

CONTROL It's easiest to eradicate young seedlings in fall, before they get established. Because this weed has a long taproot, pulling the plant can be difficult. To make it easier, moisten the soil or wait until after a rain. Regular mowing, or cutting off the top of the plant just under the soil, will remove the flower stalk and prevent seed production. However, the deep roots will remain and continue to grow back. Selective broadleaf herbicides are effective, especially for plants growing in lawn situations. Be careful when using herbicides near other plants and always follow all label instructions. ☐

Long taproot

1st year rosette
2nd year growth

Fuller's teasel
Dipsacus fullonum

IDENTIFICATION Originally introduced from Europe for use as a dried flower, Fuller's teasel has naturalized in much of North America. The first year, this biennial forms a rosette of oblong leaves that may grow to nearly 12 in. long. During the second year, several flower stalks with spines shoot up nearly 6 ft. The spiny, egg-shaped lavender flowers bloom from June to October. After flowering and producing seed, the plant dies.

FAVORITE CONDITIONS Fuller's teasel prefers open, sunny sites like roadsides and disturbed areas, although it may grow in your lawn or garden. It's a particular pest for restored prairies and wildlife areas because each plant is capable of producing more than 2,000 seeds and most of them will germinate. Under favorable growing conditions, it can actually out-compete native prairie plants.

CONTROL As with all biennial weeds, it's easier to manage Fuller's teasel in the rosette stage. Use a dandelion-puller to pull out the long tap root or slice it off, below the soil, with a sharp spade. And as with dandelions, be sure to get as much of the root as possible so it won't resprout. You can cut off the flower head to prevent it from going to seed. Herbicides that contain triclopyr or glyphosate can also be used, but are most effective when applied while the plants are in the rosette stage before they flower. ☐

Stinging nettle
Urtica dioica

IDENTIFICATION If you've ever walked along a wooded path, you've probably encountered stinging nettle. This perennial weed, with bright- to dark-green leaves, can grow to 3 to 6 ft. high. The square stems are covered with fine hairs, which break and release a sap when you brush against the plant. If the sap gets on your skin, it causes a stinging feeling that lasts for a few minutes or longer, depending on how sensitive you are. From May to October, pale green flowers open along the stem between the leaves.

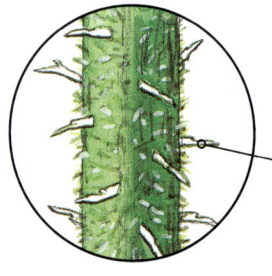

FAVORITE CONDITIONS You'll find stinging nettle in damp, fertile, shady locations. In the wild it grows well along stream banks and at the edge of wooded areas. But it'll also tolerate more sunny spots, such as an open field or roadside. In the garden, stinging nettle may pop up on bare soil, too.

CONTROL Stinging nettle spreads by seed and by rhizomes, which allow it to colonize an area quickly. To control small patches or individual plants, pull them by hand, but be sure to wear long sleeves and gloves so you don't get "stung." If you're dealing with a large colony of plants, try mowing them off and using a garden fork to remove the roots. Herbicides, such as glyphosate or 2, 4-D, are also effective and spraying them keeps you from coming in contact with the plant. ☐

Needlelike hairs on square stems

Dandelion
Taraxacum officinale

IDENTIFICATION Dandelions can be found throughout most of North America and are easily identifiable by their yellow blossoms. Depending on where you live, you may find this perennial blooming from March until frost. The flowers sprout from the center of a low rosette of jagged leaves. Each flower is held on a single hollow stalk that can be from 2 in. to almost 2 ft. tall. Break this stem or the root or pull off a leaf, and it will exude a sticky white liquid. After the flower fades, it's followed by a fluffy seedhead. The short hairs attached to each seed allow it to be carried great distances by even the slightest breeze.

FAVORITE CONDITIONS Although they're usually found in lawns, dandelions grow in almost any sunny spot where there's enough soil and moisture for the seeds to take hold. They can even take up residence in cracks in your sidewalk or driveway. However, you'll rarely find this pest growing in heavy shade.

CONTROL Pulling dandelions by hand can be successful if you can get them out before the taproot grows deep. For the best success, try pulling when the soil is wet. Once the plant's established, the root can grow several feet deep. If the taproot breaks and remains in the soil, it will resprout. Herbicides are most effective if you apply them when the weed's actively growing in spring or fall. Even so, if the plant's in full bloom when you spray, it may have enough energy to produce a crop of seeds before it dies. After you apply the herbicide, wait a day to allow the chemical to enter the plant's system and then cut the flower stems to the ground.

— Tap root

Puncturevine
Tribulus terrestris

IDENTIFICATION Don't grab this annual weed and pull! After the five-petaled yellow flowers fade, they're replaced with hard seed clusters. Each cluster is divided into five pods. And every pod has two spines that are so sharp they can puncture a bicycle tire or even the sole of your shoe.

Puncturevine can sprout, flower and set seeds within three weeks. And it'll continue to grow and flower until killed by frost. Growing from a single tap root, the wiry stems are only a couple of inches tall, but can spread over an area 6 ft. wide. The stems and all of the leaves are covered with short, stiff hairs.

FAVORITE CONDITIONS Most common in the Southwestern United States, puncturevine can be found in much of North America. It prefers full sun., so you don't find it growing in dense shade or in the center of a bed of tall perennials. But watch out along the edges of the bed where it won't have to compete for sunlight. And this prickly pest loves the heat along a sunny driveway or sidewalk.

The small, sharp pods of puncturevine can injure you or your pets.

CONTROL Get rid of this weed before it sets seeds. Both selective and nonselective herbicides are effective. Since puncturevine grows from a single root, it's easy to slice the plants off with a sharp hoe. Then, if your municipality allows it, send the stems away in the trash or burn them. Or bury any weeds with seeds in a trench at least 3 ft. deep to keep ripe seeds from sprouting. If the pods have turned brown, pick the plant up carefully so you don't shake seeds loose. They drop off easily and you could end up spreading the weed even further. And puncturevine seeds can live up to 20 years before sprouting.

Canada thistle
Cirsium arvense

IDENTIFICATION This tenacious perennial spreads by seeds and by roots. Each plant can grow 2 to 5 ft. tall with a grooved stem that's smooth or slightly hairy. Along the edges of the leaves, you'll encounter lots of sharp spines. From early to midsummer, small fuzzy, fragrant, lavender flowers bloom at the tips of the branches. By July, the pale brown seedheads form. Later, they'll split open, releasing seeds to be carried away by the wind. Seeds can survive in the soil for 20 years. Roots extend several feet down into the soil, while others spread out horizontally, just under the surface. As the horizontal roots fan out from the parent, they send up new plants, eventually forming a dense colony.

FAVORITE CONDITIONS You'll find Canada thistle growing in full sun — rarely in shade. It'll tolerate almost any soil, but prefers rich, moist conditions. Since it's perennial, this weed isn't usually found in frequently tilled gardens. Perennial gardens, shrub borders, fencerows and even lawns are much more attractive to this pest.

CONTROL Canada thistle is tough to get rid of! You can dig it up, but make sure to get all of the roots out or it'll grow back. Herbicides, both selective and nonselective types, are the weapons of choice. For the quickest results, apply them just as the flower buds form. This pest goes into a dormant state after flowering, making it harder for the herbicide to work. The next best time to spray is in fall when you see new growth sprouting near the base of old stems.

Underground runners produce new plants.

know YOUR zone

WHAT'S A ZONE AND WHY DOES IT MATTER?

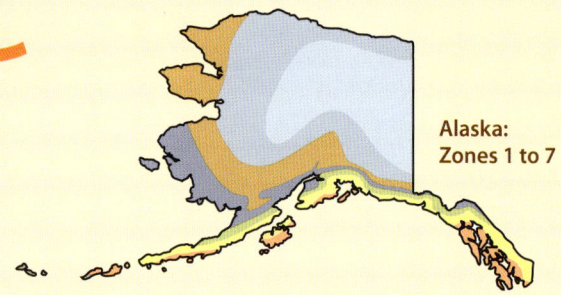

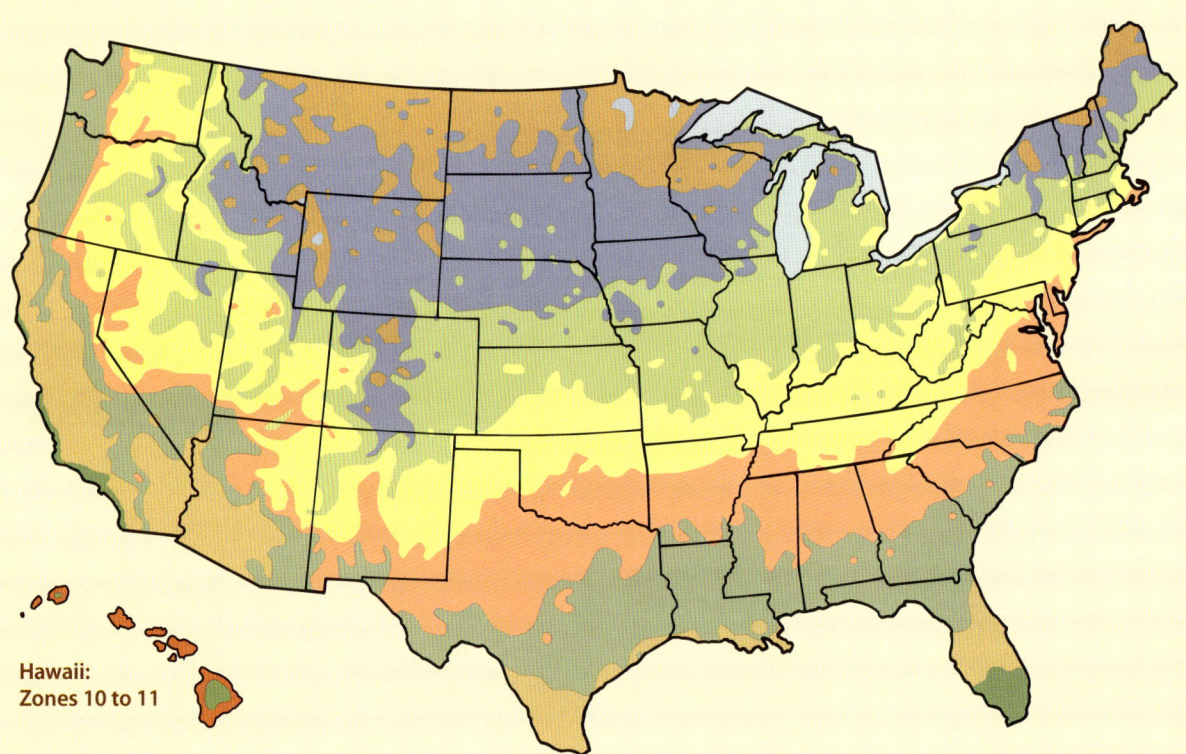

Alaska: Zones 1 to 7

Hawaii: Zones 10 to 11

COLD Hardiness

The USDA cold-hardiness map has long been the authority to help gardeners pick plants that will survive through the winter. It creates zones based on coldest average annual temperatures throughout the United States. A plant's cold-hardiness zone rating indicates where it's likely to survive the winter.

NOTE: For zones in Canada and Mexico, visit www.usna.usda.gov/Hardzone/ushzmap.html.

AVERAGE LOW TEMPERATURE	ZONE
Below -45	1
-40 to -45	2
-30 to -40	3
-20 to -30	4
-10 to -20	5
0 to -10	6

AVERAGE LOW TEMPERATURE	ZONE
10 to 0	7
20 to 10	8
30 to 20	9
40 to 30	10
Above 40	11

308 *the* YEAR IN GARDENING   www.GardenGateMagazine.com

Alaska:
Zones 1 to 2

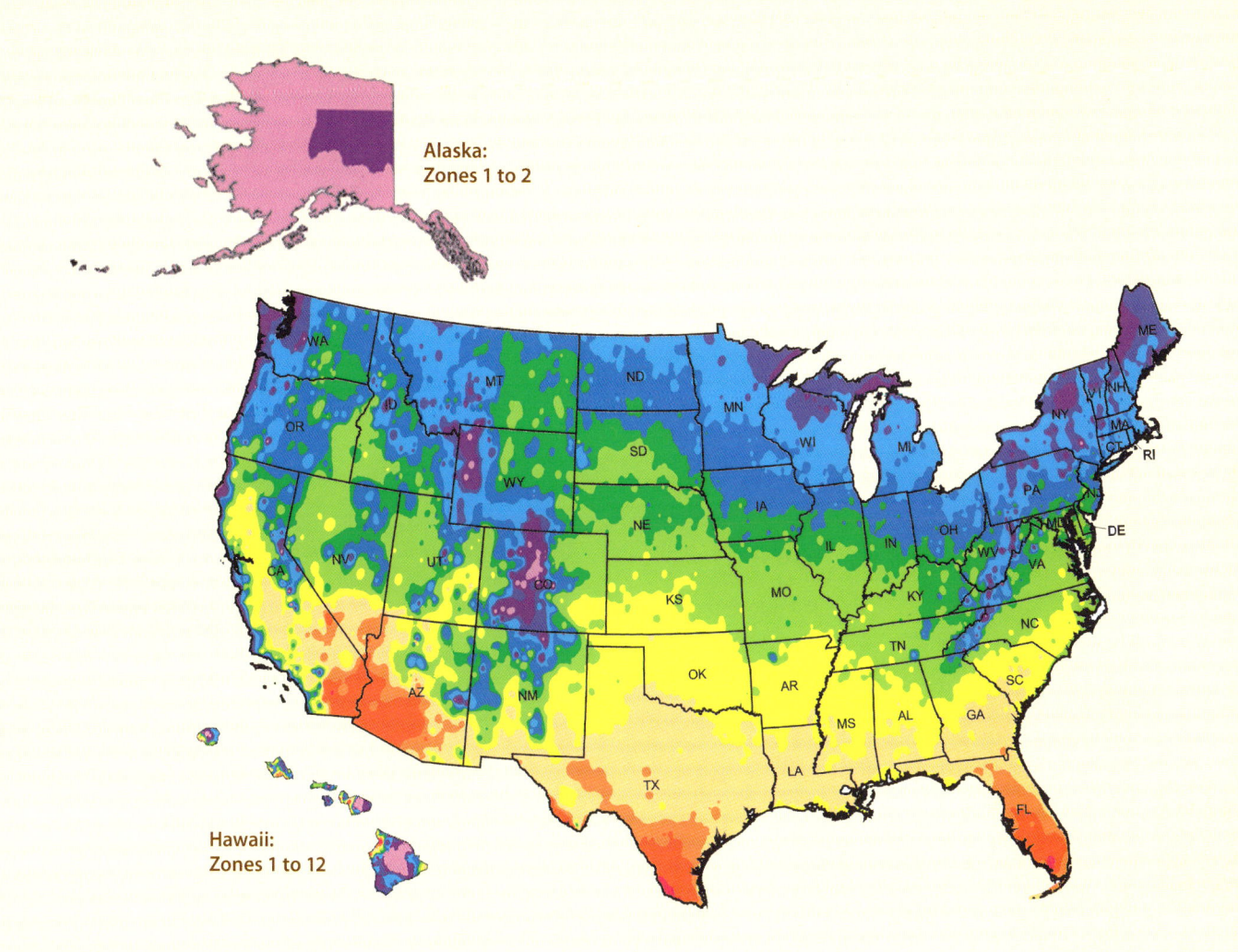

Hawaii:
Zones 1 to 12

DAYS ABOVE 86°	ZONE	DAYS ABOVE 86°	ZONE
Fewer than 1	1	60 to 90	7
1 to 7	2	90 to 120	8
7 to 14	3	120 to 150	9
14 to 30	4	150 to 180	10
30 to 45	5	180 to 210	11
45 to 60	6	More than 210	12

HEAT Tolerance

The American Horticultural Society's heat-zone map can help you determine how plants will cope with heat.

This map of the country is divided into 12 zones to indicate the average number of days in a year when the temperature goes above 86 degrees F. This is the temperature at which plants begin suffering and are unable to process water fast enough to maintain normal functions. Zone 1, the coldest zone, has less than one day. Zone 12, the hottest zone, has more than 210 days above 86 per year.

did you know...

Arbor Day Foundation changes zones

The National Arbor Day Foundation (NADF) has updated its hardiness zone map. Starting with the USDA zone map as a base, researchers examined 15 years of temperature information from the National Oceanic and Atmospheric Administration's 5,000 climatic data centers across the country. When everything was tabulated, the NADF decided to make some changes. Many areas of the country have moved up a full zone because of temperature changes over this time period. Check out www.arborday.org for the new cold-hardiness zone recommendations.

The YEAR IN GARDENING Volume 15 INDEX

aconite — butterflies

aconite, winter *see Eranthis hyemalis*
air conditioners
  shade for energy savings, 264
Allium
  top pick spring bulb, 91
alyssum, sweet *see Lobularia maritima*
Amaranthus caudatus
  top pick reseeding annual, 76
annuals
  fall cleanup, 303
  fertilizer, 254
  overwintering, 243
  vs. perennials, 302
  season-long color, 112
  top picks, 60, 74
  turning perennial, 53
Arabidopsis thaliana
  from annual to perennial, 53
arbors
  from cattle panels, 294
ash borer, emerald, 305
Asparagus densiflorus
  tuberous roots not bulbs, 57
Astilbe
  top pick for shade, 81
Athyrium niponicum pictum
  plant profile, 30
autumn daffodil *see Sternbergia lutea*
azalea *see Rhododendron*
Bacillus thuringiensis (Bt)
  eco-friendly, 258
bacterial leaf scorch, 305
bagworm caterpillars, 56
Balsam *see Impatiens*
Baptisia
  top pick new perennial, 63
barrenwort, red *see Epimedium* x*rubrum*
bat, little brown, 304
beds
  recycled concrete for raised, 183
  starting in lawn, 298
before & after
  formal garden, 106
  retaining walls, 120
  season-long color with annuals, 112
  spring color, 110
  update for privacy, 124
  water-wise beauty by region, 116
Begonia
  top pick new annual, 61
bellflower *see Campanula*
beneficial creatures, 304
Bergenia cordifolia
  top pick spring-bloomer, 72
berms, 196, 198
birds
  design to attract, 178
  feeders, 292
  perches, 184
  weeds from seed, 293
bittersweet, American *see Celastrus scandens*
blanket flower *see Gaillardia*
bleeding heart *see Dicentra*
Bletilla striata
  top pick spring bulb, 91
bloodroot *see Sanguinaria canadensis*
books
  The Ever-Blooming Flower Garden, 185
  Perennial Companions, 185
  The Truth About Organic Gardening, 295
  When Perennials Bloom, 55
borers
  emerald ash, 305
  squash vine, 305
boxwood *see Buxus*
brick edging, 284
Brunnera macrophylla
  top pick for shade, 85
bugs, minute pirate, 304
building projects
  retaining walls, 120
bulbs
  foliage support, 270
  mail-order web sites, 267
  naturalizing vs. perennializing, 302
  overwintering, 243, 269
  planting tools, 288
  protecting, 269
  top picks for three seasons, 88
burning bush *see Euonymus alatus*
butterflies
  easy tips to attract, 172
  fountain feeder, 184
  garden plan, 174

How to use your index

The index is divided by main topics with specific references following. All plants are referred to by botanical name.

For example, if you are looking for information about lily-of-the-valley, the entry will look like this:

  lily-of-the-valley *see Convallaria majalis*

Then turn to the reference for *Euonymus,* which looks like this:

Main topic (in this case, genus and species names)

  Convallaria majalis — *Page number*
    house plant, 244
    top pick for shade, 82

Specific reference to topic

You also might come across a topic that gives you specific references as well as an idea of other places in the index to look for similar information. For example:

  pests and pest controls
    see also insects; *specific pests and controls*
    buried burriers, 292
    eco-friendly pesticides, 258

Buxus
  for shade, 51
Calendula officinalis
  top pick reseeding annual, 79
Campanula
  evaluation of hardy, 53
candytuft *see Iberis sempervirens*
carts
  wheeled garbage can, 271
Castilleja indivisa
  top pick reseeding annual, 77
caterpillars, bagworm, 56
catmint *see Nepeta*
Celastrus scandens
  top pick new plant, 67
Cercis canadensis
  top pick spring-bloomer, 72
Chamaecyparis pisifera
  for shade, 51
Chionodoxa luciliae
  top pick spring bulb, 90
Chrysanthemum
  plant profile, 14
Cirsium arvense
  weed watch, 307
Clematis
  shading roots, 52
  growing conditions, 102
  slug deterrent for, 57
  top pick, 65,
  top pick new vine, 96
Cleome hassleriana
  top pick reseeding annual, 78
clumps, dividing, 260
coleus *see Solenostemon*

color
  see also garden plans
  professional secrets, 164
  three-season, 110
companion planting
  for longer blooming, 280
compost and composting
  actively aerated tea, 256
  nut shells, 299
  shower curtain drop-cloth, 270
coneflower *see Echinacea*; *Rudbeckia*
conifers, triangular, 147
Consolida ajacis
  top pick reseeding annual, 76
containers and container gardens
  adding height to, 244
  Better than Rocks for, 247
  bird baths as, 182
  cleaning, 240
  concrete, 246
  FabricPot™, 247
  for filling bare spots, 281
  hanging bags, 246

hanging baskets, 222
homemade molded "feet," 245
leaves in bottom, 244
mulch with seashells in, 244
ornamental grasses in, 228
pruning, 238
readers' best, 230
repairing terra-cotta, 246
vines in, 143
with focal plant, 214
Convallaria majalis
  house plant, 244
  top pick for shade, 82
coral bells *see Heuchera*
Corydalis
  plant profile, 24
Cosmos bipinnatus
  top pick new annual, 60
cowslip *see Primula veris*
crabapple *see Malus*
cress, thale *see Arabidopsis thaliana*
Crocosmia
  top pick summer bulb, 93

crowns, dividing, 260
cuttings, notched bottle for, 270
Cyclamen hederifolium
  top pick fall bulb, 88
cypress, false *see Chamaecyparis pisifera*
daffodil *see Narcissus*
daffodil, autumn *see Sternbergia lutea*
daisy, African *see Gazania rigens*
daisy, gerbera *see Gerbera jamesonii*
daisy, gloriosa *see Rudbeckia*
daisy, shasta *see Leucanthemum* ×*superbum*
dandelion *see Taraxacum officinale*
daylily *see Hemerocallis*
deadheading
  container gardens, 239
deer deterrents, 273, 274

ILLUSTRATIONS: Mavis Augustine Torke

design
  see also before & after; color; garden plans; specific plant profiles
  container, 214
  do-it-yourself, 130, 134
  drought tolerance, 116
  fall combos, 168
  large scale, 152
  from scratch, 130
  quick getaway, 158
  set your style, 134
  small, shady back yard, 160
  snowscaping, 272
  transitions, 138
  with triangles, 144
design challenge
  berm planting, 196
  cramped entry, 188
  simple to stunning back yard, 208
  simplified entry, 200
  steep slopes, 204
  uglies disappear, 192
Dicentra
  top picks new perennial, 65
  top pick for shade, 82
Dieffenbachia
  propagation, 54
Dipsacus fullonum
  weed watch, 306
dividing in summer, 260
dock, curly see Rumex crispus
drop cloth, shower curtain, 270
drought tolerance, design for, 116
dumb cane see Dieffenbachia
Echeveria rudofhii
  top pick new plant, 67
Echinacea
  'Doubledecker', 50
  top pick new perennial, 62
edging
  in large gardens, 154
  primer, 284
  for weed reduction, 265
emerald ash borer, 305
entries, 188, 190, 200, 202
environmental issues
  drought tolerance, 116
  invasive plants, 276
  pest control, 258
  rain gardens, 148
Epimedium ×rubrum
  plant profile, 38
Eranthis hyemalis
  top pick spring-bloomer, 69
ergonomics, garden
  emptying heavy bags, 273
Eryngium
  top pick new perennial, 64
Eschscholzia californica
  top pick reseeding annual, 77
Eucomis bicolor
  top pick summer bulb, 93
Euonymus alatus
  pruning, 51
exotics, 276
fasciation, 302
fences as transitions, 139
fern, asparagus see Asparagus densiflorus
fern, Japanese painted see Athyrium niponicum pictum
fern, lady see Athyrium niponicum pictum
fertilizers and fertilizing
  organic vs. inorganic, 255
  perennials, 301
  primer, 254
fish, plants toxic to, 53
flag, crimson see Schizostylis coccinea
forks, 287
Fritillaria meleagris
  naturalizing, 302
furniture
  double duty, 265
  for small getaway, 159
Gaillardia
  top pick new plant, 67
Galanthus nivalis
  naturalizing, 302
garbage cans
  wheeled as cart, 271
garden design
  do-it-yourself, 130, 134
garden plans
  see also before & after; design; design challenge
  container gardens
    cool idea, 236
    flowery basket, 220
    instant spring, 218
    new twist on traditional formula, 217
    orange accent, 239
    readers' best, 230
    shade bowl, 216
    sunny sizzler, 221
    super bowl, 234

garden plans

    with topiary, 215
    warm sunshine, 235
  front yard gardens
    berm, 198
    entry, 86, 190, 202
    full shade, 86
  getaways
    for privacy, 210
  patios and decks
    back yard around, 210
    multi-level, 206
  regional gardens
    attracting birds, 180
    drought-tolerant, 116
  shade gardens
    around uglies, 194
    dry, 87
    entry, 86, 202
    full, 86
    moist and cool, 87
  slope
    with retaining walls, 206
  special situations
    attracting birds by region, 180
    attracting butterflies, 174
    berms, 198
    hiding utilities, 194
    rain garden, 151
    three-season with bulbs, 94
gardeners
  Jeff Lowenfels, 256
  Joan McDonald, 178
  Kris Medic, 264
  Rita Randolph, 228
  Lisa Reas, 148
garlic, society *see Tulbaghia violacea*
gates
  brass headboard, 184
  as transitions, 139
Gazania rigens
  Frosty Kiss Mix, 28
Geographic Information Systems (GIS), 264
Gerbera jamesonii
  overwintering, 50
getaways
  low-care, 158

Gladiolus communis byzantinus
  top pick summer bulb, 92
glory of the snow *see Chionodoxa luciliae*
gloves
  clips for, 273
  Ethel®, 293
grapeholly, Oregon *see Mahonia aquifolium*
grasses
  in containers, 228
greenhouses
  landscape fabric shades, 303
ground covers
  lawn alternative, 265
  no-mow slope, 282
  vines as, 142
handles, shovel, 272, 287
hanging baskets
  gardening in, 222
hardscape in large gardens, 156
health
  patients better with flowers, 246
Helleborus
  top picks new plants, 64
  top picks for shade, 84

Hemerocallis
  long-blooming, 26
Heuchera
  top pick for shade, 85
Hibiscus moscheutos
  yellowing leaves, 57
honeysuckle *see Lonicera nitida*
horticultural oil, 258
horticultural soap, 258
hoses
  guides, 184, 271
  holders, 182
  soaker hose caps, 300
Hosta
  planting conditions, 54
  top pick for shade, 81
humidity
  Easy Bloom monitor, 299
Hydrangea macrophylla
  top pick new plant, 67
Iberis sempervirens
  top pick spring-bloomer, 71
Impatiens
  top picks reseeding annual, 75
  top picks shade plant, 83
indigo, false *see Baptisia*

insects
  beneficials, 304
  controls, 258
  ladybugs, 293
  pests, 305
invasives, 53, 276
Ipomoea purpurea
  top pick reseeding annual, 75
Iris
  'Red at Night', 10
  top pick spring-bloomer, 70
knives
  soil, 289
ladybugs, 293
Lantana montevidensis
  for butterflies, 293
larkspur *see Consolida ajacis*
lawns
  conversion to garden, 298
  conversion to ground cover, 265
  mowing less, 265
  reducing herbicide use, 265
  which fertilizer?, 254
  winterizing, 268
leaf scorch, bacterial, 305
Leucanthemum x*superbum*
  plant profile, 40

Leucojum vernum
  naturalizing, 302
light and lighting
  Easy Bloom monitor, 298
  Soji solar lantern, 185
Lilium
  dividing, 262
  fasciation, 302
  overwintering, 55
lily *see Lilium*
lily, checkered *see Fritillaria meleagris*
lily, kaffir *see Schizostylis coccinea*
lily, pineapple *see Eucomis bicolor*
lily, surprise *see Lycoris squamigera*
lily, toad *see Tricyrtis hirta*
lily-of-the-valley *see Convallaria majalis*

Lobularia maritima
  top pick reseeding annual, 79
Lonicera nitida
  top pick new shrub, 66
love-lies-bleeding *see Amaranthus caudatus*
Lycoris squamigera
  plant profile, 36
Magnolia
  'Elizabeth', 32
Mahonia aquifolium
  for shade, 51
mail order
  fewer catalogs, 295
  web sites, 266
maintenance, easier, 106
mallow, rose *see Hibiscus moscheutos*
Malus
  pruning, 51
  top pick spring-bloomer, 73

maps
  creating a base map, 130
marigold, pot *see Calendula officinalis*
microclimate in large gardens, 156
mockorange *see Philadelphus*
moles, 292
mop heads *see Hydrangea macrophylla*
morning glory *see Ipomoea purpurea*
moss rose *see Portulaca grandiflora*
mulches
  drop-cloth, 270
  gutter guard, 182
  seashells, 244
naked ladies *see Lycoris squamigera*
Narcissus
  naturalizing, 302
  top pick spring-bloomer, 71

neem oil, 258
Nepeta
  plant profile, 12
nettle, stinging *see Urtica dioica*
orchid, ground *see Bletilla striata*
Oregon grapeholly *see Mahonia aquifolium*
ornamental grasses
  cutting back, 273
  Rita Randolph on, 228
ornaments in large gardens, 156
overwintering, 241, 269
paintbrush, Indian *see Castilleja indivisa*
pathways
  petal pavers, 182
  weed-free, 108
patios
  polymeric sand, 183
pavers
  petal path, 182
  polymeric sand, 183
pear *see Pyrus calleryana*
Penstemon
  top pick new perennial, 62
perennials
  vs. annuals, 302
  fertilizer and fertilizing, 254, 301
  invasive, 277
  mail-order web sites, 266
  overwintering, 241, 269
  Perennial Companions, 185
  planting right, 250
  quick spreaders, 126
  top pick new, 62
  When Perennials Bloom, 55
pergolas
  and hanging baskets, 224
Perovskia
  transplanting, 56
pests and pest control
  see also insects; *specific pests and controls*
  buried barriers, 292
  eco-friendly pesticides, 258

Philadelphus
  slow bloomer, 52
Phlox subulata
  plant profile, 34
photography
  as aid to pruning, 272
  and seed sharing, 272
pinching
  container gardens, 238
pirate bugs, minute, 304
plans *see* maps
plant markers
  plastic utensils, 298
  tag storage, 296
  Write+Erase, 299
pollination
  Pollinator Friendly Planting Guide, 293
poppy, California *see Eschscholzia californica*
porches
  and hanging baskets, 225
  screening with plants, 202
Portulaca grandiflora
  top pick reseeding annual, 78
pot "feet," 245
pot marigold *see Calendula officinalis*
potatoes
  growing in hanging bags, 246
potting benches
  double duty, 265
potting soil
  Better Than Rocks®, 247
  Monrovia® Nurseries, 245
Primula veris
  top pick spring-bloomer, 70
privacy
  getaways, 158
  quick and easy update, 124
  "screen" porch, 202
pruners and pruning *see also specific plants*
  Fiskars™ bypass, 297
  photo aid to, 272
  vegetables, 272
puncturevine *see Tribulus terrestris*

pyrethrum, 258
Pyrus calleryana
  invasive hybrid, 53
rabbits
  protecting trees from, 56
rain gardens, 148
rakes as tool rack, 296
raspberries
  growing different colors together, 295
redbud *see Cercis canadensis*
regional gardens
  bird-friendly, 180
  right climbing roses for, 20
  water-wise beauty for, 118
rhizomes, dividing, 260
Rhododendron
  for shade, 51
Rosa
  All-American Rose Selection, 50
  avoiding thorns of, 271
  fertilizer, 254
  regional recommendations for climbers, 18
  top pick new shrub, 66
rose mallow *see Hibiscus moscheutos*
rose, moss *see Portulaca grandiflora*

Rudbeckia
  rust on, 55
  top pick new annual, 61
Rumex crispus
  weed watch, 306
rust, 55
sage *see Perovskia*
Salix
  getting rid of suckers, 303
sand, polymeric, 183
Sanguinaria canadensis
  top pick spring-bloomer, 69
Saponaria ocymoides
  plant profile, 44
scale (size)
  in large gardens, 154
Schizostylis coccinea
  top pick fall bulb, 89
sea holly *see Eryngium*
Sedum
  top pick new perennial, 63
seed starting
  containers, 270, 300
  lighting for, 301
  Sprout House and Relocation Station, 301
seeds
  SeedCalculator, 295
  sharing, 272

shade gardens
  readers' top picks for, 80
shoes
  slip-on, 296
  Sloggers boots, 296
shrubs
  fertilizer, 254
  under five feet tall, 264
  invasive, 279
  overwintering, 243, 269
  for shade, 51
  top pick new, 66
  as vine supports, 143
slopes
  design on, 197, 204, 206
  no-mow, 282
slug deterrent, 57
snakes, bull, 304
snow
  for garden space planning, 272
snowballs *see Hydrangea macrophylla*
snowdrop *see Galanthus nivalis*
snowflake *see Leucojum vernum*
soap, insecticidal, 258
soapwort *see Saponaria ocymoides*

society garlic *see Tulbaghia violacea*
soil moisture
  Easy Bloom monitor, 298
  super-absorbent polymers, 227
Solenostemon
  cuttings, 270
  managing size, 52
  top pick new plant, 67
spades
  favorites, 286
  handles as measuring devices, 272
spider flower *see Cleome hassleriana*
spinosad, 258
spirea, false *see Astilbe*
squash vine borer
  pest profile, 305

squirrels
  thorny canes as deterrent, 292
stakes
  fireplace screen, 270
  /watering system, 272
Sternbergia lutea
  top pick fall bulb, 89
stone edging, 284
string dispensers, 270
structures in large gardens, 156
suckers, 303
sudden oak death, 53
sweet alyssum *see Lobularia maritima*
Taraxacum officinale
  weed watch, 307
Taxus
  for shade, 51
teasel, Fuller's *see Dipsacus fullonum*

temperature
  Easy Bloom monitor, 298
  Freeze-Pruf, 295
  hardiness zones, 308
terra-cotta
  repairing containers, 246
thistle, Canada *see Cirsium arvense*
tomatoes
  cushioned supports, 294
  fertilizer, 254
  watering, 272
  watering/staking system, 272
tools and equipment
  as bird perches, 184
  for bulbs, 288
  drop cloth, 270
  Easy Bloom monitor, 298
  forks, 287
  Garden Gear Organizer, 297

  handles, 272, 287
  hangers, 296
  maintenance, 268
  measuring devices, 272
  spades, 286
  timesavers, 290
transitions, 138
transplants, shading, 298
trees
  fertilizer, 254
  invasive, 279
  overwintering, 269
  overwintering in containers, 243
  protecting from rabbits, 56
  suckers, 303
  trunk flare, 302
trenches and trenching
  edging, 284
Tribulus terrestris
  weed watch, 307
Tricyrtis hirta
  top pick for shade, 84
Trillium grandiflorum
  top pick for shade, 83
tropicals, overwintering, 243
trowels
  soil knives, 289
tubers, overwintering, 242
Tulbaghia violacea
  top pick summer bulb, 92
Tulipa
  top picks spring bulbs, 73, 90
twine dispensers, 270
undercutting container gardens, 239
utilities
  planting to disguise, 192, 194
Urtica dioica
  weed watch, 306
vegetables
  on arbors, 294
  fertilizer, 254
  how many to feed a family, 295
  pruning, 272
Verbena
  top pick new plant, 67

vines

vines
  invasive, 279
  new ways to use, 142
  top pick new, 65
voles, 292
walls, retaining, 120
water conservation
  design for, 116
  rain gardens, 148
water gardens
  old firepit, 184
watering
  container plants in pools for short term, 271
  laundry detergent containers as cans, 300
  /staking system, 272
  while you weed, 300
weeds and weeding
  from birdseed, 293
  pathways, 108
  to watch, 306
  while you water, 300
willow *see* Salix
yew *see* Taxus
Zinnia
  plant profile, 48

Want helpful garden advice delivered EVERY WEEK?

Then you'll LOVE our weekly e-notes. They're filled with:

- At-a-glance plant guides
- Pests and weeds to watch (and how to eliminate them)
- How-to videos and projects
- Practical tips that make gardening easier

Visit **www.GardenGateNotes.com** to become a member today!

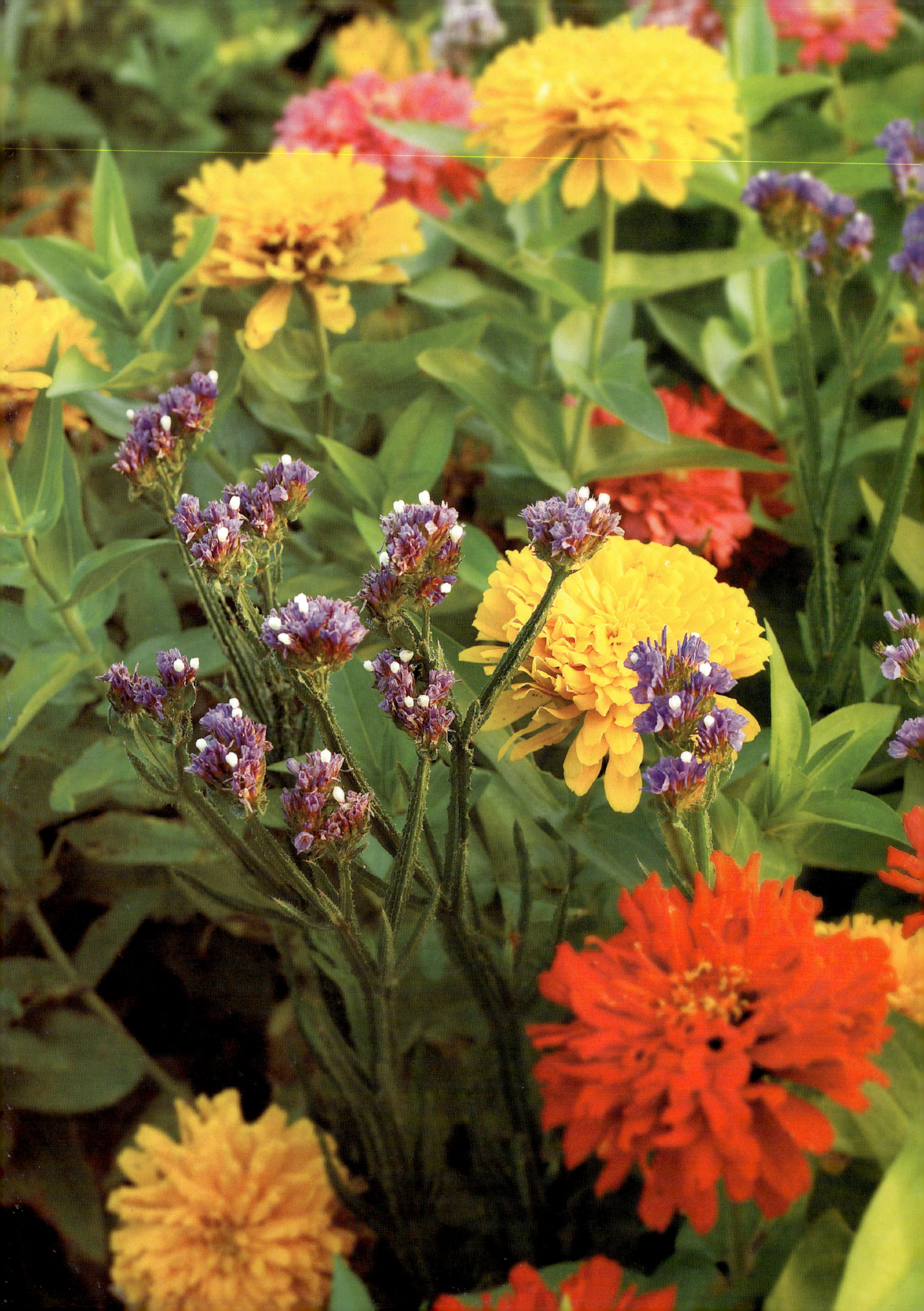

*"A life without love
is like a year
without summer."*
— *Swedish Proverb*

Garden Gate
The YEAR IN GARDENING

www.GardenGateMagazine.com